KAFKA'S ITALIAN PROGENY

Kafka's Italian Progeny

SASKIA ELIZABETH ZIOLKOWSKI

UNIVERSITY OF TORONTO PRESS
Toronto Buffalo London

© University of Toronto Press 2020
Toronto Buffalo London
utorontopress.com
Printed in Canada

ISBN 978-1-4875-0630-8 (cloth)
ISBN 978-1-4875-3380-9 (EPUB)
ISBN 978-1-4875-3379-3 (PDF)

Toronto Italian Studies

Publication cataloguing information is available
from Library and Archives Canada.

This book has been published with the assistance of Duke University.

University of Toronto Press acknowledges the financial assistance to its
publishing program of the Canada Council for the Arts and the Ontario Arts
Council, an agency of the Government of Ontario.

 **Canada Council
for the Arts** **Conseil des Arts
du Canada**

ONTARIO ARTS COUNCIL
CONSEIL DES ARTS DE L'ONTARIO

an Ontario government agency
un organisme du gouvernement de l'Ontario

Funded by the   Financé par le
Government   gouvernement
of Canada   du Canada

Canadä

MIX
Paper from
responsible sources
FSC® C016245

Contents

Acknowledgments

This book took me too long, and these acknowledgments may reflect the years that have passed between the book's conception and its existence. I have been thinking about Kafka and Italian literature since I wrote my dissertation, although the book is completely distinct from it. Mark M. Anderson and his vast Kafka knowledge were inspirational from the beginning. His focus on thorough research and emphasis on historical context prompted me to follow Kafka's Italian trails in detail. Martin Puchner's insightful questions about the particularities of Italian literary history have repeatedly led me to reconsider the framework of the project. His advice and intellectual generosity have been guiding forces.

Italianist friends from graduate school, Stephen Twilley, Lillyrose Veneziano Broccia, Juliet Nusbaum, Susanne Knittel, Rebecca Bauman, Vlad Vintila, and Gabrielle Elissa Popoff have probably all heard more about Kafka and Italy than they wanted to over the years. I am grateful to have been with them during a formative time and to continue to learn from them.

The two years spent in the company of Barbara Spackman, Mia Fuller, Albert Ascoli, and the late Steven Botterill at the University of California at Berkeley offered me the chance to have valuable conversations, teach productive courses, and present my research to them and their great graduate students. They created a welcoming space for the book to develop. Mia also, this time in Durham, was especially encouraging during the final stages of the book.

I am grateful to my colleagues at Duke, Roberto Dainotto, Luciana Fellin, Kata Gellen, Martin Eisner, Helen Solterer, Matteo Gilebbi, Laura Lieber, Michael Valdes Moses, Malachi Hacohen, Norman Keul, Toril Moi, Richard Rosa, and Gennifer Weisenfeld, who have supported me and my work in various ways. Thank you for your conversations, comments, and understanding. Thank you also to the exemplary librarians of Perkins, Lilly, and interlibrary loan for making my research possible. I am especially fortunate to have at Duke my Kafka friend, Kata Gellen, who read the entire manuscript, was always available to talk (often about Kafka), and co-directed the 2014–15 Franklin Humanities Center and Philosophy, Arts, and Literature Mellon seminar, "Whose Kafka," with me. This seminar also led to having productive conversations with several scholars, including Ruth V. Gross, Vivian Liska, Jean-Michel Rabaté, Davide Stimilli, and John Zilcosky, whose thoughts and work have been fundamental to my concept of Kafka.

Especially since there are not many scholars who study German and Italian literature, it has been a pleasure to encounter several generous and friendly scholars in this comparative field. The perspectives of Thomas Harrison, Elena Coda, Elizabeth Schächter, and Salvatore Pappalardo have all been motivating.

Because comparative work requires thinking about different audiences, I am grateful for the conferences and invited lectures where I have spoken about parts of my book. Mimmo Cangiano's intellectual energy, whether from afar or in person in Durham or Jerusalem, is always appreciated. The research group *Storia e mappe digitali della letteratura tedesca in Italia nel Novecento: editoria, campo letterario, interferenza* gave me a chance to speak to its especially knowledgeable members, including Michele Sisto, Daria Biagi, Anna Baldini, and Irene Fantappiè, about my project in Rome in 2014.

A few ideas from the introduction and chapter 5 have appeared in edited volumes and journals: "Kafka and Italy: A New Perspective on the Italian Literary Landscape" in *Franz Kafka for the Twenty-First Century* (Rochester, NY: Camden House, 2011), edited by Ruth V. Gross and Stanley Corngold; "Primo Levi and Jewish Kafka in Italy" in the special issue, "Kafka and the Holocaust," of the *Journal of the Kafka Society of America*, vol. 35/36 (2012), edited by Maria Luise Caputo-Mayr; "Svevo's Dogs: Kafka and the Importance of Svevo's Animals" in *Italo Svevo and His Legacy for the Third Millennium*, vol. 2 (Leicester, UK: Troubador, 2014), edited by Giuseppe Stellardi and Emanuela Tandello Cooper; and "Morante and Kafka: The Gothic Walking Dead and Talking Animals" in Elsa Morante's *Politics of Writing: Rethinking Subjectivity, History and the Power of Art* (Madison, NJ: Fairleigh Dickinson University Press, 2015), edited by Stefania Lucamante. These scholars' conferences, panels, and editing raised questions that I continued to consider as I developed the book.

For the last stages of the book, I have been grateful to find such a responsive and thoughtful editor in Mark Thompson at the University of Toronto Press. The two anonymous readers offered generous, thorough, and productive feedback that greatly improved the book manuscript. I very much appreciate their time and kind consideration. The copy editor, Stephanie Stone, has been both a pleasure to work with and thorough.

The kind individuals who read chapters, Roberto Dainotto, Kata Gellen, Gabrielle Elissa Popoff, Juliet Nusbaum, Martin Eisner, Elizabeth Ziolkowski, Jan Ziolkowski, and Theodore Ziolkowski, provided crucial feedback. These people come from my current institution, my graduate school, and my family. I am very lucky to have family members willing to read my work. It is impossible to recognize fully how my family has shaped me. I would most likely not know Italian had my parents, Elizabeth and Jan Ziolkowski, not bravely taken a family of five to Florence and put their three children, including my lovely sisters, Ada and Yetta, in Italian schools. I probably would not have pursued German if my parents had not used it as their secret language when I was a child. I know I would know much less German if it were not for my grandparents, Yetta and Theodore Ziolkowski, who have provided so many entries into German culture, history, and literature.

Martin's always valuable suggestions have come at every stage of my work. He has listened to innumerable tales about my authors and their works, including many things that did not make it into the book. His conversations have been fundamental not only because of how they have helped me form *Kafka's Italian Progeny* but also because of the joy they bring. Our children, Nola and Tullia, similarly bring much happiness, even if their thoughts on literature are at this point less extensive. Their patience while I work is much appreciated, and their distractions, which bring so much light into my life, even more so. I will refrain from playing on the title of the book, which is dedicated to Martin.

KAFKA'S ITALIAN PROGENY

Kafka, World Literature, and the Italian Literary Landscape

> If I am not mistaken the heterogeneous selections I have mentioned resemble Kafka's work: if I am not mistaken, not all of them resemble each other, and this fact is the significant one. Kafka's idiosyncrasy, in greater or lesser degree, is present in each of these writings, but if Kafka had not written we would not perceive it; that is to say, it would not exist.
>
> – Jorge Luis Borges,
> "Kafka and His Precursors"

Whereas Kafka has been mobilized and deployed in discourses on minor literature, as formulated by Deleuze and Guattari, and world literature, as examined by Damrosch and Casanova, *Kafka's Italian Progeny* uses him to examine the dimensions of the questioned and, at times, ignored modern literature of one national assignation, Italy.[1] Through an exploration of a distinct but hitherto unexamined Kafkan tradition in Italy, this study brings together disparate but well-defined groups to fill gaps left by previous methods of organization. Revisiting canonical authors such as Italo Svevo and Italo Calvino, as well as investigating lesser-known authors such as Tommaso Landolfi and Lalla Romano, *Kafka's Italian Progeny* analyses many figures who have been described as isolated from the Italian literary scene and, therefore, hard to place.

In addition to adding to the critical view of these writers, this book integrates new combinations of Italian authors into significant debates, an examination that, in turn, contributes to these discourses. Because

---

1 See Deleuze and Guattari, *Kafka*; Damrosch, *What Is World Literature?*; and Casanova, *The World Republic of Letters*.

most important critical discussions of twentieth- and twenty-first-century literature include Kafka, but not the literature of modern Italy, one goal is to bring the richness of Italian fiction to a larger audience by way of the German-language author. These literary-critical motivations are complemented by the historical fact of Kafka's remarkable, but frequently overlooked, Italian reception.[2] The first section of this introduction addresses the larger literary-critical stakes before describing Kafka's distinctive reception in Italy.

The Place of Italian Literature in World-Literature Debates

While one line of world literature studies has proceeded on the assumption that national literatures are fixed, *Kafka's Italian Progeny* reveals how complex the notion of a national literature is. Wai Chee Dimock and Lawrence Buell's *Shades of the Planet: American Literature as World Literature* questioned the category of American literature within global, transnational, and international perspectives, showing the difficulties of defining a national literary tradition. American, like any national, literature presents its own challenges and opportunities (the pervasiveness of the English language, the prominence of the United States in the global economy, etc.). At first glance, the Italian case may appear simpler: a peninsula with borders seemingly predetermined by geography and geology; no other dominant, same-language literary tradition; a long history emphasizing Italian-ness; and a strong medieval literary tradition. Many of Italy's best-known authors knew each other. In contrast to the cultural contexts described in *Shades of the Planet*, the Italian literary world can seem extremely small.

Nonetheless, American and Italian studies share at least one quality, although it stems from different factors. In *Shades of the Planet*, Jonathan Arac comments on the resistance Americanists face when engaged in comparative work: "In the United States all forms of comparative and international study always carry an implicit critique of the continental insularity that marks this country."[3] Comparative work on the literature of Italy faces similar challenges, in part because of peninsularity and an apparent need to protect the debated modern tradition from outside influences. Because critics often avoid putting Italian authors into conversation with non-Italian ones, like Kafka, some of their exciting

---

2 For more on Kafka's Italian reception, see Hösle, "Italien"; Cusatelli, "Kafka e i suoi lettori italiani"; Caputo-Mayr, "Kafka and Romance Languages"; Ziolkowski, "Primo Levi and Jewish Kafka in Italy"; and Ziolkowski, "Kafka and Italy."

3 Arac, "Global and Babel," 23.

qualities have been overlooked. The comparisons of these authors with Kafka offered here aim to shed new light on them.

Italy's twentieth-century literary scene is both expansive in terms of who is considered significant and, at the same time, often (relatedly) isolated from other literary discussions. The modern canon of Italy is more debated than are those of (for instance) France, Germany, and England. Many have been called Italy's most important or greatest modern author: Gabriele D'Annunzio, Luigi Pirandello, Italo Svevo, Elsa Morante, Alberto Moravia, Carlo Emilio Gadda, Eugenio Montale, Italo Calvino, and Pier Paolo Pasolini. Because of the long-standing idea that Italian literature defines Italy, determining an Italian author's significance may be particularly vital.

While not having a nation has been proposed as one of the reasons for Goethe's promotion of *Weltliteratur*, one can see the opposite tendency among the Italian intellectuals who looked to their own unique linguistic-literary traditions to see their national future. In response to Klemens von Metternich's jab at the Congress of Vienna that Italy was a "geographical expression," Giosuè Carducci claimed that it was instead "a literary expression, a poetic tradition."[4] The sense that Italy and her literature were one and the same continued well after the Risorgimento.[5] In 1960, Carlo Levi characterized the relationship between Italy and her literature in a similar manner: "All of her artists and poets have, in describing the country, determined it."[6]

Strategies for approaching and trying to describe the Italian scene more broadly than examinations of individual authors include attention to regional differences, literary journals, and literary movements or groups, such as *frammetismo, ermetismo, novecentismo, futurismo, crepuscolarismo, neorealismo,* and *neo-sperimentalismo.* As with the journals (*La voce, Lacerba, La ronda, Il Baretti, 900, Solaria, Il selvaggio, Letteratura, La riforma letteraria, Il Frontespizio, Primato, Il Politecnico, Officina,* and *Il menabò di letteratura*), many of these groups and terms, these various *ismi,* are specific to the Italian literary landscape. Although

---

4 "Un'espressione letteraria, una tradizione poetica" (Carducci, quoted in Jossa, *L'Italia letteraria*, 20). In 1847, Francesco De Sanctis's student Luigi La Vista expressed an analogous sentiment: "A history of Italian literature would be a history of Italy" ("Una storia della letteratura italiana sarebbe una storia d'Italia"; La Vista, quoted in Jossa, 21.) Unless otherwise noted (with page numbers), translations into English are my own.

5 Stefano Jossa's *L'Italia letteraria* [Literary Italy, 2006] explores how Italy's late founding and literary history gave its literature a large role in the country's perception of itself.

6 "Tutti i suoi artisti e i suoi poeti l'hanno, descrivendola, determinata" (Levi, *Un volto che ci somiglia*, viii).

the description of any modern literature confronts numerous issues, modern Italian literature is particularly problematic. Several challenges owe not only to the subject matter and the qualities of modern Italian authors but also to how Italian literature has tended to be examined.

As the lists above attest, Italy is notable for the number of its movements. One history of Italian literature proclaims, "Since the death of Pascoli the century has hardly witnessed two consecutive years without the creation of some new literary movement, formalized or otherwise, the publication of new cultural journals or the growth of affiliations of littérateurs loosely classifiable in 'schools.'"[7] Since many of these terms and journals are relevant only or primarily to Italy, numerous studies that concentrate on them, like those that concentrate on individual authors, add a great deal to the critical details of the Italian literary landscape, but often do not bring Italian literature into broader conversations. There are, of course, exceptions, including several works on the journals that aimed to bring broader literary traditions to Italy, such as *Solaria* and *Botteghe oscure*, and studies like those of Francesca Billiani, who put these journals into transnational contexts.[8] In general, however, by concentrating on local trends, particular figures, or regional clusters of authors, critics of Italian literature have developed refined understandings of Italy's authors and movements, but have tended to isolate Italian literature from international perspectives. Breaking up the categories that prevent some authors from being compared, since they have been classified using different, specific, terms, will highlight new connections among several works, such as those of Lalla Romano, Giorgio Manganelli, and Antonio Tabucchi, discussed in the second chapter.

Studies of European or world literature often relegate modern Italian literature to a brief mention.[9] Although Italy's strong medieval tradition guarantees that Italian works have a prominent place in discussions of world literature, W.H. Auden declared Kafka, not a modern Italian author, the Dante of our time.[10] Whenever Italian authors are mentioned, they are regularly compared, generally to their disadvantage, with French- and English-language ones. Authors from Italy, even Italo Svevo, Carlo Emilio Gadda, and Luigi Pirandello, are frequently

---

7 Woodhouse, "The Fascist Era," 289.

8 See Billiani, *Modes of Censorship and Translation*; and Billiani, la Penna, and Milani, special issue, *Modern Italy*.

9 See Dainotto, "World Literature and European Literature," on the complex relationship between European literature and world literature.

10 See W.H. Auden: "Had one to name the artist who comes nearest to bearing the same kind of relation to our age that Dante, Shakespeare and Goethe bore to theirs, Kafka is the first one would think of" (Auden, *Prose*, 2:110).

omitted from the canon of modern writers, where James Joyce, Marcel Proust, and Franz Kafka reside.[11] The modern Italian literary tradition is often described as in the shadow of, or overshadowed by, the corresponding French one. In their analysis of Émile Zola's role in Italy, Ann Hallamore Caesar and Michael Caesar point out that French authors are seen both as the primary influencers of, and also as more modern than, Italian authors, who have been recognized, but not necessarily embraced, by the Italian public.[12] Pascale Casanova affirms and codifies the capital city of France as the centre of literary relations in *The World Republic of Letters*: "And so it was that Paris became the capital of the literary world, the city endowed with the greatest literary prestige on earth."[13] Since critics often assume the centrality of Paris, they at times overlook the cultural, historical, and intellectual connections between Italy and other nations.

Examining a German-language author against Italian ones complements the more numerous studies that concentrate on Italy's literary connections to France.[14] While the relationships between French and Italian literatures are undeniably multiple and important, the focus on this geographical, cultural, and literary association has, at times, obscured other significant relationships. In *1910: The Emancipation of Dissonance*, Thomas Harrison draws attention to this problem: he examines how

---

11 For works on Kafka and world literature, see Engel and Lamping, *Franz Kafka und die Weltliteratur*; Damrosch's chapter, "Kafka Comes Home," in *What Is World Literature?*; and Zyla, *Franz Kafka*.

12 "The critical reception of Zola in Italy was a microcosm of the establishment's views of French culture and its influence on the Italian public in general. He was held in high esteem by literary critics and was a literary model for writers who later acquired a canonical status in Italy. But at the same time he was the scourge of clerics and commentators, who felt he and alongside him many other French writers were a nefarious influence on susceptible readers" (Caesar and Caesar, *Modern Italian Literature*, 125).

13 Casanova, *The World Republic of Letters*, 24. As Ram has stated, "In its evident Gallocentrism, Casanova's theory can certainly be faulted for perpetuating the very logic it seeks to expose" (Ram, "Futurist Geographies," 319). Casanova's examination of Paris as the model is both convincing and, at the same time, makes for some awkward observations about Italy. She calls attention to this issue, which she in part explores, however generally, from a French vantage point (Casanova, 23). In her description, French humanists aimed to challenge the power of Italy, a country that would not exist for centuries (Casanova, 49). For her, "Italy" failed to produce a literary capital, despite Dante, Boccaccio, Petrarch, and Machiavelli, because it was not a country (Casanova, 81). Meanwhile, Italy's sense of unity was in large part based on its literary (non-national) past, and the medieval tradition continues to have a stronger presence than the modern one that arose during nationalism.

14 This critical tendency is present in the broader discussion of Italian literature as much as in individual studies – say, on Proust.

the scholarly emphasis on Dino Campana's French, symbolic lineage "obscured a proper view of the more raw, 'Teutonic,' expressionistic dimensions of his verse."[15] By taking a German-language author as the point of comparison, *Kafka's Italian Progeny* approaches Italian literature from a different vantage point. For instance, this book does not focus on existentialism and surrealism, although these terms have been discussed in regard to Kafka, since concentrating on them would put Kafka and Italian literature onto French terrain without necessarily changing the perspective on the Italian literary landscape. Even though several authors discussed in *Kafka's Italian Progeny*, including Moravia, Vittorini, Ginzburg, Pavese, and Buzzati, have been examined in light of existentialism, the category can be awkward in the Italian context, revealing how using critical categories can determine the parameters of a discussion.[16] In contrast to early French writers, Italian critics, in fact, repeatedly discussed why Kafka was not an existential or surrealist author, and proposed their own views of him, in the 1940s, 1950s, and 1960s.

Discussions of Italian modernism exemplify the often difficult relationship between Italian literary traditions and broadly international ones. While *romanticism* and *existentialism* appear in the index of *The Cambridge History of Italian Literature*, revised in 1999, *modernism* does not. This absence, which would be unimaginable in a similar reference work for many other national literatures, reveals how little critical traction the term has had in Italian studies, a fact that has contributed to its relative isolation. The study of Italian modernism has been partially hindered by the association between early avant-garde movements, or early modernist groups, and fascism. Italy has often been treated as if it had an avant-garde, futurism, subsequently linked to fascism, but no modernism.[17] Indeed, *modernism* has been consistently used to describe

---

15 Harrison, *1910*, 36. Ragusa comments on how the Italian "habit of self-denigration" began to extend itself beyond just comparison with French culture to include Anglo-Saxon and Germanic (Ragusa, *Narrative and Drama*, 4).

16 "Every reader with even the slightest knowledge of Italian literature is well aware that, unlike France, Italy does not claim in its roster of writers any names that could match those of such distinguished, articulate and highly vocal personalities as Jean-Paul Sartre, Gabriel Marcel, Simone de Beauvoir, Maurice Merleau-Ponty who, along with a score of novelists and essayists, are mainly responsible for the popularity and fame currently being enjoyed by Existentialism" (Pacifici, "Existentialism and Italian Literature," 79).

17 Emilio Gentile, Walter L. Adamson, and Martin Puchner have pointed to the limitations of making this sharp distinction since there are "alliances and shared projects across the presumed line separating high modernism and manifesto-driven or avant-garde Modernism" (Puchner, *Poetry of the Revolution*, 7). Ram puts the Italian movement in its international context (Ram, "Futurist Geographies").

modern Italian literature only since the beginning of this century, with Luca Somigli and Mario Moroni's field-changing edited volume, *Italian Modernism* (2004).[18]

Accommodating modernism to the Italian literary landscape can be a struggle. The problems of applying it in discussions of Italian literature are evidenced by the fact that one of the primary ways to bring many authors of modernism together is to comment on how different they are, as in Robert Dombroski's "The Foundations of Italian Modernism," which summarizes the situation: "Geography played a crucial role in defining the Italian experience of 'modernity.' ... Pirandello, Svevo, and Gadda represent three different stages and ways of portraying and interpreting reality."[19] In addition, a modernism that not only encompasses but even begins with Svevo's and Gadda's novels (*Senilità*, 1898; *La coscienza di Zeno*, 1923; *Quer pasticciaccio brutto de via Merulana*, 1957; and *La cognizione del dolore*, 1963) is less chronologically concentrated than most other modernisms. *Modernism*, a much-debated term in general, can become particularly vague when applied to Italy's chronologically diffuse and geographically diverse literary scene. While several of my chapters will comment on the modernist qualities of Italian authors, my analysis is not intended to fit all the authors discussed into the category of modernism. The awkwardness of Italian modernism potentially prompts new ways to bring together a variety of important modern Italian authors.

I propose a Kafkan perspective on Italian literature as an alternative approach, one that allows for a diverse and complex portrait of the Italian literary landscape, but that also brings Italian literature into broader conversations. The comparison with Kafka, who came from a multilingual, contested area and whose works have been seen as, in part, a result of these conflicts, sheds light on Italian authors' multilingual, marginal, and contested contexts.[20] From representations of crises, animal imagery, and oppressive familial relations to extremely short fiction and literary detective novels, the disparate elements of Kafka's work are reflected throughout modern Italian literature. This Kafkan tradition encompasses a more diverse group of authors than headings

---

18 Since Somigli and Moroni's collection appeared, a series of other critics, notably Roberto Luperini and Massimiliano Tortora, have engaged in a sustained consideration of what *modernism* means in the Italian context.

19 Dombroski, "The Foundations of Italian Modernism," 102.

20 See, in particular, chaps. 4 and 5. *Multilingual* in the Italian context refers primarily to the prominence of dialects (which are often further from Italian, linguistically, than Spanish is), although many Italian authors also knew French, English, German, etc.

such as *frammentismo* allow, without assimilating the particularity of the Italian scene into one larger modernist movement.

David Damrosch has analysed how a viewer's origins change the picture of any literary scene: "For any given observer, even a genuinely global perspective remains a perspective *from somewhere*, and global patterns of circulation of world literature take shape in their local manifestations."[21] His quote addresses a problem he saw in Franco Moretti's characterization of world literature.[22] Moretti claimed a division between seeing "trees" and "waves" for scholars working on national and world literature: "national literature, for people who see trees; world literature, for people who see waves."[23] One of the issues with this formulation is that of perspective. We create our trees; they are not solid and unchanging.[24] While not discounting the many other "trees" that have been discussed, this book offers a new perspective and proposes that those of national literature are frequently more fluid, or rhizomatic in the Deleuze and Guattarian sense, than rooted.[25]

Kafka's Italian Reception: An Overview

Critics generally characterize Kafka as "barely known to his contemporaries" at the time of his death in 1924, and they describe his fame as a post–Second World War phenomenon.[26] While French, German, American, and British studies tend to credit the French, Germans, Americans, and British for bringing Kafka to the world's attention, he had a strong presence in Italy even before the Second World War. Italian

---

21 Damrosch, *What Is World Literature?*, 27.
22 Damrosch, 25.
23 Moretti, *Distant Reading*, 61.
24 Apter has clarified how a nation acts as the proprietor of its literary tradition in a way that is analogous to an author's own works: "Literary communities are gated: according to Western law and international statute, authors *have* texts, publishers *have* a universal right to translate (as long as they pay), and nations *own* literary patrimony as cultural inheritance" (Apter, *Against World Literature*, 15). We critics describe these gated communities and, in part, decide how the outside world views them.
25 This continues with a critical trend that Saussy, in "Exquisite Cadavers Stitched from Fresh Nightmares," and Jonathan Culler note, that comparative literature suggests approaches that national literature and culture departments should also consider (Culler, "Comparative Literature, at Last," 237).
26 This quote is from Caputo-Mayr, "Introduction," 331. She has written several other articles on Kafka's reception (for his reception in Italy, see, in particular, Caputo-Mayr, "Kafka and Romance Languages") and is the co-editor, with Julius M. Herz, of *Franz Kafka*.

authors such as Carlo Emilio Gadda, Natalia Ginzburg, Tommaso Landolfi, Eugenio Montale, Elsa Morante, Alberto Moravia, Cesare Pavese, Italo Svevo, and Elio Vittorini mention Kafka's importance before 1945. Lavinia Mazzucchetti states that the "first non-German notice" of Kafka came from Italians, and she herself wrote of Kafka in 1926.[27] The Italian translations of "Ein Brudermord" ("Un fratricidio"), "Ein altes Blatt" ("Un vecchio foglietto"), "Vor dem Gesetz" ("Davanti alla legge"), and "Der neue Advokat" ("Il nuovo avvocato") in 1928 were prefaced with the translator's remark that he worried about daring to present an author of Kafka's stature.[28] This comment comes not long after the posthumous publication in German of Kafka's three novels, *Der Prozess*, 1925 (*The Trial*); *Das Schloss*, 1926 (*The Castle*); and *Amerika*, later *Der Verschollene*, 1927 (*Amerika*, or *The Man Who Disappeared*), which had yet to gain much notice.

Kafka's precocious appearance in the Italian literary landscape was due, in part, to the Austro-Hungarian and later Italian city of Trieste. Under Habsburg rule, Trieste was not allowed a university, so many of its citizens went to universities in Florence, Vienna, and Prague, returning with a deeper interest in the literature of those cities. Because many Triestines knew German, in addition to Triestine, Italian, and Slovene, a number of them could read Kafka in the original, even before he was translated.[29] The labours of the Triestine Roberto "Bobi" Bazlen exemplify the city's role in spreading recognition of Kafka. Bazlen recommended Kafka's works to Italians who wanted to improve their German as early as 1919 and to notable Italian authors, such as the poet Eugenio Montale in 1924.[30]

For most of Kafka's life, Trieste was the major port of the Austro-Hungarian Empire. Even after its fall in 1918, many of the cultural connections among Trieste, Prague, Vienna, and the rest of the Habsburg territories remained. Kafka's own experiences reflect the connections between Prague and Trieste. Kafka began studying Italian in 1907, when he considered moving to Trieste since he worked for the insurance company Assicurazioni Generali, whose headquarters were located in the port city. Many Triestine authors, including Italo Svevo,

---

27 See the citation in Mazzuchetti, *Novecento in Germania*, 188. See also Mazzuchetti, "Franz Kafka e il Novecento."
28 See Kafka and Menassé, "Franz Kafka," 383.
29 For examinations of the category and works of Triestine authors, see Ara and Magris, *Trieste*; Pizzi, *A City in Search of an Author*; and Klopp, *Bele Antiche Stòríe*.
30 See Mattioni, *Storia di Umberto Saba*, 82; La Ferla, *Diritto al silenzio*; and Montale, *Lettere Italo Svevo*, 178.

Giani Stuparich, Alberto Spaini, Stelio Mattioni, Susanna Tamaro, and Claudio Magris, draw on Kafka in their literary works.[31]

After the Second World War, Kafka remained a prominent figure, especially as Italian authors considered what foreign novels could add to Italian literature. Especially since many Italians read Kafka not only in Italian translation but also in French and German, among other versions, some early Italian criticism of Kafka mirrors that of other countries.[32] In keeping with other critics, when they first encountered Kafka, Italian writers often used the terms *labyrinthine, mystical*, and *metaphysical* to describe him. Calvino saw learning from Kafka as an important step for Italians to become world authors. Calvino was drawn to Kafka, in part, out of a desire to rejuvenate Italian literature: "With this meagre assortment of values to save from our own recent tradition, we threw ourselves with impatience into the crucible of the world literature of our century: Proust, Joyce, Kafka."[33] The hope that Kafka's work would help revive Italian prose more generally relates to a long tradition of Italian authors (not just translators) who brought German, French, and Anglo-American works to the Italian public. From the 1930s (Alberto Spaini) to today (Paola Capriolo), several notable Italian authors have dedicated their time to translating Kafka. At times, authors were drawn to Kafka on their own; in other cases, publishers (such as Primo Levi's) facilitated a connection between the German-language author and an Italian one. In the 1980s, Einaudi's Authors Translated by Authors series published both Levi's translation of *The Trial* (1983) and Franco Fortini's translation of Kafka's short stories (1986).[34]

---

31 While not all of them make it into *Kafka's Italian Progeny*, all would be productive to discuss with regard to Kafka. However, the existing category, Triestine authors, is often considered somewhat foreign to the Italian literary landscape, and this book aims to show how Kafka suggests new groups of authors rather than modifying existing ones.

32 Svevo, who called Kafka his last literary love, read the Prague author in German. See Ziolkowski, "Svevo's Dogs."

33 "Con questo scarno bagaglio di valori da salvare della nostra ultima tradizione, ci buttavamo con impazienza nel crogiuolo della letteratura mondiale del nostro secolo: Proust, Joyce, Kafka" (Calvino, *Saggi*, 65). This quote is from a version of a talk published in Italian ("Tre correnti del romanzo italiano d'oggi," 1960). The earlier English talk, given at Columbia University in 1959 and then published in 1960 ("Main Currents in Italian Fiction Today"), does not contain this sentence.

34 See Mauro's discussion of Franco Fortini's translation in Mauro, *Il ponte di Glienicke*, 111–24.

Emily Apter has argued that world literature relies on a "translatability assumption" (often into English), ignoring the untranslatability of works and phrases.[35] Complementing her arguments about untranslatability, Kafka's Italian reception shows the specificity of translation from one tradition to another. The presentation of a work and the texture of its text changes depending, in part, on the culture of the target audience. For instance, Kafka's early translator, Alberto Spaini, not only chose which of Kafka's novels to translate first due to his specific reading of Kafka's realism, but his views also affected his translation practices. Translations have a specificity that is sometimes overlooked in discussions of world literature.[36] Many studies on Kafka and his influence concentrate on him and English-language authors, just as many works on Kafka's world reception focus on works originally written in, or translated into, English.[37] I argue that the unique relationship between Kafka and Italian literature offers another way to complicate the dominance of global English in literary studies.

Italian critics, in fact, have a notable tradition of contributing to Kafka criticism.[38] As Italian reviewers of Angel Flores's 1946 English-language collection *The Kafka Problem* pointed out, it contained two translations of Italian essays, Renato Poggioli's "Kafka and Dostoevsky" and Alberto Spaini's introduction to *The Trial*. Roberto Calasso's introduction to and edition of *Zürau Aphorisms*, originally in Italian, has been used for German, English, French, Spanish, Polish, and other editions of the work. In a 2013 review of Reiner Stach's *Kafka: The Decisive Years* and *Kafka: The Years of Insight*,[39] as well as Saul Friedländer's *Franz Kafka: The Poet of Shame and Guilt*, John Banville singles out both Pietro Citati

---

35 "In a counter-move, I invoke untranslatability as a deflationary gesture toward the expansionism and gargantuan scale of world-literary endeavors. A primary argument of this book is that many recent efforts to revive World Literature rely on a translatability assumption" (Apter, *Against World Literature*, 3).

36 See Woods, *Kafka Translated*. See Sofri, *Una variazione di Kafka*, for a discussion of the interpretative difference that one word can make.

37 See the impressive online project, "Kafka Atlas," which documents Kafka's reception in numerous countries (Russia, China, Brazil, India, and Canada, etc.): Haring, "Kafka-Atlas."

38 Italians who travelled to other countries also often introduced others to his work. Lorenza Mazzetti recalls that her London colleagues had not heard of Kafka before she started making a film based on *The Metamorphosis*, and Viktor Nekrasov recounts that Alberto Moravia was the first to mention Kafka to him and several of his fellow Russian writers.

39 The review is of the two English translations by Shelley Frisch.

and Roberto Calasso: "In the matter of originality one should mention Pietro Citati's *Kafka* (English translation 1990) and Roberto Calasso's *K.* (English translation 2005). These are not biographies but deeply perceptive and poetic meditations on the unique phenomenon that Kafka represented."[40]

The fact that the two works Banville mentions are Italian suggests how Italy's position in the critical landscape can lend itself to creating unusual, provocative works.[41] The Italian background of these works is rarely mentioned: Italian criticism is not far enough from the primary Western critical tradition for it to be of note (were Citati and Calasso both Japanese, their nationality would probably have been mentioned), but it is also not dominant enough (unlike French- or English-language writers) for Italian critics to be considered central to the critical discussion. Relatedly, while Agamben's writing on Kafka has had a strong international *fortuna*, critics often overlook the importance of his Italian background in shaping his views. Primo Levi's translation of *The Trial* and his subsequent reflection on the idea of shame in the novel significantly informed Agamben's concept of Kafka.[42]

To give a sense of the extent of Kafka's influence in Italy, I offer an example from each decade since the 1940s, in which significant Italian intellectuals refer to and use Kafka directly in their work.[43] In 1942, Tommaso Landolfi publishes the story "Il babbo di Kafka" ("Kafka's Dad"), in which Kafka encounters a large spider with the head of his father. In 1953, Italian author and director Lorenza Mazzetti produces a cinematic version of "Die Verwandlung" ("The Metamorphosis") in England, called *K.* She discusses the process of making the film in *Diario londinese* (*London Diary*) and notes the appeal of Kafka to someone, like her, who felt like an outsider. A notable number of other Italian works on Kafka are called "*K*," including Edoardo Sanguineti's dramatic

---

40 Banville, "A Different Kafka."
41 In addition to Levi, Elsa Morante, Massimo Cacciari, and Davide Stimilli are all important points of reference in his discussions of Kafka. Agamben's piece, "K.," in *Nudities* reflects on the idea that K. in *Der Process* stands for *kalumniator*, an idea he expands from Davide Stimilli's analysis of Kafka.
42 Snoek argues that while the fascination with Agamben and Kafka is rooted in their "seemingly gloomy political world views" (Snoek, *Agamben's Joyful Kafka*, 1), Agamben, in fact, uses Kafka as an exit strategy from unbearable political situations.
43 While *Kafka's Italian Progeny* engages Kafka's reception to analyse groups of Italian authors, this method is not the only way to combine Kafka and Italy or Kafka and Italian literature. Italian Kafka is a rich source for study. While direct references to Kafka in Italian literature, film, and art guide the readings in several chapters in this book, there are many more examples of Kafka's influence in Italy.

rendering of Kafka's purported conversations with Gustav Janouch, Calasso's book, and Agamben's piece in *Nudità* (*Nudities*). Since *K* is not part of the standard Italian alphabet, the use of this letter immediately marks the upcoming reading as foreign and is perhaps even more closely linked to Kafka than it is in German or English.

In 1964, Pier Paolo Pasolini's "Progetto di opere future" ("Plan for Future Works") includes the lines "oh Kafka – tutto è terrore"[44] ("oh Kafka – everything is terror"). Nobel prize-winner Eugenio Montale includes a poem, "Verboten," in the *Diaries from 1971 and 1972* that begins by describing Kafka's grammar as missing the future. One of the premises of Federico Fellini's *Intervista* (1987) is that the famous director is finally realizing his dream of filming Kafka's *Amerika*. Claudio Magris describes a visit to the room where Kafka died in *Danubio* (*Danube*, 1990). Cristian Martini's travel story draws on Kafka in content and title: *La vendetta di Kafka* (*Kafka's Revenge*, 2005). In 2015 at Italy's Embassy in Washington, DC, Francesco Nonino showed his series of photographs, "Come se la vergogna" / "As If the Shame of It," inspired by Kafka's *The Trial*. One of the photographs from this series provides this book's cover image.

The early fascination of Italian readers with Kafka stems, in part, from the numerous references to Italian names, characters, and locations in his oeuvre.[45] Italian consistently appears in Kafka's works, partially because of his travels. He travelled to Italian locations on multiple occasions, visiting Trieste, Lugano, Milan, Stresa, Brescia, Verona, Venice, Desenzano, Merano, and Riva on Lake Garda. Kafka's experience in Brescia, analysed in Peter Demetz's *The Air Show at Brescia, 1909*, led to his first published article, which included a couple of not very flattering comments about D'Annunzio: "Gabriele d'Annunzio, short and fragile, dances about in an apparently bashful way in front of the Count Oldofredi, one of the most important gentlemen of the Committee. Looking out over the rail of the stand is the strong face of Puccini, with a nose that might be called the nose of a drinker."[46] Curzio Malaparte discusses D'Annunzio's annoyance at the description during a 1928 visit, during which the authors looked at an Italian translation of the article: "'Look,' he said to me, 'even him! Would you have imagined it? He comes to Italy, and cannot find anything better

---

44 Pasolini, *Poesia in forma di rosa*, 204.
45 For more on Kafka's Italian journeys, see Caputo-Mayr, "Kafka and Romance Languages"; Demetz, *The Air Show at Brescia, 1909*; Crespi, "Kafka e l'Italia," 107–12; and Stach, *Kafka*.
46 Kafka, *The Transformation*, 7.

to do but insult me. He was a miserable office worker, in an insurance company for Prague, but he was a great artist, with a noble mind. And look who comes forward to talk about me, the poor office worker.' I read the name: it was Kafka's."[47] Because Kafka had written about D'Annunzio (even if in a critical manner), the Italian author was interested in Kafka.

The early Italian view of Kafka was distinct from other national traditions in several ways and continues to affect the view of him in Italy today.[48] In 1954, Ladislao Mittner published "Kafka senza kafkaismi" (Kafka without Kafkaisms), in which he argued that the time to reassess Kafka had finally come because Kafka's fame had moved beyond its apex. Italian Germanists, such as Mittner, often resisted the more popular ideas of Kafka as existentialist, surrealist, or a religious prophet.[49] Kafka's strong presence among Italian authors and intellectuals, before he was internationally famous, affected the course of his Italian reception: Italian criticism was at the forefront of calling attention to the significance of Prague, Jewish culture, Austria-Hungary, and humour for understanding Kafka.[50] Multiple factors contribute to these noticeable elements of Italian criticism of Kafka.

From before the Jewish periodical *La rassegna mensile di Israel* (*Monthly Review of Israel*) published an overview in 1936 to De Angelis's *Qualcosa*

---

47 "'Guarda,' mi disse, 'anche lui! Lo avresti immaginato? Viene in Italia, e non trova di meglio da fare che insultar me. Era un misero impiegatuccio, in una società di assicurazioni di Praga, ma era un grande artista, una nobile mente. E guarda chi vien fuori, per parla di me: l'impiegatuccio.' Io lessi il nome: era quello di Kafka" (Malaparte, *Battibecco*, 101–2).

48 The particular Italian context also affects which works of Kafka's are taught in schools. For instance, Panebianco, Seminara, and Gineprini's "Percorso Tema" gives a selection of texts that are connected to the students inspired by Marco Polo's *Milione*, including selections from Coleridge's "Kubla Khan," Kafka's "Un messsaggio dell'imperatore," and Calvino's *Le città invisibili*. Calvino's introduction to *Le città invisibili*, in fact, suggested this connection.

49 Mittner began his 1954 article, "Camus, in a kafkaesquely vivid style, wrote regarding *The Castle*, 'The destiny and perhaps the greatness of this work consists of offering everything and confirming nothing.' Kafkomania has been in definite decline for the past ten years, and perhaps it has reached the ideal moment to liberate Kafka from the various *kafkismi*" (Mittner, *La letteratura tedesca del Novecento*, 249).

50 Although it is now a commonplace to claim that Kafka's humour is overlooked, Renato Barilli (1982) and Guido Crespi (1983) dedicated entire books to the issue of Kafka's humour over a decade before David Foster Wallace's better known "Laughing with Kafka" (1998). My chapter on the Italian understanding of Kafka as a realist and the significance of *Amerika*, or *Der Verschollene* (*Amerika*, or *The Man Who Disappeared*) in Italy goes into the background of this in the greatest detail since Kafka's humour and realism are related.

di più intimo, 2006 (*Something More Intimate*) and beyond, Kafka's Jewish heritage has been a point of focus and a significant reference point in discussions of Jewishness in Italy.[51] In the 1920s and 1930s major Italian authors, such as Svevo and Ginzburg, remarked on the importance of Kafka's Jewishness. For many Italian authors, Kafka helped them to define elements of their own Jewish heritage. Kafka's appeal as a Jewish author to many Italian authors with Jewish backgrounds also highlights the prominence of these authors in modern Italian literature.

In certain areas of Italy, interest in Kafka and his Jewishness really grew after the racial laws were instituted in 1938. These laws forced people of Jewish background out of the main school system and caused them to run their own middle and high schools, often with Jewish instructors who had been professors at universities. This separation promoted an interest in Judaism and in the meaning of being Jewish. Kafka was a significant part of the schools' program of Jewish discovery. Much of the Italian reception of Kafka's Jewishness reflects past studies of Jewishness in Italy: attraction to Kafka's Jewish heritage, negative feelings related to his Jewish background, and ignorance of Kafka's Jewishness occurred simultaneously and reflect the various responses of Italians more generally to Italians of Jewish background before, during, and soon after the Second World War.[52]

Whereas Kafka's background and context are now considered central for understanding the author, this shift took place at a broader level over fifty years after his death. *Franz Kafka: International Bibliography of Primary and Secondary Literature* lists Giuliano Baioni's *Kafka: Romanzo e parabola*, 1962 (*Kafka: Novel and Parable*) first in its summary of works dedicated to Kafka's Jewishness and "affinity to Eastern European culture."[53] Trieste's strong connections to the Austro-Hungarian world contribute to the important role that Italian critics have played in understanding the importance of Prague and Austria-Hungary to Kafka's work. Jacques Le Rider characterizes the German translation of Claudio Magris's *Il mito absburgico nella letteratura austriaca moderna* (*The Habsburg Myth in Modern Austrian Literature; Der habsburgische Mythos in der*

---

51 See Luzzatto's piece on Kafka ("Franz Kafka") in *La Rassegna Mensile di Israel*.
52 I have discussed elsewhere, in more detail, Svevo's, Ginzburg's, and Primo Levi's comments on Kafka's Jewishness (Ziolkowski, "Primo Levi and Jewish Kafka in Italy"). Kafka's early reception reflects the difficulty of trying to define the existence and character of Italian Jewishness as well as Italian anti-Semitism. For works that explore Italian authors with Jewish background as modern Italian Jewish authors, see, e.g., Hughes, *Prisoners of Hope*; and De Angelis, *Qualcosa di più intimo*.
53 Caputo-Mayr and Herz, *Franz Kafka*, xxxvii.

österreichischen Literatur), which includes discussions of Kafka, as marking the "early beginning of the rediscovery of 'Viennese modernity.'"[54]

Even before Magris and Baioni, in a review of the first Italian edition of
The Castle (1948), Giovanni Papini proposed that it made no sense to read
the novel as an allegory about God or a search, but that, if it had meaning, it was about Austro-Hungarian bureaucracy: "*The Castle* would be,
in this way, a gray and bitter parody of the Habsburg administration, or
even of the imperial government, which for the Slavs of Prague, was a
foreign government and, therefore, even more ridiculous and odious.
But this contingent symbolism will seem too modest to the abstracters of
sleep-walking criticism."[55] Like many Italian writers, Papini took issue
with how his contemporaries tended to read Kafka, even though, unlike
most Italian critics and authors, he reached fairly negative conclusions
about Kafka's work. Attention to Kafka's cultural contexts, humour, and
realism are interrelated. *The Castle,* for instance, is more likely to seem
amusing if it is read as a realistic parody of Habsburg bureaucracy.

Papini's view contrasts with the world-literature perspective of
his time.[56] David Damrosch, in his chapter, "Kafka Comes Home,"
in *What Is World Literature?* describes the shift from viewing Kafka
as a universal author in most of the twentieth century to considering him a representative of a "marginal" culture in this century:
"Following Brod's lead, the Muirs and their publisher Schocken,
worked to produce a universalist Kafka, a creator of symbolic quests
for spiritual meaning, a writer who could become a central figure for
modern self-understanding rather than someone who needed to be

---

54 Le Rider, *Modernity and Crises of Identity,* xxxvii. Magris provided one explanation
    for the Italian sense of Austro-Hungarian contemporaneity: "Habsburg civilization
    is fashionable because it highlights the irreality that has taken over the world." ("La
    civiltà asburgica è di moda perché ha posto in evidenza l'irrealtà che ha investito
    il mondo"; Magris, *Itaca e oltre,* 42.) Magris commented that journeying to another
    part of the Italian peninsula was necessary to realize the Austro-Hungarian nature
    of his Italian home (Magris, "Genesi di un 'mito,'" 15).

55 "*Il Castello* sarebbe, così, una grigia e amara parodia dell'amministrazione
    absburgica, o addirittura del governo imperiale, che per gli slavi di Praga, era
    un governo straniero epperciò ancor più ridicolo e odioso. Ma questo simbolo
    contingente sembrerà troppo modesto agli strologatori della critica sonnambula"
    (Papini, *La loggia dei busti,* 255).

56 Papini is not the only early reviewer to find the work boring – a piece in the
    New Yorker informed the reader, "I warn you that the book is dull. I also warn you that
    the allegory is often obscured and fogged beyond all reason" (Smith, "The Castle,"
    106) – but he can be distinguished as seeing the relationship between *The Castle* and
    Austro-Hungarian culture at this point, whereas the *New Yorker* reviewer, Agnes
    W. Smith, follows the Muirs in her interpretation and frames the work as an allegory.

read in the context of turn-of-the-century Prague or even of German culture at large."[57] Damrosch's narrative represents well the Anglo-American, German, and French reception of Kafka, but, as discussed, Italians underscored the significance of Kafka's cultural background and Jewish heritage earlier and more often than other critics.

Do the differences between the Italian situation and Damrosch's description mean that Italian Kafka is not part of world-literature Kafka? Damrosch asks, "If we now see a Prague Jew where an earlier generation saw an international modernist, are we getting closer to the essence of the writer and his work, or simply projecting our current interests into both?"[58] One might also ask, does the "we" exclude Italian authors and critics? Anglophone critics are at times stuck within their own perspective, that the world-literature view of Kafka is the Kafka whom we, English speakers, know. This view shifts over time, but is especially recognizable to the American or British scholar, even though Kafka is a widely accepted world author, in part, because of his strong receptions in places that are frequently considered more peripheral, like Japan, Argentina, and Israel.

Also changing with time, Russian Kafka, Chinese Kafka, Spanish Kafka, and Italian Kafka are all a little different. These various Kafkas are significant for adding to the critical understanding of Kafka and his reception as well as to help reconsider what is meant by the *world-literature* view of an author. In a discussion of world literature, centres, and peripheries, Martin Puchner remarks upon "the provincialism of the centre as a feeling that the world comes to you anyway, a provincialism associated with cultural (as well as political) hegemony."[59] This provincialism of the centre is often true not only of individual authors, like Ibsen, whom Puchner analyses, but also of reception. World-literature Kafka tends to describe the Kafka of the centre, whereas Italian, Russian, and Japanese Kafka can be seen as peripheral and, therefore, offering something new.

Modifying Heinz Politzer's earlier comment that Kafka's work is like a Rorschach test for the critics, Stephen Dowden posits that

57 Damrosch, *What Is World Literature?*, 189. He provides an important, often-used reference to world literature: "I take world literature to encompass all literary works that circulate beyond their culture of origin, either in translation or in their original language" (Damrosch, 4). He describes how Brod and the Muirs framed *The Castle*, quoting Brod's description of it as a "book in which everyone recognizes his own experience" before moving to more culturally specific interpretations of the work.
58 Damrosch, 198.
59 Puchner, "Goethe, Marx, Ibsen and the Creation of a World Literature," 5.

Kafka criticism itself now looks like a "vast and shapeless Rorschach blotch."[60] World-literature discussions give shape to the blotch, but often minimize, distil, and flatten it, while revealing which countries are considered part of world literature. Altering this view can help change the Rorschach blotch of Kafka, add to the critical understanding of Kafka, complicate world-literature narratives like those of Damrosch, and give a different shape to the Italian modern literary tradition.

Morante and Buzzati: Two Cases of Kafka Reception

Morante and Buzzati offer two examples of Kafka's early Italian reception and what it can reveal about both Italian literature and its study. Morante was at the forefront of Kafka reception, and she comments on one of the first visual representations of Kafka's work, Max Ernst's depiction of Odradek in the French journal *Minotaure* (1937), which accompanied André Breton's surrealist description of Kafka.[61] This image prompted Morante to dream of Kafka's death as well as associate herself and Moravia with the author from Prague. In her note to her collection *Lo scialle andaluso* (*The Andalusian Shawl*), Morante claims that Kafka was the only author to influence her: "This however was the first and last time that E.M. – it is to be said in all fairness – was influenced by any other author in the world."[62] Moravia referred to Kafka as Morante's "master" and "religion."[63] Morante's consideration of Kafka and playing with Kafkan modes of narration were fundamental to the Italian author's process of creating her narrative style.[64] She saw Kafka's stories as more truthful, more real, than attempts to represent reality naturalistically or documentarily: "Kafka writes surreal fables: and yet no photographic or documented report expresses certain atrocious truths of this century, as his surreal fables."[65] Morante's interest in and

---

60 Dowden, *Kafka's Castle and the Critical Imagination*, 1. Dowden used *The Castle* to give shape to the immense, seemingly blotch-like criticism.

61 For Morante's comments on Odradek, see *Diario 1938*, 32; for my discussion of the relationship between her comments on Kafka and her own work, see Ziolkowski, "Morante and Kafka."

62 "Questa però fu la prima e l'ultima che E.M. – sia detto a sua giustizia – risentì l'influsso di un qualsiasi altro autore al mondo" (Morante, *Lo scialle andaluso*, 215). This is, of course, arguable; see, e.g., Lucamante, *Elsa Morante e l'eredità proustiana*.

63 See Moravia's "master" comment (*Life of Moravia*, 190) and "religion" comment (Paris, 50).

64 See Ziolkowski, "Morante and Kafka."

65 "Kafka scrive delle favole surreali: eppure nessun resoconto fotografico e documentato esprime certe atroci verità del presente secolo, come le sue favole surreali" (Morante, *Opere*, 2:1511). See Leavitt, "Una seconda fase del realismo," for a discussion of Morante and realism.

connections with Kafka's work are multiple. The two authors could be read together in terms of Jewish identity, realism, and the gothic, among other topics. In this book, Morante's work plays an important role in chapter 4 on the family and chapter 5 on the human-animal boundary.

Morante focused particularly on Kafka in the 1930s, when his important collection *Il messaggio dell'imperatore* (*The Imperial Message*) was published. This short story collection brought together most of Kafka's short works (thirty-nine of them), including "The Hunter Gracchus." Set in Riva, which Kafka visited in 1909 and 1913, "The Hunter Gracchus" features the "only geographically specific setting in any of Kafka's short fiction."[66] Revealing how Kafka's settings could shape Italian authors' views of their own country, Kafka's description of an Italian city influenced Morante's experience of another Italian coastal city. She sees the story of the Hunter Gracchus reflected in her trip to Cefalù in 1937: "Windows closed, it makes one think about death. It seems like the boat of a dead pagan, tired of wandering and come ashore (Kafka's 'The Hunter Gracchus')."[67] Kafka was in Morante's dreams, her mind as she travelled, and her thoughts as she wrote.

Many other Italian authors, such as Lalla Romano and Cesare Pavese, discuss the significance of their encounters with Kafka's work in 1935, the year *Il messaggio dell'imperatore* was published. In his 1945 introduction to *America* (*The Man Who Disappeared*, originally published as *Amerika*), Alberto Spaini insinuated that certain Italian authors had made Kafka-like literature popular before he was well known in Italy, and he dated the beginning of this influence to 1935: "For ten years we have been invaded by *Kafkaini* and by a *Kafkaismo* that so far the critics have not identified, perhaps because his name would not have meant anything to anyone, but which has made Kafka more popular in Italy than one can imagine."[68] Critics often read this comment as referencing Buzzati.[69] The potential Buzzati-Kafka connection is a long-standing issue in Buzzati criticism.[70] In 1947, Montale wanted to meet Buzzati, partly because so many had associated him with Kafka, revealing both

[handwritten margin notes: This year for Kafka]

---

66 Gross, "Hunting Kafka," 249.
67 "Finestre chiuse, fa pensare alla morte. Sembra una barca di un morto pagano, stanca di errare e approdata a questa riva ('Il cacciattore gracco' di Kafka)" (Morante, *Opere*, 1:xxix).
68 "Da dieci anni siamo invasi da kafkiani e da un kafkismo che la critica non ha finora identificato, forse perché il nome non avrebbe dette nulla a nessuno, ma che hanno reso Kafka assai più popolare in Italia di quanto di immagini" (Spaini, "Prefazione," vii).
69 See, e.g., Cusatelli, "Kafka e i suoi lettori italiani," 3.
70 See, e.g., Baumann's "Buzzati: Ein 'Kafka italiano'?" in *Dino Buzzati*, 215–20. In a review of *The Tartar Steppe*, Tim Parks argues, "Much, far too much, has been made of Buzzati's debt to Kafka" (Parks, "Throwing Down a Gauntlet").

his own continued interest in Kafka and the prominence of questions about Kafka's influence on Buzzati.[71] Critics often compared Buzzati's early works to Kafka's in an unflattering manner.[72] Moravia, for instance, suggested that Buzzati's work was unoriginal and derivative of Kafka's: "The book [Buzzati's *The Tartar Steppe*] enjoyed a popularity precisely because the success of Kafka, a true writer, had prepared the ground for the work of his imitator."[73]

Showing that he thought as little of Moravia's work as Moravia did of his, Buzzati posited Kafka as a model for literary production, in contrast to the type of fiction Moravia wrote: "I have the distinct impression that all veristic literature that is being written today, from the classic novels of love to stories like Moravia's, really have no reason to exist. One should write something about which the public cannot help but be interested in, even if, in the case of Kafka, the public does not read it."[74] In this letter from 1935, Buzzati, who often aimed for the same effect in his own work, categorizes Kafka's as a new kind of writing that offers a denaturalizing perspective. He read Kafka in both Italian and German, highlighting Kafka as one of the German authors whose works he chose to read in the original on account of the accessibility of Kafka's language: "Because Kafka's German is very limpid, very easy."[75]

The Longanesi publishers asked Buzzati to change the originally proposed title of his *Tartar* novel from "La fortezza" (The fortress), with its strong military connotations, in part perhaps because it would recall Kafka's *The Castle*, which Buzzati discussed reading, again in 1935: "I read 140 pages of *The Castle* and then I stopped, although it is impressive. But in this period, I need to read stupid and gay books like those of Wodehouse. Write me what you think of *The Castle*. It seems

---

71 Montale, quoted in Arslan, *Invito alla lettura*, 19.
72 See, e.g., Bárberi Squarotti, *Dal tramonto*, 56. For an overview of the Kafka-Buzzati relationship with regard to the broader issues of intertextuality in Buzzati, see Polcini, *Dino Buzzati and Anglo-American Culture*, 9–33.
73 Moravia and Elkann, *Life of Moravia*, 269. ("Il libro ha avuto una diffusione dovuta proprio al fatto che il successo di Kafka, scrittore autentico, aveva preparato il terreno all'opera del suo imitatore"; Moravia and Elkann, *Vita di Moravia*, 223.) While Moravia accused Buzzati of being successful merely because Kafka was, other critics commented that Buzzati drew on Kafka before Kafka was popular, even before many of his works had been translated into Italian.
74 "Ho la netta impressione che tutta la letteratura veristica, quale oggi si va praticando, dal classico romanzo d'amore ai racconti tipo Moravia, non abbia una vera ragione di esistere.... Bisognerebbe scrivere qualcosa di cui il pubblico non possa non interessarsi, anche se, come nel caso di Kafka, non la legge" (Buzzati, *Lettere a Brambilla*, 230).
75 "Perché è un tedesco molto limpido, molto facile, quello di Kafka" (Buzzati and Panafieu, *Dino Buzzati*, 29).

to me it is even more Kafkaesque than *The Trial*."[76] Buzzati's proposed alternative titles, "Il messaggio del Nord" (The message from the north) and "Il deserto dei Tartari" (The desert of the Tartars), also recall works by Kafka.[77] Adriano Buzzati mentioned giving *Il messaggio dell'impera-tore* (*A Message from the Emperor*, or *The Imperial Message*) to his famous brother.[78] Linked by their titles and content, both the collection's titular story and Buzzati's "I sette messaggeri" ("The Seven Messengers") highlight the theme of hoped-for occurrences that are doomed to failure.[79] In "The Seven Messengers," a king's son sets out to reach the frontier beyond his kingdom, but never arrives. Similarly, Kafka's "The Imperial Message" narrates an ongoing, hopeless process: "No one can force his way through here, least of all with a message from a dead man. – But you sit at your window and dream up that message when evening falls."[80]

Of Buzzati's three proposed titles, the final one, *Il deserto dei Tartari* (*The Tartar Steppe*) reflects the most subtle connection to Kafka.[81] In Kafka's "Before the Law," which has also been associated with Buzzati's novel, the man from the country notes the doorkeeper's "long thin black Tartar beard."[82] In part because he closely observes the doorkeeper's appearance, the man "decides that it would be better, after all, to wait until he has permission to enter,"[83] suggesting that the

---

76 "Ho letto 140 pagine del Castello poi mi sono fermato, benché sia una cosa impressionante. Ma in questo periodo ho bisogno di leggere libri stupidi e gai come quelli di Wodehouse. Scrivimi cosa ti sembra il Castello. È più Kafkiano ancora del Processo, mi sembra" (Buzzati, 230–1). For a discussion of the title change, see Nerenberg, *Prison Terms*, 33. For more on the history of the original title and the production of the manuscript, see Germani, *L'attesa e l'ignoto*, 92.

77 Viganò, *Album Buzzati*, 157.

78 Ioli, *Dino Buzzati*, 86. See also Asquer, *La grande torre*, 83–4.

79 Lazzarin refers to "The Imperial Message" as the Kafka text that Buzzati had "best memorized" (Lazzarin, "Note sulla contaminazione delle fonti nella narrativa breve di Buzzati," 11). See Bárberi Squarotti for an analysis of the two stories ("Forme simboliche," 115–17).

80 Kafka, *The Transformation*, 175. "Niemand dringt durch und gar mit der Botschaft eines Toten. – Du aber sitzt an Deinem Fenster und erträumst sie Dir, wenn der Abend kommt" (Kafka, *Erzählungen*, 306).

81 Giulio Savelli has read "Before the Law" as the model parable for tracing the theme of destiny in Buzzati's work, especially in his famous novel (Savelli, "Una struttura del destino in Buzzati," 126).

82 Kafka, *Kafka's Selected Stories* (hereafter cited as *KSS*), 68 ("den langen, dünnen, schawrzen tatrischen Bart"; Kafka, *Erzählungen*, 162).

83 *KSS*, 68. ("Das Gesetz soll doch jedem und immer zugänglich sein, denkt er, aber als er jetzt den Türhüter in seinem Pelzmantel genauer ansieht, seine große Spitznase, den langen, dünnen, schwarzen tatarischen Bart, entschließt er sich, doch lieber zu warten, bis er die Erlaubnis zum Eintritt bekommt"; Kafka, *Erzählungen*, 162.)

beard contributes to the man's decision to wait forever by the door. The unusual detail of the Tartar beard raises the question of where this door is located, suggesting the work's "transnational" character.[84] Similar to how the meaning of the guardian's strange, specifically described beard remains a point of examination, the Tartars in Buzzati's novel prompt various theories about its setting. The protagonist himself wonders about the desert's unusual name: "'That's right – a desert. Stones and parched earth – they call it the Tartar steppe.' 'Why Tartar?,' asked Drogo. 'Were there ever Tartars there?' 'Long, long ago, I believe. But it is a legend more than anything else.'"[85]

The double answer to Drogo's question about the Tartars, that the desert's name is inspired both by fiction and by history, provides one answer to the debate about whether Kafka's literature or Buzzati's experience inspired Buzzati's novel. Both led to it, and it is difficult to know the comparative degrees of their influence. At the same time, the novel is separate from them as the desert exists regardless of the origins of its name. Although reading Kafka influenced Buzzati, Buzzati's work is not derivative. Comparing Kafka and Buzzati will also put into relief elements of Buzzati's fiction that distinguish his work from Kafka's.

Since some critics used Kafka to degrade Buzzati, Buzzati and some of his supporters responded by proclaiming that there his writings show few similarities to Kafka's. Buzzati goes so far as to claim that he had not read Kafka until after having written his most Kafkaesque works, although, as mentioned, his personal correspondence reveals that he had read Kafka in the 1930s, before writing *The Tartar Steppe*.[86] Following in the footsteps not only of Kafka but also of past Italian authors like Renato Poggioli and Italo Calvino, who looked for traces of Kafka in

---

84 Suchoff, *Kafka's Jewish Languages*, 43.
85 Buzzati, *The Tartar*, 11. ("'Un deserto effettivamente, pietre e terra secca, lo chiamano il deserto dei Tartari.' Drogo domandò: 'Perché dei Tartari? C'erano dei Tartari?' 'Anticamente, credo. Ma più che altro una leggenda'"; Buzzati, *Il deserto*, 13.)
86 Following Buzzati's suggestion, his friend Indro Montanelli argues that Buzzati's *The Tartar Steppe* was inspired by his experiences at *Il Corriere della Sera*, not Kafka (Montanelli, "Nella malattia," 75). The relationship between Kafka and Buzzati became a point of debate not only for Italian authors discussing Buzzati's literary merits and inspirations but also for critics discussing Kafkaesque literature, what this category could mean, and intertextuality. Kafka is a starting point in Valentina Polcini's broader discussion of Buzzati and intertextuality, *Dino Buzzati and Anglo-American Culture*. Joseph Strelka summarizes the public debates about Kafka and Buzzati: "When the Italian writer Dino Buzzati, whose novel *Il deserto dei Tartari* (*The Tartar Steppe*) appeared in 1940, received the high literary award, *Premio Strega*, in 1958, the jury was accused of having wasted the prize on an author who had achieved nothing but to popularize a difficult author, namely Kafka" (Strelka, "Kafkaesque Elements," 439).

Prague, Buzzati journeyed to the northern European city and then wrote about the experience.[87] He reflected on his reaction to being constantly compared with Kafka in the resulting piece in *Corriere della Sera*:

> From the very beginning of my writing career, Kafka has been my cross. I have not written a story, novel, or play in which someone has not perceived resemblances, derivations, imitations or simply shameless plagiarisms at the Czech writer's expense. Several critics proclaimed guilty analogies even when I sent a telegram or filled out official forms. All this has determined my attitude toward Kafka for many years: I have suffered not from an inferiority complex but from an annoyance complex. The result has been that I have lost any desire to read his work, as well as biographies and essays that deal with him.[88]

Finding the constant comparison to Kafka irritating, Buzzati suggests that if a critic is looking for Kafka's influence, it can be seen everywhere, even in routine communications. Is there anything in the modern world that is not Kafkaesque? In "Le case di Kafka" ("Kafka's Houses"), Buzzati humorously points to the danger of over-identifying his work with Kafka's. Throughout much of his life, he campaigned to distance himself from Kafka as much as possible.

The critical focus on how much Buzzati was perhaps influenced by Kafka contrasts with Morante's open dedication to Kafka, which critics generally ignore. Both authors read Kafka in the 1930s and discussed in personal correspondence the influence of his prose.[89] Morante also publicly related Kafka's effect on her. The potential reasons that Kafka's significance to Morante's development have often been overlooked are numerous, including her less familiar conception of Kafka's work, her putative distance from literary scenes, and the fact that she is a woman.

---

87 | Renato Poggioli went to Prague to discuss Kafka with Max Brod and then published an article on him in *Solaria* in 1934. Calvino commented on looking for Kafka's ghost during his 1947 trip to Prague.

88 Buzzati, "Kafka's Houses," 143; trans. modified. ("Da quando ho cominciato a scrivere, Kafka è stato la mia croce. Non c'è stato mio racconto, romanzo, commedia dove qualcuno non ravvisasse somiglianze, derivazioni, imitazioni o addirittura sfrontati plagi a spese dello scrittore boemo. Alcuni critici denunciavano colpevoli analogie con Kafka anche quando spedivo un telegramma o compilavo il modulo Vanoni. Tutto questo da molti anni ha determinato in me, nei riguardi di Franz Kafka, non un complesso di inferiorità ma un complesso di fastidio. Da allora non ho voluto più leggere cose sue, né biografie, né saggi che lo riguardavano"; Buzzati, "Le case di Kafka.")

89 Lazzarin and Zangrilli have discussed this; see, e.g., Lazzarin, *Il Buzzati "secondo,"* 92–3.

Kafka's Italian Progeny complements the field-changing studies by Sharon Wood, Adalgisa Giorgio, Stefania Lucamante, Danielle Hipkins, and Laura Lazzari, which concentrate on women authors, by putting these authors in a different genealogy.[90] Both Lalla Romano, discussed in the second chapter, and Paola Capriolo, analysed in the third chapter, have been compared to Kafka in a pejorative manner. While Italian and non-Italian male authors have also been framed as sub-par Kafkas or poor Kafka imitators, the comparison of female Italian authors with Kafka has on more than one occasion suggested misogynistically that they dared to compare themselves with Kafka or write like him. The modern Italian canon itself is debated, and the place of women writers in it is even more varied. This book puts Italian female writers into conversation with Kafka and male co-nationals, with the aim of showing how Kafka's work, and critical studies on him, can reveal less noted elements of Italian fiction, including certain women writers.[91] Although Natalia Ginzburg, Elsa Morante, Lalla Romano, Paola Capriolo, and Elena Ferrante will be discussed, and while issues of gender are significant in several of the examinations, the primary aim is to rethink the categories in which Italian authors are placed, including "women writers."

Kafka's Italian Progeny: An Overview

In "Kafka and His Precursors," Jorge Luis Borges discusses recognizing Kafka in writers that came before him, including Han Yu, Kierkegaard, Browning, Léon Bloy, and Lord Dunsany.[92] Borges's project can be distinguished from the idea of influence since, first of all, the authors he mentions were not ones whom Kafka necessarily read. Like any author's personal list (one need think only of Calvino's examples in *Six Memos*), Borges's precursors for Kafka appear idiosyncratic, which is part of his point. He proposes that Kafka's body of work means that other authors are read differently in light of it. Just as every powerful author creates his or her own precursors, so an author creates his or her own successors. *Kafka's Italian Progeny* draws on the Borgesian idea of Kafka's successors, concentrating on one nation, Italy.

---

90 See Lucamante, *A Multitude of Women*; Giorgio, "The Passion for the Mother";
      Wood, *Italian Women's Writing*; and Hipkins, *Contemporary Italian Women Writers*.
91 Many of the authors discussed, including Ginzburg, Morante, and Capriolo, also
      resisted or resented being categorized as a "female" or "woman" author.
92 "Once I planned to make a survey of Kafka's precursors. At first I thought he was
      as singular as the fabulous phoenix; when I knew him better I thought I recognized
      his voice, or his habits, in the texts of various literatures and various ages" (Borges,
      "Kafka and His Precursors," 199).

This book's idiosyncrasies are primarily based on the critical reception of Kafka in Italy, and each chapter groups together different authors based on their "family resemblance" to a particular element of Kafka's work. In Borges's words, "Not all of them resemble each other," but all resemble Kafka. While Kafka's reception helps guide the choice of authors, analysing the extent of Kafka's influence is not the goal of *Kafka's Italian Progeny*.[93] Although many of the Italian successors I discuss mention Kafka's impact, more significant is how putting their work into conversation with Kafka modifies the critical conception of Italian literature.

Several studies explore various authors using Kafka as the particular lens. While they generally have chapters or sections dedicated to an individual author, such as Coetzee, Roth, Sebald, Bellow, Mailer, Salinger, Camus, Robbe-Grillet, Beckett, or Ionesco, my chapters treat multiple Italian authors.[94] The groupings are based on readings of Kafka, and the members of each group share certain similarities, but the qualities that link the authors together will vary. Instead of focusing on direct, linear inheritances, these Italian authors are connected through Kafka and each other through family resemblances. In an exploration of how to link together all the things we call *games*, "board-games, card-games, ball-games, Olympic games,"[95] Ludwig Wittgenstein employs the term "family resemblances" to define the characteristics that group extremely different entities together.[96] As the terms *family resemblances* and *progeny* imply, the chapters do not aim to present a uniform picture of Kafka or Italian literature; rather, they draw on the diversity of both to fill in gaps that discussions of Italy's literary movements, regions, and authors have left.

Drawing attention to unnoted aspects of well-known Italian authors and some lesser-studied ones, this investigation of a Kafkan tradition suggests one way to construct an identity of modern Italian literature that is not primarily determined by chronological or geographical criteria. Using diverse approaches to explore the thematic, generic, *crucial*

---

93 "The word 'precursor' is indispensable in the vocabulary of criticism, but one should try to purify it from every connotation of polemic or rivalry. The fact is that each writer *creates* his precursors. His work modifies our conception of the past, as it will modify the future" (Borges, 201).

94 See Sandbank, *After Kafka*; Whitlark, *Behind the Great Wall*; Weinberg, *The New Novel in America*; and Medin, *Three Sons*.

95 Wittgenstein, *Philosophical Investigations*, 27e.

96 "I can think of no better expression to characterize these similarities than 'family resemblances'; for the various resemblances between members of a family" (Wittgenstein, 28e).

historical, and cultural connections between Kafka's works and those
of Italian authors, this book analyses a Kafkan tradition in Italian modern literature that encompasses a diverse group of authors, thereby
complementing other works, such as Gino Tellini's "The Wine and
the Cellars: On the Twentieth-Century Italian Novel" and Luca Somigli's work on modernism, both of which have put a range of Italian
authors into conversation with each other and aim to reorient the critical perspective in Italian literary studies. While not dedicated to one
methodology, since each chapter requires distinct theories, context, and
critical thought, this book is based on productive comparisons and attention to the formation of the Italian canon.

The first three chapters examine how the unique Italian readings of
Kafka lead to new understandings of Italian literature. Although generally less well known in the context of Kafka's oeuvre, the strange
American landscape that Kafka describes in his novel *Der Verschollene*
(*The Man Who Disappeared*), also entitled *Amerika*, has appealed to
a number of Italian authors, critics, and directors, who drew on the
work in their writing and films. Chapter 1, "*Amerika* in Italy: Kafka's
Realism, Pavese, and Calvino," examines the convergence of factors
that contributed to the novel's popularity in Italy as well as what this
particular perception of *Amerika*, in turn, reveals about Italian literature, especially Calvino's and Pavese's. The Italian tradition of reading Kafka as a realist writer helps explain the Italian fascination with
Amerika and raises the question of how much categories guide critical readings. Revealing Kafka's significance for Italian depictions of
the United States, the chapter concludes with an examination of the
commonalities between Kafka's and Pavese's portrayals of America.
This particular Italian understanding of Kafka points to the problems
of limiting which nations are examined in the reception of works and
ideas, which in turn shapes how critics read literature.

What Kafka means for the novel has been a source of debate for decades. Edoardo Sanguineti comments that Kafka, along with Proust and
Joyce, changed our perception of the novel: "If today we speak about
narration, of the novel, how can we still talk of a well-made, organically
conceived form, according to solidified models, after Proust, Joyce, and
Kafka?"[97] While Sanguineti's other two examples of great novelists are
almost synonymous with their famous novels (*In Search of Lost Time*

---

97 "Se noi oggi parliamo di narrazione, di romanzo, come possiamo parlare ancora
di una forma ben fatta, organicamente pensata, secondo modelli consolidati, dopo
Proust, Joyce, Kafka?" (Sanguineti and Galletta, *Sanguineti/Novecento*, 49–50).

and *Ulysses*), whether Kafka is more often referred to as the author of *The Trial* or "The Metamorphosis" is debatable.[98] Indeed, in his lifetime, Kafka published primarily extremely short fiction.

The second chapter asks, building on Sanguineti, "If today we speak about narrations, short stories, how can we still talk about a well-made form after Kafka?" "Dreams of Short Fiction after Kafka: Lalla Romano, Giorgio Manganelli, and Antonio Tabucchi" examines the Kafkan tradition from a formal perspective. Concentrating on a few of Kafka's very short works, the chapter follows a different sort of Kafka, one that resonates with the dream-like, hard-to-define, short fiction of Tabucchi, Manganelli, and Romano. These authors explore different gender identities, generic possibilities, and ask the reader to imagine with them. They aim not to represent reality but to alter the reader's view of reality. The Italian authors, pressed by readers who sometimes resisted their modes of writing, present ideas not only on how to understand their works but also on how to understand the experimental short fiction more broadly, ideas that, in turn, can help readers approaching Kafka's very short fiction.

Like chapter 2, chapter 3 concentrates, in part, on the formal resemblances between the works of Kafka and those of Italian authors. It turns from Kafka's fragmented, lyrical, very short fiction to the more recognizable Kafka of *The Trial* and *The Castle*, and proposes how these novels can be understood within the framework of detective fiction. "*Processi* without End: The Mysteries of Dino Buzzati and Paola Capriolo" discusses the relationships between Kafka and Italian authors, such as Gadda, Camilleri, Sciascia, Tabucchi, and Eco, who wrote non-traditional detective novels, before analysing Buzzati's *Il deserto dei Tartari* (*The Tartar Steppe*) and Capriolo's *Il doppio regno* (*The Dual Realm*) in light of these considerations of Kafka and detective fiction. While literary detective novels often provide a critique of how society works and ask readers to question the government, instead of reassuring them, the works of Kafka, Buzzati, and Capriolo ask the reader to question all elements of society. The novels of Buzzati

---

98 Sanguineti himself engaged a very different sort of Kafka, one that has a great deal in common with Kafka's aphoristic works, the Kafka of Gustav Janouch. Janouch, whose "hagiographic" work has been shown to have numerous factual problems and to be better for inspiring fiction than using as a reliable reference, records conversations he had with Kafka when he knew him towards the end of his life. Sanguineti plays on Janouch's material and Kafka's works in his 1959 play, *K*, which stages a conversation between K (Franz K.) and J (Gustav J.), but which undercuts the seriousness with which Janouch took Kafka.

and Capriolo suggest the potential significance of literature and art in attempts to find community and question society.

The last two chapters are based on themes and critical conversations. Following the theme of family throughout Kafka's fiction and autobiographical work, chapter 4, "Kafka's Parental Bonds: The Family as Institution in Italian Literature," examines how Kafka's work leads to a re-examination of one of the most significant parts of society, the family. The chapter complements Italian studies that concentrate on the figure of the mother in women's writing by exploring the idea of familial oppression in Kafka and Svevo, Ginzburg, Calvino, and Ferrante. It then offers close readings of familial dynamics in Massimo Bontempelli's *Il figlio di due madri* (*The Son of Two Mothers*, published in English with the title *The Boy with Two Mothers*) and Elsa Morante's *L'isola di Arturo* (*Arturo's Island*), which interrogate whether the family unit is escapable and what an escape would look like. "Kafka's Parental Bonds" provides an example of how re-imagining critical categories – that is, the institution of motherhood versus parenthood – provides a different view of Italian authors' works.

While in chapter 4 Kafka adds to a lively debate on the family within Italian studies, the last chapter uses him to bring Italian literature into a broader discussion. Chapter 5 returns to the introduction's discourse on world literature by calling attention to Italian talking animals, which have frequently been ignored by animal studies. "The Human-Animal Boundary, Italian Style: Kafka's Red Peter in Conversation with Svevo's Argo, Morante's Bella, and Landolfi's Tombo" compares Red Peter from Kafka's "A Report to an Academy" with some of the talking animals of Landolfi, Svevo, Morante, and Buzzati to explore how the human-animal boundary is expressed in twentieth-century Italian literature. Following this thematic connection between Kafka's and these Italian authors' stories suggests a similar set of cultural problems: as multi-lingual, multi-ethnic Austria-Hungary and its language crisis partially explain Kafka's Red Peter, Italy's also complex linguistic situation can be viewed as one of the reasons for the many Italian realistically talking animals.

The epilogue brings together the various threads of the chapters, with the aid of Calvino, who plays a role in every chapter. The variety of his work that can be associated with Kafka provides a lens through which to view the diversity of Kafkan-Italian encounters and how Kafka can be used to reconfigure the Italian literary landscape. Calvino's readings of Kafka, discussed earlier in the book, as a realist and lyrical, also point to how the more peripheral views of Kafka can lead to a new understanding of the author as well as our concept of the world-literature views of a famous author. While *Kafka's Italian Progeny* is about (roughly in order of appearance) Italo Calvino, Cesare Pavese, Amelia Rosselli, Lalla Romano, Giorgio Manganelli, Antonio Tabucchi, Paola Capriolo, Dino Buzzati, Natalia Ginzburg, Elena Ferrante, Italo Svevo, Elsa Morante, Massimo Bontempelli, and Tommaso Landolfi, it is also about Franz Kafka: my analysis of Italian views of Kafka aims to contribute to the international understanding of Kafka. *Kafka's Italian Progeny* may also prompt a Kafka lover or two to discover some of Kafka's wonderful Italian family members you never knew he had. My other intention is to advance efforts to reorient the field of modern Italian studies and shed light on unnoted qualities of great modern Italian literature – to reconsider, in other words, what we mean by a national literary tradition.

Chapter One

Amerika in Italy: Kafka's Realism, Pavese, and Calvino

Amo Kafka perché è realista.
I love Kafka because he is a realist.

– Italo Calvino

Non sarei mai arrivato a Kafka senza aver letto Pavese ... penso che si assomiglino parecchio.
I would never have come to Kafka without having read Pavese ... I think that they resemble each other a great deal.

– Jean-Marie Straub

In Franz Kafka's novel, *Amerika,* or *Der Verschollene (Amerika,* or *The Man who Disappeared*), the protagonist's boat sails past the Statue of Liberty, which memorably holds a sword in the air, and a bridge connects Manhattan to Boston.[1] Although less well known among Kafka's works, the strange American landscape Kafka describes has appealed to a number of Italian authors, critics, and directors, who drew on it in

---

1 *Amerika* is the title Max Brod gave to the work; *Der Verschollene* is a name Kafka mentioned wanting to give it. Many editions now include both titles, and some update it to just *Der Verschollene*. The issue is made even more complicated in English since "the actual title *Der Verschollene* defies any simple English translation" (Anderson, *Kafka's Clothes,* 104). *Der Verschollene* has been translated as *The Castaway, The Man Who Disappeared, The One Who Sank Out of Sight, The Missing Person, The Lost One, Lost without a Trace, The Man Who Was Lost Sight Of, Missing Presumed Dead, The Boy Who Was Missing, The Boy Who Was Never Heard of Again, The Boy Who Was Never More Heard Of,* and *The Boy Who Was Lost and Never Heard from Again.* Given the growing tendency to refer to Kafka's book using a version of "his" title (*Der Verschollene*) and the sheer number of English translations, I would refer to it as *Der Verschollene,* but the figures discussed in this chapter (Pavese, Calvino, Fortini, Fellini) knew the work as *America* (*Amerika*), and the connotations of the title remain important for this chapter.

their writing and films. Italo Calvino mentioned more than once that *Amerika* was his favourite novel: "My author is Kafka and my favorite novel is *Amerika*."[2] Often included with Kafka's other short stories, the first chapter of *Amerika*, "Der Heizer" ("The Stoker") has been issued repeatedly as a free-standing volume in Italy, as "The Metamorphosis" frequently is in many countries.[3]

The order in which Kafka's three novels were published reveals both a reason for, and provides evidence of, *Amerika*'s remarkable place in the Italian literary landscape: instead of being the last of Kafka's novels published, as it was in German, English, French, Polish, Norwegian, Japanese, Danish, Dutch, Russian, Turkish, Chinese, Czech, and Hungarian, it was published after *The Trial* and before *The Castle*.[4] Revealing how publication order influences interpretation, Walter Benjamin calls the novel's protagonist, Karl Rossmann, "the *third* and happier incarnation of K."[5] This chapter will examine the convergence of factors that contributed to the novel's popularity in Italy as well as what this particular perception of *Amerika* reveals about Italian literature, especially Italo Calvino's early works and Cesare Pavese's *La luna e i falò* (*The Moon and the Bonfires*).

The Italian interest in Kafka's *Amerika*, published in Italian in 1945, is, in part, due to the presence of America in the Italian cultural imagination, which also relates to Italian immigration to the United States. In 1950, critic and author Giuseppe Antonio Borgese published a review of *Amerika* from the United States, in which he compared his experiences of the country with the America portrayed by Kafka: "After almost twenty years in this country, it is time to visit it with Kafka's guidance."[6]

---

2 Calvino, "The Art of Fiction." The interview is a collage of materials from the interviews with Calvino owned by the *Paris Review*, and Calvino's statement is a response to the question, "Were you influenced by Joyce or any of the modernists?"

3 "Il fochista" was published as "Il melangolo" (Kafka, *Il fochista*, 1993) and "I racconti di Repubblica" (Kafka, *Il fochista*, 1997).

4 Shimon Sandbank surmises, "The particular influence of *The Castle* (in English) may have to do with the fact this was the first work by Kafka to be published in English" (Sandbank, *After Kafka*, 116), and he examines four novels influenced by *The Castle* that existed before the Italian translation was available. The prefaces of the English-language and Italian publications of *America* locate *The Castle* in very different places within Kafka's oeuvre.

5 Benjamin, *Illuminations*, 119 (emphasis added).

6 "Dopo quasi vent'anni in questo paese, è tempo di visitarlo sotto la guida di Kafka" (Borgese, "In Amerika con Kafka," 253). Borgese left Italy because of fascist policies and married Thomas Mann's daughter in 1939. Mann was an early supporter of Kafka as well. The circulation of Kafka among German émigrés in America is perhaps best known in the story about Thomas Mann lending Einstein Kafka. While there has been a sizeable focus on German émigrés in America and Italians in America, both in isolation, of course they also frequently interacted (and sometimes even married).

neorealism

Although Kafka himself had never seen America, his novel belongs to the group of literary and cinematic works portraying America that contributed to the Italian idea of the United States. The myth of America as a land of opportunity was especially prominent in 1940s and 1950s Italy.[7] Several Italian authors associated it with a concept of realism, especially during the fascist period.[8] Many important Italian works from the 1930s to the 1950s, such as Carlo Levi's *Cristo si è fermato a Eboli* (*Christ Stopped at Eboli*, 1945), Mario Soldati's *America primo amore* (*America First Love*, 1935, reissued by Einaudi in 1945), and Cesare Pavese's *La luna e i falò* (*The Moon and the Bonfires*, 1950), explore or employ this myth. Starting with his 1930 essay on Sinclair Lewis, Pavese played a particularly significant role in propagating the myth of America.[9]

Critical studies generally focus on three main sources for these Italian literary depictions of America: the reports, oral and written, of Italians who spent time there (such as Soldati), the Italian reception of literary works by Americans (such as Pavese's translations and essays), and the Italian consumption of American films.[10] While not arising directly out of Italian-American exchanges, other European representations of America helped shape it in the Italian literary imagination. These works are not only part of a broader European image of America; they also often influenced each other. Because the American-Italian relationship is usually considered to be one between two countries, the United States and Italy, Kafka's *Amerika* tends to be ignored in discussions of Italian depictions of the United States, despite the novel's presence. Given its notable Italian reception and publication date, it merits attention when examining Italian literary depictions of the United States. This chapter outlines the reasons for *Amerika*'s Italian reception, including the idea

---

7 In an article from 1959, Golino notes the widespread popularity of mythic America in Italy: "Strange as this may seem it is even stranger to realize that until very recently this mythical concept of America has existed in Italy, not only for the peasants, but for people of all classes" (Golino, "On the Italian 'Myth' of America," 19). For an interesting discussion of the role of the American west and cowboys in postwar Italy (and how these concepts intersected with Italy's own self-conception), see Leake, *Tex Willer: Un cowboy nell'Italia del dopoguerra*.

8 See Cecchi, "Introduzione."

9 Dominique Fernandez dates the beginning of the Italian intellectual myth of America to Pavese's 1930 essay on Sinclair Lewis and its end to Pavese's death in 1950.

10 See, e.g., Heiney's discussion of Pavese's sources for *The Moon and the Bonfires*, which include American films, talking to emigrants, and American literature (Heiney, *America in Modern Italian Literature*, 174–6, 178). Pavese's encounter with American actress Constance Dowling, to whom *The Moon and the Bonfires* is dedicated, is also a source of investigation and comment.

of Kafka's realism, before concluding with an analysis of Pavese's and Kafka's representations of America.

Kafka's *Amerika* in Italy

Kafka's representation of America is often characterized as a European-ized one. From Klaus Mann's preface to *Amerika*, in which he claims that the country home portrayed is "built like an ancient European castle – a typical Kafka castle,"[11] to Michael Hofmann's more recent introduction, which refers to Kafka's America as "an exploded Bohemia,"[12] many see Kafka's Prague in his America.[13] The practice of overlaying one's own European streets with the idea of America was particularly prominent in mid-twentieth-century Italy. In *Christ Stopped at Eboli,* Carlo Levi recounts the power that America, especially New York, had in relatively isolated, southern Italy.[14] Not only did New York feel closer to the cit-izens of Gagliano than other Italian cities, as they were more likely to move to the United States than to Rome or Naples, but American prac-tices also became common in parts of the town: "Life at Gagliano was entirely American in regard to mechanical equipment as well as weights and measures, for the peasants spoke of pounds and inches rather than of kilograms and centimetres."[15] Kafka's strange, at times ultra-modern, and also partially European America was especially appealing to an Italian audience, many of whose members could have experienced the overlap of American and European culture in their own country.

America, Giorgio Barberio Corsetti's theatrical adaptation of Kafka's *Amerika,* first performed in 1992, drew on the aforementioned connec-tions among Karl Rossmann's America, Kafka's European background, and Italy. The play was performed in productions that took advantage of different spaces in the cities of Cividale di Friuli and Milan, a place Kafka visited and one that shaped his ideas about the modern city. Close to the Slovenian border, Cividale del Friuli, meanwhile, reminds

---

11 Mann, "Introduction to *Amerika*," 138.

12 Hofmann, Introduction to *Amerika*, xiii.

13 "Remarkably enough, *Amerika* is also Kafka's only narrative work in which Prague is explicitly mentioned" (Stach, *Is That Kafka?*, 203).

14 "Non Roma o Napoli, ma New York sarebbe la vera capitale dei contadini di Lucania, se mai questi uomini senza Stato potessero averne una" (Levi, *Cristo si è fermato a Eboli*, 108).

15 Levi, *Christ Stopped at Eboli*, 128. ("La vita di Gagliano, per quello che riguarda i ferri dei mestieri, è tutta americana, come lo è per le misure: si parla, dai contadini, di pollici e di libbre piuttosto che di centimetri o di chilogrammi"; Levi, *Cristo si è fermato a Eboli*, 115.)

Barberio Corsetti of Kafka's birthplace, and he points to the similarities between northern, medieval cities in Italy and Prague: "When we actualized *Amerika* in Cividale di Friuli, people followed the action, moving in the streets in the lay-bys of an ancient geography: it had a very beautiful, remote character, and in some ways it reminded me of Prague. In this case, the route prompted other thoughts: that which I detected was Kafka walking around Prague and imagining America."[16] The Cividale del Friuli production points to shared images of America, which drew, in part, on a common European landscape.

Because of the popularity of Kafka's first novel in Italy, Barberio Corsetti's play is one among several theatrical and cinematic adaptations of *Amerika*. The most famous of the numerous Italian adaptations of and references to the novel, Federico Fellini's *Intervista* (1987), portrays the director realizing his dream of adapting *Amerika* to the screen.[17] Like Calvino's, Fellini's interest in Kafka began in the 1940s, spanned several decades, and focused especially on *Amerika*. Kafka was an important part of Fellini's education and artistic development.[18] The director comments, "Kafka moved me profoundly. I was struck by the way he confronted the mystery of things, their unknown quality, the sense of being in a labyrinth, and daily life turned magical."[19] Many of the reasons for Fellini's particular attraction to *Amerika* reflect the broader Italian fascination with the novel. Although Kafka is more famous for his grown-up male characters, *Amerika*'s Karl Rossmann is a teenager, like so many of the protagonists of Fellini's films.[20] The

---

16 "Quando abbiamo realizzato *America* a Cividale del Friuli, la gente seguiva l'azione, muovendosi nelle strade, negli slarghi di una geografia antica: era una dimensione molto bella, remota, per certi versi mi ricordava Praga. In quel caso il percorso suggeriva ben altre suggestioni: quello che percepivo era Kafka che camminava per Praga e si immaginava l'America" (Barberio Corsetti, *America*, 44).

17 Robertson also ends his comprehensive introduction with the argument that it is time for another cinematic adaptation of Kafka's novel; see his introduction to *The Man Who Disappeared (America)*, xxvi–xxvii.

18 Comedian Marcello Marchesi introduced Fellini and others to Kafka when they were working at *Marc' Aurelio* (Kezich, *Fellini*, 35); "*Marc' Aurelio* was Fellini's university" (Chandler, *I, Fellini*, 330). Tullio Kezich and Peter Bondanella posit that Fellini's *Il mio amico Pasqualino* (composed while working at *Marc' Aurelio*) "may well reflect Fellini's early reading of Franz Kafka" (Bondanella, *The Films of Federico Fellini*, 12; and Kezich, *Fellini*, 35).

19 Testa, *Masters of Two Arts*, 35.

20 In his chapter on the reasons for Fellini's interest in Kafka's first novel, Carlo Testa remarks upon the youth of the novel's protagonist (Testa, 36). A Russian critic, Knipovich, talked about the similar potrayals of childhood in Kafka and Fellini even before Fellini produced *Intervista*; see Mallac, "Kafka in Russia," 70.

prominent focus on youth and the illuminating nature of an adolescent perspective in Fellini, Pavese's *The Moon and the Bonfires,* and Calvino's *The Path to the Spiders' Nests,* to name just a few examples, indicate two reasons why many Italian intellectuals in the 1940s and 1950s would have been drawn to Karl's revealing naiveté.

The absurdity of youth in Fellini's films suggests another connection between the director's vision and *Amerika.* Whereas considerations of Kafka and the absurd often underline the more horrifying or hopeless qualities of his representations, putting Kafka into conversation with Fellini highlights his potentially amusing, Chaplinesque elements.[21] Noting the connection between Fellini and Kafka highlights Kafka's humour, not just the connections between Kafka and Chaplin, one of Fellini's favourite directors. Although it is now it is a commonplace to mention that readers overlook Kafka's humour, Italian critics have focused on Kafka's humour for decades.[22]

More recently, Roberto Calasso also characterizes comedy as being integral to understanding Kafka: "In *whatever* he writes it's enough for him to be meticulous and exacting in his description of developments and rigorous in observing their phases – and the comic erupts, invincible, sovereign. *Comedy is in the details,* that's the rule. Kafka formulated it but then crossed out the passage in which it appeared."[23] Gregor, transformed, worries about getting to work on time. As this example indicates and Guido Crespi argued, focusing on Kafka's humour often leads to a realist reading of his work: "In order to identify and enjoy Kafka's humour even more, we have arrived, by necessity, to a more realist interpretation of the work."[24] In the next section, I will examine how

comic elements → realism

21 From Max Brod on, critics have drawn attention to the commonalities between Kafka (particularly his *Amerika*) and Charlie Chaplin. Ladislao Mittner distinguished Karl Rossmann from *The Trial's* Josef K. and *The Castle's* K. for several reasons, particularly his goodwill, which evokes Chaplin (Mittner, *La letteratura tedesca del Novecento,* 281). Already in 1950, Borgese notes that the Chaplin-Kafka connection has often been made (Borgese, "In Amerika con Kafka," 254). Tyler notes the "general resemblance of the plot of *Amerika* to the plot of Chaplin comedies" (Tyler, "Kafka's and Chaplin's *Amerika,*" 301). Klaus Mann's introduction to *Amerika* also refers to Charlie Chaplin.

22 See, e.g., Barilli, *Comicità di Kafka;* and Crespi, *Kafka Umorista.*

23 Calasso, *K.,* 63.

24 "Per individuare e gustare maggiormente l'umorismo di Kafka siamo arrivati, per necessità, ad una interpretazione più realista dell'opera" (Crespi, *Kafka Umorista,* 125). Crespi points to Klaus Wagenbach's discussion of the village of Wossek (where Kafka's father was born) and how the topography corresponds to that described in *The Castle.* Crespi discusses how the people of Wossek called the villa on the hill "the castle" and that Kafka depicts a caricature of this in his last novel.

hinges on his reception as a realist

the Italian view of Kafka as a realist, an important factor for the appreciation of *Amerika*, both leads to a particular understanding of Kafka's works and provides insight into Italy's intellectual scene and literature.

The Italian View of Kafka's Realism

While Kafka's works have been analysed as belonging to numerous modern *isms*, including surrealism, modernism, magical realism, expressionism, and existentialism, *realism* is one of the least common terms applied to Kafka's oeuvre. Italy, however, has a strong tradition of reading Kafka as a realist writer. Pavese, Calvino, Fortini, Moravia, and Eco all describe his realism. The Italian emphasis on Kafka's realism develops from the importance of the term *realism* in twentieth-century Italian literary criticism, Georg Lukács's role in Italian criticism, and Kafka's early Italian reception. From the 1920s to today, realism holds a significant place in Italian literary debates. It occupies a larger space in the twentieth-century Italian critical lexicon than modernism does. Federico Bertoni's *Realismo e letteratura: Una storia possibile* (*Realism and Literature: A Possible History*) analyses the shifting meaning of realism and the difficulty of establishing one definition:

> It is perhaps the original paradox of realism, the first root of its semantic drift: the fact of being anchored, in its theoretical foundations, to a culturally changing term of reference, subject to continuous adjustments and epistemic redefinitions. If modernist culture seems to have realized an "ontological degradation of objective reality" resulting in an apparent "absence of the world in literature" it is because the focal point has moved, because the hierarchy of phenomena has inverted, because that which passed for *the* reality (physical, biological, environmental, social) has become inert literary material, supplanted by a more essential and decisive interior reality. "Only the spiritual world exists," notes Kafka, the world of a "spirit" desperately unknown and unknowable.[25]

---

25 "È forse il paradosso originario del realismo, la radice prima della sua deriva semantica: il fatto di essere ancorato, per statuto, a un termine di riferimento culturalmente mutevole, soggetto a continui assestamenti e ridefinizioni epistemiche. Se la cultura modernista sembra avere attuato una 'degradazione ontologica della realtà oggettiva,' sfociando in un'apparente 'assenza del mondo nella letteratura,' è perché si è spostato il baricentro, perché si è invertita la gerarchia dei fenomeni, perché quella che passava per essere *la* realtà (fisica, biologica, ambientale, sociale) è diventata materiale letterariamente inerte, soppiantata da una ben più essenziale e decisiva realtà interiore. 'Non esiste che il mondo spirituale,' annota Kafka, il mondo di un' 'anima' disperatamente ignota e inconoscibile" (Bertoni, *Realismo e letteratura*, 266).

Bertoni discusses the mutability of realism in different epochs, and his summary of the term reveals part of why the term has been (and continues to be) so significant in Italy. The Kafka quotation "There is nothing beyond the spiritual world" helps demonstrate how the reality of the interior world receives greater attention in the twentieth century. For Bertoni, as for many Italian critics, considering Kafka and his work challenges the critical concept of realism. The terms of the debate on realism are vast, especially in the Italian context, and this section will focus on the elements related to the Italian idea of Kafka as a realist.

The importance of realism for early twentieth-century Italian critics and authors explains, in part, the number of Italian thinkers who proposed that Kafka's work could be described using this term. While it was often considered in terms of post-war neorealism, critics and authors also explored realism during the fascist period, as Ruth Ben-Ghiat demonstrates in "Fascism, Writing, and Memory: The Realist Aesthetic in Italy, 1930–50."[26] In his book on German realism, Giovanni Necco includes a chapter from 1934 entitled "Il problema Kafka o della simbolomania" ("The Kafka Problem or about Symbolmania"), which argues for Kafka's realism in a discussion of symbolism, allegory, and expressionism.[27] In the 1930s, 1940s, and 1950s, allegorical readings of Kafka were popular, but, situating Kafka's realism between expressionism and *Neue Sachlichkeit*, Necco proposed that the realism of Kafka's work, especially his detailed descriptions, resists symbolic interpretations.[28] While early Kafka critics moved between labelling Kafka using terms from German movements (*Neue Sachlichkeit* or expressionism) and appropriating him to the Italian context (*novecentismo*), the term realism could be used to navigate between national and international considerations.

The debate over Kafka's realism grew in the 1940s. The translator of the first Italian edition of *Amerika*, Alberto Spaini, contributed to this more realistic reading with his translation practices and criticism.[29]

---

26 "Realism represents an example of how the fascist beliefs of Italian intellectuals mediated their reception and practice of modernist literary techniques" (Ben-Ghiat, "Fascism, Writing, and Memory," 665).

27 "Kafka's realism is too circumstantial and precise ... to yield to the allegory game." ("Il realismo del Kafka è troppo circostanziato e preciso, ... per piegarsi al gioco dell'allegoria"; Necco, *Realismo e idealismo*, 214.)

28 Necco's presentation of Kafka's realism (Necco, 189) fits the argument that Ben-Ghiat makes about the growing Italian concept of realism in the 1930s (Ben-Ghiat, "Fascism, Writing, and Memory," 665).

29 "Spaini sembra quindi, anche in modo pratico, allontanarsi dalla critica psicologica della scrittura di Kafka e ad avvicinarsi ad una sua interpretazione più realistica" (Galinetto, "Alberto Spaini germanista," 320).

From the first sentence of *Amerika*, in which the Statue of Liberty holds a sword in a sudden burst of incredible sunlight, the novel could easily be associated with other categories, such as surrealism and modernism. While *Amerika*'s position in Kafka's oeuvre has been debated and even labelled postmodernist because of its mix of genres and humour, Spaini and early Italian readers focused particularly on the work's realistic elements. Spaini proposes that the unusual publication in Italy of *Amerika* after *The Trial* is due to an artistic arc, one that starts with *The Trial* and ends with *The Castle*. His view of Kafka's realism helps to explain his interpretation, and his introduction to *Amerika* foregrounds realistic details of Kafka's work: "Yet this story, so simple and candid, takes place in the most open, Kafkan atmosphere: everything is of the most meticulous, illustrated, legitimate reality, that step by step, centimeter by centimeter, one continually expects to feel the floor fall out from under one's feet."[30] Promoting *Amerika*, rather than *The Trial* and *The Castle*, several Italian critics praised Kafka's first novel for its realism.

Noting how it builds from a realistic situation to become ever stranger, Franco Fortini described *Amerika* as "perhaps Kafka's most successful novel."[31] Emphasizing the differences between their beginnings, Fortini contrasted *Amerika* with "The Metamorphosis" and lauded the opening of the novel in his 1947 essay: "In this book, the supernatural develops together with the conventionally real, and almost is mixed up with it; in contrast to 'The Metamorphosis' where the scandal is declared in the first lines."[32] Extolling *Amerika*, especially in contrast to "The Metamorphosis," is unusual. For both Fortini and Spaini, *Amerika*'s difference among Kafka's works was a point of praise rather than a dismissal, as it has been for many other international critics.[33]

Considering Fortini's essay on Kafka indicates two primary, different, although often intertwined qualities of Kafka's *Amerika* that critics reference when categorizing the work as realist: the novel's potentially

---

30 "Eppure questa storia, così semplice ed ingenua, si svolge tutta nel più schietto clima kafkiano: tutto è di una realtà così minuziosa, chiarita, giustificata, a passo a passo, centimetro per centimetro, che continuamente si trema di sentirsi mancare il terreno sotto i piedi" (Spaini, "Prefazione," xi–xii).

31 "Forse la massima riuscita di K" (Fortini, "Capoversi su Kafka," 684). Fortini's article was first published in 1947 in *Il Politecnico*, a journal that had published Calvino's "Abbandonato al commando" the year before and would publish selections from Lukács later the same year.

32 "In questo libro il sovrannaturale si sviluppa insieme al reale di convenzione, e quasi a questo confuso; a rovescio della *Metamorfosi*, dove lo scandalo è dichiarato nelle prime righe" (Fortini, "Capoversi su Kafka," 684).

33 Sgorlon similarly praised the work (Sgorlon, *Kafka narratore*, 49).

verisimilar representation of the world and its descriptions of the plight of the working class. Parts of Fortini's article focus on how the novel's narrative techniques convey realistic representations, similar to Spaini's introduction, and it was also, in the words of Lucia Re, "in effect a defense of Kafka against his Marxist critics."[34] Fortini's article first appeared in *Il Politecnico*, an important but short-lived journal (1945–7) that had many communist contributors. The focus on whether Kafka could be convincingly read within a communist or socialist framework grew in the 1940s.

The high point of the debate about Kafka's realism coincided with discussions about neorealism, although it lasted well after.[35] Elio Vittorini, a key figure in the development of neorealism, made use of Kafka to argue with a certain line of communist criticism. Kafka became a symbol and a point of contention, central in arguments over what acceptable Marxist fiction was and could be. In a well-known, open letter to Togliatti in *Il Politecnico*, Vittorini proposes that authors should be judged by different standards than their politics.[36] Distancing himself from the Communist Party, Vittorini focuses on the problems with the communist tendency to evaluate authors based on their political engagement, or lack thereof: "It happens that we want to judge if an author's poetry tends toward progressive or reactionary depending on his political displays, or on how explicit he was."[37] For Vittorini, Kafka offers an important example of an author that remains overlooked if critics adhere to this policy: "We ignore completely, for example, Kafka, who represented with great force of mythic depictions the conditions in which man is reduced to living in contemporary society."[38] Vittorini

---

34 Re, *Calvino and the Age of Neorealism*, 101.

35 The chronological and contextual boundaries of realism overlap with neorealism, depending on the critic's definition; see, e.g., Baldini, "Il Neorealismo," 110.

36 Two issues of *Il Politecnico* later (no. 39, 1947), Vittorini dedicated a sizeable portion of the journal to Kafka. It included Fortini's article, "Capoversi su Kafka"; Antonio Ghirelli's biography; Carlo Bo's "Il problema di Kafka"; and five unedited pieces by Kafka. Vittorini had emphasized the significance of Kafka earlier, in *Il Politecnico* no. 35 (December 1946) (Vittorini, *Diario in Pubblico*, 256).

37 "Avviene che noi si voglia giudicare dalle manifestazioni politiche di un poeta, o da quanto egli ha dato di esplicito, se la sua poesia è a tendenza progressista o a tendenza reazionaria" (Vittorini, "Politica e cultura," 188). Originally published in *Il Politecnico*, it was reprinted in the anthology edited by Marco Forti and Sergo Pautasso, *Il Politecnico*.

38 "Ignoriamo completamente, per esempio, Kafka, che pure ha rappresentato con la forza grandiosa delle raffigurazioni mitiche la condizione in cui l'uomo è ridotto a vivere nella società contemporanea" (Vittorini, 188).

was not the only author to debate Kafka in a communist journal. *L'Unità*, for instance, critiqued an anonymous commentator (Pavese) for describing Kafka using the term *realism*. Pavese wrote his friend Giolitti a response to this criticism in 1949: "In any case, I confirm that Hemingway is a great writer, that Kafka is a realist, and that 'cattolicità' is good Italian."[39]

Lukács's work was vital to the development of this lively debate over Kafka's realism and whether he was appropriate communist reading. Examining how his writings on Kafka were received in Italy reveals his important role as a mediator of German-language culture as well as the complexity of Italy's intellectual situation in the 1950s and 1960s. While the translation of Auerbach's *Mimesis* into Italian in 1957 is also of great significance for the understanding of realism in Italy (and the work mentions Kafka once), it is much less crucial to the debates on Kafka's realism than Lukács's work. In the 1950s, Italy was in a particular cultural position when it came to Lukács and Kafka: receptive to Kafka, as opposed to many communist countries, where he was more or less banned, and also more receptive to Lukács's criticism than many non-communist countries.[40]

In 1963, René Wellek commented on the American reluctance to engage Lukács: "But today no genuine Marxist criticism seems to be written in the United States. This is not, I think, due to McCarthyism or to anti-Soviet bias. It seems rather ignorance or lack of interest in the kind of criticism practiced by Georg Lukács or T.W. Adorno with such great acclaim on the Continent."[41] In contrast, a notable number of twentieth-century

---

39 "Comunque confermo che Hemingway è un grande scrittore, che Kafka è realista e che 'cattolicità' è buon italiano" (Pavese, *Officina Einaudi*, 362). Whereas the potential significance of Hemingway to Pavese has often been explored, the next part of Pavese's statement, about the realism of Kafka and this statement's relevance to his writing, has rarely been noted.

40 Kafka remained unpublished or ignored in many Communist countries during the 1940s, 1950s, and 1960s. At times, he was published with reluctance – e.g., as with the Russian edition of Kafka's works from 1965. The collection's preface is described as having "but one purpose: to talk the reader into not reading the book – provided of course he has somehow managed to get his hands on it. The Russian Kafka selection is the only book I know of which informs its owner already at the outset, that his reading of the book is sheer waste of time. For some 60 pages Suchkov takes elaborate pains to demonstrate that Kafka's writings are devoid of all literary merit" (Karst, "Kafka and the Russians," 186).

41 Wellek, *Concepts of Criticism*, 331.

politics

Italian critics could be described as Lukácsian.[42] Italian criticism, not just politics, reflects the view that "Communism attracted more adherents in Italy than in any other country in the West."[43]

In 1963, intellectuals gathered in Liblice, Czechoslovakia, to debate Kafka's role in the Eastern Bloc; this had become an important symbolic discussion that went well beyond a literary analysis.[44] Sartre has been described as claiming, "Kafka is a cartload of dynamite standing between East and West which each side tries to wheel into the other's camp so it will explode there."[45] Ernst Fischer finished his Liblice talk with a call to reclaim Kafka: "I hope this conference will contribute decisively to rescuing Kafka from the arena of the cold war, to no longer reserving him to the commentators, but to turning him over to the socialist reader. I appeal to the socialist world: Bring Kafka's work back from its involuntary exile! Give it a permanent visa!"[46]

In addition to contributing to the Prague Spring, the conference made Kafka a frequent topic of conversation. The 1966 Italian translation of the conference proceedings reveals both the Italian attention to communist criticism of Kafka, given that the volume was translated so quickly (as it has never been in its entirety into English), and the Italian emphasis on

---

42 As Preve writes, "In summary there existed the preconditions for an 'understanding' of Lukács's language and problematics, and it is not by chance that particularly during the fifties many left intellectuals in Italy became in various ways and more or less enthusiastically, 'Lukácsian.'" ("Esistevano insomma, le precondizioni per una 'comprensione' del linguaggio e della problematica lukacsiana, e non è a caso che in particolare nel corso degli anni Cinquanta molti intellettuali di sinistra in Italia diventarono in vario modo 'lukácsiani,' più o meno entusiasti"; Preve, "Lukács in Italia," 80.) Maslow, in contrast, identifies Galvano della Volpe and Rocco Musolino as Italian critics who attack Lukács (Maslow, "Lukacs' Man-Centered Aesthetics," 543).

43 Gilmour, *The Pursuit of Italy*, 345.

44 The conference proceedings were then published in German.

45 Bondy interviews Mayer, who discusses a talk that Sartre gave (in Moscow) (Bondy, *European Notebooks*, 56). See Sartre, "Die Abrüstung der Kultur." Sartre is an example of French writers who often inhabited this space between communist and non-communist writers, but often with a more established view of Kafka (existential, surreal), as opposed to engaging in a more extensive manner with him as a realist, as happened in Italy. For a description of the "battle for Franz Kafka" during the Cold War, see Kusin, *The Intellectual Origins*, 63–7. See also Bondy, "The Struggle for Kafka and Joyce," in *European Notebooks*, 55–67.

46 Fischer, "Kafka Conference," 94. ("Es ist zu hoffen, daß diese Konferenz entscheidend dazu beiträgt, Kafka aus der Region des kalten Krieges zu retten, sein Werk nicht Kommentatoren vorzubehalten, sondern dem sozialistichen Leser zu übergeben. Ich appelliere an die sozialistische Welt: Holt das Werk Kafkas aus unfreiwilligem Exil zurück! Gebt ihm ein Dauervisum!"; Fischer, "Kafka-Konferenz," 168.)

Kafka + Communism

Lukács.[47] The translator, Saverio Vertone, dedicates a sizeable portion of his introduction to discussing Lukács: "One is shocked by the attitude of the majority of critics in terms of the most important – or better – the most notable theorizer of the Marxist aesthetic of the contemporary world: Georgy Lukács. Lukács is generally ignored."[48] The introduction highlights the remarkably small role Lukács plays in the volume, which many critics have read as purposeful, since some view the Liblice conference as anti-Lukácsian and a retort to Lukács's essay "Franz Kafka or Thomas Mann?"

Lukács, characterized as "the most influential denigrator of Kafka among Marxist literary critics,"[49] is at times censured for contributing to, or even being the source of, the resistance to Kafka's work in communist countries.[50] However, some instead hold Lukács's "Franz Kafka or Thomas Mann?" as the beginning of Kafka's acceptance in Czechoslovakia, the Soviet Union, and other communist countries since, previously, Kafka had been almost completely ignored.[51] In other words, while Lukács's conclusions about Kafka were negative, he was speaking about him in detail, something few communist critics had done. Indeed, many Soviet authors had not read or even heard of Kafka. Viktor Nekrasov recalls the embarrassment he felt at Alberto Moravia's question about the author from Prague, whom many communist authorities did not condone: "Here I remember how uncomfortable we felt, a group of us Soviet writers, including Panova and Granin, when six years ago in Leningrad, Alberto Moravia asked us what we thought

---

47 Several of the essays were translated into English in Kenneth Hughes's *Franz Kafka*. A few were not translated into Italian, but the volume contains twenty-four essays. The introduction explains the reasons for excluding a few of the essays, most of which have to do with Kafka's reception in other countries.

48 "Stupisce l'atteggiamento della maggior parte degli studiosi nei confronti del più importante – o meglio – del più noto teorizzatore di estetica marxista del mondo contemporaneo: Georgy Lukács. Lukács viene di solito ignorato" (Vertone, *Franz Kafka da Praga* 1963, 99).

49 Caute, *Politics and the Novel*, 235.

50 "In *'Que faire de Kafka?'* André Gisselbrecht blamed Lukács for banishing Kafka from the realist canon; Kafka's work amounted to the *témoignage bouleversant* of a victim of inhuman capitalism" (Caute, 237). "His position has been condemned as orthodox and dogmatic by non-Marxist critics, while Marxists East and West have called him a revisionist, a misinterpreter of classical texts, a theoretician with idealistic and Hegelian tendencies rather than a strictly materialistic and Marxist philosopher" (Maslow, "Lukacs' Man-Centered Aesthetics," 543).

51 One critic summarizes the situation this way: "Between 1948 and 1957 no book on Kafka had been published on the Communist attitude towards Kafka" (Bahr, "Kafka and the Prague Spring," 20). For a reading of *Realism in Our Time* as a work that represents a shift in Lukács's thinking, see Kadarkay, *Georg Lukács*, 425.

of Kafka. We looked back and forth at each other and couldn't say a word: at that time we had never heard of him."[52] This anecdote provides an example of how several Italian writers moved between eastern and western countries, intellectually and physically, and also suggests the significance of Italian authors for Kafka's international reception.

The several co-existing, overlapping, and, at times, contradictory theories on Lukács's role in Kafka criticism take a particular shape in Italy.[53] His *Il significato attuale del realismo critico* (*Realism in Our Time*), which contains the much discussed essay "Franz Kafka or Thomas Mann?," was first published in Italian in 1957, before it was published in German.[54] By 1955–6, Lukács had already presented much of the material in the work in Rome, Florence, Bologna, Turin, and Milan, where he had given a series of talks.[55] His writings on Kafka varied in their estimation of the author, and several critics posit that Lukács changed his mind about Kafka after having written *Il significato attuale del realismo critico*. Even in "Franz Kafka or Thomas Mann?," which comes out clearly in favour of Mann and aligns him with fruitful critical realism, as opposed to Kafka's aesthetically appealing but decadent modernism, Lukács makes several comments that, if extrapolated from the essay, seem to praise Kafka's work, especially in translation: "Content is here the immediate determinant of aesthetic form – that is why Kafka seems to belong with the great realistic writers. Indeed, from a subjective point of view, he is one of the greatest of all, if we consider how few writers have ever equaled his skill in the imaginative evocation of the concrete novelty of the world."[56] While Lukács argues that Kafka

---

52 Nekrasov, *Both Sides of the Ocean*, 47.
53 "È possibile dire che l'ingresso di Lukács (anzi, del Lukács 'marxista') nella cultura italiana avenna sulla base di una complessa dialettica continuità-rottura con la tradizione nazionale del marxismo italiano di tipo 'gramsciano'" (Preve, "Lukács in Italia," 79).
54 In German, the title has also shifted: from *Die Gegenwartsbedeutung des kritischen Realismus* to *Wider den missverstandenen Realismus*.
55 The talks were given at a crucial moment in the Italian reception of Kafka and Musil.
56 Lukacs, *Realism in Our Time*, 77; trans. modified slightly to follow the Italian more closely. ("Esso stesso, nella sua schietta immediatezza, determina la sua propria espressione. Questo aspetto formale sembra collocare Kafka nella famiglia degli insigni realisti. E – da un punto di vista soggettivo – egli appartiene tanto più a questa famiglia in quanto vi sono pochi scrittori in cui l'originarietà elementare nell'appercezione e riproduzione del mondo, lo stupore davanti al suo non-esserci-ancora-mai-stato, fosse così potentemente sviluppato come in Kafka"; Lukács, *Il significato attuale del realismo critico*, 88.) Critics reference several moments as the turning point in Lukács's changing view of Kafka. The difference among the various editions of the work can change the critical idea of Lukács's view of Kafka; see Kadarkay, *Georg Lukács*, 425.

ultimately is not a realist writer, he calls attention to Kafka's representation of worldly details and places him not only among a certain kind of seemingly realist authors but even among the very best.

A trajectory towards a different view of Kafka can be read in the first two essays of *Il significato attuale del realismo critico*, and Italian critics often followed Lukács's ideas on Kafka's realism, but came to different conclusions: that Kafka was a realist and therefore a valuable author. The preface to the original Italian edition of *Il significato attuale del realismo critico* inspires this line of interpretation: "At the center of the work appears or, to be more exact, is revealed (almost as a mountain thinned out by the fog) the great figure of Kafka, the champion of modern allegorical art, to whom Lukács renders, indirectly, perhaps the greatest homage he has been given up until now."[57] Viewing Lukács as offering one of the best appraisals of Kafka requires a distinct perspective since, by 1957, other well-known figures had provided clearly positive appraisals, including a piece by Thomas Mann actually called "Homage." Italian readers were more disposed than many others to see the debatable homage to Kafka in Lukács's work.

 In part because they developed Lukács's comments about Kafka beyond the parameters that Lukács had set up, Italian intellectuals were at the forefront of cultural interpretations of Kafka that study how his Austro-Hungarian and Jewish heritage shaped his writing.[58] Lukács remarks on the relationship between Kafka's understanding of life in Austria-Hungary and the fact that Kafka's works have been read as prophesizing modern anxiety: "What he described and 'demonized' was not the truly demonic world of Fascism, but the world of the Habsburg Monarchy acquires this haunting objectivity in the light of 'prophetic' Kafkaesque *Angst*."[59] While Lukács did not present Kafka as a writer that should be read, many of his interpretations are ones that critics who value Kafka still debate today. The question of Kafka as a

---

57 "Al centro di essa appare o per meglio dire si discopre (quasi montagna al diradarsi della nebbia) la grande figura di Kafka, il campione dell'arte allegorica moderna, a cui Lukács rende, indirettamente, l'omaggio forse piú alto che gli sia stato reso finora" (Lukács, *Il significato attuale del realismo critico*, 1).

58 See, e.g., the works of Caputo-Mayr and Ziolkowski for discussions of Kafka's Italian reception.

59 Lukacs, *Realism in Our Time*, 77–8; trans. modified slightly to follow the Italian. ("Ciò che egli descrive ed eleva al diabolico, non è il mondo effettivamente e realmente diabolico del fascismo, ma la vecchia monarchia asburgica acquista, alla luce della 'profetica' angoscia kafkiana, questa spettrale oggettività"; Lukács, *Il significato attuale del realismo critico*, 89.)

crucial quote on Kafka reception

prophet of the Holocaust and fascism, including how his background contributes to this understanding of his work, continue to appear in criticism of his work.[60]

When Italian critics wanted to save certain authors from Lukács's disapproval, they tended to do so on his terms, proving why Kafka or Musil was in fact "realist" (and therefore worthy of being read) instead of abandoning Lukács's categories altogether.[61] Remembering Lukács's aforementioned lectures in Italy, Sanguineti refers to him as the basis for conversations on Kafka's realism and mentions how Lukács eventually changed his mind in old age, deciding that Kafka was a realist, as many Italian intellectuals before him already had:

> I remember Lukács in Turin with his famous lecture about realism that, comparing Mann to Kafka, made the latter the negative emblem of decadence, reaffirming his thesis about the clear continuity between naturalism, decadentism, and the avant-garde. Naturally I could not agree. Later however, in old age, Lukács declared that Kafka was a great realist, understanding finally everything that was "prophetic" in the author of *The Trial*. It was a recognition that started the moment in which Lukács was able to overcome certain external and internal censors, rereading in a freer and more faithful way the story of European culture.[62]

Sanguineti holds that, at his most intellectually open, Lukács believed that Kafka was a realist. Sanguineti references the well-known story of Lukács describing Kafka as a realist, based on statements he made while being kept in the Snagov Castle for his involvement in the Nagy government. In this bizarre situation, held in a castle in which the guards claimed not to speak Hungarian but clearly did, and awaiting a trial by unclear authorities (a Soviet court, the KGB, the new Hungarian authorities were all options), several companions reported hearing

---

60 See, e.g., *Journal of the Kafka Society of America*, vol. 35/36 (2012), which is dedicated to the idea of Kafka as a Holocaust prophet.

61 See Bárberi Squarotti, *Dal tramonto*, 17.

62 "Ricordo Lukács a Torino con la sua famosa conferenza sopra il realismo, che, contrapponendo Mann a Kafka, e facendo di quest'ultimo l'emblema negativo della decadenza, ribadiva la sua tesi sulla continuità netta tra naturalismo, decadentismo e avanguardia. Naturalmente non potevo essere d'accordo. Più tardi però il vecchio Lukács dichiarò che Kafka era un grande realista, cogliendo finalmente tutto quello che di 'profetico' c'era nell'autore del *Processo*. Era un riconoscimento che nasceva nel momento in cui Lukács riusciva a superare certe censure esterne e interne, rileggendo in maniera più libera e leale la storia della cultura europea" (Sanguineti and Gambaro, *Colloquio con Edoardo Sanguineti*, 39).

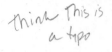

Lukács remark to his wife, "Kafka war doch ein Realist" ("Kafka was a realist after all").[63]

Sanguineti's emphasis on Kafka as a realist contrasts with the general idea, held outside Italy, of Kafka as a realist and reveals, again, both the prominence of Lukács in Italy and the significance of the term *realism* for Italian considerations of Kafka. In a discussion of this same incident, Reiner Stach, known for his authoritative Kafka biographies, represents the more popular view of Kafka and realism: "The communist literary scholar and social scientist Georg Lukács was one of Kafka's strongest critics but after his arrest in 1956 in Budapest, he is said to have admitted, 'Kafka was a realist after all.' This about-turn was as narrow-minded as his earlier indictment because both missed the point of Kafka's work."[64] Many critics consider using the term *realism*, affirmatively or negatively, to describe Kafka as too restrictive.[65]

Sanguineti's comment about internal and external censures indicates another theory about Lukács and Kafka, that Lukács had always liked Kafka privately and that describing Kafka as a problematic, modernist author was merely following the party line. Suggesting that the official communist view of Kafka prevented Lukács from saying everything he ideally would have about the author from Prague, Cesare Cases discusses the "two sides" of Lukács, one as a public figure who condemned the decadent literature of Kafka and one as a private reader. In his statement on the contrast between Lukács the speaker and Lukács as a thinker in person, Cases emphasizes that Lukács could be an insightful critic of Kafka and modernists: "In private he could be a wonderful critic of the 'decadent' literature, from Kafka to Musil..., a complete incomprehension he showed only in terms of Proust and Joyce."[66] Cases particularly highlights Lukács's understanding of German-language authors, in contrast to others.[67]

Sanguineti's and Cases's reflections on the talks Lukács gave in Italy and Lukács's Italian experiences in the 1950s raise the idea of the

---

63   Raddetz, *Georg Lukács in Selbstzeugnissen und Bilddocumenten*, 116. For further discussion of Lukács's quote, see Löwy, "Fascinating Delusive Light," 183.

64   Stach, "Death by Data."

65   Of course, there are important non-Italian critics who examine Kafka's realism. Robertson, e.g., discusses Kafka's relationship to nineteenth-century realism (Robertson, "Reading the Clues," 59).

66   "In privato poteva essere un ottimo critico della letteratura 'decadente' da Kafka a Musil ..., un'incomprensione totale la rivelava solo per Proust e Joyce" (Cases, "L'uomo buono," 12).

67   Cases also mentions that Lukács was reading Hermann Broch's *The Sleepwalkers* (*Der Schläfwandler*) at the time (Cases, 12).

potential significance of Italian thought to Lukács beyond the Italian authors he cited, such as Pavese and Morante. In terms of Kafka and realism, Lukács and Italian intellectuals exchanged views in person that most likely helped to shape their interpretations of Kafka. Among the many theories about the origins of Lukács's shifting view of Kafka's realism, I would include the idea that his conversations in Italy furthered his understanding of Kafka.

Lukács's interpretation of Kafka as a realist continued to have a cultural weight past the 1950s. Partly because of the political and cultural context of the 1950s in Italy, there are notable parallels between Italian and communist criticism of Kafka, such as a greater emphasis on the novel *Amerika*.[68] Many communist critics emphasized the importance of Kafka's *Amerika* (in contrast to *The Trial* or *The Castle*) when discussing why Kafka should be acceptable reading in their countries. In Italy, there was less of a need to argue for Kafka's acceptance, but there was an analogous emphasis on the novel. This realist view of *Amerika* continues to shape Italian considerations of the novel. For instance, a comment from Eduard Goldstücker, one of the organizers of the 1963 Liblice conference, was chosen as one of the seven introductory quotes to Dalai editore's 2011 paperback edition of *Amerika*:

> It is difficult to find, in the literature before the First World War, a work by a bourgeois author that supports with so much "partitarietà" the proletariat cause, a work which vibrates with a sincere desire to see the proletariat make a more combatant and consistent effort in the defense of their rights and, above all, a work in which the author shows with extreme clarity (even in his incapacity to break its too solid chains of its own social origins) that the best part of him, his real heart, is with the working class, with the stoker.[69]

An English-language editor would be unlikely to include this quote as one of the few with which to preface the novel. Examining the early

---

68 For Kafka's relationship with socialism, see, e.g., Politzer, *Franz Kafka: Parable and Paradox*, 118–21; and Stach and Frisch, *Kafka*, 191–2. For examples of Marxist criticism of Kafka in English, see Hughes, *Franz Kafka*.

69 "È difficile trovare, nella letteratura anteriore alla prima Guerra mondiale, un'opera di autore borghese che sostenga con tanta partitarietà la causa proletaria, un'opera in cui vibri un così sincero desiderio di vedere il proletariato impegnarsi in modo più combattivo e conseguente nella difesa dei propri diritti e, soprattutto, un'opera in cui l'autore dimostri con tanta chiarezza (pur nella sua incapacità a spezzare le troppo solide catene della propria origine sociale) che la parte migliore di sé, il proprio cuore, è con la classe operaia, con il fochista" (Goldstücker in Kafka, *America*, 24).

tangled up in communism + realism

Italian reception of *Amerika* not only sheds light on Italy's particular intellectual situation in the 1940s, 1950s, and 1960s but also reveals how this situation continues to influence views of Kafka in Italy.[70]

Both Moravia and Eco discuss the author from Prague using the term *realist*. In 1969, Moravia published a piece in the *Corriere della Sera* entitled "Kafka scrittore realista" (Kafka, realist writer): "In a historical sense Kafka was a realist writer, one of the best of his time. His novels and stories describe with exactitude and truth the state of mind of modern man when confronting absurd and inhumane complications of the world in which we are condemned to live."[71] In *Six Walks in the Fictional Woods* (1994), Umberto Eco situates the beginning of "The Metamorphosis" in the realist tradition: "The description seems to intensify the unbelievable nature of what has happened, yet reduces it to acceptable proportions. It's amazing that a man wakes up to find himself transformed into an insect; but if in fact he has done so, this insect must have the normal features of a normal insect. These few lines of Kafka's are an example of realism, not surrealism."[72] While these Italian authors often have different approaches to realism, they are disposed to engage this critical category.

Calvino's Realist Kafka

Although Italian intellectuals refer to Kafka as a realist in part because of Lukács, the traces of Lukács are frequently lost. Even some of the authors who esteemed Lukács in the 1950s later underestimate his significance. Although not framed in this way, Calvino's statement from 1959, "Amo Kafka perché è realista" (I love Kafka because he is a realist),[73] reflects the intense debates about Kafka's realism in the 1940s and 1950s. While in 1984 Calvino said he had preferred Brecht to Lukács,[74]

---

70 To offer another example, Barberio Corsetti's adaptation of *Amerika* made explicit its interpretation as a critique of capitalism: in one of the first scenes of the play, a man exclaims, "Non è il caso di sperare in un po' di misericordia. In America solamente la gente fortunata pare che possa godere la propria fortuna, in mezzo ai volti indifferenti che la circondavano" (Barberio Corsetti, *America*, 90).

71 "In senso storico, Kafka è stato uno scrittore realista, uno dei maggiori dell'epoca. I suoi romanzi e i suoi racconti descrivono con esattezza e verità lo stato d'animo dell'uomo moderno di fronte alle assurde e disumane complicazioni del mondo in cui è condannato a vivere" (Moravia, "Kafka scrittore realista," 227).

72 Eco, *Six Walks in the Fictional Woods*, 79.

73 Baranelli and Ferrero, *Album Calvino*, 91.

74 Calvino, *Italo Calvino*, 87. ("Non m'importanta più granché né di Brecht né di Lukács. Ma a quell'epoca, fra Brecht e Lukács, sceglievo Brecht"; Calvino, *Sono nato in America*, 572.)

in 1953 he repeatedly mentioned the importance of Lukács's *Il marxismo e la critica letteraria* (*Marxism and Literary Criticism*): "He is – perhaps – the first Marxist I've read who when he talks about literature deals with the flesh and blood of works, and he sets out the problems before you in a way that leaves you gasping."[75]

Calvino includes Lukács's writing in a list of works, along with Fortini's and Auerbach's, that are "fenomeni generali,"[76] truly significant works of criticism. In other words, Lukács changed Calvino's understanding of literature: "I have something sensational to tell you. I've been unexpectedly bowled over by reading Lukács: all my aesthetic ideas have been thrown overboard, I found that book (I'm talking especially about the second part) more stimulating and clarifying than I'd ever have believed, and I can only think now by starting out from his categories."[77] Calvino ultimately found the parameters of Lukács's debates on realism too restrictive, but the power of the term *realism* for Calvino meant that he often continued to read authors, including Kafka, using this category.[78]

For Calvino, representing the reality of the world directly in literature is impossible: writing always distorts reality. He presents Kafka as a primary example of an author who walks the line between the real world and the written world: "But is mimesis the right way? My starting point was the irreconcilable contrast between the written and unwritten world; if their two languages merge, my argument goes to pieces. The true challenge for a writer is to speak about the tangled mess of our century using a language so transparent that it reaches a hallucinatory level, as Kafka did."[79] Due to the clarity with which he

---

75 Calvino, *Italo Calvino*, 87. ("È il primo – forse – marxista che leggo che parlando di letteratura tocca proprio la carne e il sangue delle opere, e ti mette davanti problemi da lasciarti senza fiato"; Calvino, *Lettere*, 379.)

76 Calvino, *Lettere*, 489.

77 Calvino, *Italo Calvino*, 546. ("Tutte le mie idee estetiche sono scombussolate, ho trovato quel libro [parlo soprattutto della seconda parte] stimolante e chiarificatore come non avrei mai creduto, e non riesco più a pensare senza prescindere dalle sue impostazioni"; Calvino, *Lettere*, 379.)

78 Lucia Re analyses Calvino's lasting realism: "Even after its official 'death,' neorealism was indeed to leave its indelible mark, the traces of its 'passion for the real,' on Calvino more than on any other Italian writer of the postwar era" (Re, *Calvino and the Age of Neorealism*, 36).

79 Calvino, "The Written and Unwritten Word," 38. ("Ma sarà proprio la mimesi la via giusta? Ero partito dall'opposizione inconciliabile tra mondo scritto e non scritto; se i loro due linguaggi si fondono, il mio ragionamento crolla. La vera sfida per uno scrittore è parlare dell'intricato groviglio della nostra situazione usando un linguaggio che sembra tanto trasparente da creare un senso d'allucinazione, come è riuscito a fare Kafka"; Calvino, *Mondo scritto e mondo non scritto*, 122.)

describes the contradictions and unknowability of the world, Kafka's abstraction from reality makes his stories more successful and more realistic for Calvino. Calvino even contends that Kafka could be a realist despite himself: "Kafka, thinking he was writing metaphysical allegory, described the alienation of contemporary man in a way that has never been surpassed."[80]

Calvino ends the posthumously published essay "Leggerezza" ("Lightness") with an analysis of Kafka's story "Der Kübelreiter" ("The Bucket Rider"). Calvino's discussion of this lesser-known story reveals his unique view of Kafka, which is partly due to his individual perspective, but which also relates to the fact that he came to Kafka at an early point, both in his own development and in the reception of Kafka. Calvino's description of "The Bucket Rider" fits with his earlier interpretations of Kafka: "This is a very short story written in 1917 in the first person, and its point of departure is plainly a real situation in that winter of warfare, the worst for the Austrian Empire: the lack of coal."[81]

While many critics examined the traces of Kafka's life in his literature, such as Elias Canetti in his analysis of how Kafka's engagement to Felice Bauer relates to *The Trial*, direct comparisons between Kafka's works and historical events were less common in Calvino's lifetime. Calvino, however, emphasized the historical origins of "The Bucket Rider" as well as how the story is abstracted from reality and ends with a fantastical flight. After being denied coal, the bucket rider flies off into the unknown on his bucket: "'You bad woman! I begged you for a shovelful of the worst coal and you would not give it me.' And with that I ascend into the regions of the ice mountains and am lost forever."[82]

Alessia Ricciardi views Calvino's end-of-life reading of Kafka as a sign of how removed he is from his earlier, more realist fiction: "In his final testament of *Six Memos*, Calvino sadly assumes the position of a narcissistic censor proselytizing for his own bellelettrist tastes. Precisely because he bemoans in this treatise the debilitating effects

---

80 Calvino, *Why Read the Classics*, 192. ("Kafka, credendo di fare dell'allegoria metafisica, ha descritto in modo ineguagliabile l'alienazione dell'uomo contemporaneo"; Calvino, *Saggi*, 1381.)

81 Calvino, *Six Memos for the Next Millennium*, 27–8. ("È un breve racconto in prima persona, scritta nel 1917 e il suo punto di partenza è evidentemente una situazione ben reale in quell'inverno di guerra, il più terribile per l'impero austriaco: la mancanza di carbone"; Calvino, *Lezioni americane*, 34.)

82 Kafka, "The Bucket Rider," 414. ("'Du Böse! Um eine Schaufel von der schlechtesten habe ich gebeten und du hast sie mir nicht gegeben.' Und damit steige ich in die Regionen der Eisgebirge und verliere mich auf Nimmerwiedersehn"; Kafka, *Erzählungen*, 270.)

What exactly is specific in Kafka?

of consumer culture, his found antidote of a literature of style that celebrates its own removal from all social meaning remains in the end deeply unsatisfactory.... The shortcomings of Calvino's poetics become manifest in his weirdly optimistic reading of Kafka's short story."[83] Although Ricciardi comments on the strangeness of Calvino's "optimistic" reading of "The Bucket Rider," equally unusual is Calvino's choice to associate the text with a historical period of time. Adorno claimed that Kafka avoids "almost every reference to the historical."[84] Walter Sokel has argued that Kafka "equates the call of literature with a hidden, powerful inner world that ... stands in complete opposition to ordinary life."[85] Talking specifically about "The Bucket Rider," Stanley Corngold speaks of the work's depiction of the heavens: "The late pieces are full of delicately staged invocations of 'the heavens' and also mockeries of this passion, such as 'The Coal-Scuttle Rider' ('Der Kübelreiter', 1917) in which the heavens figure as a 'silver shield against anyone looking for help from there.'"[86] All this to say that, while Calvino's reading of Kafka's "The Bucket Rider" may seem optimistic and ahistorical in an Italian context, what distinguishes it in Kafka criticism is its emphasis on the historical.

Calvino's interpretation of "The Bucket Rider" as a story that grows out of a historical event connects Kafka to Calvino's own early work, which is often considered realist or neorealist. "Lightness," an examination of how fantasy sheds light on reality, begins with a reflection on the Italian author's first writings. Although Calvino emphasizes Kafka's importance to his early development as writer, anglophone critics have most often associated Kafka with Calvino's later work, like *Le città invisibili* (*Invisible Cities*), which is best known in the United States. Harold Bloom begins his introduction to an edited volume on Calvino with an abstract comparison of *Invisible Cities* and Kafka: "Like much of Kafka, *Invisible Cities* will survive its admirers' modes of apprehension, because it returns us to the pure form of romance, genre of the marvelous, realm of speculation."[87] Focusing on Calvino's later works, English-language writers connect Calvino and Kafka to help introduce Calvino to Americans. The emphasis on the better-known Kafka, as opposed to the Kafka of Calvino's favourite Kafka novel, *Amerika*, have hindered comparisons of Kafka and Calvino's early work.

---

83 Ricciardi, *After La Dolce Vita*, 10–1.
84 Adorno, *Prisms*, 269.
85 Sokel, *The Myth of Power and the Self*, 69.
86 Corngold, "Kafka's Later Stories and Aphorisms," 96.
87 Bloom, *Italo Calvino*, 1.

Calvino's first extant, autobiographical description reveals Kafka's importance at the beginning of his career: "He is from the most recent draft of writers and therefore prefers dry and pitiless narrations, badly dressed and rude characters, and open and rocky landscapes, like Liguria's. However, in him there is a subtle taste for fairytales and enchanted discovery: perhaps because of this he loves gothic and lively cities, and here we see him as he is visiting Prague and consulting Kafka's ghost."[88] The 1947 text accompanies a photo of Calvino in Prague. Many elements of this description are familiar: young Calvino's neorealism (dry narrations, rude characters), the significance to him of the Ligurian landscape, and his attraction to fairy tales, whereas the mention of Kafka stands out as placing Kafka more centrally and earlier in Calvino's development than is generally discussed. Tracing Calvino's mentions of Kafka supports Lucia Re's argument that Calvino's style did not radically alter in the 1960s, but that these earlier writings already reflect much of his later development.[89]

Calvino's "Impiccagione di un giudice" ("The Hanging of a Judge," 1948–9, translated as "A Judgment" in its English publication) shares numerous stylistic and thematic analogies to Kafka's works, most notably *The Trial*, "The Judgment," and "In the Penal Colony." In "The Hanging of a Judge," a judge signs a series of papers, among which he discovers his own death sentence: "And now, suddenly the Clerk of the Court slipped the top sheet off completely: and there, on the sheet underneath Judge Onofrio Clerici read: 'Onofrio Clerici, judge, guilty of having for a long time insulted and derided us other poor Italians, is condemned to die like a dog.' And beneath this was his signature."[90] The judge is sentenced to die, "like a dog," as was Josef K. at the end of *The Trial*, famous lines that Primo Levi examined after translating the novel: "'Like a dog!' he said; it seemed as if the shame was to outlive

---

88 "È dell'ultima leva di scrittori e come tale preferisce le narrazioni secche e crude, i personaggi malvestiti e maleducati, i paesaggi aperti e sassosi come Liguria. Però c'è in lui un gusto sottile di fiaba e scoperta incantata: forse per questo ama le città gotiche e colorate, e qui lo vediamo mentre gira per Praga e interroga il fantasma di Kafka" (Calvino, quoted in Ribatti, *Italo Calvino e l'Einaudi*, 26). Both Calvino's photo and the image of the manuscript are in Baranelli and Ferrero, *Album Calvino*, 88–9.

89 See Lucia Re's field-changing *Calvino and the Age of Neorealism*.

90 Calvino, *Adam, One Afternoon*, 140. ("Ecco, ora il cancelliere faceva scorrere via il primo foglio, e via e via: sotto, sul secondo foglio, il giudice Onofrio Clerici lesse: Onofrio Clerici, giudice, reo d'aver insultato e deriso per lungo tempo noialtri poveri italiani, e condannato a morire impiccato come un cane. Sotto lui aveva firmato"; Calvino, *Romanzi e racconti*, 1:351.)

him."[91] The comparison to a dog emphasizes the characters' lack of power over their deaths and how the enforcers seem to stop considering the guilty men to be human. In "The Hanging of a Judge" and *The Trial*, the shame can also be read as social since both protagonists had an intense concern for their status in society.

Other elements of the court scene in Calvino's story, such as the descriptions of the crowd and the two guards, also echo *The Trial*. Mirroring Josef K.'s final moments, the two guards who accompany Clerici expect him to kill himself. Like Josef K., Clerici dies in a deserted area. In *The Trial*, the empty square could represent Josef K.'s removal from society: "When K. noticed that, he stopped, causing the others to stop as well; they were on the edge of an open, deserted square decorated with flower beds."[92] In "The Hanging of a Judge," the meaning of the square's desolation is made more overt: "Meanwhile the darkness was growing thicker in the arcades of the deserted courtyard; deserted because those filthy Italians had not even come to see him die."[93] The last lines of the story share the judge's condemnation of the Italian people and, with their absence, their condemnation of him. The judge dies without understanding the harm he has perpetrated. Both the judge and Josef K. die without a fair trial. One of the last lines of *The Trial* reflects on this lack: "Where was the judge he'd never seen? Where was the high court he'd never reached?"[94] The Italian judge signed his own death warrant, in part due to his inattentiveness to what the law meant in individual cases. The judge's mistake of obeying the authorities is clear when read in the context of fascism, but requires bringing outside context to the story.

While Josef K. spends a portion of *The Trial* looking for justice, Onofrio Clerici believes that, as a judge, he is executing justice. Like the officer

---

91 Kafka, *The Trial*, 231. ("Con occhi ormai spenti K., vide ancora come i signori, guancia a guancia davanti al suo volto, spiavano l'attimo risolutivo. – Come un cane! – disse, e fu come se la vergogna gli dovesse sopravvivere"; Kafka, *Il processo*, 250.) ("Mit brechenden Augen sah noch K. wie nahe vor seinem Gesicht die Herren Wange an Wange aneinandergelehnt die Entscheidung beobachteten. 'Wie ein Hund!' sagte er, es war, als sollte die Scham ihn überleben"; Kafka, *Der Proceß*, 241.)

92 Kafka, *The Trial*, 227. ("Als K. das bemerkte blieb er stehn, infolgedessen blieben die andern stehn; sie waren am Rand eines freien menschenleeren mit Anlagen geschmückten Platzes"; Kafka, *Der Proceß*, 237.)

93 Calvino, *Adam, One Afternoon*, 141 ("e intanto il buio s'andava addensando ai pilastri del cortile deserto; deserto perché quella gentucola italiana non era nemmeno venuta a vederlo morire"; Calvino, *Romanzi e racconti*, 1:351).

94 Kafka, *The Trial*, 231. ("Wo war der Richter den er nie gesehen hatte? Wo war das hohe Gericht bis zu dem er nie gekommen war?"; Kafka, *Der Proceß*, 241.)

from "In the Penal Colony," the judge believes in the punishments he disperses. Kafka's story asks what a participant or spectator of a judicial system that is condoned by history and society, but seems unjust, should do. Both "In the Penal Colony" and "The Hanging of a Judge" indicate how an individual's sense of justice sometimes needs to supersede official or historically constructed justice. The ominous building of the gallows in Calvino's story recalls the officer's description of the machine in Kafka's. The officer explains in great detail how the machine works and was built, before he himself gets into it. Wondering how it functions, Calvino's judge watches the making of his gallows: "And outside that hammering and dragging about of planks never seemed to stop.... Now, on the other side of the window had appeared a rope, and two hands unrolling it, as if to see how long it was. What on earth was it for, that rope?"[95]

In both stories, the men pay greater attention to the mechanics of the death apparatus than to the fairness of the death sentences they facilitate. In Kafka's story, the officer is most interested in describing the machine, how it operates, and the traditions that have grown up around it, less so in the humans whom the machine will torture. In Calvino's story, the judge distractedly metes out verdicts as he watches the construction of the gallows. Both stories ask the reader to consider carefully what happens when a society is more fixated on the system of punishment than the individual who is going to be punished. With their violent ends and the deaths of the judge and officer, the stories express the need to be critical of systems of justice rather than assume that they function properly.

Like the officer in "In the Penal Colony," as well as Georg in "The Judgment," the judge in Calvino's story is compelled to commit suicide, ostensibly for justice. The English title of the story, "A Judgment," draws attention to the similarity with Kafka's "The Judgment." While Georg's supposed crime, like Josef K.'s, can be interpreted as moral or psychological, in "The Hanging of a Judge" the judge has more clearly erred, but has not necessarily committed any legal crime. As in many of Kafka's stories, the grounds for judgment shift, and the arbitrary nature of official justice lies exposed. Although Calvino gives his tale a more obvious historical setting than Kafka, many of the story's references to fascism are, however, abstract or vague. Calvino's other works, such

---

95 Calvino, *Adam, One Afternoon*, 139. ("E quel martellare e quel trasportare di tavole, che non smetteva mai, là fuori.... Ora, di là dalle finestre, si vedeva una corda, e due mani che la svoltolavano, come per vedere quant'era lunga. A che mai poteva servire, quella corda?"; Calvino, *Romanzi e racconti*, 1:349–50; ellipses in original.)

as *The Path to the Spiders' Nests*, what is known about his development as a writer, and the timing of the story's publication help contextualize the historical setting of "The Hanging of a Judge." The suppression of most direct historical references leaves the story open to broader interpretations about justice. Read alongside Kafka's works, instead of the neorealist works with which it is usually associated, the abstraction of Calvino's story becomes more evident.

Both experimenting with Kafkan techniques and portraying life in fascist Italy were significant for Calvino's development as an author, but the latter has received much more attention. Kafka's and Calvino's stories are connected not only thematically but also through their narrative techniques. The reader constantly needs to evaluate the primary perspective of the work. Calvino's story is told from the fascist judge's perspective to the end, even when he might be dead. The reader of "The Hanging of the Judge" experiences the shock of surviving the story's point of focalization: "And his eyes strained out of their sockets like big black snails as if the light they were looking for could be converted to air."[96] Kafka also uses this notable technique of having the point of focalization die and the story continue. For instance, the narrator disappears (or dies) but still narrates at the end of "The Bucket Rider." Because the narration continues even after the disposal of Gregor's body, the end of "The Metamorphosis" can be unsettling for similar reasons.

The technique of having a story continue after the death of the character whose thoughts have formed the basis of the story contributes to why several of Kafka's works are described as dream-like or surreal. This narrative technique may be one reason that the journal *Rinascita* agreed to publish Calvino's story with the title "Il sogno di un giudice" (A judge's dream). *Rinascita* may also have requested the alternative title and, moreover, presented Calvino's story under the subheading "Imaginary Stories" because of the horror of the situation described and its relationship to 1940s strife.

While "The Hanging of a Judge" provides one example of Calvino's literature, set during the Second World War, that is revealed to be more symbolic and abstract when put into conversation with Kafka's work, other early Calvino stories are even further removed from historical contexts and also reflect Kafkan themes and methods. Calvino's early short story "Chi si contenta" ("Making Do") discusses people who are allowed to play only one game, *lippa* (translated as "tip-cat") and,

---

96 Calvino, *Adam, One Afternoon*, 141. ("E gli occhi, come grandi lumache nere, gli uscivano dal guscio delle orbite, quasi la luce che cercavano potesse convertirsi in aria"; Calvino, *Romanzi e racconti*, 1:351.)

even when allowed to do anything, continue to play just this one game: "'Understand?' the messengers insisted. 'You are free to do what you want.' The people went on playing tip-cat. 'Good,' replied the subjects. 'We're playing tip-cat.'"[97] To force the people to stop playing *lippa*, the game is outlawed, which causes the people to revolt: "That was when the people rebelled and killed the lot of them."[98] Humorous and violent, the story reflects upon people's inconsistent reactions to power. Like many of Kafka's short tales, including "Before the Law," "The Great Wall of China," and "Give It Up," the story reveals the often illogical nature of official judgment and the paradoxical nature of human freedom.

While certainly written before Calvino read Borges, the page-long story "Making Do" is Kafkan-Borgesian in its humour and structure. Calvino described Borges as the "maestro" of the short form, but Borges did not inspire Calvino to write short, paradoxical works. Calvino was instead drawn to Borges, in part, because of feelings of literary kinship: "I began reading Borges when much of my work had already been written and the training for what I wrote was already confirmed, but certainly the presence of Borges reinforced some of my inclinations and tendencies that I already had."[99] The potential Kafka-Borges-Calvino connections reveal the frequent problems of attempting to untangle and dissect influence. Borges was also an avid reader of Kafka and pays him homage in stories like "The Lottery in Babylon," with the playfully named Quaphqa (pronounced "Kafka").

Reading Borges added to Calvino's concept of Kafka. If, as Davide Messina suggests, Calvino may also have been playing on Kafka's name with his character of the *Cosmicomics* (Qfwfq), this particular Kafkan genealogy may be received through Borges (Quaphqa).[100] Between Kafka and Calvino, there exists paths of literary influence, kinship, and then the influence of similar earlier authors.[101] Unlike with Borges,

---

97 Calvino, *Numbers in the Dark*, 11. ("'Avete capito? Insistettero i messi.' 'Siete liberi a fare quel che volete.' 'Bene' risposero i sudditi, 'Noi giochiamo alla lippa'"; Calvino, *Romanzi e racconti*, 3:782.)

98 Calvino, *Numbers in the Dark*, 12. ("Fu la volta che il popolo fece la rivoluzione e li ammazzò tutti"; Calvino, *Romanzi e racconti*, 3:782.)

99 "Ho cominciato a leggere Borges quando parte della mia opera era già scritta e l'impostazione di quello che scrivevo era già affermata, ma certamente la presenza di Borges è servita a rafforzare certe mie inclinazioni, certe tendenze che già erano in me" (Calvino, *Sono nato in America*, 368).

100 Messina, "Qfwfq as Kafka?"

101 As *Six Memos* attests, Calvino read widely, including associated authors that are often not put together. Kafka and Borges, meanwhile, is a more expected conjunction.

Calvino discovered Kafka before either he or Kafka was established in the world canon. Kafka was especially significant to Calvino when the Italian author was first establishing his narrative voice and experimenting with narrative techniques. Examining Calvino's early sources of influence, such as Kafka, sheds light on his development as a writer and his first stories, and it engages his work of the 1940s in conversations that complement the in-depth work that has been done on his early Italian context by critics such as Lucia Re, Andrea Dini, and Eugenio Bolongaro.[102]

Kafka's presence can be seen in Calvino's work not just when he became an internationally known author but also, and perhaps especially, at the beginning of his career. Calvino is one of several important Italian authors in whose literary development Kafka played a crucial role. Calvino's attention to international literature and literary techniques was part of a desire to rejuvenate Italian literature.[103] He wrote about the need to move from intra- to intercultural, national to international comparisons (and then back again): "The classics help us to understand who we are and the point we have reached, and that consequently Italian classics are indispensable to us Italians in order to compare them with foreign classics, and foreign classics are equally indispensable so that we can measure them against Italian classics."[104] Calvino read Kafka while keeping in mind the potential gap between the popular view of Kafka's work and the reality of Kafka's work, between Kafkaesque Kafka and less Kafkaesque Kafka: "When reading Kafka, I cannot avoid approving or rejecting the legitimacy of the adjective 'Kafkaesque,' which one is likely to hear every quarter of an hour, applied indiscriminately."[105] Calvino's personal idea of Kafka brings me back to his preferences for *Amerika* and what this means for understanding his first novel.

---

102 See Bolongaro, *Italo Calvino*; Re, *Calvino and the Age of Neorealism*; and Dini, *Il Premio nazionale "Riccione" 1947*.

103 "Con questo scarno bagaglio di valori da salvare della nostra ultima tradizione, ci buttavamo con impazienza nel crogiuolo della letteratura mondiale del nostro secolo: Proust, Joyce, Kafka" (Calvino, "Tre correnti del romanzo italiano d'oggi," 49).

104 Calvino, *Why Read the Classics?*, 9.

105 Calvino, *The Literature Machine*, 128. ("Leggendo Kafka non posso fare a meno di comprovare o di respingere la legittimità dell'aggettivo 'kafkiano' che ci capita di sentire ogni quarto d'ora, applicato per dritto e per traverse"; Calvino, *Perché leggere i classici*, 8.) Calvino's own work suffered from what he felt was a mischaracterization when it came to Kafka (Calvino, *Lettere*, 1511).

Amerika and *The Path to the Spiders' Nests*: Finding and Losing the Way, All Over Again

Calvino considered *Amerika* the utmost novel of the twentieth century. In one of his last letters, he promised to write an introduction to a new edition of *Amerika*, but unfortunately died before doing so. Describing them as fundamental in his development, Calvino pairs *Pinocchio*, a significant symbol of Italian culture and the work he considered the foremost model of narration, with Kafka's *Amerika*:[106] "If a continuity can be identified in my first formation – let's say between six and twenty-three years old – it is one that goes from *Pinocchio* to Kafka's *Amerika*, the other decisive book of my life, that I have always considered 'the novel' *par excellence* of twentieth-century world literature, and perhaps not just that."[107] Calvino marks the end of his "first formation" as the age at which he wrote *The Path to the Spiders' Nests*, a novel that could be summarized using Calvino's characterization of *Pinocchio*'s and *Amerika*'s shared qualities: "The unifying element could be defined like this: the adventure and solitude of an individual lost in the vastness of the world, moving toward the initiation and construction of the self."[108] While Pinocchio's development remains one of the charms of that work, the progress of Pin in *The Path to the Spiders' Nests* and Karl in *Amerika* is less straightforward. How, and if, they develop is open to interpretation.

I will offer a description of *Amerika* that emphasizes its commonalities with *The Path to the Spiders' Nests*. In Kafka's novel, the young protagonist, effectively orphaned, tries to navigate a cruel and capricious world. Karl stumbles into national and class squabbles and, at times, tries to take part. He searches for a father figure or friend (categories he confuses), and these men always disappoint him.[109] Karl has been seen

---

106 "Quando ho cominciato a scrivere ero un giovano di poche lettura; tentatrela ricostruzione di una biblioteca *genetica* vuol dire risalire rapidamente ai libri d'infanzia: ogni elenco credo deve cominciare da *Pinocchio* che ho sempre considerato un modello di narrazione" (Faeti, "Note su Italo Calvino e la scuola," 66).

107 "Se una continuità può essere ravvisata nella mia prima formazione – diciamo tra i sei e i ventitré anni – è quella che va da *Pinocchio* a *America* di Kafka, altro libro decisivo della mia vita, che ho sempre considerato 'il romanzo' per eccellenza nella letteratura mondiale del Novecento e forse non solo in quella" (Calvino, *Sono nato in America*, 650).

108 "L'elemento unificante potrebbe essere definito così: avventura e solitudine di un individuo sperduto nella vastità del mondo, verso una iniziazione e autocostruzione interiore" (Calvino, 650).

109 Like Pin and Cugino at the end of *Il sentiero*, Karl frequently grasps and holds hands with these father figures.

as experiencing a cycle of banishment, disorientation, and relocation that repeats in a sort of never-realized Bildungsroman.[110] *The Path to the Spiders' Nests* could be similarly described, with adults continuing to lie to Pin to the very end and Pin hoping to be able to trust someone. Even though Karl is older, he – forever tricked and tormented – seems unable to learn some of the lessons that Pin believes he knows, that "i grandi sono sempre ambigui e bugiardi [deceptive and liars]"[111] ("grown-ups are always so double-faced"[112]).

Despite their notable similarities and Calvino's proclamations about *Amerika*, Kafka's and Calvino's first novels are generally placed into different groups of authors and works. Calvino's later preface to *The Path to the Spiders' Nests* emphasized the particular historical context of the novel's composition since he read his novel as a book born of its time: "This is what strikes me most today: the anonymous voice of that age, which comes across more strongly than my own individual inflections, which were still rather uncertain."[113] Critics have noted that Calvino's preface put his work in a certain light, which had perhaps as much to do with his 1964 views of the 1940s historical context as it did with the novel's production. Comparison with Kafka draws attention to a different literary genealogy and places the work in a more personal, literary context. The ambiguity of Kafka's first novel puts into relief the related ambiguity of Calvino's first novel.

A comparison of the endings (or, in Kafka's case, the beginning of an ending) of *Amerika* and *The Path to the Spiders' Nests* reveals how the youth of the protagonists helps establish a world view that the reader should question. Instead of successfully navigating the New World, Kafka's protagonist Karl Rossmann falls deeper into poverty and increasingly inhumane jobs. In later chapters, his chance to hold a real job in the United States appears unlikely and his ability to acclimate productively questionable. Partially because *Amerika* is unfinished, critics have read Karl's final position differently: Karl dying and Karl getting a heavenly job have both been suggested as possibilities.[114]

---

110 See Zilcosky's summary of critics who have discussed the novel as a Bildungsroman (Zilcosky, *Kafka's Travels*, 214). See also Moretti, *The Way of the World*, 229, 239.

111 Calvino, *Il sentiero*, 67.

112 Calvino, *The Path*, 94.

113 Calvino, *The Path*, 8. ("Che impressione mi fa, a riprenderlo in mano adesso? Più che come un'opera mia lo leggo come un libro nato anonimamente dal clima generale di un'epoca"; Calvino, *Il sentiero*, v–vi.)

114 In a diary entry, Kafka mentions that Karl would die. Max Brod mentioned in his introduction that Kafka had planned the Oklahoma chapter to provide an optimistic end to the work.

Calvino and Pavese would have read the more "optimistic" version of
Amerika, in which the Nature Theater of Oklahoma, or "Oklahama,"
as Kafka wrote it, employs Karl. Even when considering this potentially more positive version, with "Nature Theater" as the title of the
last chapter, the end is not unequivocally positive.

A poster informs Karl about the Nature Theater, and a number of
signs indicate that the poster's content is suspect: "There were so many
posters, no one believed posters anymore. And this poster was still
more incredible than posters usually are."[115] When Karl first learns
about the poster, he and the reader are made aware of its potential lack
of credibility. It contains other suspicious elements: "Above all, it had
one great drawback, there wasn't a single word in it about payment.
If it had been at all worth mentioning, then surely the poster would
have mentioned it; it wouldn't have left out the most alluring thing of
all. No one wanted to be an artist, but everyone wanted to be paid for
his work."[116] The assurances that the theatre in Oklahoma offers promise utopia, but could end in an unpaid work camp. The application
deadline on the poster (midnight) is the same time that Karl's capitalist
uncle had arbitrarily set to remove Karl from his life and that Karl had
called unfair. The similar timing indicates the potential injustices of the
Nature Theatre as well.

Karl, who has made mistake after mistake in judgment, overlooks all
this and focuses on the fact that he would be welcome at the theatre:
"But for Karl there was a great lure in the poster. 'All welcome' it said.
All, even Karl. Everything he had done up until now would be forgotten,
no one would hold it against him."[117] Although Karl expresses doubts,
the message's inclusion attracts him: "Maybe all the grandiloquence of
the poster was just a trick, maybe the great Theatre of Oklahoma was
just a little touring circus, but it was taking people on, and that was
enough. Karl didn't read the poster through again, he just looked out

---

115 Kafka, *Amerika*, 1996, 202. ("Es gab so viel Plakate, Plakaten glaubte niemand mehr.
Und dieses Plakat war noch unwahrscheinlicher, als Plakate zu sein pflegen";
Kafka, *Der Verschollene*, 1:387.)

116 Kafka, *Amerika*, 1996, 202. ("Vor allem aber hatte es einen großen Fehler, es stand
kein Wort von der Bezahlung darin. Wäre sie auch nur ein wenig erwähnenswert
gewesen, das Plakat hätte sie gewiß genannt; es hätte das Verlockendste nicht
vergessen. Künstlerwerden wollte niemand, wohl aber wollte jeder für seine Arbeit
bezahlt werden"; Kafka, *Der Verschollene*, 1:387–8.)

117 Kafka, *Amerika*, 1996, 202. ("Für Karl stand aber doch in dem 'Jeder war
willkommen', hieß es. Jeder, also auch Karl. Alles was er bisher getan hatte,
war vergessen, niemand wollte ihm daraus einen Vorwurf machen"; Kafka,
Der Verschollene, 1:388.)

the sentence 'All welcome' once more."[118] Karl knows that the poster may be an exaggeration, but he does not bother to reread it; he instead returns to the most promising line. He, like many early readers faced with interpreting Kafka's work, draws on the sentences that fit his understanding and forces himself to overlook the ones that contradict it.

Karl may experience anything from utopia or abuse in the theatre. Although he encounters his friend Giacomo, with whom he forms a group, this new community may not necessarily be trusted, just as the earlier characters Delamarche and Robinson were not reliable. Karl reveals that members of his group are physically abusive: "Karl thanked them – Giacomo's English wasn't comprehensible to everyone – and as time passed, as happens with people sharing a compartment, they became much friendlier, though their friendliness often took trying forms, for instance each time they dropped a card and looked for it on the floor, they pinched Karl or Giacomo in the leg as hard as they could."[119] Only Karl understands Giacomo, while his other supposed friends manufacture situations in which they can hurt him. What they would do outside the train compartment could be worse.

Giacomo is not the only friend that Karl rediscovers in the Nature Theater. Before his train trip, he sees Fanny, with whom he briefly reunites. He climbs up a ladder to greet her:

> "Am I allowed to go up?" asked Karl. "Who is going to tell me we can't shake hands with each other," cried Fanny, and looked around wrathfully, as if in fact someone with just such a message was coming. Karl ran up the stairs. "Not so fast!" cried Fanny. "The pedestal and the pair of us will fall over."[120]

---

118 Kafka, *Amerika*, 1996, 202–3. ("Mochte alles Großsprecherische, was auf dem Plakate stand, eine Lüge sein, mochte das große Teater von Oklahama ein kleiner Wandercirkus sein, es wollte Leute aufnehmen, das war genügend. Karl las das Plakat nicht zum zweitenmale, suchte aber noch einmal den Satz: 'Jeder ist willkommen' hervor"; Kafka, *Der Verschollene*, 1:388.)

119 Kafka, *Amerika*, 1996, 218. ("Karl dankte ihnen – Giacomos Englisch war nicht jedem verständlich – und sie wurden im Laufe der Zeit, wie es unter Coupeegenossen nicht anders sein kann, viel freundlicher, doch war auch ihre Freundlichkeit oft lästig, da sie z. B. immer wenn ihnen eine Karte auf den Boden fiel und sie den Boden nach ihr absuchten, Karl oder Giacomo mit aller Kraft ins Bein zwickten"; Kafka, *Der Verschollene*, 1:418.)

120 Kafka, *Amerika*, 1996, 205. ("Ist es erlaubt, hinaufzugehen?" fragte Karl. "Wer will uns verbieten, daß wir einander die Hand drücken!" rief Fanny und blickte sich erzürnt um, ob nicht etwa schon jemand mit dem Verbote käme. Karl lief aber schon die Treppe hinauf. "Langsamer!" rief Fanny. "Das Postament und wir beide stürzen um!"; Kafka, *Der Verschollene*, 1:392.)

Fanny warns Karl to be careful since reaching her is potentially treacher-
ous. Her behaviour suggests that someone in the Nature Theater will not
allow his friendship with her to continue, that their symbolic handshake
will break some rule. Indeed, although Karl plays Fanny's instrument
better than she and her companions do, he is not taken to be a musician,
leaving it unclear whether he and Fanny will ever touch hands again.
The holding of hands in *Amerika* is multivalent, often symbolizing not
only friendship but an erotic connection as well. Karl's holding of the
stoker's hand in the first chapter seemed confirmation of a connection, of
a friendship, and perhaps of more. As with Fanny, the ephemeral connection ends, and the stoker is never seen again. Friendships in the work are
temporary. Interpreting Karl as having found stability with Giacomo in
a train moving towards an unknown place requires reading the ending
against the novel that preceded it, against Karl's previous adventures
in America. Generic conventions or assumptions, not the fragmentary,
potentially final chapters, suggest a positive conclusion to the story.

Relatedly, to understand the ending of *The Path to the Spiders' Nests* as
revealing that Pin has found a lasting friendship entails ignoring whole
sections of the work. Similar to how Karl and Giacomo reunite in the
theatre, Pin and Cugino reunite in Pin's "nest," a spot that the boy has
hoped to share with someone special throughout the novel. Resembling
Karl's finding, then losing, and then finding again Fanny and Giacomo,
Pin repeatedly finds and then loses Cugino. He appears to lose Cugino
one last time with Cugino's departure, apparently to sleep with Pin's
sister: "Instead of which Cousin is like all other grown-ups; there's
nothing to be done about it, Pin understands these things."[121] Although
disappointed in Cugino, Pin believes he has grown up and therefore
has relinquished the idea of finding a unique friend, a "grande amico."

Pin hears a shot and Cugino returns, explaining, "You know, I got
disgusted and came away without doing anything."[122] In his joy at
Cugino's return, Pin forgets about the earlier shot, which suggested
that Cugino killed his sister: "Pin is delighted. He really is the Great
Friend, Cousin is."[123] Despite his earlier claims about comprehending
adults, Pin easily reverses his opinion in his search for true friendship. Disregarding his earlier experiences with grownups and their

121   Calvino, *The Path*, 184. ("Invece Cugino è come tutti gli altri grandi, non c'è niente
      da fare, Pin capisce bene queste cose"; Calvino, *Il sentiero*, 158.)
122   Calvino, *The Path*, 184. ("Sai m'è venuto schifo e me ne sono andato senza far
      niente"; Calvino, *Il sentiero*, 159.)
123   Calvino, *The Path*, 184. ("Pin è tutto contento. È davvero il Grande Amico, il
      Cugino"; Calvino, *Il sentiero*, 159.)

inconsistencies, he clings to Cugino. The story ends with hand-holding, a sign of friendship, community, and resolution. The last line reads, "And they walk on, the big man and the child, into the night, amid the fireflies, holding each other by the hand."[124] As with *Amerika*, believing that this consecrates an unending friendship requires a leap of faith and discounting earlier moments. Even the *lucciole* (fireflies, but collo-quially also prostitutes) hint at what may have just happened between Cugino and Pin's sister. Believing that Karl has rediscovered a lasting friend in Giacomo entails ignoring his fleeting interaction with Fanny.

Contrasting the hand-holding in *Amerika* and *The Path to the Spiders' Nests* with the famous hand-holding scene from *The Aeneid* helps shed light on the ambiguity in the modern texts. Evander recounts to Aeneas not only his friendship but also the power of holding hands: "I yearned, in a boy's way, to approach the king / and take him by the hand. So up I went to him, / eagerly showed him round the walls of Pheneus. / At his departure he gave me a splendid quiver / bristling Lycian arrows, a battle-cape shot through / with golden mesh, and a pair of gilded reins my son, / Pallas now makes his. So the hand you want / is clasping yours. We are allies bound as one."[125] Potential erotica, desiring a father figure and, most of all, longing for a community are present in this moment, as they are in Karl's with the stoker or Pin's with Cugino.[126] But, while the grasping of hands in *The Aeneid* consecrates a friendship, proves permanent alliances, and ultimately indicates the beginning of an empire, in *The Path to the Spiders' Nests* and *Amerika* it consecrates a moment that may soon be lost and a desire for friendship, but not necessarily friendship itself.

There are too many modernist ambiguities at play in both novels for a reader to be left with a real sense of stability, no matter who holds hands at the end. Reading the hand-holding in *The Path to the Spiders' Nests* as indicative of a permanent change flattens the novel's complex portrayals of friendship and anti-fascism. While Kafka's ambiguous modernity is now generally treated as assumed, the contradictions of Calvino's early texts are still at times overlooked or explained away; putting the two works into conversation highlights their similarities.[127]

---

124 Calvino, *The Path*, 185. ("E continuano a camminare, l'omone e il bambino, nella notte, in mezzo alle lucciole, tenendosi per mano"; Calvino, *Il sentiero*, 159.)
125 Virgil, *The Aeneid*, 8.193–4, 246–7.
126 For a discussion of this in *The Path*, see, e.g., McLaughlin, *Italo Calvino*, 26–7.
127 Re argued, "Both structuralist and Marxist critics of *The Path* tend to presuppose that every textual detail must work to confirm the governing logic or organic totality of the text. This basic aesthetic assumption leads such critics to ignore or exclude what does not fit into their interpretation of the text's (presumed) unity and coherence" (Re, *Calvino and the Age of Neorealism*, 261).

Both novels raise various questions about class that have been analysed from opposing viewpoints. As already discussed, *Amerika* has been read as the Kafka work that most clearly offers a social critique: some scholars have labelled the novel a socialist text, while others discuss it as problematic because of its representation of the proletariat as opportunists and the naiveté of the protagonist. Similarly, some Calvino commentators critiqued the ambiguous portrayal of the partisans, many of whom *The Path to the Spiders' Nests* depicts as fighting due to circumstances or opportunity, not necessarily belief or heroism.[128] Others claimed it was a communist work. The ambiguities of both works that leave them open to these contrasting readings contribute to the ways the works can be read as realist or modernist.

The Americas of Kafka and Pavese: Class Relations and Solitude

The comparison of Kafka's *Amerika* to Calvino's early works reveals how much a discourse's frame shapes the critical view of these authors. While Kafka's work may seem an unusual choice to compare to Calvino's *The Path to the Spiders' Nests* and Pavese's *The Moon and the Bonfires*, which is the focus of the rest of the chapter, all three authors play with the limited hope of finding community. An interpretation of the novels, especially their endings, depends in large part on what the reader brings to the texts. How one's personal perspective changes one's understanding of Kafka has been a trope of Kafka criticism, from Heinz Politzer's calling Kafka a Rorschach test for the interpreter to today, but it applies to *The Path to the Spiders' Nests* and *The Moon and the Bonfires* as well. Comparing Pavese and Calvino to Kafka helps to reorient the critical view of all three works and calls attention to their ambiguities.

Both Pavese and Kafka were Europeans who read Whitman, saw American movies, and represented the United States without having seen it. America represented an imaginative space in which Pavese and Kafka intertwined their reading and study of the country with their perceptions of modern society. It provided a space for contemplating the plight of living in the modern world. For both authors, it also offered a potential alternative to life in Europe. For years, Pavese wished to leave Italy for America: "I'm swept along by the wanderlust. I swear here to you that I cannot stay here in Italy any longer. My army-duty is over

---

128 For an extensive discussion of Calvino's novel, the critical reactions to it, and a
     reading of what is overlooked in many of these reactions, see Lucia Re, "Between
     the Imaginary and the Symbolic," in *Calvino and the Age of Neorealism*.

at last. I've no news of my old fixing with Columbia, and don't speak about blues, boy! I dream, hope, long, die after America."[129] America represented the hope for a new start.[130]

Kafka also wrote about wanting to escape to America: "If someone had told me last night I could be whatever I wanted, I would have chosen to be a small Jewish boy from the East, standing there in the corner without a trace of worry, ... and in a few weeks one will be in America. Of course it's not that simple."[131] Like many Italians, Kafka dreamed of leaving his country for a faraway place, which America embodied.[132] Although it represented a model place for escape, neither Kafka nor Pavese describe an idealized America. Both authors used it to question the modern condition and ask whether its loneliness and violence was escapable. Neither of their novels provides optimistic answers.

While Kafka and Pavese have occasionally been grouped together among other European authors because of their stark, negative depictions of America, the direct connections between them have been left fairly unexplored. Pavese's letters reveal that he knew of and was interested in Kafka before 1935.[133] He asked for Kafka's newest work in exile: "Frassinelli's new Kafka (Free of charge, of course)."[134] Frassinelli published Pavese's translation of *Moby Dick* in 1932.[135] The

---

129 Pavese and Chiuminatto, *Cesare Pavese and Anthony Chiuminatto*, 158. ("Ti giuro che non ne posso più di stare in Italia. Finalmente sono libero da obblighi militari. Non ho più notizie del mio vecchio impegno con la Columbia University; non ti dico la malinconia! Sogno, spero, aspiro, fino a morirne, l'America. Devo andarci"; Pavese, *Lettere*, 209.)

130 "The truth is that Pavese, Vittorini, and Pintor never even mythified the United States of America, or at least not in the way that the vast majority of critics would have us believe" (Ferrari, *Myths and Counter-Myths of America*, 68).

131 Kafka, *Letters to Milena*, 190–1. ("Wenn man mir freigestellt hätte, ich könnte sein was ich will, dann hätte ich ein kleiner ostjüdischer Junge sein wollen, ... und in [ein] paar Wochen wird man in Amerika sein"; Kafka, *Briefe 1918–1920*, 338.)

132 "In the end, the place itself is not as important as is the fact that it is elsewhere – beyond Prague, beyond the family, beyond the office" (Zilcosky, *Kafka's Travels*, 3).

133 Like many Italians, Pavese knew of Kafka well before Kafka had gained unquestionable status as a world author. Many thanks to Juliet Nusbaum for drawing my attention to the Pavese-Kafka connection when she shared Pavese's thoughts on Kafka, recorded in *Il mestiere di vivere*.

134 "Il nuovo Kafka di Frassinelli (*Cela gratuit de sa part, bien entendu*)" (Pavese, *Lettere*, 443). Many of Pavese's requests in exile are more general (e.g., for a German novel).

135 "The most important of Pavese's early works was undoubtedly his translation of *Moby Dick*, which was published by Frassinelli in 1932 when he was barely out of the university. For the young Italians of Pavese's generation this one novel more than any book stood for America and the Myth of America" (Heiney, *America in Modern Italian Literature*, 61).

"new Kafka," one of Pavese's few requests for a specific author, refers to the collection of Kafka's short stories published in 1935, in contrast to Spaini's translation of *The Trial* in 1933.

For Pavese, as for many other writers in the twentieth century, Kafka may have held a particular appeal after the experience of being punished without a trial and without necessarily knowing the exact reasons for his punishment. Pavese continued to write about Kafka in the 1940s, arguing for his realism.[136] In 1949, he mentioned that he considered Kafka a rare writer who could truly transform symbolism from the past into great literature: "There exists in this regard an affable group of narrators, who apply certain symbolic modes from the past – magic, divine authority – without really believing in it. Generally they ironize (Cabell), sometimes they pose (Powys, Yeats, Lisi), rarely do they create poetry (Kafka)."[137] As Pavese's quote suggests, there are several other productive connections between him and Kafka, such as their use of symbolism and myth, views on women, and representations of exile, in addition to their portrayals of America and modernist ambiguities.[138]

Since this section concentrates on the connections between *Amerika* and *The Moon and the Bonfires*, I will briefly outline Pavese's potential reception of Kafka's first novel fragment. Pavese helped found the publishing house Einaudi, which published *Amerika* in 1945.[139] It was published in the series *Narratori stranieri tradotti* (Foreign Authors, Translated), which Pavese co-directed. Einaudi had previously published Pavese's translation of *David Copperfield*, a novel that Kafka claimed *Amerika* imitated.[140] In 1945, the journal *Il Politecnico*

---

136 In the 1940s, Renato Poggioli, who visited Max Brod in Prague, wrote Pavese from America to discuss his article on Kafka.

137 "Esiste a questo proposito, tutta un'amabile provincia di narratori, i quali applicano senza troppo crederci modi simbolici del passato – la magìa, l'arbitrio divino. Solitamente ironizzano (Cabell), qualche volta si atteggiano (Powys, Yeats, Lisi), rarissimo fanno poesia (Kafka)" (Pavese, *La letteratura americana*, 308).

138 Several of the works related to Pavese's exile, such as "Terra d'esilio" and *Il carcere*, have been briefly compared to Kafka's works; see Gioanola, *Cesare Pavese*, 73; Lauretano, *La traccia di Cesare Pavese*, 62; and Hösle, *Cesare Pavese*, 39, 44. Kafka and Pavese, like several of the Italian authors in this book, could be the focus of an entire monograph.

139 The publication had been ready almost ten years before (Spaini, "Prefazione," vii).

140 On 8 October 1917, Kafka wrote about the connection, "Dickens's *Copperfield*. 'The Stoker' a sheer imitation of Dickens, the projected novel even more so" (Kafka, *The Diaries*, 388). ("Dickens' Copperfield ['Der Heizer' glatte Dickensnachahmung, noch mehr der geplante Roman]"; Kafka, *Tagebücher*, 840–1.)

recommended Kafka's *Amerika*, along with Dickens's *David Copperfield*, Pavese's *Feria d'agosto*, and other works as books to purchase for Christmas.[141] Pavese and Vittorini had been in communication about *Il Politecnico* before this issue appeared.[142] Pavese, had he not already been aware of *Amerika* based on his interest in Kafka, may have been drawn to the novel when it was included in a list with his translation (*David Copperfield*) and recent work (*Feria d'agosto*) in a journal for which he had been invited to write.

In addition, and as discussed, Pavese's interlocutor Calvino loved *Amerika*. Calvino's letter from 3 September 1950 suggests that Calvino would have mentioned one of his preferred novels to his friend: "Not only was [Pavese] one of my favorite writers, one of my best friends, a work colleague for many years, a person I spoke with every day, but he was one of the most important people in my life. He was someone to whom I owe almost everything I am, who had been crucial to me becoming a writer, had always guided and encouraged and followed my work, who influenced the way I thought, my tastes, even my life habits and attitudes."[143] Especially since Calvino described Pavese and Kafka as formative for his development as an author, he most likely discussed the latter with the former.

Although the potential points of contact between Pavese and *Amerika* are many and the novel probably added to Pavese's image of America, Pavese and Kafka have seldom been compared, in part because of their different critical *fortunae* and also because their representations of America come from two sides of Europe.[144] In *Cesare Pavese and America: Life, Love, and Literature,* Lawrence G. Smith states that "not one American book dealing with Pavese appeared between 1988 and 2007."[145] Before Pavese's prominence in international criticism began to wane, Lienhard Bergel (1962) and Richard Ruland (1976) mentioned the potential connections between his and Kafka's

---

141 *Il Politecnico*, "Libri per Natale," 22–29 December 1945, supplement 13–14, 8.

142 "Caro Vittorini, ho visto con ammirazione l'immenso progetto per il *Politecnico* (o il Nuovo Politecnico). È una summa del mondo moderno" (Pavese, *Officina Einaudi*, 160). Catalfamo examines why Pavese did not contribute to *Il Politecnico*, despite Vittorini's invitations (Catalfamo, *Cesare Pavese*, 77–86).

143 Calvino, *Italo Calvino*, 65.

144 Pavese and Kafka have also been briefly compared because of their use of symbols and perspectives on women.

145 Smith, *Cesare Pavese and America*, 1–2. This comprehensive monograph considers Pavese's connections and ideas of America from numerous angles, but does not mention Kafka's *Amerika*. Calvino's love for *Amerika* is also not a point of investigation in Raveggi, *Calvino americano*.

America.[146] After the 1970s, Pavese was more likely to be considered in a primarily Italian context, with attention paid to his interest in America and English-language translations. This comparison between Pavese and Kafka is part of a growing conversation about Pavese's modernism, which comes as critics re-evaluate the terms traditionally used to label the great Italian authors of the twentieth century.[147]

Pavese and Kafka are a specific instance of the problem with considering Italian representations of America as a two-way street rather than the result of a combination of factors. The potential significance of reading Kafka's *Amerika* and Pavese's *The Moon and the Bonfires* together has often been overlooked since Pavese and Kafka tend to be considered such distinct authors, partly because of the "world author" view of Kafka, based primarily on "The Metamorphosis," *The Trial*, and *The Castle* and partly because, for a long time, debates surrounding Pavese often focused on his realism, whereas Kafka's modernism was frequently assumed. When the Marxist directors Straub and Huillet, often referred to collectively as Straub-Huillet in discussions of their co-directed films, discussed their 1984 cinematic adaptation of *Amerika*, tellingly entitled *Klassenverhältnisse* (*Class Relations*), they pointed to the significance of Pavese for their understanding of Kafka. Before filming *Klassenverhältnisse*, Straub-Huillet had made *Dalla nube alla Resistenza* (*From the Clouds to the Resistance*, 1979), an adaptation of Pavese's works that translated *Dialoghi con Leuco* (*Dialogues with Leuco*) and *The Moon and the Bonfires* to the screen:

> I would never have come to Kafka without having read Pavese, whose work we adapted in *Dalla nube alla Resistenza,* says Straub, I think that they resemble each other a great deal. In any case, I am convinced that metaphysical and existential readings of Kafka are deceptive. I see him as the first (and perhaps the last) great poet of industrialized civilization. His life is all a great political experience. The anxiety of his characters is typical for those who live in a productive machinery and are afraid to lose their place in the machinery. Class relationships are fundamental in his novels, even

---

146 Ruland, *America in Modern European Literature*, 86; and Bergel, "*Amerika*: Its Meaning," 123. Bergel argues that Pavese's and Kafka's representations of America can be opposed to that of Whitman, who was the subject of Pavese's thesis for the University of Turin and an author whom Kafka mentioned reading (Bergel, 123). Pavese, e.g., is absent from Elbeshlawy, *America in Literature and Film*, which includes a chapter on Kafka.

147 See Riccobono and Thompson, "*Onde di questo mare*"; and Comparini, "Una proposta per il modernismo italiano."

if as a good little employee he tended to interiorize everything, to live the class struggle by himself.[148]

Straub insists that Kafka not be understood as an existential or metaphysical writer, but as an author who represents the anxieties of industrialization and conflicts of social class. The perhaps surprising comment that he and Huillet were led to Kafka through Pavese becomes less strange when examining the modernization and class relations in *The Moon and the Bonfires* and *Amerika*. Their vision of Kafka and Pavese helps a viewer to understand their films and a reader to see the significance of class relations in *Amerika* and *The Moon and the Bonfires*.

Kafka and Pavese have been considered alternately apolitical and to have written works that should be read within a communist or socialist framework.[149] Major class shifts occur in the two novels. The protagonists, Karl in *Amerika* and Anguilla in *The Moon and the Bonfires*, not only go through reversals of fortune but also discuss their reversals with numerous characters of different means. As with Pavese, describing Kafka's work as realist and a critique of capitalism paints a partial picture, but does call attention to important elements of the novel.[150]

Several critics have read *Amerika* as a critique of modern, capitalist society: "The novel belongs to the most clairvoyant poetic revelations of modern industrial society known in world literature. The secret economic and psychological mechanisms of this society and their satanic consequences

---

148 "Non sarei mai arrivato a Kafka senza aver letto Pavese, da cui abbiamo tratto *Dalla nube alla Resistenza*, dice Straub, penso che si assomiglino parecchio. E comunque sono convinto che le letture metafisiche e esistenzialistiche di Kafka siano fuorvianti. Io lo vedo come il primo (e forse l'ultimo) grande poeta della civiltà industriale. La sua vita è tutta una grande esperienza politica. L'angoscia dei suoi personaggi è tipica di coloro che vivono in un meccanismo produttivo e hanno il terrore di perdere il proprio posto all'interno di tale ingranaggio. I rapporti di classe sono fondamentali nei suoi romanzi, anche se da bravo impiegatuccio lui tendeva a interiorizzare tutto, a vivere la lotta di classe sulla propria pelle" (Straub, interview by Crespi, "Kafka ha due soli registi," 11).

149 Lukács, e.g., mentions a few Italian authors in his work. He esteemed Morante and cites Pavese's views on Dos Passos in the first essay of *Il significato attuale*. "La posizione di Pavese nei confronti dell'impegno e dell'azione politica fu di totale, quasi costituzionale, indifferenza: la politica non rientrava nella sfera dei suoi interessi culturali o umani" (Lukács, quoted in Pappalardo La Rosa, *Cesare Pavese e il mito dell'adolescenza*, 73). Kafka has often been described as apolitical. See, e.g., Friedlander: "One of his best-known diary entries is that of August 2, 1914: 'Germany has declared war on Russia. Swimming in the afternoon'" (Friedlander, *Franz Kafka*, 140–1). Critics now argue against the idea that this quote means Kafka was uninterested in politics, but it remains a popular view of this author.

150 See Finzi, *Come leggere "La luna,"* 66.

are pitilessly bared in it."[151] Uncle Jacob's business provides an example of how capitalist practices shape and influence human interactions in *Amerika*: "It was a kind of consignment and shipping business, the likes of which – so far as Karl could recall – could perhaps not be found in Europe. The business involved intermediary trading, which rather than, say, conveying goods from producers to consumers or perhaps to merchants, handled the distribution of all goods and components and their transport to and fro between the large manufacturing cartels."[152]

The "so far as Karl could recall" and "perhaps" throw into doubt whether this type of business exists only in America or in all industrialized societies. The funny description of American business also accurately represents many modern companies. Kafka's imagined American landscape is part of a European tradition depicting a version of America influenced by Europeans' own urban, industrial experiences: "Even in Kafka's time Europeans regarded America ambivalently. 'Americanization' was often envisaged as Europe's future and as meaning the destruction of traditional culture by materialism and technology."[153] While certain European cities also offer sites with which to consider modernization, in Kafka's America technology and industry have progressed faster than in Europe.

Karl next describes the workers at their jobs, and the vision turns increasingly alarming: "No one said hello, such greetings had been dispensed with; each person followed in the steps of the person before him, either looking at the floor, which he wanted to cross as quickly as possible, or glancing at the papers in his hands and probably managing to catch only isolated words or numbers from the papers fluttering in his hand, as he ran along."[154] In *Amerika*, people have become machines

---

151 Emrich, *Franz Kafka*, 227.
152 Kafka, *Amerika*, 2008, 43. ("Es war eine Art Kommissions- und Speditionsgeschäftes, wie sie, soweit sich Karl erinnern konnte, in Europa vielleicht gar nicht zu finden war. Das Geschäft bestand nämlich in einem Zwischenhandel, der aber die Waren nicht etwa von den Produzenten zu den Konsumten oder vielleicht zu den Händlern vermittelte, sondern welcher die Vermittlung aller Waren und Urprodukte für die großen Fabrikskartelle und zwischen ihnen besorgte"; Kafka, *Der Verschollene*, 1:65–6.)
153 Robertson, introduction to *The Man Who Disappeared*, xiv. "The big city – *die Großstadt* – was a common theme in German literature at the turn of the century, and New York often served the European imagination as a hyperbolic vision of its own urban and futuristic tendencies" (Anderson, *Kafka's Clothes*, 100).
154 Kafka, *Amerika*, 1996, 44. ("Keiner grüßte, das Grüßen war abgeschafft, jeder schloß sich den Schritten des ihm Vorhergehenden an und sah auf den Boden, auf dem er möglichst rasch vorwärtskommen wollte, oder fing mit den Blicken wohl nur einzelne Worte oder Zahlen von Papieren ab, die er in der Hand hielt und die bei seinem Laufschritt flatterten"; Kafka, *Der Verschollene*, 1:67.)

or cogs, without community or even the time to think. Communication and the meaning of language have broken down. Later Karl's cohort, Delamarche, directly disparages Uncle Jacob's business practices: "This was a fraudulent way of hiring people, it was utterly disgraceful, and the Jakob corporation was notorious all over the United States."[155] Despite having been adversely affected by his uncle's view of how the world should work, Karl continues to esteem him at this point and dismisses Delamarche's characterization of his business. Delamarche and his friend Robinson, meanwhile, steal from and abuse Karl. Karl's cluelessness repeatedly leads him to be an unwitting victim in multiple situations. Delamarche's and Robinson's behaviour contributes to understanding the novel as an investigation of how capitalism erodes human relationships. The uncle's treatment of Karl calls into question whether even familial bonds can survive the pressures of capitalism.

The Moon and the Bonfires also offers a bleak picture of American consumerism and its impact on human interactions. The narrator, nick-named Anguilla (his official name is never given), travels back to the small village in Italy where he grew up. He has been gone for twenty years, a period that covers the majority of the fascist *ventennio*. Setting up contrasts among three primary time periods, the narrator's descriptions move between his youth in Italy, his time in America, and his return to Italy. In the America the narrator describes, everyone wants more, which disrupts any sense of community: "There were women, there was land, there was money. But nobody had enough, nobody stopped no matter how much he had, and the fields, even the vine-yards, looked like public gardens, fake flower beds like those at rail-way stations, or else wilderness, burned over land, mountains of slag. It wasn't a country where you could resign yourself, rest your head and say to others 'For better or worse, you know me. For better or worse, let me live.' That was the frightening part."[156]

The constant desire for more destroys connections among humans and a sense of safety. Everyone in America is divorced from the land-scape, and nature has been replaced by "fake flowerbeds." Community

---

155 Kafka, *Amerika*, 1996, 94. ("Diese Art, Leute aufzunehmen, sei ein schändlicher Betrug, und die Firma Jakob sei berüchtigt in den ganzen Vereinigten Staaten"; Kafka, *Der Verschollene*, 1:142.)

156 Pavese, *The Moon*, 16. ("C'erano donne, c'era terra, c'era denari. Ma nessuno ne aveva abbastanza, nessuno per quanto ne avesse si fermava, e le campagne, anche le vigne, sembravano giardini pubblici, aiuole finte come quelle delle stazioni, oppure incolti, terre bruciate, montagne di ferraccio. Non era un paese che uno potesse rassegnarsi, posare la testa e dire agli altri: 'Per male che vada mi conoscete. Per male che vada lasciatemi vivere.' Era questo che faceva paura"; Pavese, *La luna*, 17.)

does not exist. This lack of human companionship eventually leads to violence: "A day would come when just to touch something, to make himself known, a man would strangle a woman, shoot her in her sleep, crack her head open with a monkey wrench."[157] One of the few ways to get to know someone, to feel as if a meaningful interaction has occurred, is to kill. The loneliness of modern society often leads to sexualized violence.

In Karl's world, violence and potentially sexual struggles also appear to be one of the few ways to really "touch" someone. Karl's reaction to being raped reflects this connection between violence and a need for human relationships: "He felt as though she were a part of him, and perhaps for that reason he felt seized by a shocking helplessness (*Hilfsbedürftigkeit*)."[158] *Hilfsbedürftigkeit* has been translated as "helplessness" (Hofmann), "yearning" (Muir), "need" (Wensinger), and, in Italian, "*vuoto*" (Spaini), which expresses the feeling that this abusive sexual act forced Karl to desire a genuine human connection. While the sexual intercourse with Johannes is unwanted, it caused Karl to realize the extent to which he would like to relate to others.

Sexualized violence can be seen in Klara's and Karl's interactions as well. In the United States, Karl spends his time at Klara's house, hoping to form a relationship with her and her father, but feels uncomfortable. Klara makes an effort to put Karl at ease: "Couldn't you feel a little more at home? Come with me, I'll make one final effort."[159] ("Wollen Sie sich hier nicht ein wenig heimisch fühlen? Kommen Sie, ich will den letzten Versuch machen."[160]) Once alone, though, Klara and Karl become involved in a weird physical altercation: "'I'm going to push you down again.' And she put her arms round him, he was so surprised he forgot to make himself heavy, and with her sport-toughened body she carried him almost as far as the window."[161] The interaction could be read as a sexual one or one potentially leading to death.

157 Pavese, *The Moon*, 16. ("Veniva il giorno che uno per toccare qualcosa, per farsi conoscere, strozzava una donna, le sparava nel sonno, le rompeva la testa con una chiave inglese"; Pavese, *La luna*, 17–18.)

158 Kafka, *Amerika*, 1996, 22. ("Ihm war, als sei sie ein Teil seiner Selbst, und vielleicht aus diesem Grunde hatte ihn eine entsetzliche Hilfsbedürftigkeit ergriffen"; Kafka, *Der Verschollene*, 1:43.)

159 Kafka, *Amerika*, 1996, 44.

160 Kafka, *Der Verschollene*, 1:87.

161 Kafka, *Amerika*, 1996, 46. ("'Ich stoße Sie noch einmal hinunter.' Und wirklich umfaßte sie ihn und trug ihn, der verblüfft sich zuerst schwer zu machen vergaß, mit ihrem vom Sport gestählten Körper fast bis zum Fenster"; Kafka, *Der Verschollene*, 1:90.)

As in Pavese, trying to relate to another in the New World seems to entail violence. After their odd struggle, Klara uses *Du* instead of *Sie* as a sign of familiarity: "I'm sorry for you, you're quite a good-looking boy really, and if you'd learned ju-jitsu, you would probably have given me a thrashing. Even so – seeing you lying there, I feel an enormous urge to smack your face."[162] ("Du tust mir ja leid und bist ein erträglich hübscher Junge und hättest Du Jiu-Jitsu gelernt, hättest Du wahrscheinlich mich durchgeprügelt. Trotzdem, trotzdem – es verlockt mich geradezu riesig Dich zu ohrfeigen so wie Du jetzt daliegst."[163]) Klara comments on Karl's physical attraction and that she would like to smack him, again linking attraction and violence. With traditional senses of community destroyed, violence brings lonely people closer together.

In Pavese's and Kafka's novels, America embodies the modern condition of loneliness. Although its cities are more populated than Europe's, their America is a lonelier place. Anguilla remembers lamenting the lack of wine (or anything, really) in the United States in a conversation with another Italian: "'But if I'd known they drank stuff like this.... Not that it doesn't warm you, of course, but a good table wine they don't have....' 'They don't have anything,' I said. 'It's like the moon.'"[164] Comparing the United States to the moon, Anguilla emphasizes the emptiness of his American experience. While life in Italy is connected to the moon based on agrarian, natural ties, in the United States the moon represents a place totally alien to human life. Anguilla's and Karl's reflections highlight the solitude they experience in the country, partly because, as immigrants, they do not seamlessly acculturate and their Americanization remains debatable throughout the works, and partly because everyone in America seems lonely.

As in the wine and moon discussion, several of the episodes Anguilla narrates about his time in America involve contrasting it with Italy. Similarly, Kafka's depiction of America frequently includes nostalgic references to Europe. Karl comments on the differences between the landscape he observes and what he remembers from home: "There were no pedestrians, no market women making their way into town, as existed in Karl's home."[165] Expectations as well as nostalgia, however,

---

162 Kafka, *Amerika*, 1996, 47.
163 Kafka, *Der Verschollene*, 1:91.
164 Pavese, *The Moon*, 14. ("'Ma se sapevo che si beve questa roba.... Mica da dire, riscalda, ma un vino da pasto non c'è....' 'Non c'è niente,' gli dissi, 'è come la luna'"; Pavese, *La luna*, 16; ellipses in original.)
165 Kafka, *Amerika*, 1996, 93. ("Fußgänger gab es keine, hier wanderten keine einzelnen Marktweiber zur Stadt, wie in Karls Heimat"; Kafka, *Der Verschollene*, 1:141.)

are both undercut by Anguilla's and Karl's experiences. The novels allude to the interplay among memory, fantasy, and reality, not only when confronting a new place but also when remembering the old.

The loneliness the characters experience in the United States is not limited to their experience as foreigners. Both novels question the idea of returning home to find a community. Anguilla doubts his decision to come to America: "Was it worth it to have come? Where could I go now? Throw myself off the breakwater?"[166] On the other hand, when he goes back to Italy, he finds it hard to reintegrate into the community he left behind. What would have happened to him had he stayed is also framed negatively. Anguilla discovers, in large part through his friend Nuto, that many of the villagers, including the beautiful Santa, who was only a child when Anguilla left, have been killed or died. Santa's symbolic death calls into question the village's ability to recover from the strife of the 1940s as well as Anguilla's ability to re-enter a community that has gone through so much.

For Karl, Europe frequently represents a positive model of life, one where his education would have continued. He dreams of going home: "Many of these sights reminded Karl of his homeland, and he was not sure whether it would make sense for him to leave New York and head inland. In New York there was the sea and always the possibility of returning to his homeland."[167] It is unclear, however, what the results of remaining at home would have been. Karl's parents shipped him off to America because the woman who had seduced him was pregnant. His father mocked him before he left, doubtful that Karl would do well in the New World. While Karl searches for community and understanding in America, it is debatable whether he ever had this at home, with his fraught parental relations, or would have it if he returned. His yearning for human connection began before he arrived in America.

The endings of *The Moon and the Bonfires* and *Amerika* are ambiguous about the main characters' ability to form meaningful relationships. The novels leave unresolved the question of whether their incapacity is constitutional or due to life in the twentieth century. In *The Moon and the Bonfires* and *Amerika*, the United States represents a place where it is possible to be completely lost, without any lasting connections to

---

166 Pavese, *The Moon*, 16. ("Valeva la pena esser venuto? Dove potevo ancora andare? Buttarmi dal molo?"; Pavese, *La luna*, 17.)

167 Kafka, *Amerika*, 1996, 95. ("Vieles erinnerte Karl an seine Heimat und er wußte nicht, ob er gut daran tue, New-York zu verlassen und in das Innere des Landes zu gehn. In New-York war das Meer und zu jeder Zeit die Möglichkeit der Rückkehr in die Heimat"; Kafka, *Der Verschollene*, 1:143.)

another human being. Pavese wrote about how America shed light on his contemporary society: "During those years of study, it dawned on us that America was not 'another' country, a 'new' beginning in history, but only the gigantic theater where with greater freedom than elsewhere the drama of all was being acted out."[168] The idea that America represented a place that exposed the "drama of all" is one reason the country proved to be such a productive space for authors such as Pavese and Kafka. Both works raise the question of whether everyone in the modern world is "American," in the sense of being unable to form meaningful communities.

Using the United States, Kafka and Pavese explore various hopes and fears about modern society in their novels. The Americas of Pavese, "the poet of solitude," and of Kafka, whose novels form a *"Trilogie der Einsamkeit"* ("trilogy of solitude"), repeatedly reveal the potential loneliness of humankind. Pavese viewed Kafka as a master of describing the anxiety and uprootedness of twentieth-century society, something that became even clearer after Kafka's death: "The war's lesson of anxiety that we all experienced beat into our consciences many years before the bombs began to fall. It is not an accident that Kafka, the most authentic poet of humanity uprooted by persecution and racial terror, wrote in the period of the first world war."[169] Pavese emphasizes Kafka's portrayals of uprootedness and persecution. Pavese's and Calvino's reading of Kafka as a realist lead, in turn, to the ambiguities and the potential modernism of their own early works. Putting Kafka's *Amerika* into conversation with Calvino's *The Path to the Spiders' Nest* and Pavese's *The Moon and the Bonfires* highlights the slippage between neorealism and modernism.

While neorealism in literature has always been an issue for debate, the contours of neorealist film have appeared clearer. Similar to how Kafka's *Amerika* sheds light on the potential modernism of literary works categorized as neorealist, the adaptations of it discussed in this

---

168 Pavese, *American Literature*, 198. ("Ci si accorse durante quegli anni di studio, che l'America non era un *altro* paese, un *nuovo* inizio della storia, ma soltanto il gigantesco teatro dove con maggiore franchezza che altrove veniva recitato il dramma di tutti"; Pavese, *La letteratura americana*, 174.) Pavese's views on America and the significance of American literature to Italy shifted over time. This essay refers to what America used to mean to him.

169 "La lezione d'angoscia della Guerra da noi tutti vissuta martellava le nostre coscienze già molti anni prima che le bombe cominciassero a cadere. E non è un caso che il piú autentico poeta dell'umanità sradicata dalle persecuzioni e dal terrore razziale, Franz Kafka, scrivesse ancora al tempo della prima guerra mondiale" (Pavese, *La letteratura americana*, 250).

section contribute to studies that focus on the connections between neorealism and other movements like modernism, revealing neorealism as less distinct than is sometimes argued.[170] Many neorealist films, such as *Ladri di biciclette* (*Bicycle Thieves*, 1948), actually adapt a literary work to the screen. While it focuses on daily life and uses amateur actors, the film draws on the narrative plot of Luigi Bartolini's *Ladri di biciclette* (*Bicycle Thieves*, 1946). Since it is easy to forget that a text prompted the film, a viewer does not necessarily focus on the relationship between the film and its source. In fact, neorealism is frequently described, in part, by how it portrays "reality," in contrast to films that adapt literary works.

Both Straub-Huillet and Fellini, meanwhile, employ techniques that make viewers aware that they are watching a film that adapts Kafka's first novel. In *Intervista*, part of the plot of the film is that the viewer observes Fellini working on adapting Kafka's novel. Actors try out for the roles of various characters. Fellini unites documentary and fantasy in his treatment of Kafka's *Amerika*, presenting an "American Street" with blown-up photographs of Americans in period clothing, showing how a film weaves together reality and the literary to form something new.[171]

Straub-Huillet's actors read lines directly from *Amerika* in a flat mode that calls attention to the written nature of the lines. The startlingly sharp edits between scenes call attention to the process of filming itself, enacting a Brechtian distance from the work, but also suggesting the unfinished nature of Kafka's novel. While *Class Relations* is set in America, most of it was filmed in Hamburg, Germany, reflecting how Karl is weighed down by his – literal and metaphorical – European baggage as well as the fact that Kafka himself never travelled to America. Although several of Straub-Huillet's and Fellini's techniques developed out of neorealism, their films do not neatly fit into this category, especially the way they display an openness about the adaptation process. This openness could be seen as more realistic than trying to represent reality through a literary work without calling attention to the tension between the two.

The films comment on the difficulty of representing reality as well as adapting literary works. Whether their discontinuities cause them to be more realist, modernist, or fantastical depends, in part, on one's

---

170 See Leavitt, "Cronaca, Narrativa, and the Unstable Foundations of the Institution of Neorealism" for an analysis of this.

171 "Fellini, like Kafka, has no intention of presenting a real America, but in thinking about fictionality and place and the nature of reality as it is mediated through the imagination and sight" (Woods, *Kafka Translated*, 219).

definitions of these terms. The view of realism that *Class Relations* and *Intervista* portray adds to Bertoni's explanation, discussed at the beginning of the chapter, of how the concept of realism shifts depending on what one focuses on as real: "That which passed for *the* reality (physical, biological, environmental, social) has become inert literary material, supplanted by a more essential and decisive interior reality. 'Only the spiritual world exists,' notes Kafka, the world of a 'spirit' desperately unknown and unknowable."[172] Kafka, especially his *Amerika*, reveals the modernism of several of Italy's realist works.

---

172 "Quella che passava per essere *la* realtà (fisica, biologica, ambientale, sociale) è diventata materiale letterariamente inerte, soppiantata da una ben più essenziale e decisiva realtà interiore. 'Non esiste che il mondo spirituale,' annota Kafka, il mondo di un' 'anima' disperatamente ignota e inconoscibile" (Bertoni, *Realismo e letteratura*, 266).

Chapter Two

Dreams of Short Fiction after Kafka: Lalla Romano, Giorgio Manganelli, and Antonio Tabucchi

Whereas the last chapter discussed a particular Italian view of *Amerika* for the purpose of examining Calvino and Pavese, this one explores how Kafka's lyrical, fragmented, and aphoristic short works suggest connections among three authors not usually associated with one another: Lalla Romano (1906–2001), Giorgio Manganelli (1922–90), and Antonio Tabucchi (1943–2012). Repositioning the critical view of Italian authors' connections, I explore how Kafka's extremely short works informed and can be fruitfully compared to three Italian short-work collections: Romano's *Le metamorfosi* (*Metamorphoses*, 1951), Manganelli's *Centuria* (*Centuria*, 1979), and Tabucchi's *Sogni di sogni* (*Dreams of Dreams*, 1992). I analyse how the brevity, language, and abstraction of Romano's, Manganelli's, and Tabucchi's short pieces, like those of Kafka, offer spaces of experimentation in terms of genre, gender, and time. An investigation of Kafka's short, short works and Italian literature reveals how lyricism, brevity, fragmentation, and the hypothetical are interrelated in these works. These authors ultimately also shed light on one way to read lyrical Kafka, which contributes to an alternative world view of the author.

While this chapter concentrates on Italian authors to examine the particular shape of Italian literature and draw attention to new elements of Italian fiction, the contrast between the Kafka of *The Trial* and the lyrical, fragmented, and shorter Kafka could be extended internationally and would paint two very different pictures of Kafka's role in world literature. Rather than bring together authors such as Kobo Abe (*The Woman in the Dunes*), J.M. Coetzee (*The Childhood of Jesus*), Dino Buzzati (*The Tartar Steppe*), and Haruki Marakami (*After Dark*), whose works are often associated with *The Trial* and *The Castle*, the Kafka who inspires lyrical works would focus on authors such as Amelia Rosselli

(*War Variations*) and Louise Glück (*Faithful and Virtuous Night*), both of whom mention Kafka's importance to their work.[1]

Lyrical, Short Kafka

In a reflection on the various received Kafkas that emerge in different historical periods in Italy, Italo Calvino points to an alternative tradition of understanding Kafka as lyrical: "But from the lyrical Kafkaism of the forties we have moved to the (much more pseudo) sociological Kafkaism of the sixties, when, in other words, all the numerous intellectual functionaries of Olivetti wrote a novel in which the company became mysterious and allegorical."[2] Lamenting the shift away from the attention paid to Kafka's works originally published in Italy that prompted conversations about Kafka's lyricism, Calvino sees lyrical Kafka as a stronger interpretation of Kafka than the sociological, allegorical, and more "Kafkaesque" (as it is generally understood) Kafkaism that followed.[3]

What Calvino means by *lyrical Kafka* may not be immediately clear: this chapter offers one perspective on lyrical Kafka in the Italian context. Since the first Kafka works published in Italy were much shorter than "The Metamorphosis," often only a couple of pages, or sentences, long and sometimes characterized as prose poems, many critics initially placed Kafka in different literary traditions than they typically would with the Kafka of the famous novels. In 1928, twenty years before the Italian publication of *Das Schloss* (*The Castle*), the journal *Il Convegno* (*The Convention*) published translations of "Vor dem Gesetz" ("Before the Law"), "Ein altes Blatt" ("An Old Manuscript"), "Ein Brudermord" ("A Fratricide"), and "Der neue Advokat" ("The New Advocate"). The translator ended his note to the selection by mentioning the relevance to Kafka of Baudelaire and Poe.[4] Silvio Benco introduced this early

---

1 Giraldi, "Internal Tapestries: Conversation with Louise Glück," 44. Rosselli will be discussed.

2 "Ma dal kafkaismo lirico degli anni '40 siamo passati al [molto più pseudo] kafkaismo sociologico degli anni '60, quando cioè ognuno dei numerosi letterati funzionari dell'Olivetti ... ha scritto un romanzo in cui l'Olivetti diventava un'azienda misteriosa e allegorica" (Calvino, *Lettere*, 872–3). Calvino's comment raises questions about what he meant by "Olivetti novels," which Giuseppe Lupo has addressed in an article that analyses Ottiero Ottieri, Giancarlo Buzzi, Paolo Volponi, and Libera Bigiaretti, among others (Lupo, "Calvino, Kafka e il romanzo olivettiano").

3 As seen in my chapter "*Amerika* in Italy," Calvino often evaluated Kafka against common ideas about him. For more on Calvino and Kafka, see chap. 1 and the epilogue.

4 Kafka and Menassé, "Franz Kafka," 383–4.

selection, and his later review of *The Trial* in 1933 begins, "We can at last read a *book* of Kafka's in Italian,"[5] giving a sense of both the desire for Kafka's works to be translated into Italian and the earlier prominence of Kafka's shorter texts.

The first piece by an Italian in the 1974 collection of Kafka criticism, *Introduzione a Kafka: Antologia di saggi critici* (*Introduction to Kafka: An Anthology of Critical Essays*) is Giovanni Battista Angioletti's "Il poeta Kafka" ("The Poet Kafka"), originally published in 1960, the end of the period that Calvino marked as being influenced by Kafka's lyricism. Although *poet* can be meant more broadly, as referring to any powerful, literary author, regardless of whether he or she writes in prose or verse (which is the way the anthology's previous selection by Herman Hesse uses the word to refer to Kafka), Angioletti discusses Kafka's poetry in the more restricted sense of the term. He describes Giacomo Leopardi (1798–1837) and Kafka as moving between poetry and prose in their writing processes.[6] He claims that Kafka's poetry is still evident, although the author ultimately arrives at prose, whereas Leopardi starts with prose and ends with poetry.[7] Angioletti goes on to characterize Kafka as the heir of expressionism and lyrical fragmentism, which led Kafka to produce the "first existential poetry."[8] Angioletti locates the "fragment" as the form in which Kafka achieves the greatest force because his powerful language and contradictory ideas are distilled in the fragment.[9]

Critics have read Kafka's fragmentation as manifesting itself in a number of ways, from titles ("The Stoker: A Fragment") and form (notes that could function as stories and unfinished novel fragments) to syntax.[10] Although often complete in the sense that they are finished, Kafka's short published works tend to embody fragmentation because of their internal contradictions. Their contrasts have been framed in different ways – for instance, as existing between a desire for

---

5   "Si legge finalmente in italiano anche un libro di Kafka" (Benco, *Scritti di critica*, 174). The review originally appeared under his name in *Il Piccolo della Sera* (Trieste), 19 October 1933.

6   The poetry of Kafka's language has been approached from a few angles outside Italian criticism as well. For instance, Ryder comments on the previously unnoted metricality of Kafka's work (Ryder, "Kafka's Language 'Poetic'?," 320).

7   Angioletti, "Il poeta Kafka," 45.

8   Angioletti, 45.

9   Angioletti, 44. According to him, these short-short works convey all the ideas that are in Kafka's novels, but more effectively because of their concise nature, which is also why they are more closely tied to their language.

10   See Miles on how Kafka's "poetics of the fragment" influence his prose style (Miles, "Pleats, Pockets, Buckles, and Buttons," 338).

inconclusiveness (or infinity) and clarity (or reality).[11] The tensions of Kafka's works contribute to why his works are generally read as open, no matter how brief. Kafka combines two modes of perception in very short, as well as longer, works.

Poetic, fragmented Kafka has a particular literary tradition in Italy. A surprisingly notable portion of early Italian criticism on Kafka engages the term *ermetismo* (hermeticism), which describes non-political, spiritual, obscure, and enigmatic poetry and is one of the many intriguing Italian movements of the twentieth century.[12] The journal *Il Frontespizio* (*The Frontispiece*), which has been associated with *ermetismo*, published several pieces on Kafka. In 1933, it published Rodolfo Paoli's article "Spavento dell'infinito" (The terror of the infinite), which discussed Kafka's ability to unsettle reality: "After having seen it with Kafka's eyes, even reality becomes dreamlike and mysterious, although it was so clear before."[13] *Il Frontespizio* published Paoli's translation of a series of Kafka's aphorisms the following year. Four years later, again in *Il Frontespizio*, Carlo Bo published "Letteratura come vita" (Literature as life), often characterized as a manifesto for *ermetismo* and hermetic poetry. Bo wrote several pieces on Kafka, starting in 1934. Bo's and Paoli's views of Kafka can be considered part of a hermetic approach to Kafka.[14]

Carlo Sgorlon's 1961 monograph on Kafka, *Kafka narratore* (*Kafka, Narrator*), begins with a list of critics who were interested in Kafka because of how his work seemed to support their theories. While many of the terms invoked are still familiar in international discussions of Kafka, Sgorlon included *ermetici* in his list, along with *Freudian, existential, Marxist, surreal,* and *Jewish.*[15] Related to Italian readings of

weird!

---

11 "Indeed, characteristic of Kafka's innovative narrative technique is an internal tension arising from the desire for conclusiveness and apodictic certainty on the one hand, and, on the other, a labyrinthine openness and inconclusiveness which incessantly frustrates this drive for closure" (Gray, *Constructive Destruction*, 2–3). For more on Kafka and infinity, see, e.g., Liska, "Kafka's Other Job."

12 "According to Bo, what unites the Hermetic poets is a shared appreciation of the spiritual value of literature, intended as a supreme truth reflected in the essential nature of life itself" (Sica, "Ermetismo," 929).

13 "Dopo averla spiata cogli occhi di Kafka anche la realtà diventa sogno e misteriosa, essa così chiara prima" (Paoli, "Spavento dell'infinito," 213).

14 Ursula Vogt explicitly connects Bo's views on *ermetismo* and his article "Intorno a Kafka" ("About Kafka," 1946) in a discussion of the concentrated and closed nature of Bo's examinations of literature (Vogt, "Carlo Bo e Franz Kafka," 52). Bo's work on Kafka caused several authors to write pieces that took issue with his views, which Bo referred to as *antibo* opinions. Since his views provoked discussion, the idea that there was an affinity between *ermetismo* and Kafka was a matter of consideration.

15 Sgorlon, *Kafka narratore*, 10.

Kafka as a Catholic, spiritual writer,[16] the understanding of Kafka as mysterious, lyrical, and hermetic is particular to his early reception in Italy.[17] Leopardi was an important point of reference for the poets and theorists of *ermetismo*, a fact that provides clarifying context for Angioletti's unusual comparison of Leopardi and Kafka. Anceschi, editor of the anthology *Lirici nuovi, antologia di poesia contemporanea* (*New Lyric: An Anthology of Contemporary Poetry*), which is important for understanding *ermetismo*, wrote an article on Kafka that took issue with interpretations prioritizing Kafka's historical context over his writing, and he dismissed existential interpretations of Kafka as inaccurate. Aligning Kafka's work with many principles of *ermetismo*, Anceschi argued for an appreciation of the author's interiority.[18]

While critics discussed Kafka in terms of *ermetismo* mostly in the 1930s to the early 1960s, the fragmented, poetic nature of Kafka's work continued to be a source of inspiration afterwards. The work of poet Amelia Rosselli provides a literary example of the potential connections between Kafka and *ermetismo*. Whereas some critics made the *ermetici*-Kafka association to advance their own views of literature, Rosselli wrote works that drew on both hermetic poetry and Kafka without a critical agenda. She comments, "The poems reflect this melancholy privation of life, but I think and hope also a more accurate linguistic rigor, and an acknowledgement, with greater humility, of all the cultural debts (not only the usual Rimbaud, Kafka, Campana, Montale!) in terms of a generation of writers considered 'minor' or surpassed (Saba, *ermetismo*, Mallarmé, Verlaine, Rilke, etc.)."[19] Both the closed, poetic language of the *ermetici* and the unsettling contradictions of Kafka's prose can be traced in Rosselli's powerful work, drawing attention to Kafka's hermetic use of precise, but abstract, language to suggest new ways to view reality.

Although in the previously cited interview Rosselli was specifically discussing her work *Serie ospedeliera* (*Hospital Series*), she mentions Kafka as a source of inspiration several other times as well, as she

---

16   Carlo Bo, e.g., associates Georges Bernanos, author of *The Diary of a Country Priest*, and Kafka's works (Bo, *Della lettura*, 239).

17   Carlo Sgorlon's monograph, like Angioletti's article, appears at the end of the period that Calvino marked as being attentive to and influenced by Kafka's lyricism. For a discussion of *Il Frontespizio* and religion, see Mazza, *Not for Art's Sake*, 137.

18   Anceschi, *L'esercizio della lettura*, 115.

19   "Le poesie rispecchiano questa melanconica privazione di vita, ma credo e spero anche un rigore linguistico più accurato, e un risconoscere con maggiore umiltà i molti debiti culturali (non solo i soliti Rimbaud, Kafka, Campana, Montale!) nei confronti di una generazione di scrittori considerati o 'minori' o sorpassati (Saba, l'ermetismo, Mallarme, Verlaine, Rilke, ecc.)" (Rosselli, *Una scrittura plurale*, 284).

does Rimbaud, Dante, Michelangelo, Leopardi, Campana, Montale, and Pavese (specifying his poetry), thus putting Kafka primarily in the company of poets.[20] Kafka seems not to belong in this group for numerous reasons: in addition to being a prose writer, he writes in a language Rosselli was not fluent in, as opposed to French, Italian, and English.[21] Rosselli repeatedly expresses surprise at Kafka's influence on her: "For the real inspiration of this series of poems, strange to say, is Kafka, the prose of Kafka."[22] Here she reflects on Kafka's significance to the development of *Variazioni belliche* (*War Variations*), a work that she highly esteemed, as did critics: "With *War Variations* it is perhaps the only time in which I had the sensation of being able to have an effect on reality through poetry."[23] Kafka helped Rosselli develop the imagery and questions raised in *War Variations* that make it such an urgent work.[24] Rosselli's interest in Kafka and her works' affinities to him indicate how he has served as a source of inspiration for authors not generally thought of as being "like Kafka."[25]

---

20 Although Rosselli mentions a few Kafka works, such as *The Castle,* it can be difficult to locate the specific texts that she found most inspiring. Even when asked directly which works influenced her, her answer remains vague: "No, I was asking, which texts?" "Well, the best texts of Kafka are well known, those that are well known. There is a mathematical, grammatical intelligence in Kafka, the grammatical in Kafka which is secret, hidden, and that is productive in poetry as well." ("No dicevo, quali testi?" "Beh, i migliori testi di Kafka son noti, quelli più noti. E v'è una intelligenza matematica, grammaticale in Kafka che è segreta, sotto sotto, e in poesia dà frutta anche"; Rosselli, *È vostra la vita che ho perso*, 302.)

21 While Rosselli's narration of her experience of Kafka varies, she frequently mentions his influence on both her content and her language. In his wide-ranging works on Rosselli, several of which discuss Kafka, Antonio Baldacci focuses on their shared visualization of horror, the materialization of a nightmarish atmosphere, the fear of living, and the idea of literature as a refuge or escape: see Fusco, *Amelia Rosselli*, 148; Baldacci's article "Amelia Danza Kafka"; and Baldacci's monographs *Fra tragico e assurdo*, 13–15, and *Amelia Rosselli*.

22 "Quanto a vero ispiratore di questa serie di poesie, strano a dirsi, è Kafka, la prosa di Kafka" (Rosselli, *È vostra la vita che ho perso*, 302).

23 "Con *Variazioni* è forse l'unica volta in cui ho avuto la sensazione di poter agire sulla realtà tramite la poesia" (Rosselli, 128).

24 "Battagliero Kafka non lo era, ma nella sua prosa razionalizzante pone un enorme problema, ed era forse quello che sotto sotto volevo anch'io porre: egli ricerca le cause del suo disastro e di quello degli altri" (Rosselli, 104; "Kafka was not a fighter, but in his rationalizing prose he posed an enormous problem, and it was perhaps that which subconsciously I also wanted to pose: he searched for the cause of his disaster and of others").

25 Mark M. Anderson connects the lyricism of "Description of a Struggle" and *Meditation,* showing how Kafka's lyricism can be traced more broadly throughout his works (Anderson, *Kafka's Clothes*, 36).

Although Rosselli frequently mentions Kafka, she rarely references specific works. The title of Kafka's "Beschreibung eines Kampfes" ("Description of a Struggle," or "Battle" or "Fight") suggests potential connections between this story and Rosselli's bellicose poetry.[26] Arguing that the story stages a grand enactment of the destabilization of language, Vivian Liska has demonstrated how the poem that initiates "Description of a Struggle" foreshadows linguistic instability and struggle: "And humans stroll about in clothes / Swaying on the gravel pathways / Under this enormous sky / Stretching out from hills in the distance / To distant hills."[27] The idea that the people and ground are shaky relates to the sense that our place in the world is unsteady, that the boundaries between interior insecurity and our external existence have been ruptured. The sky itself seems distanced from itself, as it stretches to distant hills.

Even ordinary language can completely unsettle one's sense of place in the world. This breakdown is reflected in Kafka's language use as well as his themes.[28] Many of Rosselli's memorable moments similarly collapse the distinctions between literal and metaphorical meanings. In *War Variations*, the sky becomes a trap: "Se per il cielo che tutto guida alla sua prigionia io / non provassi interessse per te – non ne morirei di questa / noia."[29] ("If for the sky that leads everything to its prison I / felt no interest for you – I would not die of this / boredom."[30]) The personal relationship to the sky, which here is threatening, erodes a sense of peace.[31] While the speaker in *War Variations* seems to want to

---

26 Baldacci highlights connections between Kafka's diaries and "Description of a Struggle" in his examinations of Rosselli (Baldacci, *Amelia Rosselli*, 63–4).

27 Many thanks to Vivian Liska for providing this translation for a seminar at Duke University, held 11 December 2014, when she also discussed her interpretation of it. For a published translation, see Kafka, "Description," 9. ("Und die Menschen gehn in Kleidern / schwankend auf dem Kies spazieren / unter diesem großen Himmel, / der von Hügeln in der Ferne / sich zu fernen Hügeln breitet"; Kafka, *Nachgelassene Schriften*, 54.)

28 "In Kafka's fictions, we know well enough, the distinction between literal and metaphorical meanings itself tends to collapse" (Koelb, "The Turn of the Trope," 59).

29 Rosselli, *War Variations / Variazioni belliche*, 300.

30 Rosselli, 301.

31 In Kafka's "Die Brücke" ("The Bridge"), which will be discussed in more detail later in this chapter, the narrator is a bridge that tries to connect with others, revealing the difficulty of communicating with them. This issue of connection appears repeatedly in *War Variations*. For instance, Rosselli reflects on the fear of living and stretching between two points in order to communicate: "Dalle coste non oso più / affrontare, temo la rossa onda / del vero vivere, e le piante che ti dicono addio. Rompi- / colo accavalco i tuoi ponti, e che essi siano / la mia / nature" (Rosselli, 28). ("From the coast I no longer dare / to face, I fear the red wave / of actually living, and the plants that say goodbye. Tom- / boy I straddle your bridges, and make them maybe / my own / nature"; Rosselli, 29.)

break out and in "Descriptions of a Struggle" to be overwhelmed by a sense of insecurity, in both works the sky and world collude with inner concerns. The two poems express the unreliability of boundaries between humans and the sky and therefore between self and world.

Rosselli mentions the appeal of Kafka's "desperation" and how his "grammar" inspired hers: "The first part of *Variations* are very short free verses, the second part is inspired, if one wants to say, by Kafka, on a grammatical level. I was then reading Kafka with great attention, in my opinion, something in my treatment of Italian grammar is similar to his hardness [*durezza*], his use of Latinisms, as far as I can understand Kafka's grammar in translation."[32] Part of the "hardness" or "harshness" that Rosselli mentions relates to how necessary every word is in Kafka's, as in her own, texts.[33] Montale also discusses the unique power of Kafka's grammar. His poem "Verboten" describes Kafka's grammar as having no future: "Dicono che nella grammatica di Kafka / manca il futuro. Questa la scoperta / di chi serbò l'incognito e con buone ragioni." ("They say the future tense is missing / in Kafka's grammar – the discovery of someone / who remained anonymous, and with good reason.")[34] To paraphrase, the tight, clear abstraction of Kafka's work appears to suggest a world without a future. This world's grammar is recognizable, inspiring, and terrifying; whoever discovered this should remain unknown. Montale's and Rosselli's concept of Kafka's "grammar" points to elements of Kafka's fiction inherently "Kafkan" that go beyond content, plot, or events.[35] The tight construction of his particular

---

32 "La prima parte di *Variazioni* sono versi liberi molto brevi, la seconda parte si ispira se vuole a Kafka sul piano grammaticale. Allora stavo leggendo Kafka con molta attenzione, qualcosa, secondo me, nel mio trattare la grammatica italiana rassomiglia, per quanto posso capire la grammatica di Kafka in traduzione a una sua certa durezza, all'uso dei latinismi" (Rosselli, *È vostra la vita che ho perso*, 164).

33 Ruth V. Gross has analysed how Kafka's short works often play upon the connotations of a single word (Gross, "Hunting Kafka"). Rosselli's poetry also builds from the multiple possible significations and interplay of words. As she states, her language is less transparent than Kafka's. For instance, while the connotations of a word in Kafka (e.g., *Klamm*) support critics' interpretations of *The Castle*, it is almost impossible to understand Rosselli's poetry without noting the often multilingual connotations of her vocabulary.

34 Montale, *Poetic Diaries, 1971 and 1972*, 128 (in Italian), 129 (in English; translation on facing page).

35 "Ma non è l'unico. È forse l'autore che mi ha ispirato di più la seconda parte delle *Variazioni*, quelle del '60–'61. L'avevo letto molto prima, e credo che si possa parlare di un'ispirazione, anche se formalmente il linguaggio kafkiano è molto diverso da quello di *Variazioni Belliche*. Vi è una specie di ricerca kafkiana sul piano logico. Poi anche il linguaggio ricorda Kafka qua e là ma non ha la stessa trasparenza" (Rosselli, *È vostra la vita che ho perso*, 125).

grammar becomes especially clear in his shorter works since nothing can be removed without destroying the meaning of an entire piece.

While Kafka's novels *The Trial* and *The Castle* hardly require an introduction, what Calvino means by "lyrical," the *ermetici*, with regard to interiority and fragmentation, and Montale and Rosselli by "Kafka's grammar," require an example from Kafka's oeuvre. A brief examination of "Wunsch, Indianer zu werden" ("The Wish to Become an Indian") will delineate many of the qualities of Kafka's short works that I then put into conversation with Romano, Manganelli, and Tabucchi. The entirety of Kafka's one-sentence piece reads:

> Wenn man doch ein Indianer wäre, gleich bereit, und auf dem rennenden Pferde, schief in der Luft, immer wieder kurz erzitterte über dem zitternden Boden, bis man die Sporen ließ, denn es gab keine Sporen, bis man die Zügel wegwarf, denn es gab keine Zügel, und kaum das Land vor sich als glattgemähte Heide sah, schon ohne Pferdehals und Pferdekopf.[36]

> If one actually were an Indian, instantly ready, on the running horse, slanting into the air, trembling again and again over the trembling ground, until one shed the spurs, because there were no spurs, until one threw away the reins because there were no reins, and hardly saw the land ahead as a smooth-mown heath, already without horse's neck and horse's head.[37]

Walter Benjamin characterized this piece as Kafka's wish for rebirth, an escape fantasy, but one could more accurately see it as a desire for a fantasy than a fantasy since every description is abstracted or taken away, beginning with the title, in which the image of an American Indian is encased and mitigated by *Wunsch* (wish, desire, longing) and *werden* (to become).[38] That is to say, the title points to the speaker's wish to become, rather than becoming, which is already transitional. There is even distance in terms of the desirer since there is no "I" longing, just an impersonal "one." In other words, the abstract piece reflects not upon being or becoming, but the idea or dream of someone becoming. Kafka's very short works often describe a wish or possibility. Since everything in it is past or hypothetical, "The Wish to Become an Indian" fits Montale's characterization of Kafka's work as missing the future.

Sometimes called a dream, contemplation, reflection, prose-poem, and meditation, "The Wish to Become an Indian" raises questions of genre. If the piece is a dream, the narrator is already waking up from it

---

36   Kafka, *Erzählungen*, 7.
37   Kafka, *Contemplation*, 52.
38   Benjamin, *Illuminations*, 119.

as he is writing. As the horse's head and neck disappear, the sentence undoes what it tries to establish before it is over. Everything is past or hypothetical, gone before it is fully realized. There would be spurs, but they are gone. There would be a horse, but it is gone. There would be a wish, but it is gone. Many of the words repeat, but become less concrete in their repetition, not more so (*erzitterte, zitterneden Boden, die Sporen, keine Sporen, die Zügel wegwarf, keine Zügel, Pferde, ohne Pferdehals und Pferdekopf*). Kafka's short pieces often seem to reverse themselves. At the end, all that remains is the literary artefact, this one sentence.

The presentation of this piece contributes to what makes it literature. Especially since the text itself is generically unstable, how it is anthologized and labelled often reveals an interpretation of the work. Kafka was deeply concerned with the amount of space "The Wish to Become an Indian" would take up on the page. He wrote to his publisher:

> I have too much respect for the books you have published to interfere with any proposals in regard to this book. I would only ask for the largest possible typeface consistent with your plans for the book. If it were possible to give the book a dark cardboard binding with tinted paper somewhat like the Kleist *Anecdotes*, I would like that very much.[39]

Kafka wanted his short text to appear as large as possible. When a work is so short and seems to sit among several genres, its paratextual identification and the accompanying works become even more important. Kafka's concern for how his very short, often hypothetical pieces would be visualized relates to the increased concern that critics and authors have about what to call very short works as they have become more accepted and studied in the last few decades.

"The Wish to Become an Indian" raises questions of form with one sentence, an unanswered *if* clause. The issue of Kafka's fragmentation, which has received increased attention with the publication of editions of his works that follow his manuscripts more closely, is revealed not only in his unfinished novels (now often referred to as "novel fragments") but also in his many short works. The works from Kafka's *Betrachtung*, which includes "The Wish to Become

---

39 Kafka, *Letters to Friends, Family, and Editors*, 85. ("Ich habe vor den Büchern, die ich aus Ihrem Verlage kenne, zuviel Respekt, um mich mit Vorschlägen wegen dieses Buches einzumischen, nur bitte ich um die größte Schrift, die innerhalb jener Absichten möglich ist, die Sie mit dem Buch haben. Wenn es möglich wäre, das Buch als einen dunklen Pappband einzurichten, mit getöntem Papier, etwa nach Art des Papieres der Kleistanekdoten, so wäre mir das sehr recht"; Kafka, *Briefe 1900–1912*, 1:168.)

an Indian," and *Oktavhefte* provide key examples of Kafka's very short, lyrical, and fragmented fiction. *Betrachtung* (*Meditation*, or *Contemplation*) was the first book of Kafka's that was published. As Andreas Huyssen discusses in *Miniature Metropolis*, the collection's eighteen short pieces, often referred to as prose poems, establish Kafka as an experimenter with form.[40] The *Oktavhefte*, the *quaderni in ottavo* in Italian, and the octavo notebooks or the blue notebooks in English, are a series of small octavo notebooks (smaller than Kafka's diaries, which were written in quarto notebooks). They have been distinguished from his diaries because of their size as well as their content.[41] They contain some of Kafka's most famous short, short works, such as "The Silence of the Sirens," "The Truth of Sancho Panza," "The Bridge," "A Report to an Academy," and *The Zürau Aphorisms*.

Although Kafka's experimentation with the extremely short form also represents a continuity in his literary production, critics have described the period in which the *Oktavhefte* were written, between 1917 and 1919, as representing a new phase of Kafka's creativity, one characterized by the production of these extremely short works, including short vignettes, descriptions, parts of plays and poetry, aphorisms, and narratives, which have been removed, by Kafka and his later editors, given titles, and published. In 1952, Ignazio Silone wrote to Marguerite Caetani that the *Oktavhefte*, because of their form, fragmentation, and content, seemed of little interest to the general public and therefore unworthy of publication: "Even the title *Oktavhefte*, which seems to contain a musical allusion but refers simply to the octavo format of the notebooks, seems vaguely mystifying."[42] The fact that the *Oktavhefte* have now not only been published as a free-standing volume for a wider public but also inspired music and much commentary is a sign

---

40 He analyses the experimental nature of the collection: "With his parables and aphorisms, Kafka is of course known as a major practitioner of the small form, and the texts collected in *Betrachtung*, opaque as they seem at first sight, demonstrate Kafka's willed and self-conscious departure from the longer realist narrative of story, novella, and novel and from the impressionist urban feuilleton sketch" (Huyssen, *Miniature Metropolis*, 57). Kübler-Jung discusses the poetry of these works in detail, beginning with an overview of critics who compare the works to poetry, calling the pieces "near poetry," "lyrical Prose," and "musical prose" (Kübler-Jung, *Einblicke in Franz Kafkas "Betrachtung,"* 45).

41 For an overview of this idea, see the entry on the *Oktavhefte* in Richard T. Gray et al., *A Franz Kafka Encyclopedia*, 210–2.

42 "Anche il titolo *Octavhefte*, che sembra contenere un'allusione musicale, pur riferendosi semplicemente al formato in 8* dei quaderni, mi sembra vagamente mistificatorio" (Caetani, *La rivista Botteghe oscure*, 253).

[handwritten margin note: Comments / reception of short fiction]

of Kafka's increased popularity as well as the growing interest in fragmentation and brevity.[43]

While Kafka's short works have now increasingly become objects of study in their own right, for decades his shortest works played a central role as establishing texts for interpreting his oeuvre. Many Kafka monographs begin with an exemplary reading of one of his short works, before moving on to his novels and longer short stories.[44] The growing tendency to concentrate on just Kafka's short works represents not only a shift in Kafka criticism but in literary studies more generally, as short works gain an increasing amount of recognition from readers, critics, and literary establishments.

Experimenting with Short, Short Works after Kafka

[handwritten margin note: Questions of form + genre]

The elements examined above in the discussion of Kafka's "The Wish to Become an Indian," such as transformations, the work's hypothetical nature, issues of genre, and the materiality of the text, frame my interpretations of *Metamorphoses, Centuria,* and *Dreams of Dreams.* Like Kafka, the Italian authors I discuss share concerns about their works' status as literary objects and how they will be read, concerns that relate to their works' short form. Romano, Manganelli, and Tabucchi's collections span over forty years and are generally not discussed together. Although their works have been associated separately with Kafka because of their plot details, another significant similarity is their notable brevity and the related difficulty of defining their genre. Each of *Metamorphoses, Centuria: One Hundred Ouroboric Novels,* and *Dreams of Dreams* consists of a series of works that are about a page long.

Praised by Elio Vittorini (who published it as one of the inaugural works in his Einaudi "*Gettoni*" series), Natalia Ginzburg, and Cesare Pavese (who read it before its publication), *Metamorphoses* is a collection of over fifty dreams narrated in the first person, originally published in 1951.[45] *Centuria* (1979) is a collection of one hundred, to use Manganelli's definition, *romanzi fiume* (river-like novels), short works that describe a

---

43   Max Richter's *The Blue Notebooks* (2004, re-released as a two-disc set in 2018) includes Tilda Swinton reading selections from Kafka's *The Blue Notebooks.*

44   Heinz Politzer, e.g., began with an examination of "Give It Up!" before discussing the rest of Kafka's oeuvre (Politzer, *Franz Kafka*). Elizabeth Boa regarded "Up in the Sky" as a model for her approach (Boa, *Kafka*).

45   The number of dreams in the collection changes based on the edition. The three main editions (1951, 1967, 1983) contain some major differences, as will be discussed. Cesare Segre wrote the introduction for Mondadori's publication of Romano's collected works, *Opere.*

[handwritten note at bottom: 1) this section focuses on the experience of reading + classifying these works 2) they work together to reveal something]

range of situations. Described as "extraordinary" by Italo Calvino,[46] it has been translated into English, unlike many of Manganelli's other works. Tabucchi's *Dreams of Dreams* (1992) is a collection of twenty dreams of famous artists and authors, organized chronologically, from Daedalus and Ovid to García Lorca and Freud.

Works from *Centuria*, along with those of Kafka, have been anthologized in some short, short fiction anthologies, such as *Short: An International Anthology of Five Centuries of Short-Short Stories, Prose Poems, Brief Essays, and Other Short Prose Forms* and *Flash Fiction International: Very Short Stories from around the World*.[47] These two collections, from 2014 and 2015, respectively, point to the rise in popularity of this form, and their titles indicate the difficulty of giving this form a name. In contrast to the numerous critical debates about the novel and short story, these microfictions, flash fictions, short-shorts, shorts, or short, short stories, as they have variously been labelled, have been less theorized. In "Microfiction: What Makes a Very Short Story Very Short?," William Nelles describes several defining features of "microfictions," which I will refer to, both to point to what could be seen as typical for the short forms I examine and what distinguishes them from many other short, short works.

While Nelles characterizes microfiction as a genre that experiences a real growth after 1980, he notes a few earlier exceptions, including Kafka's, and ends his article by commenting on the significance of microfiction within his oeuvre: "We sometimes forget that the eighteen stories in *Betrachtung* (*Meditations*, 1913), Kafka's first published collection of short fiction, average a mere 325 words in length; indeed, some two-thirds of the stories he published during his lifetime qualify as microfiction by my definition."[48] In Kafka's lifetime, "The Metamorphosis" was the longest work he published, and many of his published works were only about a paragraph long. Kafka's striking short pieces have been objects of increased attention in this century,[49]

---

46   "Libro straordinario" (Calvino, *Centuria*, 2012, 13).

47   Thomas, Shapard, and Merrill include Franz Kafka's "An Imperial Message" and Giorgio Manganelli's "An Ourboric Novel" (number "Seventy-Five" in Manganelli's collection) in their *Flash Fiction International*. Ziegler includes Kafka's "Poseidon" and Manganelli's "This thoughtful and pointlessly melancholic man ..." from *Centuria*'s "Forty-Four" in *Short*.

48   Nelles, "Microfiction," 98.

49   Clayton Koelb proposed at a roundtable at Duke University, January 2015, that the future of Kafka criticism was his short works. In 2008, a conference on Kafka and the short form examined a range of aspects and approaches to his short fiction and situated his short works among those of his contemporaries. Jorge Luis Borges, an early editor and promoter of Kafka, positioned Kafka as supreme in the short form (Borges, Foreword, 8).

but they put him in the company of early twentieth-century writers like Gottfried Benn, Peter Altenberg, Robert Walser, and Karl Kraus, all of whom produced memorable short, short works.[50]

After Kafka's death, his editor and friend, Max Brod, worked to make him known as a great novelist, not just as a master of the short form, both because he believed that all his works were worthy of publication and also because having written *novels* would help promote him as an international author worthy of fame. Similarly, while Romano, Manganelli, and Tabucchi had concerns about how their short works were going to be approached and shared varying degrees of resistance to the category of the novel, they have also been described as novelists, in part to establish their significance. The first word *The Oxford Companion to Italian Literature* uses to describe all three authors is "novelist," not the most apt term for them.[51] A better description would be "authors who experiment with form," but "novelist" has more visibility internationally. As for Kafka, "novelist" was more accessible to the potential reading public than the more complicated truth. Discussing Kafka, Romano, Manganelli, Tabucchi, and their short forms leads quickly to the power of publishers, critics, and public expectations to determine the perceived genre of works, a long-standing matter of debate with Kafka's fiction.

Tabucchi discusses this issue in a comment about why he uses different publishers: "Unfortunately the cultural industry is made in such a way that it often asks of writers very sizable books, of a certain number of pages, possibly of novels, because in Italy there is still a certain mistrust in terms of the short story or of *pastiche*, of figments of the imagination, or of that which one calls the 'text.' Many times I have talked with editors who ask me, 'But what did you write,' and I respond, 'I wrote a text, so called by narratology.' ... And they insist, 'But it isn't a novel?' And I, 'No, it is

---

50   In their preface to a 2008 conference proceedings on Kafka's short prose, Engel and Robertson write, "In the period when Kafka was writing, this generic fluidity was especially notable among short prose forms; (Engel and Robertson, preface to *Kafka und die kleine Prosa der Moderne*, 7). The advertisement of Kafka's first book highlighted his similarities to another master of the short form, Robert Walser (Stach, *Is That Kafka?*, 100). Kafka's first surviving postcard, from age seventeen, reveals his attention to Peter Altenberg's short, impressionistic works (Stach, 89).

51   In Robey and Hainsworth, eds., *The Oxford Companion to Italian Literature*, the full first sentence for Romano reads, "Novelist from Piedmont" (520) and, for Tabucchi, "Novelist who studied in Pisa and teaches Portuguese literature at the University of Siena" (575).

a text.'"[52] Tabucchi believes that generic differences are hard to maintain, and "at this point in the twentieth-century the boundary between various literary genres has completely fallen."[53] Although Tabucchi points to how the many prose experiments of the twentieth century make it hard to distinguish between novels and "not novels" (or how "not novels" were as likely as not to be called novels), there remains a critical emphasis on them, as the title of the book that contains his comments on not novels reveals: *Conversazione con Antonio Tabucchi: Dove va il romanzo?* (*Conversation with Antonio Tabucchi: What Is the Future of the Novel?*).

Romano describes readers' resistance to *Metamorphoses* being due, in part, to its form since it faced a "prejudice in terms of an ambiguous, unclassifiable literary genre."[54] Romano comments that she should have known that *Metamorphoses* would not be popular because of the works' brevity: "I should have expected it, not only because they are dreams, a non-canonical genre, but also because people usually do not like extremely short stories."[55] Romano, who reordered *Metamorphoses* differently for three distinctive editions of the work, regretted her second order, which proposed that the dreams could be read as a sort of novel; it was perhaps an attempt to bring the work to a wider audience: "It was not an easy genre, in fact, only writers liked it. So, in 1967, I reprinted it with modifications that should have made it more readable. But it was an error, a *forzatura*. For this reason, I wanted to reintroduce it in its original form. It was important to return it to its proper structure."[56] Trying

---

52   "Purtroppo l'industria culturale è così fatta che si chiede spesso allo scrittore
     dei libri molto consistenti, di un certo numero di pagine, possibilmente dei ro-
     manzi, perché in Italia c'è ancora una certa *méfiance* nei confronti del racconto o
     del *pastiche*, dell'allucinazione, o di quello che si chiama il 'testo.' Molte volte ho
     degli scambi d'opinione con degli editori, i quali mi chiedono, 'Ma che cosa hai
     scritto?', e io rispondo: 'Ho scritto un testo, lo dice la narratologia.' ... E quelli
     insistono: 'Ma non è un romanzo?', e io, 'No, è un testo'" (Tabucchi, "Incontro con
     Antonio Tabucchi," 664). Botta has commented on Tabucchi's resistance to not
     only the term *novel* but also *short story* (Botta, "The Journey and the Quest," 155).
53   "Ormai nel novecento il confine tra i vari generi letterari è completamente ca-
     duto" (Tabucchi, *Conversazione con Antonio Tabucchi*, 10).
54   "Pregiudizio nei confronti di un genere letterario ambiguo, inclassificabile"
     (Romano, *Le metamorfosi*, 207). "Staordinario lettore di romanzi, Manganelli non
     era, né desiderava essere, un romanziere" (Barenghi, "Narrazione," 408).
55   "Avrei dovuto aspettarmelo, non solo per via dei sogni, genere non canonico, ma anche
     perché di solito i racconti troppo brevi non piacciono" (Romano, *Le metamorfosi*, 209).
56   "Non era un genere facile e, infatti, piacque solo agli scrittori. Così, nel '67, lo
     ristampai con delle modificazioni che avrebbero dovuto renderlo più leggibile.
     Ma era un errore, una forzatura. Per questo l'ho volute riproporre nella sua forma
     originaria: mi premeva molto restituirolo alla sua giusta struttura" (Petrignani
     and Romano, *Le signore della scrittura*, 15).

to make *Metamorphoses* more readable to an audience that expected prose in the form of novels ruined the work's integrity.

Although both produced numerous experimental works, Romano and Tabucchi also published works that they and others call novels without qualification.[57] Manganelli, meanwhile, is even more adamant about not writing novels. In 1986, when asked why he had never written a novel, he responded, "Because I do not know how to do it. And because I don't want to."[58] This resistance represents a consistency in his career. His contribution to Gruppo 63's discussion of the experimental novel (*romanzo sperimentale*) begins: "I feel little interest in the novel in general – understood as a protracted narration of verisimilar events or situations – and sometimes I feel a sentiment closer to disgust than simple annoyance, I have the impression that today this genre has fallen into such an irreparable dilapidation that the problem is just that of removing the rubble."[59] In part because of the disgust that novels inspire in him, he suggests that the genre should perhaps be, or has already essentially been, retired.

While a few critics insist that some of Manganelli's works are, in fact, novels, most critics take their cue from the author in categorizing his works.[60] Manganelli emphasizes the brevity of the collection's one hundred approximately one-page works with his full title, *Centuria: Cento piccoli romanzi fiume*. Partly, perhaps, in an attempt to avoid them being called a novel *in toto*, he refers to each piece as a *piccolo romanzo fiume* (little river-like novel, or little *roman-fleuve*). The Italian subtitle has been rendered into English as *One Hundred Ouroboric Novels* and into German as *Hundert Romane in Pillenform* ("*A Hundred Novels in Pill Form*"), one of which emphasizes their experimental nature and the other their condensed form.[61]

---

57   In terms of their experimental works, see also Romano's *Letture di un'immagine* [Readings of an image] and Tabucchi's *Racconti con figure* [Stories with figures], which combine text and images.

58   "Perché non lo so fare. E perché non voglio" (Manganelli, interview by Maek-Gérard, "La ditta di Manganelli," 178).

59   "Io provo uno scarso interesse per il romanzo in genere – inteso come protratta narrazione di eventi o situazioni verosimili – e talora un sentimento più prossimo alla ripugnanza che al semplice fastidio; ho l'impressione che oggi codesto genere sia caduto in tanto irreparabile fatiscenza che il problema è solo quello dello sgombero delle macerie" (Manganelli, "6," 173).

60   Grazia Menechella, e.g., states, "He wrote essays, commentaries, stories, and dialogues, but he did not write novels. *Centurie* is an experiment." ("Scrive trattati, corsivi, racconti, dialoghi ma non scrive romanzi. *Centuria: Cento piccolo romanzi fiume* [1979] è un esperimento"; Menechella, "Centuria," 207; Menechella, *Il felice vanverare*, 143.)

61   These translations suggest part of why Manganelli's German audience has been larger than his English one since his experiments are framed in a more accessible, fun way. Certainly, more readers have had experience with pills than with the ouroboros.

Although Manganelli resisted the category of the novel, he spent a great deal of time evaluating novels, as the collection of his reviews, *Impero romanzesco* (*Novel Empire*), makes clear. The contrast between his statements about disliking the novel as form and the amount of writing he did about it provides another indication of the novel's almost inescapable dominance in the twentieth century. In part because of the novel's prominence, for some critics it has made more sense to stretch what a *novel* means to its limits, instead of discussing the potential significance of Manganelli's work not being a novel. Despite his resistance to *Centuria*, or any of his works, being labelled a novel, and despite their experimental form, Linda Hutcheon, for instance, discusses them as novels: "Manganelli's texts do not touch or imitate any empirical reality: they remain autonomous linguistic entities which invent new realities, new fictive universes. They remain novels."[62]

The comparison with Kafka's very short works provides one way to discuss the works of Romano, Manganelli, and Tabucchi that starts with the smallest unit, resisting the critical urge to discuss all twentieth-century literature in terms of a poetry-novel dichotomy. This divide is perhaps especially marked in Italy, where, traditionally, poetry has been considered more distinguished: "There is a commonplace in Italian criticism that at times resurfaces, especially in journalistic criticism, that sees Italy as a country of great poets, but not of great narrators."[63] Many associations accompany this commonplace – that, for instance, poetry is more important to the Italian literary landscape and that poetry has a more esteemed tradition. In *Six Memos for the Next Millennium*, Calvino used this dichotomy to point to the Italian tradition of brevity and to argue for short, short prose fiction: "In this preference for short literary forms I am only following the true vocation of Italian literature, which is poor in novelists but rich in poets, who even when they write prose give of their best in texts where the highest degree of invention and thought is contained in a few pages."[64]

---

62 Hutcheon, *Narcissistic Narrative*, 202.
63 "Esiste un luogo comune della critica italiana, che qualche volta riaffiora soprattutto nella critica giornalistica, che vede l'Italia come un paese di grandi poeti, ma non di grandi narratori" (Tabucchi, in Gumpert and Tabucchi, "La letteratura come enigma," 72).
64 Calvino, *Six Memos for the Next Millennium*, 49. His first example is Leopardi's *Operette morali*, which again points to the convergence of prose-poetry, Leopardi, and *ermetismo*. The idea that Italy is poor in novelists can certainly be disputed (see Benedetti, *Pasolini Contro Calvino*), but the special admiration for poetry in the Italian literary landscape is clear.

While in an international context it may be best to consider Italian works, like the collections I discuss, strange novels, in Italy many regard poetry as the most significant art. Romano called *Metamorphoses*, her first prose work, "a path from poetry to prose."[65] She suggests that the dreams could be read as "ballets, short sonatas, pantomimes."[66] Wondering whether her work would have fared better had it been labelled poetry originally, she writes at one point that *Metamorphoses* is, in fact, a book of poetry, just not in verse.[67] Manganelli compared his *romanzi fiume* to sonnets: "It's a little bit the myth of the sonnet, in other words it has a rigid and restrictive structure with which the writer necessarily has to challenge oneself."[68] This comment may aim to ameliorate the critical views of Manganelli's short, short works, which, as in Romano's case, faced some generic prejudice. When asked about writing a novel (which he did not believe to be his form), Tabucchi's response included prose poems: "If one day I were able to write a novel perfectly appropriate to me, I would write a work that contained prose-poems."[69] The dedication to *Dreams of Dreams* takes the form of a very short poem. Romano's, Manganelli's, and Tabucchi's terms call attention to how quickly short works cross the boundary between genres as well as between poetry and prose.

Whereas aspects of a novel's form are its aspiration to autonomy, development of tensions within itself, and ability to create a world, the short, short fiction of these authors often references or relies upon another world, literary or otherwise. Nelles describes this act of citation as a quality of microfiction, in contrast to the short story.[70] The fact that Tabucchi and Manganelli cite other texts contributes to why critics have labelled them postmodernist authors. Tabucchi's *Dreams of Dreams* offers rewritings and new perspectives, in condensed form,

---

65 "Un cammino dalla poesia alla prosa"; see the interview of Romano by Vincenti, *Lalla Romano*, 1).

66 "Balletti, sonatine, pantomime" (Romano, *Le metamorfosi*, 208).

67 "Per me *Le metamorfosi* sono un libro di poesia; forse se fosse stato presentato allor come tale, avrebbe avuto maggior fortuna tra il pubblico. Penso che il lettore fatichi a capire, crede di trovarsi di fronte a un libro di prosa, invece le narrazioni sono brevi, lapidarie: sono poesie non in verse" (Romano, quoted in Segre, "Nota Biogragrafica," *Opere*, 1:XXVII).

68 "È un po' il mito del sonetto, cioè di una struttura rigida e vessatoria con la quale lo scrittore deve necessariamente misurarsi" (Manganelli, *Centuria*, 2012, 289).

69 "Se un giorno riuscissi a scrivere un romanzo perfettamente aderente a me, scriverei un'opera che contenga 'poemes en prose'" (Tabucchi, *Conversazione con Antonio Tabucchi*, 34).

70 Nelles, "Microfiction," 95.

on other literary figures and their worlds. Many of Kafka's short works from the Octavo notebooks, which include reconfigurations of Sancho Panza from *Don Quixote*, the sirens from the *Odyssey*, Prometheus, and Abraham, rewrite previous works. Like Tabucchi's *Dreams of Dreams*, these prose works bear a close and often unsettling relationship to other texts: they draw on them, rewrite them, and undercut them. Romano's short works refer not to a text, but to dreams. They rewrite oral narrations of dreamed experience: "This book, composed of short prose, courageously confronts, in the first place, a risk of being ordered essentially for practical reasons: they are not short stories, they are not poems, they are not essays, what are they? They are lyric visions, they are metamorphoses, they are dreams. In fact, it is book made of transcribed and reported dreams."[71] The works invite the reader to consider what the original dream was, as Manganelli's short texts prompt the reader to consider what they would be like as novels.

All these authors' short works can be distinguished by how they rewrite and hypothesize. From Manganelli's use of the term *romanzi fiume* to Tabucchi's title *Dreams of Dreams*, which frames the contents as imagined dreams, the authors point to the abstract nature of their works and how their works frequently hypothesize narrative rather than simply narrate. The first piece of *Centuria* begins "Supponiamo che" ("Let's suppose"), and the last piece opens, "A writer is writing a book about a writer who is writing two books about two writers."[72] Each story invites the reader to think of it not as a short story, but as a work that describes a different work. Each piece, therefore, presents the reader with an opportunity to re-imagine. The main title, *Centuria*, links Manganelli's work with the novella tradition of the *Decameron*, but the work lacks a frame, and the subtitle, *One Hundred Ouroboric Novels*, points to the individual works' distinctiveness rather than unity. With his use of *Novels* in the subtitle, Manganelli positions his work to be not a novel, but a collection of experiments that perhaps describe potential novels he would never write.

---

71   "Questo libro di ora, tutto di prose brevi, affronta coraggiosamente, in primo luogo, un rischio d'ordine essenzialmente pratico: non sono racconti, non sono poesie, non sono saggi: che cosa sono? Sono 'visioni liriche,' sono metamorfosi, sono sogni. Anzi, è un libro fatto di sogni trascritti e riferiti" (Sereni, "Sogni che parlano da sé," vii). Vittorio Sereni's "Sogni che parlano da sé" originally appeared in *Corriere della Sera*, 1951, and then was reprinted as the introduction to the 1986 Mondadori edition of *Le metamorfosi*.

72   Manganelli, *Centuria*, 2005, 97. ("Uno scrittore scrive un libro attorno ad uno scrittore che scrive due libri, attorno a due scrittori"; Manganelli, *Centuria*, 215.)

The first Manganelli piece presented at the founding Gruppo 63 conference was a play, "Iperipotesi" (or "Hyperipotesi," "Hyperhypothesis"), which dwelled on the importance of hypothesis. The piece's tone, overblown and at times mocking, recalls the beginning of Kafka's "A Report to an Academy," which has also been performed as a play. Manganelli's monologue begins, "Ladies and gentlemen, what is important is to propose hypotheses. No activity is more noble than this, more worthy of man."[73] The piece frames trying to know, not knowing or representing actuality, as the most important activity.[74]

Tabucchi also believed that constructing the hypothetical was one of the most important ways to respond to the modern world: "'When you talk about your work, you always speak of hypotheses, of hesitations ... why?' 'I believe that it depends on a private existential fact: the incapacity to express a story, a judgment on the real, the need to propose it as a hypothesis, because perhaps to a writer like me, in a historical moment like ours, the real can appear completely hypothetical.'"[75] Emphasizing the hypothetical and impossible qualities of *Dreams of Dreams*, the prefatory note asks the reader to consider the works "poor suppositions, pale illusions, implausible projections."[76]

Kafka's short works are full of *if*s and unfinished hypothetical statements as well as guesses and queries, asking the reader to dream or imagine with the narrator, as with Kafka's unfinished "if" in "The Wish to Become an Indian." To offer another example, "Prometheus" is composed of four one-sentence "legends" that give alternative ideas about the myth of Prometheus. It is, among other things, a work about possibility. For Kafka, Romano, Manganelli, and Tabucchi, the hypothetical is a key element of their short, short fiction. This hypothetical quality distinguishes their works from many other microfictions that narrate "palpable and extreme" stories.[77] The title

hypothetical + referential

---

73 "Signori e signore, l'importante è proporre delle ipotesi. Nessuna attività è più nobile di questa, più degna dell'uomo" (Manganelli, "Iperipotesi," 259).

74 "At the founding conference Manganelli presented *Iperipotesi*, a sort of theatrical monologue in which a speaker explains why formulating a hypothesis is a useful and indispensable activity" (Contarini, "The 'New' Novel of the *Neoavanguardia*," 116).

75 "'Quando lei parla del suo codice, va sempre per ipotesi, per tentennamenti ... perché?' 'Credo che dipenda da un fatto privato esistenziale: l'incapacità di esprimere un giudizio forte sul reale, il bisogno di proporlo come ipotesi, perché forse a uno scrittore come me, in un momento storico come il nostro, il reale può apparire del tutto ipotetico'" (Tabucchi, "Incontro con Antonio Tabucchi," 2:656).

76 Tabucchi, *Dreams of Dreams*, 7. ("Povere supposizioni, pallide illusioni, implausibili protesi. Che come tali vengano lette"; Tabucchi, *Sogni di sogni*, 13.)

77 Nelles, "Microfiction," 91.

Betrachtung (*Meditation,* or *Contemplation*), perhaps, offers a suggestion of how many of Kafka's short, short texts could be approached,
in contrast to how short stories are more traditionally examined. They
are reflections, meditations, or contemplations, and reading them
as such would be different than reading them as a more traditional
short story. When the editor of Kafka's next collection tried to connect it to his first work, with the title *Der Landarzt: Neue Betrachtungen*
(*The Country Doctor: New Contemplations*), Kafka corrected it to *Ein
Landarzt: Kleine Erzählungen* (*A Country Doctor: Little Stories*).[78] These
categorical designations made a difference to Kafka and suggest
different modes of reading.

While Kafka experimented with short forms and the accompanying generic codes, Romano's, Tabucchi's, and Manganelli's paratexts
make even clearer how a reader should approach their works.[79] With
their alternatives to short story, metamorphoses, *romanzi fiume,* and
dreams, these authors indicate how their works do not fit with what
one might expect from a short story and suggest how to read their
works. Romano's title, while also potentially connecting her work to
Kafka and Ovid, indicates how her works should be read. The transformations refer not only to the content of many of her short works
but also to the fact that they are all dreams and represent the potential
transformations that happen when asleep and then when moving from
dreamed experience to literature. Romano insisted that the works in
Metamorphoses be read as dreams and that dreams establish a close relationship among the reader, writer, and dreamer.[80]

All these works complicate the relationship between the reader
and the narrative, drawing the author and reader together. Romano,
Manganelli, and Tabucchi construct gaps that can be filled in differently
depending on the reader. As mentioned, the first word in *Centuria* is
"supponiamo" (let's suppose), not "suppongo" (I suppose) or a description. In modern Italian literature, the reorientation of the reader-narrator
relationship occurs perhaps most famously in Calvino's *Se una notte un
viaggiatore* (*If on a Winter's Night a Traveler*). He was one of the first to
praise Manganelli's work and to note the parallels between this work

---

78 "Kafka insisted on the title he had chosen, *A Country Doctor: Little Stories*" (Stach,
     Is That Kafka?, 107).
79 Kafka did not usually refer to his short works, especially those taken from the
     Octavo notebooks, as short stories because he, like Romano, Tabucchi, and
     Manganelli – as far as the pieces I am discussing are concerned – resisted this
     term and the accompanying generic codes. Kafka often referred to his shorter
     works as "short prose" and gave the subtitle "fragment" to several of his works.
80 Romano, *Le metamorfosi,* 206.

key point – escape form + genre

and Manganelli's *Centuria*.[81] The distinction between Calvino's first word, "stai" (you are), and Manganelli's "supponiamo" establish different relationships with the reader. Calvino's novel begins, "You are about to begin reading Italo Calvino's new novel, *If on a winter's night a traveler*. Relax. Concentrate. Dispel every other thought."[82]

Calvino's narrator instructs the reader about what to imagine. In contrast to the fragmentation and openness of Manganelli's one hundred short works, his work can be called a novel: it presents itself as a novel in the first sentence, and its parts interlock, building upon each other. Calvino's work is about and of novels, whereas Manganelli proposes and establishes his *romanzi fiume* as experiments within the text as well as in the title. Manganelli wants to develop a way to escape form, which he attempts with his collection of short, short works. The trope that each short work is a condensed novel asks the reader to imagine beyond the narration, to re-imagine the stories in another form.[83]

Noting the fragmentation of Tabucchi's texts, an interviewer asks Tabucchi what sort of reader he hopes will approach his texts:[84] "I would like the reader to be an open, very flexible person from the point of view of imagination. I imagine him also as a fragile person, not as a strong person. I am afraid of strong people, those who have great convictions, great principles. I don't imagine my reader as a person with great convictions and principles, but rather as a person open to the world, to the randomness of life and that dose of mystery that life contains and is always unpredictable. To say it in a phrase, I would want him to be open to the unpredictability of existence."[85] Tabucchi's

love this

---

81 Calvino, *Lettere*, 1392.

82 Calvino, *If on a Winter's Night a Traveler*, 3. ("Stai per cominciare a leggere il nuovo romanzo *Se una notte d'inverno un viaggiatore* di Italo Calvino. Rilassati. Raccogliti"; Calvino, *Se una notte*, 3.)

83 This distinction between these two works aligns with the overall differences between the authors that Mario Barenghi has noted, with Calvino attentive to the geometric and Manganelli hostile to form (Barenghi, "Narrazione," 412).

84 "The fragmentary character of your narrations seems to want to presume or ask the reader's collaboration. How do you imagine your reader, and how would you like him to be?" ("Il carattere frammentario delle sue narrazioni sembra voler supporre o richiedere la collaborazione del lettore. Come immagina il suo lettore e come lo vorrebbe?"; Gumpert, quoted in Gumpert and Tabucchi, "La letteratura come enigma," 19.)

85 "Mi piacerebbe che fosse una persona molto disponibile, molto flessibile dal punto di vista dell'immaginazione. Lo immagino anche come una persona fragile, non come una persona forte. Temo le persone forte, quelle che possiedono grandi convinzioni, grandi principi. Non immagino il mio lettore con grandi convinzioni e principi, bensì come una persona aperta al mondo, alla casualità della vita e a quella dose di mistero che la vita contiene e che è sempre imprevedibile. Per dirlo in una frase, lo vorrei disponibile all'imprevedibilità dell'esistenza" (Tabucchi, in Gumpert and Tabucchi, 19).

ideal reader comes to the text willing to succumb to fragmentation. Tabucchi imagines a reader who will not necessarily have a strong or ideological interpretation of his work, but who will respond to its openness. Tabucchi, like Manganelli and Romano, wants a reader to engage with his work on various levels and to experience its fragmentation in an individual fashion.

Kafka's *Zürau Aphorisms* suggests how readers could experience Kafka's fragmentation. In 2004, Roberto Calasso published Kafka's aphorisms as a free-standing edition, taken from the Octavo notebooks, with the explanation that a reader should have the experience of encountering the texts in "exactly the form Kafka gave them."[86] This publication again demonstrates the growing attraction of fragmentation and short, short works. The Zürau aphorisms give a different impression than many of Kafka's other works, in part because of how they were recorded:

> I studied the manuscript of *The Castle.* I became accustomed to those schoolboy notebooks.... One day I came to the folder containing the *Zürau Aphorisms.* The scenery had changed utterly. Loose pages – a hundred and three of them – in horizontal format, measuring 14.5 by 11.5 centimeters. The pages were very thin and pale yellow, obtained by quartering a number of sheets of stationery. All the fragments were numbered sequentially.... Nearly all of the fragments were taken, occasionally with slight modifications, from two octavo notebooks he was writing in those months: it was as if they had been taken out of a certain *form* in order to be articulated in another.[87]

Calasso calls attention to the significance of Kafka's materiality, which is at times overlooked in the case of his short works. Kafka starts the tradition that has been particularly true of his works: how they are anthologized and with what other works they are published help determine their interpretation.

Although for decades critics have discussed the order of the chapters in *The Trial,* a work whose authorial or ideal organization remains unclear, little attention has been paid to the order of the pieces in the *Zürau Aphorisms,* a work whose contents Kafka numbered. The order has perhaps not been a wide focus of attention because it, much like the order of the stories in Romano's and Manganelli's works, relates to a certain rhythm of reading, rather than an arc or progression. Kafka's

---

86 Calasso, "Marginalia," x.
87 Calasso, viii–ix.

aphorisms build upon each other by creating a mode of attention and promoting certain understandings of individual words. Every word bears potentially great significance since it may link sequential pieces of the work. Partly because of the importance of the pieces' "opaque details," Theodor Adorno proposed the dream as a model for understanding Kafka: "Among the moments of shock, not the least results from the fact that Kafka takes dreams à la lettre. Because everything that does not resemble the dream and its pre-logical logic is excluded, the dream itself is excluded. It is not the horrible which shocks, but its self-evidence.... The attitude that Kafka assumes towards dreams should be the reader's towards Kafka. He should dwell on the incommensurable, opaque details, the blind spots."[88] A small turn of phrase, a seemingly unimportant detail often drives interpretations of Kafka's short works. Calasso's formatting of Kafka's text fits with Adorno's proposed mode of reading Kafka. Similarly, Romano's, Manganelli's, and Tabucchi's collections ask the reader to dwell on opaque details and blind spots.

Rather than overall plot, words, ideas, figures, and themes drive these Italian authors' works. Manganelli explains his work: "They have been published in the exact order of composition, this is especially because I think that in their entirety they designate, if not a plot, certainly a rhythm."[89] This rhythm forces the reader to shift attention and read differently. Repetition in Manganelli, Tabucchi, and Romano helps create their works' rhythm. For instance, Tabucchi begins many of his dreams with the same phrases, such as *si trovava*. The frame of the dreams, which locates the dreamer's physical location, also repeats. In all the authors' works, certain figures and phrases recur, and each reader will make different connections between the individual pieces, which emphasize the significance of the reader.

All these authors reflect on the writing process and, not surprisingly, the materiality of their literary objects. One distinction between a forgotten dream, or hypothetical narrative, and a literary work is the recording of it. Tabucchi's dedication to his daughter makes clear the significance of his object, his notebook, which helped inspire his *Dreams of Dreams*: "A mia figlia Teresa / che mi ha regalato / il quaderno / dove è nato questo libro."[90] ("To my daughter Teresa / who gave me / the notebook / in which

---

88   Adorno, *Prisms*, 248.
89   "Sono stati pubblicati nell'esatto ordine di composizione; questo soprattutto perché credo che nel loro insieme essi disegnino, se non una trama, certamente un ritmo" (Manganelli, *Centuria*, 2012, 289).
90   Tabucchi, *Sogni di sogni*, n.p.

this book was born."[91]) *Dreams of Dreams* was "born" in a particular notebook. Trentini has proposed that the word *quaderno* (notebook) is a fitting term with which to discuss the published work as well, in part because of its small size.[92] Both the Italian original and the English translation are printed in smaller-sized editions, drawing attention to the unusual format of the book and making a reader more aware of the texts' brevity. As mentioned, Tabucchi lamented that more publishers were not willing to print smaller books, which would encourage generic flexibility.[93]

For Manganelli, the brevity of his *romanzi fiume* were determined by his paper size, which in part inspired the form these stories took: "By chance I had a number of sheets of typing paper which were slightly larger than normal, and I found myself intrigued by the thought of writing a series of narratives which each would never exceed the length of a single page."[94] He concludes, "I think that if I had not had these papers, I would never have been able to write this book."[95] His work, like Tabucchi's, is partly the result of a particular format of a paper product, and the length of the pieces relates to the paper on which they were written. In Adelphi's edition, they are all slightly longer than a printed page, which can feel jarring. The work's original form seems to make itself known even when it is transformed for publication.

All three of these Italian authors emphasize the relationship between the work they produce and their writing materials. Tabucchi mentions that all his writing, not just that of *Dreams of Dreams*, is done in particular notebooks and that using a typewriter would change his art.[96] Romano's *Metamorphoses* originates from "little papers," *foglietti*, on which she ordered and reordered the dreams. Many of her works are largely determined by the specific materials she used.[97] For her,

---

91   Tabucchi, *Dreams of Dreams*, n.p.

92   Trentini, *Una scrittura in partita doppia*, 191.

93   Tabucchi, "Incontro con Antonio Tabucchi," 2:663.

94   Manganelli, *Centuria*, 2005, 6. ("Avevo per caso molti fogli da macchina leggermente più grandi del normale, e mi è venuta la tentazione di scrivere sequenze narrative che in ogni caso non superassero la misura di un foglio"; Manganelli, *Centuria*, 2012, 289.)

95   "Credo che se non avessi avuto quei fogli non sarei mai riuscito a scrivere questo libro" (Manganelli, *Centuria*, 2012, 289).

96   "Scrivo a mano, su dei vecchi quaderni con la copertina nera, che mi è sempre più difficile trovare.... Se scrivessi a macchina credo che potrei fare della poesia concreta" (Tabucchi, in Gumpert and Tabucchi, "La letteratura come enigma," 58).

97   For instance, *Le lune di Hvar* [The moons of Hvar], which were written in specific notebooks; see Ria and Romano, *Il silenzio tra noi leggero*, 47. *Le lune di Hvar* was published as is, and Romano described it as one of her favourite books.

fragmentation is a source of inspiration and aesthetic choice. Critics have discussed how out of place her fragmented modernist fiction was in the neorealist landscape of the early 1950s. With *Metamorphoses*, Romano may have been ahead of her time since fragmented works have gained increasing acceptance.

The Transformations of Romano, Manganelli, and Tabucchi

Romano's *Metamorphoses*, Manganelli's *Centuria*, and Tabucchi's *Dreams of Dreams* have been linked individually to Kafka because of their content, but not to each other or in an analysis of form. I will briefly outline Kafka's significance to these authors before building on the formal connections between their works and Kafka's to discuss their short, short works in more detail. *Dreams of Dreams*, written in Italian, has been characterized as a continuation of Tabucchi's more famous work, *Requiem*, written in Portuguese.[98] *Requiem* includes a discussion of Kafka in the narrator's dream conversation with a famous poet (understood to be Pessoa): "I'll tell you something, cowardice produced some of the bravest writing of the century, for example, that Czech writer who wrote in German.... There's something cowardly about his diary, but what courage he had to write that magnificent book of his, you know, the one about guilt. *The Trial?*, I asked, is that the one you mean? Of course, he said, the most courageous book of the century, he has the courage to say that we are all guilty."[99] While Flavia Brizio-Skov has analysed this discussion of Kafka as part of what leads the reader to know that Pessoa is the long-awaited poet, just as striking is the narrator's knowledge of Kafka in contrast to that of the "great poet" (Pessoa), who avoids pronouncing Kafka's name and the titles of his works.[100] Although not as significant a figure as the looming Pessoa for Tabucchi, Kafka nonetheless plays a key role in Tabucchi's concept of modern literature, as the discussion of Kafka in *Requiem* indicates.

In "Il mio tram attraverso il Novecento" (My tram through the twentieth century), Tabucchi divides literature into different tram stops and

---

98 Trentini, *Una scrittura in partita doppia*, 193.

99 Tabucchi, *Requiem*, 101. I have quoted *Requiem* in the English translation from the Portuguese. For an analysis of the meaning of the discussion about Kafka, see Botta, "The Journey and the Quest," 152. Franco Zangrilli interprets this moment of praise for Kafka as one also for Pessoa and Tabucchi himself (Zangrilli, *Dietro la maschera della scrittura*, 101): in describing Kafka, Tabucchi is also perhaps describing the authors who are discussing Kafka.

100 Brizio-Skov, *Antonio Tabucchi*, 125.

gives a personalized literary history.[101] Kafka appears repeatedly in this
description of twentieth-century literature: he is mentioned in three
parts: "A Parisian Manifesto," "The Absurd," and "Identity," more than
any other author. Tabucchi associates Kafka with Beckett, Svevo, Pirandello, García Lorca, and – again – Pessoa.[102] He characterizes Kafka as
fundamental for the modern sense of life being unhinged, of lacking a
clear purpose: "The lack of goals is one of the great Kafkan intuitions,
because he was the one to have the genius to make that which happens in our life happen without explanations and I think that this is a
manifestation of the loss of a religious sense of existence. From when
we lost the conviction that someone was watching us, our life has been
missing purpose."[103] Tabucchi also includes Kafka in a list, along with
Conrad and Kundera, of significant bilingual authors, a list that would,
of course, include Tabucchi too.[104] Several of Tabucchi's works have
been associated with Kafka, including *L'angelo nero* (*Black Angel*), *La
testa del Damasceno Monteiro* (*The Head of Damasceno Monteiro*), discussed
in chapter 3, and certain dreams from *Dreams of Dreams*, such as those
of Daedalus, Ovid, and Freud. Openness to modernist fragmentation
was a significant part of Kafka's appeal for Tabucchi, an author who has
been described as both modernist and postmodernist.[105]

As with Tabucchi and Kafka, the connections between Manganelli
and Kafka are multiple and spread across Manganelli's career. In an

---

101   His first stop is "un manifesto paragino," which discusses futurism, and his last is
      "il diritto di sognare." Before describing futurism in more detail, he suggests that
      authors could be divided into those for whom machines are to be deified and those
      for whom they represent monsters. Kafka is one of the first authors mentioned, and
      "In the Penal Colony" one of the first works, that belong in this latter category.
102   Trentini highlights Pessoa, Pirandello, Kafka, and Conrad as authors whom
      Tabucchi mentions especially often (Trentini, *Una scrittura in partita doppia*, 26).
103   "La mancanza di scopi è una delle grandi intuizioni kafkiane, perché fu lui ad avere
      la genialità di pensare che quanto avviene nella nostra vita avviene senza un perché.
      E credo che ciò sia il sintomo della perdita di senso religioso e dell'esistenza. Da
      quando abbiamo perso la convinzione che qualcuno ci osservi, la nostra vita manca
      di finalità" (Tabucchi, in Gumpert and Tabucchi, "La letteratura come enigma," 98).
      In a discussion of Milan Kundera, Tabucchi reflects on the relationship between
      realism and metaphysics and how Pirandello and Kafka offer strong examples of
      authors who engage the two (Zangrilli, *Dietro la maschera della scrittura*, 111).
104   Tabucchi, *Conversazione con Antonio Tabucchi*, 27.
105   Trentini offers a clear overview of one of the significant connections between
      the two authors' works: "L'influenza che Kafka esercita su Tabucchi non è
      determinata solo dalla struttura disossata dei suoi scritti, come abbiamo già avuto
      modo di segnalare, ma si estende anche a quel senso di impotenza che caratterizza
      i personaggi tabucchiani, che perdono, o per sbaglio o per destino, il controllo
      sulle cose" (Trentini, *Una scrittura in partita doppia*, 67).

exploration of the difficulty of placing him in an Italian literary tradition, Vecchi proposes that Kafka was one of his "literary fathers."[106] Scholars consider Kafka a key source of inspiration for Gruppo 63, a group with which Manganelli was involved when he was establishing himself as an author.[107] Klaus Wagenbach was both Manganelli's first foreign editor and an early, devoted, and important Kafka critic.[108] Partially because of his attention, Manganelli's German public was at first larger than his Italian one, and he called the Germans his "true audience."[109] Kafka's name continually appeared in Manganelli's discussions of literature and critics' interpretations of Manganelli. From his animals to his spaces of imprisonment to his transformations, a range of Manganelli's themes and works have been compared to Kafka's.[110]

Manganelli's *Centuria* will be discussed in more detail, but it offers numerous moments that suggest Kafka's importance to the Italian author. Manganelli's descriptions of ungraspable judgment, waiting, and disorientation suggest various works of Kafka's. "Five" in *Centuria* recalls *The Trial*: "A man who had not killed anyone was sentenced to death for murder."[111] "Ten" recalls "Before the Law": "The gentlemen who come to this station to await the train generally die while waiting."[112] "Eighty-Five" recalls "The Metamorphosis": "Waking up.

---

106 Vecchi, "Giorgio Manganelli," 49.

107 "In their search for models, on the theoretical level, of the neo-avant-garde novel, the group [Gruppo 63] favours the foreign triad of Joyce, Kafka, and Musil; the Italian forefathers Pirandello and Svevo are mentioned with some reservation" (Contarini, "The 'New' Novel of the *Neoavanguardia*," 103). For more on Manganelli and Gruppo 63, see, e.g., Mussgnug, *The Eloquence of Ghosts*; Contarini; and Falkoff, "Giorgio Manganelli and the Illegible Obscene."

108 "L'interesse di Manganelli per il mondo tedesco era naturalmente anche dovuto al fatto che il suo primo editore all'estero fu Klaus Wagenbach e che i suoi primi libri avevano trovato più lettori in Germania che in Italia" (Vollenweider, "Il mondo tedesco," 194). See also Wagenbach, *La libertà dell'editore*.

109 "Vero pubblico," quoted in Vollenweider, 194. Manganelli was motivated to improve his German in part because of this. Like the character in *Centuria*, he studied German on the bus: "Il signore con l'impermeabile, che tutte le mattine prende l'autobus numer 36 – un autobus sempre eccessivamente affollato – e che sull'autobus legge attentamente, astrattamente, una grammatica tedesca" (Manganelli, *Centuria*, 2012, 49). ("The gentleman wearing a raincoat, and who every morning takes the number 36 bus – an always overcrowded bus – on which he attentively studies, absent-mindedly, a German grammar book"; Manganelli, *Centuria*, 2005, 43.)

110 See, e.g., Paolone, *Il cavaliere immaginale*, 22–3; and Pulce, *Giorgio Manganelli*, 55.

111 Manganelli, *Centuria*, 2005, 19. ("Un signore che non aveva ucciso nessuno venne condannato a morte per omicidio"; Manganelli, *Centuria*, 2012, 25.)

112 Manganelli, *Centuria*, 2005, 29. ("Generalmente i signori che vengono a questa fermata ad attendere il treno, muoiono nell'attesa"; Manganelli, *Centuria*, 2012, 35.)

He always wakes with a feeling of disorientation. His disorientation does not derive from any doubt about where he is, but from absolute certainty. He is in his house, where he has lived for many years. The fact of waking up in his house, in a place he already knows to be indifferent to him, is boring; it causes him a slight irritation, like a miniaturized desperation, fit to be applied to an insect."[113]

While Manganelli's "Eighty-Five" suggests how a person can wake up feeling disoriented like Gregor Samsa without having been transformed into an insect, several of Manganelli's works in *Centuria* also contain transformations and non-human forms. In part because of this, Pietro Citati proposes a deep kinship between Manganelli and Kafka's work: "Once our common friend said that Manganelli was not 'anthropomorphic;' and he was very amused. He had always known he belonged to Gregor Samsa's family."[114] According to Citati's entertaining anecdote, Manganelli saw the connection between himself and Kafka's "monstrous vermin" (*ungeheures Ungeziefer*) with the mind of a travelling salesman: he felt a kinship with the non-human form as represented by Kafka.

Manganelli himself wrote and spoke about Kafka on several occasions. The public broadcasting service RAI has preserved one of Manganelli's presentations of Kafka, in which he describes him as an extraordinary, hypnotizing author, who "is a kind of deformed presence in our cultural, literary, and imaginary world."[115] In his probings of what literature, authorship, and criticism mean, Manganelli used Kafka as an example of one of the most important authors: "The greater an author, the more anonymous he becomes: his name serves only to be known in society. Borges and Kafka are two collections of words, of emotion, of interior tension, of ghosts, of enchantment."[116] Manganelli took up a similar line of argument in a discussion of Pietro Citati's monograph,

---

113   Manganelli, *Centuria*, 2005, 179. ("Svegliarsi. Egli si sveglia sempre con un senso di disorientamento. Il disorientamento non viene dal dubbio sul posto in cui si trova, ma dalla assoluta certezza. Si trova nella sua casa, in cui vive da molti anni. Il fatto di svegliarsi lì, in un luogo che ha già sperimentato indiffferente, gli è noioso, gli dà un fastidio lieve, come di una disperazione miniaturizzata, così da poter essere applicate ad un insetto"; Manganelli, *Centuria*, 2012, 185.)

114   "Una volta un nostro amico commune disse che Manganelli non era 'antropomorfo'; e lui si divertì molto. Aveva sempre saputo di essere della razza di Gregor Samsa" (Citati, "Giorgio, malinconico tapiro," 256).

115   "È una sorta di presenza deforme nella nostro mondo reale letterario fantastico" (Manganelli, "Giorgio Manganelli presenta Franz Kafka").

116   "Quanto più è grande uno scrittore, più anonimo diventa: il suo nome serve solo per essere conosciuto in società. Borges e Kafka sono due insieme di parole, di emozione, di tensione interiore, di fantasmi, di stegoneria" (Deidier, "Scrittori d'Italia," 207).

Kafka. His review, entitled "Ma Kafka non esiste" (But Kafka does not exist), lays out one of his theories of criticism: "But, then, what is it? It is literature. It is my personal conviction that criticism is simply literature on literature.... If a book like Citati's shows something, it is that Kafka does not exist. Events exist, that at times are written, at times are lived, that all make a story, a 'criticism,' possible."[117]

Like Manganelli, Romano wrote a review of Citati's *Kafka*, entitled "Io e Kafka" (Kafka and me). While her review of Citati's work was negative, it provided an opportunity to reflect on Kafka's impact on her when she first read him in the 1930s: "The encounter with Kafka, for those who had it, like me, in the thirties, the time of the first Italian translations, was crucial for everyone."[118] In the same review, she mentions an interlocutor who connects her piece "Le porte" (The doors) from *Metamorphoses* with Kafka's "Before the Law." The end of "The Doors," in particular, recalls Kafka's famous piece: "The doors arise one after another, all the same. I can still pass through, but it's futile. There will always be another door."[119] Unlike Kafka's man from the country, the dreamer can go through the doors, but he, like the man from the country, will never reach the end; and the effect is similar, with an unreachable destination.

Critics often cited Kafka in discussions of Romano's first book of prose, *Metamorphoses*, because of its title. Although Romano resisted the comparison to "The Metamorphosis," she had distinct ideas about the similarities between her and Kafka's works: "The Kafka whom *Metamorphoses* could recall is not that of the famous 'Metamorphosis' (perhaps also inspired by a dream but expanded to a short story and therefore no longer a dream as such), but if anything that of the short work 'The Bridge.'"[120] She compares Kafka's "Die Brücke" ("The Bridge") to her "Il palo" (The pole). Both works are narrated in the first person by the inanimate objects identified in the titles. "The Bridge"

---

117 "Ma, allora, che cosa è? È letteratura. È mia personale convinzione che la critica sia semplicemente letteratura sulla letteratura.... Se qualcosa dimostra un libro come quello di Citati è che Kafka non esiste. Esistono degli eventi, che talora sono scritti, talora sono stati visuti, che tutti insieme rendono possibile un racconto, una storia, una 'critica'" (Manganelli, *Il rumore sottile della prosa*, 118–19).

118 "L'incontro con Kafka, per chi l'ebbe, come me, negli anni Trenta – a tanto risalgono le prime traduzioni italiane –, fu fatale per ognuno" (Romano, *Opere*, 2:1558).

119 "Le porte si presentano, una dopo l'altra, tutte uguali. Posso ancora passare; ma è inutile. Ci sarà sempre ancora una porta" (Romano, *Le metamorfosi*, 150).

120 "Il Kafka a cui si potrebbero richiamare *Le metamorfosi* non è quello della famosa *Metamorfosi* (forse anche ispirata da un sogno ma dilatata a racconto e perciò non più sogno come tale), ma semmai quello della breve novella *Il ponte*" (Romano, 208).

begins with a description of the physical experience of being a bridge: "I was stiff and cold, I was a bridge, I spanned an abyss; my toes were dug in one side, my hands in the other; I had clamped myself in crumbling clay."[121] ("Ich war steif und kalt, ich war eine Brücke, über einem Abgrund lag ich. Diesseits waren die Fußspitzen, jenseits die Hände eingebohrt, in bröckelndem Lehm habe ich mich festgebissen."[122]) Romano's "palo" similarly situates itself outside: "I was a small, iron post, placed on the railing of an old bridge" ("Ero un piccolo palo di ferro, piantato sulla ringhiera di un vecchio ponte."[123])

A transformational experience happens almost immediately after the abrupt "Ich war eine Brücke" and "Ero un piccolo palo di ferro" in narrative time, but perhaps after an extremely long time in the stories' chronologies. Time stretches, shrinks, and is vague in these short, short works. Centuries pass in a moment. After its transformation, the pole narrates: "Meanwhile centuries passed. I got rusty, tilting toward the river."[124] Not only is the narrator an inanimate object, but its sense of time is also beyond the normal human understanding of time. In "The Bridge," one cannot know if almost no time passes or centuries pass: "One day, toward evening – was it the first, was it the thousandth, I cannot tell, my thoughts were always racing in confusion, always, always in circles – toward evening in the summer, the brook was roaring with a darker sound, I hear the footstep of a man!"[125] Time follows the bridge's cyclical and confused thoughts. The time of thinking here supersedes any other sense of time, including chronological. Manganelli's "Eighty-Seven" in *Centuria* offers a reflection on time's potential to be broken and stretched, which Romano's and Kafka's works enact: "Time follows no rules, yet pretends to."[126] "The Bridge" and "The Pole," in fact, highlight three kinds of time: experiential, measured, and narrative. Further complicating the depiction of time, Kafka's narrative has the notable quality of being narrated in the past, even though the bridge appears to break at the end.

---

121 KSS, 108.
122 Kafka, *Erzählungen*, 264.
123 Romano, *Le metamorfosi*, 8.
124 "Intanto passavano i secoli. Io arrugginivo, inclinandomi verso il fiume" (Romano, 8).
125 KSS, 108. ("Einmal gegen Abend war es – war es der erste, war es der tausendste, ich weiß nicht, – meine Gedanken gingen immer in einem Wirrwarr und immer in der Runde – gegen Abend im Sommer, dunkler rauschte der Bach, da hörte ich einen Mannesschritt!"; Kafka, *Erzählungen*, 264.)
126 Manganelli, *Centuria*, 2005, 183. ("Il tempo non ha regola, e finge di averne"; Manganelli, *Centuria*, 2012, 189.)

The human capacity to narrate causes the bridge's and pole's inanimate status to seem lonely and stressful. The immobility and voicelessness of the narrators exemplify the anxiety of loneliness and, at the same time, the difficulty of finding a community or communicating with others. The narrators' fixity relates to their inability to connect. The pole comments, "The fact of being a pole and not being able to escape increased my terror."[127] An attempt to move and connect with another destroys Kafka's bridge: "And I turned to look at him. Bridge turns around! I had not yet turned around when I was already falling; I fell, and in a moment I was torn apart and impaled on the sharp stones that had always gazed up so peacefully at me from the raging water."[128] While the bridge's act of turning around has been read as an attempt to understand another being and to escape loneliness, the movement results in the loss of the potential connection.[129] The danger and desperation of trying to communicate are elements of Kafka's work that Romano, like Rosselli, found appealing and expressed in her own work.

While the bridge breaks during an act of daring – the attempt to connect – the pole seems to give up when the pursuit of contact seems impossible. In comparison with the pole, the bridge appears courageous and active. The pole Romano describes tries to connect and follows a shadowy figure, which at the end of the dream disappears: "My partner left and I followed him. Along the way he stopped in front of another village just like the one near the bridge and disappeared silently."[130] Contrasting the stories generally emphasizes the sadness of "The Pole." Since the bridge may have always been a bridge, its ontological status is not necessarily negative. The narrator's status as an object in "The Pole," meanwhile, originates from a punishment, explained in the initial lines: "However I made a mistake with a signal. I was punished and transformed into a pole."[131] Being alone and voiceless results from not having

---

127 "Il fatto di essere un palo e di non poter fuggire accresceva il mio terrore" (Romano, *Le metamorfosi*, 8).

128 KSS, 109. ("Und ich drehte mich um, ihn zu sehen. Brücke dreht sich um! Ich war noch nicht umgedreht, da stürzte ich schon, ich stürzte und war schon zerrissen und aufgespießt von den zugespitzten Kieseln, die mich so friedlich immer angestarrt hatten aus dem rasenden Wasser"; Kafka, *Erzählungen*, 264–5.)

129 "On one level the bridge's motion recalls the mythological gesture of Orpheus turning around to glimpse his beloved – the epistemological impulse to 'see' the other that results in separation and loss" (Anderson, "Kafka, Homosexuality and the Aesthetics of 'Male Culture,'" 92).

130 "Il mio accompagnatore uscí e lo seguii. Per strada egli si fermò davanti a un'altra villa uguale a quella del ponte e vi sparì silenziosamente" (Romano, *Le metamorfosi*, 9).

131 "Sbagliai però un segnale. Fui punito e trasformato in un palo" (Romano, 8).

properly obeyed society's rules, a sense that one could read into Kafka's piece, but that is clear in Romano's piece. While the bridge's breaking could be due to a courageous attempt to know another, the pole remains passive.[132] While following the shadowy figure, the pole encounters dismembered bodies, which seem to reflect the pole's own lack of life.

Romano talks about how dreams are "a certain way to see life."[133] This mode of seeing relates to the work's narration as well as to the reader's relationship to the text: as she explains, "He who receives the narrated communication of the dream (the reader) enters into a direct relationship with the dreamer, with whom the reader should now and again try to identify himself."[134] Many of Kafka's short works also aim to complicate and break down the barriers between reader and writer. Adorno, among others, has commented on this: "Among Kafka's presuppositions, not the least is that the contemplative relation between text and reader is shaken to its very roots. His texts are designed not to sustain a constant distance between themselves and their victim but rather to agitate his feelings to a point where he fears that the narrative will shoot towards him like a locomotive in a three-dimensional film."[135] These works prompt the reader to establish a more personal relationship with them.

By having the bridge dream with another, an unknown figure, a man with a cane, "The Bridge" performs the rupture of assumed reader-text boundaries that Romano also wants to transgress: "But then – just as I was following him in a dream over mountain and valley – he jumped with both feet onto the middle of my body. I shuddered in wild pain, totally uncomprehending."[136] The bridge attempts to dream with the man, until the man's sudden jump onto the bridge emphasizes the gap between them. The questions the bridge-narrator then asks are similar to the ones the reader asks when trying to interpret the work: "Who was it? A child? A gymnast? A daredevil? A suicide? A tempter? A destroyer?"[137]

---

132 "Là dentro erano ammucchiati cadaveri di uomini e di bestie ormai in stato di putrefazione" (Romano, 9). ("There inside were heaps of human and animal cadavers already in a state of rot.")

133 "Una certa maniera di vedere la vita" (Romano, 9).

134 "Quello che riceve la comunicazione narrativa del sogno (il lettore) entra in un rapporto diretto col sognatore, col quale dovrebbe di volta in volta cercare di identificarsi" (Romano, 206).

135 Adorno, *Prisms*, 246.

136 KSS, 108–9. ("Dann aber – gerade träumte ich ihm nach über Berg und Tal – sprang er mit beiden Füßen mir mitten auf den Leib. Ich erschauerte in wildem Schmerz, gänzlich unwissend"; Kafka, *Erzählungen*, 264.)

137 KSS, 109. ("Wer war es? Ein Kind? Ein Turner? Ein Waghalsiger? Ein Selbstmörder? Ein Versucher? Ein Vernichter?"; Kafka, 264.) These questions have been read (and translated) in various ways.

The reader, like the narrator, wonders what the man could represent. This short work, like many of the Italian works I discuss, as much as describing or providing a narrative, supposes and asks questions: about its own narrative, about the act of reading, and about literature.[138]

Romano not only compares "The Pole" to "The Bridge" but also says that Kafka's work helped set the tone for her entire collection: "But in truth it was a 'true' collection of dreams. The tone was suggested to me by one of the phrases that my son (at that time a child) had noted to narrate one of his dreams, 'I was a small, iron pole, placed on the railing of an old bridge.' It really struck me, also because this impression of solitude and immediate transformation reminded me of Kafka."[139] According to Romano, the loneliness and transformations that Kafka's and her work express provided a basis for her work: "The collection and writing of the 'dreams' was a, involuntary, but perhaps not unaware filiation, born from the spiritual fertility of Kafka's writings."[140] Not only was Kafka a guiding force for Romano's collection, but Romano also proposes reading "The Bridge" as a dream.[141] Romano's unusual description of "The Bridge" as a dream reveals a certain interpretation that draws her first prose project and Kafka's work closer together.

Just as a Kafkan transformation, albeit not Gregor's, reminded Romano of Kafka and led her to connect him with her dream collection, so transformations often lead critics to refer to Kafka when discussing Romano, Manganelli, and Tabucchi. Unlike "The Metamorphosis," in which at least two elements of the transformation are clear – Gregor was human, and then he transformed into an *ungeheures Ungeziefer* – many of the transformations in these shorter works are more abstract, as in the desired but unrealized transformation into an American

---

138 Serpell examines how "The Bridge" promotes a certain kind of reading that causes the reader to experience various levels of distance from the work (Serpell, "Of Being Bridge," 15, 20). She interprets "The Bridge" using Jean-Luc Nancy's definition of *sovereignty*, and in her reading, the last few lines of the text reveal the difficulty of staying with any one idea in the text. Her interpretation reveals how "The Bridge" potentially enacts the complicated and changing relationship between the reader and Kafka's text that Adorno noted.

139 "Ma in realtà era una 'vera' raccolta di sogni. Il tono mi era stato suggerito da una frase che mio figlio – allora bambino – aveva annotato per raccontare un suo sogno: 'Ero un piccolo palo di ferro, piantato sulla ringhiera di un vecchio ponte.' Mi aveva colpito moltissimo, anche perché questa impressione di solitudine e di trasformazione immediata mi aveva ricordato Kafka" (Ria and Romano, *Il silenzio tra noi leggero*, 4).

140 "La raccolta e la stesura dei 'sogni' era una filiazione, involontaria, ma forse non inconsapevole, nata dalla fecondazione – spirituale – degli scritti di Kafka" (Romano, *Opere*, 2:1558).

141 "Deve essere effettivamente un sogno" (Romano, *Le metamorfosi*, 223).

Indian or the perhaps non-transformation of the bridge. As examined in chapter 1, one can speak of the realism of "The Metamorphosis" because of the post-transformation descriptions and concerns. Tabucchi's and Romano's transformations are all ones that occur in dreams and involve an extra level of abstraction since reading a work framed as a dream is different from a work narrated as a potential reality.

Manganelli's transformations are similarly abstract since his works are condensed descriptions of hypothetical, longer works and also because many of the transformations described in *Centuria* involve multiple transformations, thereby eroding the relationship between the ostensibly original being and the transformed even further. "Sixty-Seven" begins, "The animal pursued by the hunters undergoes, in the course of its silent and meticulous flight, a series of transformations which make it impossible to give of it a credible scientific description."[142] The first of the series of creatures that the animal appears to be transforming into is a fox, then it is green, has quills, and is a snake. Every description leads into a new one. At the end, the animal is "vast" and "its substance so diffuse that bullets traverse it while never, or almost never, wounding it."[143] The animal is ultimately a monster that consumes the hunters. Of course, the work also never makes clear what the animal was originally, so all elements of the transformation are conjectural, and the transformations can be imagined, but not definitively grasped.

In "Ninety-One," on the other hand, the original being and the transformed one seem, at first, clear: "In his previous incarnation, that man was a horse."[144] The following clause undercuts the factual nature of the first statement: "This is something of which he is fully aware, in light of unassailable evidence: his favorite shoes, his food, the way he laughs."[145] The sense of transformation appears to rely on opinion and hilarious evidence. As the narrative continues, it turns out, however, that the man does not realize he had, in fact, been three horses.[146] Even

---

142   Manganelli, *Centuria*, 2005, 143. ("L'animale inseguito dai cacciatori, subisce, durante la sua fuga silenziosa e accurata, una serie di trasforazioni, che ne rendono impossibile la descrizione scientificamente attendibile"; Manganelli, *Centuria*, 2012, 149.)

143   Manganelli, *Centuria*, 2005, 144. ("La sua materia è tanto rada, che le palle l'attraversano senza mai, o quasi mai, ferirla"; Manganelli, *Centuria*, 2012, 151.)

144   Manganelli, *Centuria*, 2005, 191. ("Nell'incarnazione precedente quell'uomo è stato un cavallo"; Manganelli, *Centuria*, 2012, 197.)

145   Manganelli, *Centuria*, 2005, 191. ("Di questo egli è ben consapevole, da non dubbi idizi: le calzature che ama, il cibo, il modo di ridere"; Manganelli, *Centuria*, 2012, 197.)

146   "He did not know, in fact, that he had inhabited not a single incarnation as a horse, but three consecutive ones" (Manganelli, *Centuria*, 2005, 191). ("In realtà egli ignorava che non una sola incarnazione di cavallo aveva abitato, ma ben tre consecutive"; Manganelli, *Centuria*, 2012, 197.)

if he had been a horse, it is not a singular horse that can be considered. The transformation becomes increasingly abstract, and hypothesis constantly re-enters the narrative, further undercutting reality.

In contrast to many of the other dreams in which the dreamer dreams of himself as himself, two of Tabucchi's works that most obviously connect to Kafka involve metamorphoses. Most of the works in *Dreams of Dreams* start with a description of the dreamer's physical location, followed by a sentence that contains *stava* (he was) or *si trovava* (he found himself), which situates the dreamer in his dream; these include the dreams of Daedalus, Apuleius, Rabelais, Coleridge, and Leopardi.[147] Similar sentences begin the dreams of Debussy, Majakovskij, and García Lorca. Since the dreamer is located and understood as being himself, even in the dream, the reader is prompted to imagine Rabelais, Coleridge, or García Lorca as the actor in these dreams. Ovid, meanwhile, dreams of having been transformed into a butterfly in the second piece of the work, and, in the last story, Freud dreams of being Dora, the woman from his case study.[148] Ovid's dream begins, "Publius Ovidius Naso, poet and courtier, dreamed that he had become a poet beloved by the emperor. And as such, by a miracle of the gods, he was transformed into a great butterfly."[149]

As in most of the *Dreams of Dreams*, there are many connections between a dream and the dreamer's biography and works. While generally pointing to *The Metamorphoses*, Ovid's dreamed transformation, however, does not reference a particular metamorphosis from his work, which includes a wide variety of changes into birds (swan, crow, owl, magpie, stork, crane, dove, swallow, jackdaw, hawk, osprey, etc.), but not butterflies or beetles or flies.[150] While Kafka does not own transformations into insects, there are many other creatures that one could choose that would not inspire the reference.[151] Indeed, several

---

147   "Sognò che si trovava nelle viscere di un palazzo" ("Sogno di Dedalo, architetto e aviatore," 15); "Sognò di trovarsi in una cittadina della Numidia" ("Sogno di Lucio Apuleio, scrittore e mago," 22); "Sognò che si trovava sotto la pergola di una tavern del Périgord" ("Sogno di Francois Rabelais, scrittore e frate smesso," 32); "Sognò che si trovava su un vascello imprigionato tra i ghiacci" ("Sogno di Samuel Taylor Coleride, poeta e oppiamane," 41)"; and "Sognò che si trovava in un deserto, e che era un pastore" ("Sogno di Giacomo Leopardi, poeta e lunatico," 43).

148   Tabucchi, *Sogni di sogni*, 74.

149   Tabucchi, *Dreams of Dreams*, 13. ("Publio Ovidio Nasone, poeta e cortigiano, sognò che era diventato un poeta amato dall'imperatore. E in quanto tale, per miracolo degli dèi, si era trasformato in una grande farfalla"; Tabucchi, *Sogni di sogni*, 19.)

150   Although there is, of course, the famous arachnid, Arachne.

151   Derek Attridge has made similar statements about the letter *K* in an unpublished talk, "The Question of Character in Modernist Fiction: Kafka and Coetzee." Thanks to Derek Attridge for sharing the paper version of this talk with me by email, 9 April 2015.

of the details of Ovid's transformation recall Gregor's from "The Metamorphosis."[152]

Even though the reader knows the reason for Ovid's transformation, unlike for Gregor's new state, both Gregor and Tabucchi's Ovid face many of the same issues. In the beginning, the transformed humans have little control over their bodies and, therefore, have problems getting out of the supine position. Gregor's little legs make him momentarily powerless and wave before his eyes, prompting him to ask about what has happened to him: "His many legs, pitifully thin compared to the rest of him, waved helplessly before his eyes."[153] ("Seine vielen, im Vergleich zu seinem sonstigen Umfang kläglich dünnen Beine flimmerten ihm hilflos vor den Augen.")[154] Ovid's frail legs seem similarly useless in contrast to his heavy body: "He tried to stand up, but his thin legs couldn't bear the weight of his wings, so every now and then he was obliged to recline on cushions, his feet kicking in the air."[155] ("Lui cercava di tenersi in piedi, ma le sue esili zampe non riuscivano a reggere il peso delle ali, così che era obbligato ogni tanto a reclinarsi sui cuscini, con le zampe che sgambettavano in aria."[156]) These English translations highlight the similarities between these "thin legs" (*Beine, zampe*) that prevent Ovid and Gregor from easily moving around.

Worse than the physical discomfort for these creatures is their loss of speech. Neither Ovid nor Gregor initially realizes that he will not be understood because he lacks a human voice. Gregor hilariously tries to give excuses to his supervisor for why he is late for work, but the Prokurist announces to Gregor's family: "That was an animal's voice."[157] This moment marks the first time that Gregor is referred to with the term *Tier* (animal), which is used sparingly in the text and marks a few other significant moments, such as when Gregor asks whether he really is an animal if he can enjoy his sister's violin playing. The confusion between the Prokurist's understanding of Gregor and Gregor's understanding of himself raises the issue of what Gregor is, exactly, suggesting how this problem will grow throughout the story, until Gregor's sister asserts that the Tier (animal) cannot possibly be Gregor.

---

152   Pezzin has also remarked on the similarity: "Ovidio appare come una sorta di Gregorio Samsa mitico, con una fusione dell'immagine della parola-farfalla di Groddeck e dell'insetto repellente de *Le metamorfosi* di Kafka" (Pezzin, *Antonio Tabucchi*, 88).

153   Kafka, *The Metamorphosis*, 21.

154   Kafka, *Erzählungen*, 96.

155   Tabucchi, *Dreams of Dreams*, 13.

156   Tabucchi, *Sogni di sogni*, 19.

157   Kafka, *The Metamorphosis*, 39. ("Das war eine Tierstimme"; Kafka, *Erzählungen*, 108.)

Like Gregor, when Ovid first speaks, he understands himself, although no one else does: "Don't you hear my song, cried Ovid, this is the song of the poet Ovid, the one who taught the art of love, who told of the courtiers and rogues, of miracles and metamorphoses! But his voice was an indistinct whistle, and the crowd scattered before the horses."[158] As with Gregor, Ovid's new form seems to erase everything he has done in the past. The office worker in "The Metamorphosis" and the crowd in "Sogno di Ovidio, poeta e cortigiano" ("Dream of Publius Ovidius Naso, Poet and Courtier") respond with extreme displeasure to the creature voices of the transformed humans: "But from his mouth issued a strange hiss, a shrill, unbearable whistle that made the people in the crowd cover their ears with their hands."[159] These reactions presage the negative public reactions to their transformed bodies when Ovid and Gregor finally raise themselves up onto their thin little legs.

Although they still comprehend human speech, Gregor and Ovid are unable to communicate understandably with voice or gestures. Gregor lives completely separated from his family members and cannot make them realize his thoughts or motivations.[160] When he tries to position himself so that his father will understand his harmlessness, his endeavours are futile: "But his father was in no mood to take note of subtleties."[161] Gregor's attempt to join the family leads to the famous apple scene that contributes to his death. Hoping to communicate, Ovid tries to perform his poetry with gesture: "But how to recite them, he wondered, if his voice was only the hiss of an insect. And so he decided to communicate his verses to Caesar with gestures."[162]

---

158 Tabucchi, *Dreams of Dreams*, 14. ("Non sentite il mio canto?, gridava Ovidio, questo è il canto del poeta Ovidio, colui che ha insegnato l'arte di amare, che ha parlato di cortigiane e di belletti, di miracoli e di metamorfosi! Ma la sua voce era un fischio indistinto, e la folla si scostava davanti ai cavalli"; Tabucchi, *Sogni di sogni*, 20.)

159 Tabucchi, *Dreams of Dreams*, 14. ("Ma dalla sua bocca uscì uno strano sibilo, un fischio acuttismo e insopportabile che obbligò la folla a mettersi le mani sugli orecchi"; Tabucchi, *Sogni di sogni*, 20.)

160 "To Gregor it was clear his father had misinterpreted Grete's all too brief pronouncement to assume him guilty of some act of violence. So it behooved Gregor to try to pacify his father, as he was lacking both the time and means to enlighten him" (Kafka, *The Metamorphosis*, 80).

161 Kafka, 81. ("Aber der Vater war nicht in der Stimmung, solche Feinheiten zu bemerken"; Kafka, *Erzählungen*, 136.)

162 Tabucchi, *Dreams of Dreams*, 14. ("Ma come dirli?, pensò, se la sua voce era solo un sibilo di insetto? E allora pensò di comunicare i suoi versi al Cesare facendo dei gesti"; Tabucchi, *Sogni di sogni*, 20.)

Instead of being understood, his movements disgust Caesar, who, as a result, has Ovid's wings cut off: "Ovid understood at that moment that his life was ending."[163]

The transformation had seemed positive, a sign of Ovid's important status as poet, but it quickly turned out to be a punishment, like his actual exile. Ovid's transformation hovers between gift and affliction. In the dream, Ovid obtains his desires to be loved by the emperor and blessed by the gods, but this leads to his downfall. Despite their respective dedication to Caesar and the family, Tabucchi's Ovid and Kafka's Gregor are ultimately rewarded with death. Since his physical incapacity allows him to stop working, Gregor's transformed figured has been described as a form of wish fulfilment. His transformation has also been interpreted as a manifestation of family resentment about his growing role as provider. Viewing the story in a Freudian framework highlights the father's displeasure at having been replaced, and Gregor's form potentially embodies this Freudian resentment. The works suggest that neither Gregor nor Ovid was able to remain part of society, even when seemingly fulfilling their proper roles. The works highlight the powerlessness of the individual and the crushing, often conflicting, weight of societal obligations.

Ovid and Gregor can be examined as individuals, but also as representations of certain societal roles. "The Metamorphosis" reflects upon the roles of the son and worker, while Ovid's dream comments on the role of the artist. All the pieces in *Dreams of Dreams* reflect, in some way, on the relationship among the artist, society, and imagination. Some of the dreams are inspired by the artist's work, and some are treated as what led to the artist's work. Inspiration, dreams, literature, and biography intertwine in the dreams. Apuleius is approached by his character, who asks for his help: "I am Lucius, he said. / Don't you recognize me? / Which Lucius? asked Apuleius. / Your Lucius, said the ass, the one from your adventures, your friend Lucius."[164] Freud, as a psychoanalyst rather than artist or author, as traditionally defined, could be seen as the outlier in the collection; however, Tabucchi's description of Freud makes clear how he fits with the other artists and literary authors: "His *Case Histories* can be read as ingenious novels. Id, Ego, and Superego are his Trinity. And, perhaps, ours

---

163 Tabucchi, *Dreams of Dreams*, 15. ("Ovidio capì che la sua vita finiva in quel momento"; Tabucchi, *Sogni di sogni*, 21.)

164 Tabucchi, *Dreams of Dreams*, 19. ("Sono Lucio, disse, non mi riconosci? / Quale Lucio?, chiese Apuleio. / Il tuo Lucio, disse l'asino, quello delle tue avventure, il tuo amico Lucio"; Tabucchi, *Sogni di sogni*, 24.)

too."[165] This characterization, which concludes the work, frames Freud as a powerful artist, a writer of novels that continue to inform our society.

In "Sogno del dottor Sigmund Freud, interprete dei sogni altrui" ("Dream of Doctor Sigmund Freud, Interpreter of Other People's Dreams"), the Freud in the dream wanders the streets of Vienna as Dora: "He dreamed he had become Dora, and that he was crossing a bombarded Vienna."[166] He feels uncomfortable at what the awake, real Freud has done to Dora-Freud's reputation, but he also appreciates aspects of being female: "Dr. Freud perked up. After all, it was rather agreeable to be treated familiarly by a sexy [virile] butcher boy, and, after all, he was Dora, who had sordid sexual problems."[167] While initially irritated at being confused for Dora, Freud comes to enjoy the experience, particularly as it pertains to his sexuality. Although, notably, Tabucchi writes only about the dreams of male artists and writers, Freud and Ovid experience a certain fluidity of their gender identity. Caesar's view of Ovid as feminine causes him to order Ovid's wings to be removed, which leads to the author's death: "He couldn't stand it that this indecent insect would perform that effeminate ballet in front of him."[168] In Ovid's dream, this effeminate dance represents poetry, which intimates a connection between literature and femininity. The piece suggests that literature is an open space of potential experimentation, a boundary space that is necessarily transgressive.

Manganelli's first piece in Centuria points directly to the potential openness of literature by suggesting that the reader imagine the sex of one of the described characters: "Let's suppose that [Supponiamo che] a person who is writing a letter to another person, – their sex or sexes are immaterial – should at some point hold the suspicion, or simply perhaps have the realization, of being slightly drunk."[169] In an epistolary

---

165 Tabucchi, Dreams of Dreams, 85. ("I suoi Casi clinici possono essere letti come ingegnosi romanzi. Es, Io e Super-Io sono la sua Trinità. E, forse, ancora la nostra"; Tabucchi, Sogni di sogni, 86.) Tabucchi discussed this in interviews as well, when asked about how Freud did not seem to fit with the other artists and writers; see Tabucchi, Gumpert, and González Rovira, Conversaciones con Antonio Tabucchi, 193.

166 Tabucchi, Dreams of Dreams, 75. ("Sognò che era diventato Dora e che stava attraversando Vienna bombardata"; Tabucchi, Sogni di sogni, 74.)

167 Tabucchi, Dreams of Dreams, 76. ("Il dottor Freud si ringalluzzì. Dopo tutto era bello essere trattato con familiarità da un virile garzone di macellaio, e dopo tutto lui era Dora, che aveva problemi turpi"; Tabucchi, Sogni di sogni, 75.)

168 Tabucchi, Dreams of Dreams, 14. ("Non poteva sopportare che quell'insetto indecente eseguisse davanti a lui quell femmineo balletto"; Tabucchi, Sogni di sogni, 21.)

169 Manganelli, Centuria, 2005, 11. ("Supponiamo che, ad un certo momento, una persona che sta scrivendo una lettera ad un'altra persona – il sesso o i sessi sono irrilevanti – abbia il sospetto, o forse semplicemente s'accorga di essere lievemente ubriaco"; Manganelli, Centuria, 2012, 17.)

novel, the sex of the letter writer generally determines a large part of the reader's understanding of the dynamics between writer and addressee, but the first piece of *Centuria* playfully suggests that the addressee's and writer's sexes are unimportant, leaving it up to the reader's imagination. At the same time, the narrator refers to the writer and addressee with masculine adjectives, pronouns, and nouns, potentially undercutting his original supposition and causing the reader to re-evaluate the narrator-reader relationship.

While Manganelli's narrator posits that the character's sex is potentially open to the reader's interpretation, in Romano's work the narrator's sex is often a matter of interpretation. Since the sexes of the dreamers are not identified in the first or more recent editions of the work, all the dreams could potentially involve gender transformations.[170] Contrasting this with what Freud believed made the narration of dreams significant, the descriptions of the dreams do not directly reference the personal details and life events that may have caused or relate to the dreams. The narration generally does not provide details about the relationship between the dreamer and the people mentioned. A reader would not necessarily know that "The Pole" was originally narrated by a young male child. All the dreams are narrated in the first person, but they refer to dreams of different dreamers, and the gender changes several times. While "Lo stagno" (The pond), for instance, involves a group of women, other dreams are narrated by men.[171] In many of the dreams, the indication of the speaker's gender is so small that, when translated into English, it disappears. For instance, in "Il cimitero" (The cemetery), an adjective marks the dreamer as female: "I realize I am very tired [*stanca*]."[172] The personal and original narrators, including their sexes, are often left obscured and are seemingly insignificant. The works could be divided according to the sex of the dreamer, but tone, style, and themes – not the narrator or context – link these works together.

The openness of Manganelli's character in his first piece, Freud's transformative identity experience in Tabucchi's last piece, and Romano's unclear dreamers are due in part to the brevity of the works as the confusion would be more difficult to maintain in a longer work. There are notable exceptions, such as Anne Garréta's *Sphinx* (1986), a story of love between two characters without gender. Unlike

---

170   In the second, regretted edition of the work, the dreamers are identified at the end of the dream (Anna, Giovanni, Pierino, Leda, Antonio, C., and Lydia).

171   "Finalmente, nel punto dove siamo sicure che dovrebbe esserci il negozio, troviamo una vetrina chuisa con impannate di legno" (Romano, *Le metamorfosi*, 101).

172   "Mi accorgo di essere molto stanca" (Romano, 127).

Manganelli, who posits that the sexes do not matter, but uses male pronouns throughout, Garréta, a member of the selective literary group
Oulipo, short for "Ouvroir de literature potentille" (Potential Literature Workshop), avoids using any pronouns or adjectives that would
indicate a particular gender. The work is considered experimental,
whereas, in part because of their brevity, the shorter stories of Romano,
Manganelli, and Tabucchi examined here experiment without that necessarily being the goal. In other words, these short fictions push boundaries without being explicitly about pushing boundaries. Their generic
flexibility allows for brief, non-programmatic experimentation with the
sex of narrators and characters.

These short works offer spaces of experimentation with sexual identity, and "The Bridge" reveals how Kafka's work can be interpreted
as being similarly transgressive. "The Bridge," which is feminine in
German, has been read as Kafka's only first-person female narrator
and as offering a space for sexual exploration.[173] Ruth V. Gross, Clayton
Koelb, and Mark M. Anderson have used this piece to discuss Kafka
and homosexuality as well as Kafka and femininity.[174] The sexual
connotations of the bridge's interaction with the "man" are obvious:
"He came, he knocked on me all over with the iron tip of his cane, then
he lifted my coat-tails [*Rockschöße*] with it and folded them back on me;
he thrust his spike into my bushy hair and let it stay there for a long
time while probably gazing around into the distance."[175]

In addition to examining the connotations of thrusting a spike into
bushy hair, clear in any language, Koelb and Gross have analysed in
detail the connotations of *Rockschöße*: coat, dress (*Rock*) and coat-tail,
shirt, lap, or womb (*Schoß*).[176] Koelb reads the linguistic suggestions
as contributing to the bridge's openness about gender and argues that
the "bridge links not just two sides of a geographical gap but two gen-
ders as well."[177] Gross shows how careful analysis of "The Bridge"

---

173   See Gross, "Fallen Bridge"; Koelb, "The Turn of the Trope"; and Anderson,
      "Kafka, Homosexuality and the Aesthetics of 'Male Culture.'" Gross: "She would
      also be Kafka's only female narrator, his only female voice" (Gross, 583).
174   Gross; Koelb; and Anderson.
175   KSS, 108. ("Er kam, mit der Eisenspitze seines Stockes beklopfte er mich, dann
      hob er mit ihr meine Rockschöße und ordnete sie auf mir. In mein buschiges Haar
      fuhr er mit der Spitze und ließ sie, wahrscheinlich wild umherblickend, lange drin
      liegen"; Kafka, *Erzählungen*, 264.)
176   "A 'Rock' may be either a coat or a dress, therefore either a male or a female gar-
      ment. A 'Schoß' may be either the 'tail' of a coat or shirt or a (usually female) lap"
      (Koelb, "The Turn of the Trope," 61).
177   Koelb, 61–2.

reveals the insecurity of Kafka's narrative: "When Kafkan language is pried apart, broken to pieces, the masculine, secure meaning – the universal meanings that the critics have found in Kafka's tales – will dissolve, and different – not necessarily universal and not always masculine – voices may emerge."[178] The issue of sexuality in Kafka's short work leads back to his remarkable "grammar," to quote Rosselli and Montale. Kafka breaks boundaries through his precise and layered use of language.

The bridge's multiple potentialities relate to its status as an object, which is designated with a feminine word (*die Brücke*) in German, but which is, of course, as object, open to another series of possibilities.[179] The animated inanimate objects of Kafka present opportunities to cross anthropological and narratological boundaries. In "Blumfeld, an Elderly Bachelor" ("Blumfeld, ein älterer Junggeselle"), a bachelor considers getting a dog as a companion, returns home, and discovers bouncing balls in his apartment. The balls can be read as springing from a linguistic connotation, the dog's *Bellen* (bark) transforms into *Bälle*.[180] In Manganelli's "Seventy-Five," the protagonist also has a special relationship with a ball or, rather, sphere. The story begins, "A woman has given birth to a sphere: it's a question of a globe some twenty centimeters in diameter."[181] This sphere-baby is both completely an object and completely her baby, or at least she treats it as such. The woman's sphere bears a relationship to a child (it drinks her milk), while Blumfeld associates his spheres with having a pet dog.[182] As with Blumfeld, the woman feels that the sphere responds to her, even if the reaction is not visible: "She has the impression that, no, the sphere has nothing to tell her, but all the same is a part of her."[183]

---

178   Gross, "Fallen Bridge," 581.

179   "The metaphor insists on *both* the human and object qualities of the narrator, on *both* its maleness and femaleness, and so on" (Koelb, *Kafka's Rhetoric*, 62).

180   "The imaginary dog is described by its Bellen, a trait that is almost instantly transformed by paronomasia into the *Bälle* Blumfeld finds in his room" (Koelb, 35).

181   Manganelli, *Centuria*, 2005, 159. ("Una donna ha partorito una sfera; si tratta di un globo del diametro di venti centimetri"; Manganelli, *Centuria*, 2012, 165.)

182   Donna Yari discusses Kafka's spheres along with Gregor and Odradek as hybrid creatures, which combine qualities from more than one creature or thing (Yarri, "Index to Kafka's Use of Creatures in His Writings," 270).

183   Manganelli, *Centuria*, 2005, 160. ("La sua impressione è che la sfera non voglia dire nulla, e che tuttavia le appartenga"; Manganelli, *Centuria*, 2012, 166.)

Like the balls of Blumfeld, Manganelli's spheres resist "metaphorical or symbolic reduction."[184] While described as objects, they are treated as more than just spheres. More perhaps than any creature could be, these objects are open to being male-female, alive–not alive, symbolic–not symbolic. These dichotomies that generally determine the world are broken down in their object-subject transgression. The broken boundaries often hinge on the significance of minor moments and linguistic relationships. The linguistic and other transgressions of Kafka's short form inspired Romano, Manganelli, and Tabucchi. Although numerous authors write literature that could be defined as fragmented, lyrical, or aphoristic, revisiting Kafka's work in an Italian context calls attention to the narrative and stylistic experimentations of Romano, Tabucchi, and Manganelli, asking the reader to pay special attention to the role of hypothesis in all these authors' works. These hypotheses often investigate the transgression of boundaries.

Kafka, Romano, Manganelli, and Tabucchi embody Calvino's call for writing prose like poetry. Urging the integration of poetic and prose practices, Calvino noted the Italian proclivity for poetry and brevity in his essay "Quickness": "I am convinced that writing prose should not be any different from writing poetry. In both cases it is a question of looking for the unique expression, one that is concise, concentrated, and memorable. It is hard to keep up tension of this kind in very long works."[185] Calvino's desire for poetic, brief prose fits with his earlier lament that the concentration on Kafka's lyricism was in decline. While Calvino regretted the seeming disappearance of lyrical, short Kafka decades ago, his popularity is on the rise and, looking at the Italian tradition in a different light, one that highlights Romano, Manganelli, and Tabucchi, the attraction to short, lyrical Kafka never disappeared; it was simply obfuscated by the force of his last two novels and the critical focus on this genre. Kafka wrote about his literary fortune:

> What will be my fate as a writer is very simple. My talent for portraying my dreamlike inner life [*meines traumhaften innern Lebens*] has thrust all other matters into the background; my life has dwindled dreadfully, nor will it cease to dwindle. Nothing else will ever satisfy me.... Others waver too, but in lower regions, with greater strength; if they are in danger of falling, they are caught up by the kinsman who walks beside them for

184   Gray et al., *A Franz Kafka Encyclopedia*, 47.
185   Calvino, *Six Memos for the Next Millennium*, 48–9.

that very purpose. But I waver on the heights; it is not death, alas, but the eternal torments of dying.[186]

Kafka comments on his power as an author, his ability to forcefully describe "dreamlike inner life," which separates him from others. Contrasting an ability to live and an ability to portray dream-like fiction, he describes how his powerful writing abilities are stronger than his ability to live. Without this sense, he may not have produced the literature that often causes the reader to rethink his or her reality.

While Kafka records this idea about the relationship between his writing and his lived life privately, in his diaries, the Italian authors I have discussed were frequently asked about the relationship of reality to their often dream-like, abstract works. Italian critics often return to the concept of *impegno* (commitment), not just in the 1940s or 1950s, but throughout the twentieth century.[187] When asked about the meaning of *impegno* in a conversation with Daniele Del Giudice, Angelo Giugliemi, Alberto Moravia, Roberto Pazzi, Edoardo Sanguineti, and Pier Vittorio Tondelli, Tabucchi and Manganelli are the first to answer. Tabucchi provides his interpretation: "For a writer, *impegno* cannot be anything other than moral. An *impegno* of honesty with oneself. Otherwise *impegno* becomes, as they said once upon a time, a problem of 'engagement.' And this does not work. Everyone must judge himself. If an author looks out from a window he cannot help but note the people who pass in the street. But if the window is oriented inward, he will note that which happens to him."[188] Tabucchi proposes that

---

186   Kafka, *Diaries*, 302. ("Von der Literatur aus gesehen ist mein Schicksal sehr einfach. Der Sinn für die Darstellung meines traumhaften innern Lebens hat alles andere ins Nebensächliche gerückt, und es ist in einer schrecklichen Weise verkümmert und hört nicht auf, zu verkümmern. Nichts anderes kann mich jemals zufrieden stellen.... Andere schwanken auch, aber in untern Gegenden, mit stärkeren Kräften; drohen sie zu fallen, so fängt sie der Verwandte auf, der zu diesem Zweck neben ihnen geht. Ich aber schwanke dort oben, es ist leider kein Tod, aber die ewigen Qualen des Sterbens"; Kafka, *Tagebücher*, 546.)

187   For a discussion of the significant role that *impegno* has in Italian criticism, see Re, "Pasolini vs. Calvino, One More Time."

188   "Per uno scrittore, l'impegno non può che essere morale. Un impegno di onestà con se stesso. Altrimenti l'impegno diventa, come si diceva un tempo, un problema di 'engagement.' E non va bene. Ognuno deve giudicare la propria testa. Se uno scrittore spia l'esterno da una finestra, non può che registrare le persone che passano per strada. Ma se la sua finestra è rivolta all'interno, registrerà ciò che gli accade" (Tabucchi, interview in Deidier, "Scrittori d'Italia," 171). On Tabucchi being ethical in addition to postmodern, see Klopp, "Antonio Tabucchi." For more on Tabucchi and *impegno*, see Settis, "Antonio Tabucchi

portraying "inner life" can be as engaged as portraying outside life. Manganelli was prompted to write his ideas about literature in "Letteratura come menzogna" (Literature as lie), in part because of questions about whether abstract fiction, the fiction of games, or any literature seemingly divorced from the world should exist. Romano proposed that dreams change the dreamer, as real life does: "A dream is lived, in a certain way, it should be narrated."[189] As Rodolfo Paoli said of Kafka, while his literature may not represent reality, it changes the reader's view of reality.[190] Tabucchi also described how dream literature expressed a mode of understanding literature and life: "When we write at the end we dream ... literature is a collective dream. Exactly in this way literature is also *impegno*."[191]

While the short, short works discussed in this chapter do not provide ideologically driven examples of literature, they question, rewrite, and hypothesize. They explore different gender identities and generic possibilities, and they ask us to imagine with them. They aim not to represent reality but to alter the reader's view of reality. These Italian authors, pressed by readers who sometimes resisted their modes of abstract writing, present ideas not only about how to understand their works but also about how to understand the experimental short, short fiction like Kafka's. They explain one reason for the growing attraction to the short form and indicate one way to understand the importance of an increasingly popular genre. While some critical energy has been given to the idea that short attention spans are contributing to the end of literature and that the rise of short, short fiction relates to our inability to read anything long, a more positive assessment of the form's popularity is that short, short fiction like Kafka's, Romano's, Manganelli's, and Tabucchi's can be transgressive and ask readers to rethink their world views.

possibility, hypothesese

---

contro l'eclisse dell'impegno intellettuale." For more on the postmodern and *impegno* in Italy more broadly, see the collection by Antonello and Mussgnug, *Postmodern impegno*.

189   "Il sogno è vissuto, in qualche modo; deve essere raccontato" (Romano, *Le metamorfosi*, 206).

190   Paoli, "Spavento dell'infinito," 213.

191   "Quando noi scriviamo in fondo sogniamo ... la letteratura è un sogno collettivo. Proprio in questo senso la letteratura è anche impegno" (Tabucchi, *Conversazione con Antonio Tabucchi*, 29).

Chapter Three

Processi without End: The Mysteries of Dino Buzzati and Paola Capriolo

Theodor W. Adorno compared Kafka's novels to detective stories in which the "criminal fails to be exposed."[1] While many discussions of a genre start with the caveat that it is difficult to define or contain, those about detective stories can seem refreshingly consistent: an investigation into a crime takes place, and a criminal is identified. Many critics also assert that the first example of detective fiction can be located without debate (Edgar Allen Poe's "The Murders of Rue Morgue," 1841) and that, as Roger Caillois argues, the rules have become increasingly reified with time.[2] Tzvetan Todorov claims that deviation from the usual parameters transforms detective fiction into "literature": "Detective fiction has its norms; to 'develop' them is also to disappoint them: to 'improve upon' detective fiction is to write 'literature,' not detective fiction."[3] Like Todorov, W.H. Auden, Antonio Gramsci, and Jorge Luis Borges divide investigative work into amusing or "mechanical" and literary or "artistic."[4] The critical tradition that distinguishes

---

1 Adorno, *Prisms*, 265.
2 While critics identify earlier works that bear some similarity to detective fiction, such as *Oedipus Rex*, they generally agree that Poe's story is the real beginning; see, e.g., Pyrhönen, *Murder from an Academic Angle*, 10. Mystery, cults, and conspiracy are, of course, not new; see Ziolkowski, *Lure of the Arcane*. Caillois distinguishes detective fiction from other genres because of its rules (Caillois, *The Mystery Novel*, 2). Here he uses the term *mystery novel*; some critics draw distinctions between *detective stories* and *mystery stories*, while *crime fiction* is often used as the broadest term.
3 Todorov, *The Poetics of Prose*, 43.
4 Gramsci provides a brief outline of the differences (Gramsci, *Antonio Gramsci*, 370). When discussing detective fiction (*giallo*), critics often first clarify whether they are referring to *real* detective fiction or detective fiction that is also commonly defined as *artistic* or *literary*. Studies of Italian detective fiction often make clear whether they are going to examine more traditional detective novels or these literary ones. For instance, Massimo Carloni and Roberto Borbolini begin their work on the *giallo*

between literature and detective novels often uses Kafka to illustrate the distinction.[5]

Meanwhile, Italian novelists, such as Gadda, Eco, Tabucchi, and Sciascia, have been credited with blurring the distinction between the crime novel and literature since Italy's most famous detective stories play with the boundaries of the genre.[6] The famous Italian writers of literary detective fiction – Gadda, Eco, Sciascia, Calvino, Camilleri, and Tabucchi – reference Kafka's importance.[7] They frequently refer to *The Trial*, especially "Before the Law," and *The Castle*.[8] The first section of this chapter examines the intriguing relationships between Kafka and Italian detective fiction, or *giallo*, which references the historically yellow (*giallo*) covers of Italian detective novels. These connections suggest a new approach to analysing Kafka and two other Italian authors frequently associated with him: Dino Buzzati and Paola Capriolo, examined in the last two sections.

Kafka, Detective Fiction, and Italy

Critics have alternatively framed Josef K. and K.'s searches in *The Trial* and *The Castle* as searches for God or signs that God no longer exists for the modern man.[9] Situating Chesterton's fiction between Kafka's "Before the Law" and the castle parable in John Bunyan's seventeenth-century

---

by making clear that they will not be discussing Eco, Sciascia, or other authors "like them" (Carloni and Borbolini, *L'Italia in giallo*, 11).

5 Poe and Kafka are frequently used to identify the literary qualities of detective fiction, of which Chesterton tends to be mentioned as a primary example.

6 "The barriers which separated literature from lesser forms such as the crime novel no longer hold" (Farrell, "Literature and the Giallo," 50). In contrast to other countries that are most notable for detective fiction that can be described as traditional (e.g., Sherlock Holmes), Italy contributed to breaking down this barrier. Del Monte, among others, locates the Holmes stories as the works that popularized the term *detective novel* (Del Monte, *Breve storia del romanzo poliziesco*, 10), whereas the Italian term comes from a label put on translated works. He also discusses how the localized nature of the *giallo* helped isolate Italian detective fiction (Del Monte, 9–15).

7 Calvino and Kafka were discussed in chap. 1, Tabucchi and Kafka in chap. 2.

8 There is also a visual connection between detective fiction and Kafka in Italy since the artist Guido Crepax, e.g., illustrated both the covers of crime fiction and those of Kafka, using a similar style for both. Not only did Crepax illustrate the cover of *Il processo*, but he also adapted the entire novel as a graphic work.

9 See, e.g., Maurice Blanchot's summary of this in *The Work of Fire*: "According to Max Brod, Kafka found many paths to God. According to Mme. Magny, Kafka finds his main consolation in atheism" (Blanchot, *The Work of Fire*, 5). For more details, see Stephen Dowden's discussion of *The Castle*'s reception (Dowden, *Kafka's Castle and the Critical Imagination*).

Christian allegory, *The Pilgrim's Progress*, Borges posits a spectrum from allegory without God (Kafka) to God (Bunyan).[10] Edwin Muir similarly links Kafka and *The Pilgrim's Progress* in his introductory note to the first American edition of *The Castle*, although he interprets Kafka's searches as being closer to Bunyan's than Borges does.[11] Borges's and Muir's views of the distinction between Kafka's searches and those in texts of faith point to the long-standing, ongoing debates about the role of God in readings of Kafka's novels.

Alberto Moravia uses the structure of Kafka's *The Castle* not only to assert that detective novels share analogous characteristics with Kafka's novel but also that the searches in detective fiction can be seen as akin to the search for God.[12] In Moravia's analysis, the structure and suspense in *The Castle* connect it with all detective stories, and they then shed light on the similarities between a search for God and a search for the guilty party in detective fiction.[13] Moravia's association between these searches, for God and a criminal, reveals how comparisons of Kafka with detective fiction quickly lead to ideas about meaning, specifically about the act of interpretation itself. God is one answer when a reader seems to be left only with questions. Kafka's investigative work asks whether analysis can result in an understanding of the world of the text, and the world more generally.

The searches in Kafka's most famous novels and in detective fiction have been viewed as emblematic of the search for meaning in literature,

---

10 Borges, *Other Inquisitions*, 85. Especially since his most famous detective, Father Brown, is a priest, Chesterton is known for the large role that faith plays in his works, and their relationship to faith is another reason that his work has been compared to Kafka's.

11 "*The Castle* is, like *The Pilgrim's Progress*, a religious allegory; the desire of the hero in both cases to work out his salvation; and to do so (in both cases again) it is necessary that certain moves should be gone through, and gone through without a single hitch " (Muir, "Introductory Note," iii). Muir then complicates the comparison, but he has already set up a clear analogy.

12 Commenting on Giuseppe Pontiggia's *Il raggio d'ombra* (*The Shadow's Radius*), Moravia writes, "And so, by analogy, one has to think that the search in *Il raggio d'ombra*, as in all novels structured as detective fiction, resembles the search in *The Castle*. Following therefore the logic of resemblances, the search for the mysterious person guilty of a crime, which is the primary theme of all detective fiction from Poe to Hammett, does not seem that different from the search for God." ("E allora, per analogia, non si può fare a meno di pensare che la ricerca del *Raggio d'ombra*, come del resto di tutti i romanzi di impianto poliziesco, rassomiglia alla ricerca del *Castello* kafkiano. Seguendo quindi la logica della somiglianza, la ricerca del misterioso colpevole di un delitto, che è il tema di fondo di 'tutta' la narrativa poliziesca da Poe ad Hammett, appare così non tanto diversa dalla ricerca di Dio"; Moravia, *Diario europeo*, 213).

13 For the connection between God and the detective, see, e.g., Ania on Leonardo Sciascia (*Fortunes of the Firefly*, 5).

of the act of interpretation.[14] In part because detective fiction can be seen as a reflection of literature, critics have asserted that it is fundamental in the development of postmodernism: Michael Holquist argued, "What the structural and philosophical presuppositions of myth and depth psychology were to Modernism (Mann, Joyce, Woolf, etc.), the detective story is to Post-Modernism (Robbe-Grillet, Borges, Nabokov, etc.)."[15] Kafka does not fit well into either of these categories, or rather, he could be characterized using either description, thus undermining the neat divide.[16]

Numerous critics consider Kafka's later novels to be altered detective novels or novels that play with the rules of detective fiction, but they vary in how they view the novel as following the detective story structure, and this often affects whether they consider them modernist or postmodernist works. Astradur Eysteinsson provides a description of the relationship between modernism and the detective story that positions Kafka as emblematic of modernism: "Using Kafka as a paradigmatic figure, and bearing in mind modernist obsessive explorations of the individual consciousness (the 'private eye', so to speak), it is probably not too difficult to demonstrate how the modernist hero is frequently in the role of the detective who never solves the crime, for he is of course also the guilt-ridden criminal."[17]

Whereas Eysteinsson focuses on the figure of the guilty, self-investigating detective, William Spanos emphasizes the idea of *The Trial* as an investigation without answers and therefore includes Kafka's *The Trial* in an exploration of postmodernism since "the postmodern literary imagination at large insists on the disorienting *mystery*."[18] Spanos's list of works that fit his description includes Kafka's *The Trial* (1914–15, published in 1925 after Kafka's death), Robbe-Grillet's *The Erasures* (1938), and Graham Greene's *Brighton Rock* (1953). When considered, Kafka's novels are generally the oldest examples of postmodernism.

In *The Doomed Detective: The Contribution of the Detective Novel to Postmodern American and Italian Fiction*, Stefano Tani describes Italian

---

14 Dowden analyses how Blanchot "turned *Das Schloß* into an allegory of literature" (Dowden, *Kafka's Castle and the Critical Imagination*, 70). As Lauren Marcus describes in "Detection and Literary Fiction," several critics have similarly related detective novels to the idea of literature and its analysis (Marcus, "Detection and Literary Fiction," 245).

15 Holquist, "Whodunit and Other Questions," 135.

16 Eysteinsson, in fact, posits that Holquist's definition is, in part, a result of Kafka's relatively small role in Anglo-American studies of modernism (Eysteinsson, *The Concept of Modernism*, 120).

17 Eysteinsson, 120.

18 Spanos, *Repetitions*, 25.

literature as being in a particular position in respect to these debates about detective fiction and postmodernism since it offers such a large number of significant "literary detective novels," also described as "anti-detective novels," "metaphysical detective novels," "analytical detective novels," or "postmodern detective novels," depending on the critic.[19] Luca Somigli makes the intriguing observation that, for years, the only way for Italian authors to write detective stories that would be accepted by the public were to produce postmodern (Eco) or literary (Sciascia) detective fiction.[20]

Numerous factors have contributed to Italy's strong tradition of literary detective novels despite the relatively late introduction of traditional detective novels to the Italian public.[21] Detective novels were seen as foreign to Italy, as Umberto Saba summed up: "*Bel canto* is Italian, cinema is American, and the detective novel English."[22] The term *suspense* in Italian is a 1950s English import. The Mondadori yellow-covered *gialli* series, initiated in 1929, is generally considered the beginning of the detective story in Italy.[23] Frassinelli published the Italian translation of *The Trial* in 1933.[24] The belated idea of an Italian detective story, therefore, contributes to the later flourishing of Italian literary detective novels since detective stories and novels like *The Trial*, which have been described as a postmodern take on the detective story, were received in the same

---

19 Tani, *The Doomed Detective*, xv. For an analysis of how Sciascia's works are similar to and different from traditional detective novels, see also Ania, *Fortunes of the Firefly*. In addition to the Italian authors whom Tani analyses, other critics have examined Andrea Camilleri and Antonio Tabucchi as authors of metaphysical or postmodern detective fiction. Tabucchi and Kafka are discussed in the following chapter. For Tabucchi as a writer of metaphysical detective fiction, see, e.g., Wilson, "On the Margins."

20 Somigli, "Form and Ideology," 67.

21 As Elena Past analyses, of course this does not mean that crime was not portrayed in Italian fiction and criticism earlier (Past, *Methods of Murder*, 9).

22 "Il bel canto è italiano, il cinematografo americano, il romanzo poliziesco inglese" (Saba, *Prose scelte*, 91).

23 For more detailed discussions of detective fiction in Italy than the cursory overview I provide, see Tani, *The Doomed Detective*; Rambelli, *Storia del "giallo" italiano*; Del Monte, *Breve storia del romanzo poliziesco*; Farrell, "Literature and the Giallo"; and Ania, *Fortunes of the Firefly*. *Giallo* was soon used by other publishers to mark their collections – Mediolanum, Niccoli, Casa Edit. Universale, Martucce, Alpe – all in the 1930s (see Rambelli, 16). Rambelli discusses the terminology used to discuss detective fiction in Italy (15–29) after discussing expressions for detective stories in English, French, and German.

24 For a point of contrast, the first complete Italian translation of James Joyce's *Ulysses* was published in 1960.

period, resulting in a simultaneous imagining and re-imagining of the detective form.[25]

Gadda is the most important example of how the rise of detective fiction and its transformation into "high literature" occurred essentially simultaneously in Italy.[26] Sciascia's 1975 article on the detective novel, "Breve storia del romanzo poliziesco" (A short history of the detective novel), ends with the much-cited quote, "It's enough now to end with Gadda: who wrote the most absolute *'giallo'* that has ever been written, a *giallo* without a solution."[27] The mysterious ending of Gadda's *Quer pasticciaccio brutto de via Merulana* (*That Awful Mess on the Via Merulana*) and its multiple searches without clear answers recall Kafka's mysterious, open investigations.[28] Gadda had known about Kafka since at least 1935, the year he mentioned writing publishers in the hope that they would commission him to translate the author from Prague.[29]

In 1946, when his now-famous *That Awful Mess on the Via Merulana* began to be serialized, Gadda made several references to Kafka's *The Trial* and feeling like Josef K. Lamenting all the work he had to accomplish, he wrote to Lucia Rodocanachi, "I feel like I am living 'sotto processo' (on trial), like Kafka's hero."[30] In his description of his workload,

25 "In altri termini, allora, si potrebbe affermare che in Italia la letteratura ispirata, anche in negativo, alle forme del poliziesco preceda la nascita del genere stesso, se è proprio il '29 l'anno di nascita della collana mondadoriana di 'Libri gialli'" (Crotti, *Tre voci sospette*, 65).

26 See Past's description of Gadda's significance as well as her overview of what contributed to his being a "supreme – if anomalous – example of detective fiction in Italy" (Past, *Methods of Murder*, 172).

27 "Ci basta ora finire con Gadda: che ha scritto il più assoluto 'giallo' che sia mai stato scritto, un 'giallo' senza soluzione" (Sciascia, "Breve storia del romanzo poliziesco," 1196).

28 "Perciò *Quer Pasticciaccio* ci chiude su un mistero prossimo a quelli kafkiani" (Meldolesi, "Per una storia del teatro," 20). See Meldolesi, 11–60, for more on the connections between Gadda and Kafka's *The Castle*. See also Sbragia, *Carlo Emilio Gadda and the Modern Macaronic*, 55; and Benedetti, *Una trappola di parole*, 141.

29 He discusses this in a letter to Rodocanachi (Gadda, *Lettere a una gentile signora*, 48). Triestine Lucia Rodocanachi, a translator and friend of Bazlen's, was the one who recommended Kafka. For more information on her, see Marcenaro, *Una amica di Montale*; and Dunnett, "Translation and Concealment." One of the potential reasons for Mondadori denying Gadda's request to translate Kafka in 1935 was the cultural climate under fascism. However, as Johannes Hösle has summarized, "Immerhin ist es bemerkenswert, wie stark im faschistischen Italien, besonders nach der Machtergreifung Hitlers im Jahr 1933, die Aufnahme des jüdischen Autors Kafka noch ist." ("All the same, it is notable how strong the reception of Kafka still was in fascist Italy, especially after Hitler's seizure of power in 1933"; Hösle, "Italien," 2:723.)

30 "Mi par di vivere sotto processo, come l'eroe di Kafka" (Gadda, *Lettere a una gentile signora*, 164).

again, how Kafka can be repurposed

Gadda plays on the idea that Josef K., without necessarily having done anything wrong, feels pursued and guilty. Gadda similarly used the expression of feeling under *processo* when writing a friend to apologize for not having written sooner: "I have to write to fourteen intellectuals, eleven journalists, four editors ... and with everyone I am at fault. And then there are the simple private correspondents. I am always 'sotto processo' (on trial). Just as in Kafka's *The Trial.*"[31] Like many critics, Gadda suggests that Josef K.'s guilt lies, in part, with his response to his trial itself, but that the trial itself is almost inescapable.

The range of experiences to which Josef K.'s persecution can apply, from Gadda's idea of feeling on trial like Josef K. because of having to respond to so many missives (an emotion many academics may share) to Primo Levi comparing Josef K.'s sudden arrest to his deportation, an experience often said to lie beyond language, indicates *The Trial*'s availability to diverse interpretations.[32] Umberto Eco examines the openness of Kafka's work: "The various existentialist, theological, clinical, and psychoanalytical interpretations of Kafka's symbols cannot exhaust all the possibilities of his work. The work remains inexhaustible insofar as it is open, because in it an ordered world based on universally acknowledged laws being replaced by a world based on ambiguity, both in the negative sense that directional centers are missing and in a positive sense, because values and dogma are constantly being placed in question."[33] For Eco, Kafka's symbols remain points of discussion because of their fluidity.

In *The Open Work,* Eco's reflection on Kafka represents a counterpoint to his reading of detective stories: Kafka's openness stands in contrast with the traditional detective novel, in which at the end a criminal is identified, the others are revealed as innocent, the detective has successfully read the clues, and order returns. In other words, whereas traditional detective stories often provide the reader with positive confirmations about society (everyone who is not guilty is innocent; society

---

31 "Devo scrivere a 14 letterati, 11 giornalisti, 4 editori ... e con tutti sono in colpa. E poi i semplici privati. Sono sempre sotto processo. Proprio come nel 'processo' di Kafka" (Gadda, *A un amico fraterno,* 150). For more on Gadda's frame of mind when writing this letter, see Sbragia, *Carlo Emilio Gadda and the Modern Macaronic,* 55–6.

32 For a discussion of Primo Levi and Franz Kafka, see Ziolkowski, "Primo Levi and Jewish Kafka in Italy."

33 Eco, *The Role of the Reader,* 53–4; the same quote appears in Eco, *The Open Work,* 9. ("Le varie interpretazioni, esistenzialistiche, teologiche, cliniche, psicoanalitiche dei simboli kafkiani esauriscono appena in parte le possibilità dell'opera: in effetti l'opera rimane inesauribile ed aperta in quanto 'ambigua,' poiché ad un mondo ordinato secondo leggi universalmente riconosciute si è sostituito un mondo fondato sulla ambiguità, sia nel senso negativo di una mancanza di centri di orientamento, sia nel senso positivo di una continua rivedibilità dei valori e delle certezze"; Eco, *Opera aperta,* 42.)

works), Kafka's works call into question its "values and dogmas."[34] Eco, Gadda, Sciascia, Tabucchi, and Camilleri alter the standard rules of detective fiction in order to question society.

Critics have discussed the relationship between the questioning of values in most literary detective novels and the notable number of Italian non-traditional detective stories. Gadda's choice of genre has been noted as a sign of his anti-fascism, of being against the most recent form of Italian government, in part because the genre was outlawed under late fascist rule.[35] While discussions of crime novels are now remiss if they overlook Italian ones, one of the few mentions of Italy in Howard Haycraft's 1941 study, *Murder for Pleasure*, is the fact that the fascist government eventually banned foreign mystery novels, like Agatha Christie's, because of their potentially subversive influence.[36]

Italy's lack of traditional detective fiction was frequently interpreted as an indication that its government, and perhaps its population, did not function properly.[37] While Haycraft argues that non-democratic societies such as Italy's, in contrast with those of America, England, and France, do not foster detective fiction, later critics, like Calvino, posit that Italy prompted a new kind of detective fiction, in part because of its corruption.[38] Calvino praises Sciascia for revealing with his investigative fiction the impossibility of setting traditional detective fiction in Sicily: "I read your detective thriller which is not a thriller with all the excitement with which people read detective stories, and in addition with amusement at seeing how the thriller is deconstructed, or rather how you prove the impossibility of writing a thriller in the Sicilian environment."[39]

From Gadda to today, Italian detective fiction tends to expose corruption rather than a functioning democratic society. Descriptions of more recent detective fiction continue to contrast anglophone stories,

---

34 See Ziolkowski, *Lure of the Arcane*, for a discussion of Eco's role in international detective fiction. See Bondanella, "Eco and the Tradition," for a description of how Eco can be situated in terms of detective fiction both internationally and within Italy.

35 See, e.g., Pecoraro, *Gadda*, 133.

36 Written before the Italian literary detective novel boom, earlier scholarship on crime fiction rarely mentioned Italian works. Del Monte, an early Italian examiner of detective fiction, points out that Italian criticism also took longer in contrast with German, French, English, and American (Del Monte, *Breve storia del romanzo poliziesco*, 5).

37 "In the Southern States of Europe the law is less loved and the detective story less frequent" (Sayers, "The Omnibus of Crime," 354). In Haycraft's *Murder for Pleasure*, the epigraph from Rex Stout makes an even stronger statement: "My theory is people who don't like mystery stories are anarchists" (n.p.).

38 Haycraft concentrates on American, French, and English detective fiction and emphasizes their connection with democracy (Haycraft, 28).

39 Calvino, *Italo Calvino*, 305.

which tend to offer resolutions, with the Italian tradition.[40] The British Broadcasting Corporation's 2010 hour-long special on Italian noir focuses on this interrogative, open quality of Italian detective fiction. In it, Camilleri remarks on the lack of reality in having cases end with definitive resolutions or punishment. According to him, the writer, "the poor detective novelist," of non-traditional detective fiction therefore thinks to himself: "Do I really have to be the one to sew back together the torn parts of society?"[41] For Camilleri, traditional detective fiction does not necessarily connote a highly functioning society, but rather attempts to ameliorate our picture of society.

While most famous for his Montalbano fiction set in Sicily, Camilleri has written a number of other detective works as well.[42] Based on a real nineteenth-century event, his *La mossa del cavallo* (*The Knight's Move*) narrates how Giovanni Bovara witnesses a murder, which he is then accused of having committed.[43] The novel ends with a "dream catalogue," followed by a list of the authors whose words, phrases, and images that Camilleri, in his words, "stole," including Kafka, Faulkner, Firpo, Sciascia, Hemingway, Hammett, Joyce, and Proust.[44] Kafka is the only author to appear twice, in references to "Before the Law" and "The Metamorphosis." While Kafka is not the first writer that comes to mind in a discussion of Camilleri and Sciascia, who are most often associated with each other and with Pirandello, their allusions to him suggest his significance to the development of Italian literary detective fiction or, at the very least, his appeal for the writers of these works that question how government functions.

In "Pirandello, mio padre" ("Pirandello, My Father"), Sciascia provocatively claims that all twentieth-century literature responds to Pirandello, Kafka, and Borges: "It seems to me that one can say that all of the literature of our century is an extension, a development, an echo

---

40 "A reason often given why American movies and books are very popular globally is that they have, if not a happy ending, a definite resolution. Camilleri, like many of his compatriot writers, regards such resolutions as being dishonest and unrealistic" (Davis, "Noir, Italian Style," 10).

41 Camilleri, quoted in Davis, 9. ("Davvero io devo essere colui che ricuce l'intero strappato della società?")

42 For a consideration of Camilleri's Montalbano in comparison to other detectives (such as Sherlock Holmes), see Douthwaite, "Montalbano: Type and Prototype of the Detective."

43 The story it is based on is described in Leopold Franchetti's *Politica e mafia in Sicilia* (*Politics and Mafia in Sicily*).

44 "*Il libro di Geremia* (18.3), Kafka (*Dinanzi alla legge*), Faulkner (*L'urlo e il furore*), Firpo ('*O grillo cantadò*'), Sciascia (*Il giorno della civetta*), Hemingway (*Per chi suona la campana*) e ancora Kafka (*La metamorfosi*), Hammett (*Corkscrew*), Joyce (*Ulisse*), Proust (*La prigioniera*)" (Camilleri, *La mossa del cavallo*, 247).

from (or even a debate of) these three writers."[45] Although Pirandello is Sciascia's primary focus, he also describes Kafka as a guiding figure for modern literature.[46] The unreachable castle in Sciascia's *Il cavaliere e la morte* (*The Knight and Death*) suggests Kafka's unreachable castle, as Pupo and Briziarelli have noted.[47] While the unnamed vice-chief of police investigates the murder of a lawyer, he contemplates death, focusing on the Dürer print, *Knight, Death, and the Devil*: "Death; and that castle in the background, unattainable."[48] This unreachable castle symbolizes that the detective will not discover exactly what happened, that the novel portrays a never-ending struggle against absolute power.[49]

Kafka is often associated with Italian works that portray ongoing and endless struggles against inscrutable power. While Elio Petri is most famous for adapting Sciascia's works, *A ciascuno il suo*, 1967 (*To Each his Own*) and *Todo modo*, 1976 (*Todo Modo*), the director also found in Kafka a powerful model for criticizing Italian society. In part a commentary on corruption in the Italian government, his *Indagine su un cittadino al di sopra ogni sospetto* (*Investigation of a Citizen above Suspicion*), which won the Grand Prix Spécial du Jury at Cannes and Best Foreign Film at the Oscars in 1970, ends with a quote from *The Trial*: "Qualunque impressione faccia su di noi, egli è un servo della legge, quindi appartiene alla legge e sfugge al giudizio umano." ("Whatever impression he makes on us, he is a servant of the Law. He belongs to the Law and is not answerable to human judgment.")[50] The invocation of Kafka was part of a critique of how governmental offices in Italy functioned.

---

45 "Mi pare di poter dire che tutta la letteratura di questo nostro secolo è un rameggiare, uno svolgersi, un respirare (o anche un dibbattersi) da questi tre scrittori" (Sciascia, "Breve storia del romanzo poliziesco," 1196). Not surprisingly, critics have examined the significance of understanding all three of these authors in the light of detective fiction.

46 Ivan Pupo has drawn attention to several broad similarities between Sciascia's and Kafka's worlds, including their portrayals of the nightmares of unjust justice; the enigma of guilt; and the effects, both unsettling and freeing, of imagined patricide. "Dagli incubi della giustizia ingiusta, dall'enigma della colpa e dagli effetti, insieme inquietanti e liberatori, del 'parricidio'" (Pupo, *Passioni della ragione*, 14).

47 Briziarelli, "Of Valiant Knights and Labyrinths," 6. See also Pupo, 173.

48 Sciascia, *The Knight and Death*, 2. ("La morte; e quel castello lassù, irraggiugibile"; Sciascia, *Il cavaliere e la morte*, 12.)

49 JoAnn Cannon analyses how *The Knight and Death* criticizes not just a particular system (Sicilian or Italian), but power structures more broadly (Cannon, *The Novel as Investigation*, 6). For a discussion of the relationship of Sciascia's works to governmental corruption, see Mullen, "Leonardo Sciascia's Detective Fiction."

50 Soderbergh's thriller *Kafka*, which draws on the author's writing and biography, depicts Kafka investigating his friend's murder, which leads him to discover a secret, morally suspect organization that controls the city.

In the film, a chief investigator, who has recently moved up to become the head of the political division, kills his mistress and then plants obvious clues for other investigators to find, but many of them do not want to accuse him because of his powerful position.[51] The film angered several government officials: "Many Italian films, especially those made in the aftermath of 1968, have measured their subversive ambitions against the implacable conundrum represented by the notion of the law as popularised by Kafka."[52] Again, if traditional detective stories have been associated with democratic governments and populations that respect their laws, metaphysical detective novels and unconventional detective films that invoke Kafka raise questions about how (or whether) the government works and have played a special role in the Italian literary and cultural landscape.

In *La testa perduta di Damasceno Monteiro* (*The Missing Head of Damasceno Monteiro*), which explores the problems of a judicial system, Tabucchi's narrator also directly references Kafka in a contemplation of the law.[53] A Lukács-loving journalist, Firmino, investigates the murder of Damasceno Monteiro and, in the process, uncovers widespread corruption in Portugal, or rather Oporto, which has been read as a stand-in for any European city. Firmino spends a significant amount of time talking to a powerful lawyer, who is passionate about German literature and justice. The lawyer questions the basis for Oporto law, calling it Kafkaesque: "It's a metaphysical hypothesis, purely metaphysical. And if you want, this is a truly Kafkaesque thing, it's the norm that ensnares us all and which, though it may seem incongruous, might account for the arrogance of a little squire who thinks he has the right to whip a prostitute. The ways of the *Grundnorm* are infinite."[54]

---

51 In her thorough reading of the film, Millicent Marcus calls attention to the similarities between the world potrayed in Kafka's *The Trial* and the Italy potrayed by Petri: "Like Kafka's unspecified state, Petri's Italy offers no acceptable alternatives to a corrupt and repressive status quo" (Marcus, *Italian Film in the Light of Neorealism*, 276).

52 Vighi, *Traumatic Encounters in Italian Film*, 94. For a discussion of other films he categorizes as presenting a Kafkaesque version of the law, see Vighi, 94–7.

53 Chap. 2 discussed Tabucchi's views on Kafka in more detail. For an overview of Tabucchi and detective fiction, see Diffley, "The Figure of the Detective in the Novels of Antonio Tabucchi."

54 Tabucchi, *The Missing Head of Damasceno Monteiro*, 84. ("Se vuole è un'ipotesi metafisica, disse l'avvocato, perfettamente metafisica. E se vuole questa è veramente una cosa kafkiana, è la Norma che ci invischia tutti quanti dalla quale, anche se le sembra incongruo, potrebbe discendere la prepotenza di un signorotto che si crede in diritto di frustare una puttana. Le vie della Grundnorm sono infinite"; Tabucchi, *La testa perduta*, 115.)

by word for ambiguity

Not only does the lawyer describe how society and the law functions as Kafkaesque, but he also refers to Kafka in his own introduction: "'Don't you feel you are in a scene from Kafka?' said the obese man as if he had read his thoughts, 'you surely must have read Kafka, or have seen the film *The Trial* with Orson Welles.'"[55] The lawyer's comments about Kafka hint that justice will not prevail in this story since entering a Kafkaesque scene never bodes well for achieving justice.

In fact, the lawyer later uses Kafka to examine justice during a speech he gives, with the goal of prosecuting a policeman who seems to operate beyond the law. The journalist records the conversation, and the reader has access only to a transcript of it, which contains large gaps, represented by long strings of spaced periods. The lawyer introduces Kafka: "*Es ist ein eigentümlicher Apparat*, this is an odd sort of machine. These words were written way back in 1914 by an unknown Jew, born in Prague, but who wrote in German."[56] Although much of his argument is missing, the lawyer is clearly discussing "In the Penal Colony": "A very odd sort of machine that perpetuates a barbarous law . . . . perhaps the machine of a penal colony or a terrible prediction of the monstrous event which Europe was due to witness?"[57] Because of the missing text, by the end of the lawyer's speech it is unclear whether he is commenting on Kafka's story or the torture of Damasceno Monteiro: "Because it is evident that murder is not enough . . . . torture . . . . the jailers . . . . before killing man you have to

---

55 Tabucchi, *The Missing Head of Damasceno Monteiro*, 79. ("Non pensi di trovarsi in una situazione kafkiana, disse l'obeso come se gli leggesse nel pensiero, Lei ha certo letto Kafka o ha visto *Il Processo* con Orson Welles"; Tabucchi, *La testa perduta*, 110.)

56 Tabucchi, *The Missing Head of Damasceno Monteiro*, 167. ("Es ist ein eigentümlicher Apparat, questo è un congegno davvero singolare. Così, nel lontano 1914, un ignoto ebreo di Praga che scriveva in tedesco"; Tabucchi, *La testa perduta*, 215.)

57 Tabucchi, *The Missing Head of Damasceno Monteiro*, 167–8. ("Congegno assai singolare che perpetua una legge barbara ... solo il congegno di una colonia penale o una terribile previsione dell'evento mostruoso che l'Europa avrebbe visto?"; Tabucchi, *La testa perduta*, 215–16; strings of periods shortened to preserve space.) "In the Penal Colony" is another work of note in discussions of crime fiction.

inflict pain, to savage him, to lacerate the flesh of a man."[58] The reader is invited to fill in the blanks, either with information from the case in Tabucchi's novel or details from Kafka's story. The reader is prevented from accessing the recording, with the result that a visual trace on the page shows how easily information can disappear and how this opens up a narrative to different interpretations.

Since the lawyer's words could apply to either the prisoner of "In the Penal Colony" or the death of Damasceno Monteiro, the reader is also invited to make more connections between Kafka and the case discussed in *The Missing Head of Damasceno Monteiro*. Merging Kafka's terrifying portrayals of judicial systems and its own system, Tabucchi's novel ends with a fragmented reflection on justice and a partial examination of it, a "surreal, Kafkaesque conclusion."[59] As in so many Italian detective works, the novel concludes without a satisfying resolution to the crime, leaving the reader instead with the sense that the official systems in place protect only themselves and that there is no clear path to justice.

Gadda, Sciascia, Camilleri, Tabucchi, and Eco all play with the generic codes of the detective novel. They produce literature that is considered to be going beyond the bounds of traditional detective fiction, but the parameters with which they experiment are still clearly those of the detective novel. The crime may be left unsolved, or solved in the beginning before leading to a larger societal exploration, the investigator may die, but there is a crime, a victim, an investigation, and usually an identifiable location. In *The Trial*, none of these roles are clear, and one of the mysteries is what the mystery is. Since, as Eco has claimed, *The Trial* and *The Castle* are open to myriad interpretations, discussing these two novels in the context of detective stories sheds light on their investigative role, in terms of hermeneutics and narratology, and has helped critics, from Auden to Adorno and beyond, to frame Kafka's works.

Arguing that Kafka's novels engage a number of diverse generic tropes that reflect modern times, Marthe Robert mentions thrillers as an alternative genre with which to consider Kafka and notes the clear connection between *The Castle* and detective fiction.[60] Analysing Kafka's

---

58 Tabucchi, *The Missing Head of Damasceno Monteiro*, 168. ("Perché evidentemente l'omicidio non basta ... la tortura ... gli aguzzini ... prima di uccidere bisogna far soffrire, infierire, tormentare le carni dell'uomo"; Tabucchi, *La testa perduta*, 217; strings of periods shortened to preserve space.)

59 "Si finisce con la conclusione surreale-kafkiana" (Pezzin, *Antonio Tabucchi*, 104).

60 "Kafka actually had conceived the opening of *The Castle* in the style of a detective story or spy novel" (Robert, *The Old and the New*, 202). Robert, meanwhile, reads *The Castle* productively as an epic.

work as epic, she makes the point that focusing on one genre can bring some clarity to the confusion of modernist fiction.[61] How Kafka invites the reader to consider issues of analysis is clarified when comparing his work to detective fiction. Beginning with the detective story as a point of entry into Kafka's novels, this chapter puts Kafka's *The Trial* and *The Castle* into conversation with Buzzati's *Il deserto dei Tartari*, 1940 (*The Desert of the Tartars*, published in English as *The Tartar Steppe*) and Capriolo's *Il doppio regno*, 1991 (*The Dual Realm*).[62] Like Kafka's novels, they are works without clearly defined crimes, but with mysteries, investigations, obsessions, suspense, guilt, imprisonment, officials, spectres of death, and questions of identity. These themes will be analysed by considering the novels as engaging with techniques familiar to critics of detective stories, particularly as discussed with respect to Kafka.

The connections between Buzzati and Kafka have frequently been a point of examination in discussions of influence, while Capriolo has often been referred to as a Kafkaesque author without an extended analysis of what this means. A comparison of their novels to Kafka's, within the framework of detective fiction, sheds more light on how their structure produces "Kafkaesque" situations, the significance of the differences between their conclusions, the relationship of their protagonists to their investigations, and the novels' mysteries. Putting Buzzati's and Capriolo's novels into conversation with works of Kafka and detective fiction highlights how they motivate readers to interpret their texts and potentially mislead them. While literary detective novels tend to critique how society works, particularly the government, and ask the reader to question the government, the works of Kafka, Buzzati, and Capriolo prompt the reader to question everything.

The Structures of Suspense: Questions, Identity, and Home

Josef K. of *The Trial*, K. of *The Castle*, Giovanni Drogo of *The Tartar Steppe*, and the protagonist of *The Dual Realm* are all "*sotto processo*," to quote Gadda, perhaps as a result of their own actions. Kafka's *The Castle*, Buzzati's *The Tartar Steppe*, and Capriolo's *The Dual Realm* contain mysterious edifices (castle, fort, hotel) and protagonists stuck in seemingly timeless states of limbo. In *The Castle*, K. arrives at a village, perhaps on purpose, and tries to take up the position of land surveyor with the

---

61 Robert, 199.
62 In an analysis of Capriolo's early work and Buzzati's *Il deserto dei Tartari*, Hipkins mentions that the similarities between Buzzati and Capriolo could be due to their shared attraction to Kafka's work (Hipkins, "Evil Ambiguities," 83).

castle that he claims he has been promised. But he will never reach the castle, and his position will never be clear. In *The Tartar Steppe,* Giovanni Drogo arrives at the Fortezza Bastiani (the Bastiani Fort), which he considers a mistaken posting. He decides to remain, in part because of a hoped-for battle that he will not live to see (and that may not happen). In *The Dual Realm,* the female narrator looks for a way out of a hotel that she seems to have run into at random when fleeing a gigantic, destructive wave. Although towards the end she apparently has the chance to leave, she remains there forever.

Kafka, Buzzati, and Capriolo present works that operate around a gap, an unrecoverable mystery.[63] The openness of all three authors' novels involves a mystery about what the mystery is.[64] Brantlinger contrasts concisely the clarity of detective fiction to Kafka's narration of the "Unknown": "[*The Trial*] can also be read as a parody of mystery novels. Kafka understood that ordinary mysteries are unmysterious; one of his aims seems to have been to produce a truly mysterious story, a metaphysical 'thriller.'"[65] This fits with how Eco and other critics describe traditional detective stories: as offering easy solutions, which contrast with the mysterious novels of Kafka, Buzzati, and Capriolo: "The criminal novel reduces redundancy; pretending to rouse the reader, it in fact confirms him in a sort of imaginative laziness and creates escape by narrating, not the Unknown, but the Already Known."[66]

Critics have noted that one of the significant formulae of detective novels is that the detective (and the reader) spend the majority of a novel discovering what happened before the novel started.[67] The detective novel aims to reconstruct the past so as to identify the criminal. One way in which Kafka's novels are framed as detective novels is that an undiscoverable event has occurred before the work starts.[68]

---

63 Several of Buzzati's short works have been collected into a volume called *Il Boutique del mistero*. Viganò has collected a number of Buzzati's journal stories into a collection called *La "nera" di Dino Buzzati: Crimini e misteri.*

64 Buzzati, when questioned about the genre of the *giallo*, mentioned that he found writing *gialli* impossible, although he was drawn to mystery and enjoyed reading detective fiction (Buzzati, "Il giallo in biblieteca," 30).

65 Brantlinger, "Missing Corpses," 32.

66 Eco, *The Role of the Reader*, 160. There is the sense that detective novels, unlike "literature," can be solved with a formula and data; see Siddique, "How to Spot Whodunnit."

67 "It is the peculiarity of detective fiction that the story of an investigation is made gradually to uncover the story of the crime which antedates it" (Porter, *The Pursuit of Crime*, 25).

68 "The central organizing trope in [*The Trial*] is an embedded story which refuses to surface, or open itself to rational interpretation, or even to allow itself to be read or written in the first place by the protagonist" (Brantlinger, "Missing Corpses," 25).

Someone must have, may have, falsely (or not) accused Josef K. The castle may or may not have requested K. While *The Trial* has an ending (but remains unfinished), the ending does not provide a sense a closure or order. Jean-Michel Rabaté has remarked that Josef K.'s death in fact adds to the confusion: "K.'s death is an anti-revelation by removing any possibility of illumination or final understanding. It only obfuscates the plot further."[69] *The Castle*, meanwhile, is unfinished and ends mid-sentence. The reader will never uncover the backstory.

Another way in which Kafka's later novels are often framed as being similar to detective novels is the protagonists' investigations, which are not necessarily an analysis of the past. Josef K. tries to figure out how the court works, K. to understand the castle in order to reach it. As discussed in the first section of this chapter, emphasizing one or the other of these ways in which Kafka's novels relate to detective fiction often affects whether a critic views Kafka as a modernist or postmodernist writer. These two modes of investigation also reveal two ways of understanding Buzzati's and Capriolo's novels.

In *The Tartar Steppe*, Drogo desires to know both the history of the fort and how it currently functions, in all its details. It seems that these two investigations will help him understand his role at the fort, why he stays there, and his destiny. This split between discovering the embedded story and determining the present situation is more distinct in Capriolo's novel than in those of Kafka and Buzzati. In *The Dual Realm*, Cara (dear), as other characters eventually call her, looks for a way out of a hotel she ran into when fleeing the huge wave. Cara arrives at the hotel having lost almost all her memories, including what her name is. The diary, which constitutes the novel, begins with her age, which she can assess based only on her physical appearance: "I think I'm about thirty."[70] She wonders whether she caused the wave or whether her reaction to it perhaps led to her punishment, not being able to discover a way out of the hotel: "I pass through this quarter without calling out, without giving the alarm. I can think only of saving myself. I sometimes ask myself whether this is why I'm being punished."[71] Cara tries to recover her past, which includes everything about herself and her experiences of the world before she entered the hotel. Since Cara's own memory seems to be erased, with the exception of the morning she

---

69 Rabaté, *Crimes of the Future*, 181.
70 Capriolo, *Dual*, 3. ("Credo di avere una trentina d'anni"; Capriolo, *Il doppio*, 9.)
71 Capriolo, *Dual*, 7. ("Attraverso il quartiere senza chiamare, senza dar l'allarme: riesco a pensare soltanto alla mia salvezza. A volte mi domando se non sia questa la colpa per la quale sono punita"; Capriolo, *Il doppio*, 16.)

entered the hotel, Capriolo's novel thematizes and makes obvious the idea of a missing story as its organizing force.

The current mystery for the protagonist of *The Dual Realm* is what the hotel is, exactly, including how it functions, how it is structured, what it means, whether the protagonist can leave it, and whether it is the last edifice left on earth. When Cara arrives at the hotel, she has innumerable questions about how it works: "I asked myself how the management of a hotel in which only one guest was staying – and what's more, a guest whose needs were so few – could be so demanding."[72] The mystery of who the protagonist is and what the hotel is intertwine as the novel progresses: as Cara takes on more of the hotel's routine, who she was becomes less important. By the end, she and the hotel have merged in her mind. The last page of the work, a letter to one of the people with whom she considered escaping the hotel, makes clear the symbiotic relationship between the narrator and the hotel: "Maybe you'll come back again some say, when the hotel feels the need to play with you, or maybe your person will be forgotten forever. And I too, most surely will forget it, for that will is my will, and the memory I thought was mine, isn't mine, because, dear Guido, I am nothing, or, if I am anything at all, I am the hotel."[73]

The closing lines of the work reveal Cara's acceptance of the erasure of her past, the only way that she will be able to exist peacefully with the hotel. Similarly, Drogo's interest in how the fort works increasingly forms his identity in *The Tartar Steppe*. Every time it seems that Drogo will be able to leave the fort, the combination of his desire to understand it better and his compliance with its rules prevent him. The fact that Drogo and Cara do not leave can be understood using the same dichotomy between the desire to obey and the desire to know. These two elements, one that is often framed as negative (passive acceptance) and the other as positive (curiosity and imagination) are also used to interpret the situations in Kafka's novels. For instance, Josef K. is alternately accused of having accepted his trial and of pursuing it.

---

72 Capriolo, *Dual*, 17. ("Mi domandai come potesse essere tanto impegnativa la direzione di un albergo dove era ospitato un solo cliente, e un cliente che per giunta dava assai poco da fare"; Capriolo, *Il doppio*, 31.)

73 Capriolo, *Dual*, 105. ("Tornerà forse, un giorno, quando l'albergo avrà di nuovo desiderio di giocare con Lei, o forse la Sua persona sarà dimenticata per sempre, e anch'io certamente la dimenticherò, perché quel volere è il mio volere, e la memoria che credevo mi appartenesse, neppure quella mi appartiene, perché io, caro Signore, non sono nulla, o se sono qualcosa sono l'albergo"; Capriolo, *Il doppio*, 168.)

The Castle also presents several mysteries about K.'s past: the question of whether he was summoned and whether he is indeed a surveyor are frequent points of examination. K. talks initially about his wife and child as reasons for wanting to become a surveyor: "If you're traveling so far from your wife and child as I am, you want to bring something worthwhile home."[74] Although K. mentions his family at the beginning of the novel, he later becomes engaged to a woman in the village, Frieda. The existence of both the wife and the fiancée have caused scholars to provide a range of answers for this seeming conflict, from Kafka's oversight to K.'s trickery. Walter Sokel, for instance, asserts that K. invents the wife and child out of a need for a backstory.[75]

Cara also desires a backstory, but while she proposes many, she cannot be sure of any of them. Capriolo makes the instability of her narrator and text one of the narrator's points of discussion. Her protagonist is in the position of the reader of *The Castle*, which never allows the reader to clearly see K.'s past, although there are glimpses of it. Like K., Capriolo's narrator may have a family about which she has forgotten: "I would also learn from my documents whether I was married or not. It could be that the man's face I remember, with the stern profile and high forehead, is my husband's. Perhaps I have children. But if that was so, could I really have forgotten?"[76] Readers of Kafka's *The Castle* have similarly asked whether K. could so easily forget his wife and child, but in Capriolo, the loss is underscored. Not only does the reader not know the protagonist's history, but the protagonist herself also asks how she could not know it.

The Castle, The Tartar Steppe, and *The Dual Realm* describe the increasing impossibility of the protagonists reaching their goals, their active acceptance of their positions, and the steady erasure of their past identities. As in detective fiction, identity is a key issue in these novels: "It is hardly necessary to point out that identity is the central theme of the detective novel, since the mystery of the criminal's identity is its *raison d'être*."[77] Whereas in most detective stories a key element is the affirmation of suspects' identities, the identities of the protagonists become less defined as the novels progress, in part because of the multiple

---

74 Kafka, *Castle*, 9. ("Wenn man wie ich so weit von Frau und Kind reist, dann will man auch etwas heimbringen"; Kafka, *Das Schloß*, 14.)

75 Sokel, "K. as Imposter."

76 Capriolo, *Dual*, 11. ("Dai documenti apprenderei anche il mio stato civile: chissà che quel volto d'uomo dal profilo severo, dalla fronte alta, non sia il volto di mio marito; chissà che io non abbia figli. Ma davvero, se così fosse, potrei averlo dimenticato?"; Capriolo, *Il doppio*, 21.)

77 Aisenberg, *A Common Spring*, 24.

investigations of the narratives and how they relate to the protagonists. *The Castle* leaves the reader with a "faceless hero."[78] *The Trial* recounts the "dismantling of a personality."[79] The destruction or dismantling of Drogo's and Cara's identities, as the protagonists become more dedicated to the fort and the hotel, respectively, is even more noticeable than in Kafka's novels.

The Castle and *The Dual Realm* raise questions about what parts of identity are fundamental, in part by preventing a secure view of the protagonists' pasts. Cara's dreams and flashbacks of her past are increasingly called into question and mix with her present. Her apparent, recovered memories of her former life may, in fact, be memories of texts she has read or re-imaginings of present interactions. They may also be real; neither she nor the reader can be sure. The unrecoverable past relates to the characters' unstable identities. Kafka's K. has an initial, but all Capriolo's protagonist has is a vague feeling about names: "The name 'Emma' makes me feel vindictive and fiercely antagonistic. Is she an enemy? Or a rival? Or is she me, and I have become hateful to myself through some wrong I have done but am unaware of?"[80] Although other characters call her Cara, a name often used by critics as well, she remains nameless, unsure of who she was. She thinks she may have been a poet, but some of the poetry she records is not her own but, for instance, Rilke's.[81] She questions her familial position (mother? daughter? wife? lover?) and job (author? translator?). Both who she was and who she is at the hotel are unclear. Capriolo's protagonist mentions at the beginning of her diary that she feels estranged from herself: "I use the word 'I' reluctantly, so alien and evanescent has it become for me."[82] While Kafka began *The Castle* using the first person, he found that it worked only with the distance and perspective of the third person. Written in the first person, *The Dual Realm* thematizes the difficulty of using *I* to narrate a story of lost identity.

In addition to having lost her memory and documents, Cara undergoes a series of physical changes, which dismantle her identity. She receives a masculine haircut, which makes her almost indistinguishable

---

78   Zilcosky, *Kafka's Travels*, 150.

79   Robertson, "Reading the Clues," 64.

80   Capriolo, *Dual*, 35. ("Così 'Emma' mi suscita rancore, violenta ostilità. Una nemica? Una rivale? O io stessa, resa a me stessa odiosa da una colpa che ignore?"; Capriolo, *Il doppio*, 59.)

81   For a more extensive discussion of the role of Rilke's poetry in the work, see Ania, "Cara's 'Creative' Writing"; and Hipkins, "Lost in the Art(ifice) of Male Language."

82   Capriolo, *Dual*, 3. ("È una parola [io] che adopero malvolentieri, tanto mi è divenuta estranea, evanescente"; Capriolo, *Il doppio*, 10.)

from the other male waiters: "'But you've cut it like a man's.' 'Madam, it's the only sort of cut I know.'"[83] Her hair does not grow back. Cara avoids mirrors because she now sees reflected a boy rather than a woman.[84] At the same time that she dislikes seeing her new appearance, Cara accepts a number of other changes that wear away at her identity, especially her identity as a woman: "I was maybe obeying an unconscious desire to be released as soon as possible from the external elements of my identity."[85] The protagonist gives up her own clothes to don a waiter's uniform: "It was a final invitation to capitulate, and yet the idea of wearing this uniform was disconcertingly attractive. Besides, I told myself, and not for the first time, that I really had no choice."[86] Over the course of the novel, her femininity is erased.

She adopts the rhythms of the hotel. When three strangers arrive in the second part of the novel, they mistake her for a waiter, raising the sinister idea that all "waiters" were originally "guests." With the three new guests, Laura, Bruno, and Guido, Cara experiments briefly with her female identity, putting on a borrowed dress, but ultimately decides to accept her new, ambiguous identity. Part of the loss of her former identity relates to becoming more like the other inhabitants of the hotel. In her reflection on using the word *I*, she relates that she holds onto it, in part to resist saying *we*: "However, appealing to the little faith I have left, I still make myself use it to resist that 'we' which increasingly forces itself on me with the violence of its normalcy."[87] Since the diary ends with the strong statement that Cara and the hotel are one, the reader could assume that she would use the first person plural to express herself, but she also no longer has the need to write.

While Cara's clothing, from her clothes to a waiter's uniform, temporarily to one of Laura's dresses, and then back to the waiter's uniform

---

83 Capriolo, *Dual*, 41. ("'È un taglio maschile.' 'Signora, è l'unico che io sappia eseguire'"; Capriolo, *Il doppio*, 68.)

84 "My forehead, my ears and the nape of my neck are all bare, and I see an awkard boy, not a woman" (Capriolo, *Dual*, 42). ("La fronte, le orecchie, la nuca, sono scoperte: davanti a me continua a comparire non una donna, ma un ragazzo disgraziato"; Capriolo, *Il doppio*, 70.)

85 Capriolo, *Dual*, 42. ("Forse obbendendo a un desiderio inconsapevole di liberarmi il più possibile dei tratti esteriori della mia identità"; Capriolo, *Il doppio*, 70; trans. modified.)

86 Capriolo, *Dual*, 43. ("Era la richiesta di una capitolazione finale, ma l'idea di indossare quell'abito esercitava su di me una sconcertante attrattiva. Inoltre, come già in tante occasioni, mi dissi che non potevo fare altrimenti"; Capriolo, *Il doppio*, 71.)

87 Capriolo, *Dual*, 3. ("Ma ancora mi sforzo di adoperarla [la parola *io*], ricorrendo alla poca fede che mi rimane, per resistere a quel 'noi' che sempre più mi si impone con la violenza della sua naturalezza"; Capriolo, *Il doppio*, 10.)

are sudden and their visual impact immediate, Drogo's clothing changes are more subtle, but similarly relate to the erasure of his old identity. His transformation takes place over a longer stretch of time. He feels increasingly distanced from his family, his romantic desires, his friends, and his home. He puts on a new cloak, his strongest connection to his old life, and admires himself in the mirror: "At last the trunk with Lieutenant Drogo's kit arrived from the city. Amongst it there was a brand new cloak of extreme elegance. Drogo put it on and looked at himself inch by inch in the little mirror in his own room. It seemed to him to be a living link with the world he had left and he thought with satisfaction how everyone would look at him, so splendid was the material, so proud its line."[88] He soon learns, however, that, in the military, he will be forced to forgo fashion and his sartorial desires: "'Fashion will have the collar low,' said the tailor, 'but for us soldiers fashion doesn't count.'"[89] A piece of home has arrived, but Drogo will be unable to enjoy it because he has accepted a uniform, like Cara. Another bit of his identity is chipped away as he succumbs to these new rules. Fort life prohibits him from standing out as an individual. No longer allowed to be elegant, he is distanced further from his past self and the city he called home.

The Castle, The Tartar Steppe, and The Dual Realm present assimilation as a potentially dangerous act. If K. accepts the rules of the village and the court, if Drogo accepts all the fort's routines, if Cara accepts the hotel's strictures, if they stop resisting, their identities may be lost. By accepting the rules of the places they hope to understand, they will never really be able to penetrate them, but will become part of them. While Cara cannot remember her family (if she has one), Drogo accepts his distance from his. The protagonists represent extremes on either side of The Castle: Drogo is detached from his home despite returning to it, and Cara has no idea what or where home is; with K., the situation is less clear. When Drogo later returns home to his old room, which

---

88 Buzzati, *The Tartar*, 40. ("Giunse finalmente dalla città la cassa con i vestiti del tenente Drogo. Fra l'altro c'era un mantello nuovissimo, di straordinaria eleganza. Drogo lo indossò e si guardò pezzo a pezzo nel piccolo specchio della propria stanza. Gli parve quello un vivo collegamento con il suo mondo, pensò con soddisfazione che tutti lo avrebbero guardato, tanto splendida era la stoffa, fiero il panneggiamento che ne risultava"; Buzzati, *Il deserto*, 43.) For a discussion of this and other sartorial choices in the novel that put Drogo's choices into historical and cultural context, see Nerenberg, *Prison Terms*, 51–2.

89 Buzzati, *The Tartar*, 41. ("'La moda vorrà il collo basso' disse il sarto, 'ma per noi militari la moda non c'entra. La moda ha da essere il regolamento'"; Buzzati, *Il deserto*, 44.)

has been left unchanged, he feels as though it belongs to someone else: "His bedroom was the same as before, just as he had left it; not a book had been moved, yet it did not seem to be his."[90] He feels out of place in his city: "A stranger, he wandered through the city seeking old friends; he heard that they were deep in affairs, in great enterprises, in their political careers."[91] Once Drogo's footsteps awoke his mother, while upon his return they no longer do: "There was no special reason for it, except that he was her son. But now it seemed that he was her son no more."[92] The loss of her hearing his footsteps implies a loss of the entire mother-son relationship.[93]

The woman Drogo thought he might marry also now seems to come from a different world: "And she had not changed either. But something had come between them."[94] The narrative repeatedly emphasizes the distance between Drogo and his fiancée. Their apparent past closeness occurred before the novel began: "But something had indeed come between them, an obscure indefinable veil which would not dissolve. Perhaps it had risen slowly day by day during the long separation, dividing them from each other and neither of them knew it."[95] The division between them is, in large part, due to Drogo's dedication to the fort and the loss of identity that this dedication entails. Drogo cannot be the charming, elegant fiancé and also a true participant in fort life. Only the memory of having been close to his fiancée remains.

In contrast to K.'s situation, Cara's and Drogo's transformations require the absence of love. Cara considers leaving the hotel, in part because of her attraction to the guest Guido. Rejecting this relationship leads to her decision to stay. The hotel offers an almost genderless, desire-less existence. Similarly, Drogo's rejection of love ensures that he

---

90 Buzzati, *The Tartar*, 124. ("La sua camera era rimasta identica, così come l'aveva lasciata, non un libro era stato mosso, pure, gli parve di un altro"; Buzzati, *Il deserto*, 128.)

91 Buzzati, *The Tartar*, 125. ("Straniero, girò per la città, in cerca dei vecchi amici, li seppe occupatissimi negli affari, in grandi imprese, nella carriera politica"; Buzzati, *Il deserto*, 129.)

92 Buzzati, *The Tartar*, 127. ("Nessuna speciale ragione, soltanto che lui era il figliolo. Ma adesso dunque non più"; Buzzati, *Il deserto*, 131.)

93 "Si accorge di essere divenuto estraneo a tutti: alla madre, agli amici, alla sua donna" (Asquer, *La grande torre*, 90).

94 Buzzati, *The Tartar*, 128. ("Anche lei non era mutata. Ma qualche cosa si era messo fra di loro"; Buzzati, *Il deserto*, 132.)

95 Buzzati, *The Tartar*, 130. ("Ma qualche cosa si era messo veramente fra loro, un velo indefinibile e vago che non voleva dissolversi; forse esso era cresciuto lentamente, durante la lunga separazione, giorno per giorno, dividendoli, e nessuno dei due lo sapeva"; Buzzati, *Il deserto*, 134.)

can live out his life at the fort. The hotel and the fort seem to promise a life that goes beyond the personal, beyond identity. While family, work, and love are goals in the world beyond the buildings, the protagonists instead dedicate themselves to where they are. The dismantling of identity corresponds to the protagonists' increasing dedication to their new institutions. Love and sex, meanwhile, are part of K.'s new life in the village, but are described as part of his loss of identity and assimilation into his new reality. His lovemaking with Frieda emphasizes that the experience takes him as far from home as possible:

> Hours passed there, hours breathing together with a single heartbeat, hours in which K. constantly felt he was lost or had wandered farther into foreign lands than any human being before him, so foreign that even the air hadn't a single component of the air in his homeland and where one would inevitably suffocate from the foreignness but where the meaningless enticements were such that one had no alternative but to go on and get even more lost.[96]

Being involved with Frieda is a completely estranging experience, and even his way of breathing seems changed by it; it distances him further from his previous identity.

After making love with Frieda all night, K. discovers that they had not been alone since his assistants had been watching them the whole time: "We've been sitting here all night. Being your assistants isn't an easy job."[97] Not only does sex cause K. to feel far from his former self, but he also realizes that his new location allows no privacy. Privacy in *The Castle*, as in *The Trial*, *The Tartar Steppe*, and *The Dual Realm*, is eroded or destroyed. Cara's door, one of her last vestiges of privacy, is removed and never put back. She feels constantly watched: "I didn't think I could bear being in full view of the waiters' gaze for the whole day or going through another night like the one I'd just spent."[98] Going

---

96 Kafka, *Castle*, 40. ("Dort vergingen Stunden, Stunden gemeinsamen Atems, gemeinsamen Herzschlags, Stunden, in denen K. immerfort das Gefühl hatte, er verirre sich oder er sei soweit in der Fremde, wie vor ihm noch kein Mensch, eine Fremde, in der selbst die Luft keinen Bestandteil der Heimatluft habe, in der man vor Fremdheit ersticken müsse und in deren unsinnigen Verlockungen man doch nichts tun könne als weiter gehn, weiter sich verirren"; Kafka, *Das Schloß*, 55.)

97 Kafka, *Castle*, 41. ("Hier sitzten wir die ganze Nacht. Leicht ist ja der Dienst nicht"; Kafka, *Das Schloß*, 56.)

98 Capriolo, *Dual*, 31. ("L'idea di rimanere esposta per l'intera giornata agli sguardi di camerieri e di trascorrere un'altra notte nelle condizioni della precedente mi parve intollerabile"; Capriolo, *Il doppio*, 53.)

to bed no longer provides comfort in these novels since the act of sleep (or, in K.'s case, making love) is surveilled, as K. discovers and Cara believes. While the goals of surveillance in detective fiction are justice and social order, Kafka, Buzzati, and Capriolo's novels emphasize surveillance without obvious goals.[99] The act of being watched adds to the protagonists' suspicions and the novels' suspense, but the ultimate reasons for these tensions remain obscure.

In all three novels, the protagonists lack control over their new space: "In *The Castle*, for example, every building is a potential home, but these homes are subject to the randomness of the world – and thus anathema to the notion of a true shelter."[100] Unmoored, home is everywhere and nowhere. In *The Dual Realm*, the world outside the hotel may have been destroyed, Cara does not remember where she comes from, and a hotel is necessarily not home-like, no matter what commercials may claim. Cara expresses nostalgia for the idea of home, but the idea involves even more distance than *nostalgia* generally does since she feels a longing for an empty concept: "Since my arrival here I have felt quite nostalgic, and often I linked the word 'home' with this feeling. It is almost invariably empty of meaning, simply a name with no image attached to it, but sometimes a detail will resurface unexpectedly, and so clearly."[101] Drogo visits his home, but *home* has lost all the qualities generally associated with it.

Home, in the sense of where they now dwell (the village, the fort, the hotel) is, meanwhile, neither private, nor stable, nor familiar. K. moves from temporary lodging to temporary lodging.[102] Drogo and Cara have no control over their new space; they cannot make themselves at home. Drogo describes the sounds, like water dripping from a cistern and perhaps people sleeping in his vicinity, that disrupt his sleep: "From far, far away – or had he imagined it? – there came the sound of a cough. Then close by a soft drip of water sounded in the wall."[103]

---

99 Dombroski, *Creative Entanglements*, 97.
100 Zilcosky, *Kafka's Travels*, 146.
101 Capiolo, *Dual*, 21. ("Con la nostalgia che mi affligge da quanto sono qui collego spesso la parola 'casa.' Quasi sempre si tratta di un concetto vuoto, di un semplice nome al quale non è associata nessuna imagine, ma a volte un particolare riaffiora all'improvviso e mi si para davanti con estrema precisione"; Capriolo, *Il doppio*, 38.)
102 Weinstein characterizes these spaces as stand-ins for the unreachable castle: "The Castle itself – seemingly near in the novel's opening sentence ... is of course unreachable. In its place are numerous, dreamlike, substitute spaces – inns, carriages, barrooms, classrooms (with K. and Frieda undressed as the students arrive: what could be more oneiric?), bedrooms, rooms of corridors" (Weinstein, *Unknowing*, 140).
103 Buzzati, *The Tartar*, 25. ("Lontanissimo, ma era poi vero? giunse un colpo di tosse. Poi, vicino, un flaccido 'ploc' d'acqua, che si propagò per i muri"; Buzzati, *Il deserto*, 27.)

Cara's situation is even more dire since the objects in her room are immovable: "Everything had to remain exactly as it was as time passed, and if I happened to move one of the few objects which were not fixed to the furniture or walls, the next time I left my room, someone would unfailingly take the opportunity of putting it back in its original place. I gradually got used to leaving things where they were, or putting them back in their right places myself."[104] Cara adapts herself to the hotel since the hotel cannot be adapted to her needs or desires.

Cara appears to dwell in a mysterious space that does not allow her to leave any traces of herself. Objects even lack a certain amount of physicality in her new world: "One of the strangest characteristics of this place is the fact that many things remain hidden in shadow until a light is turned on and exposes them, never very clearly, but as if they are suspended between being and non-being [*l'essere e il non essere*]."[105] In addition to objects not being movable, they hover between existence and non-existence. The idea of being able to leave a mark, that one's physical presence necessarily alters one's surroundings is an integral part of much of detective fiction. Walter Benjamin describes the idea of traces as being fundamental to the origins of the detective novel:

> The interior was not only the private citizen's universe, it was also his casing. Living means leaving traces. In the interior, these were stressed. Coverings and antimacassars, boxes and casings, were devised in abundance, in which the traces of everyday objects were moulded. The resident's own traces were also moulded in the interior. The detective story appeared, which investigated these traces.[106]

In detective novels, homes are often broken into or damaged, but, when these traces are followed, they return to safety or normalcy.[107] While in literary detective novels this interruption may not be resolved, in

---

104 Capriolo, *Dual*, 24. ("Tutto doveva mantenere nel tempo una perfetta immutabilità, e si mi accadeva di spostare uno dei pochi oggetti che non fossero fissati ai mobili o alle pareti, qualcuno approfittava immancabilmente della mia assenza per ricondurli alla posizione originaria. A poco a poco mi abituai a lasciarli dov'erano o a rimetterli a posto io stessa"; Capriolo, *Il doppio*, 42.)

105 Capriolo, *Dual*, 17. ("È una delle caratteristiche più bizzarre di questo luogo che molte cose rimangono nascoste nell'ombra finché un lume, accendendosi, le riveli, mai però con chiarezza, ma in uno stato come di sospensione fra l'essere e il non essere"; Capriolo, *Il doppio*, 31–2.)

106 Benjamin, *Charles Baudelaire*, 169.

107 On Gadda and home, see Nerenberg, *Prison Terms*, 151.

The Castle, The Tartar Steppe, and *The Dual Realm* homes no longer exist. The protagonists cannot alter their surroundings the way one would at home, and the idea of home itself has been shattered.

Eroding still further the idea of home, the disorienting geographies of the village, hotel, and fort raise questions about the idea of place. For instance, in a few sentences K. becomes confused about whether he is approaching the castle, when he is told that he is in fact "home":

> Where were they? Didn't their path go any further? Was Barnabas going to say goodbye to him now? He would not succeed. K. held Barnabas by the arm so tightly that it almost hurt his own fingers. Or could the incredible have happened, and they were already in the castle or at its gates? But so far as K. was aware they had not gone up any hill. Or had Barnabas led him along the path that climbed only imperceptibly? "Where are we?" K. asked quietly, more to himself than his companion. "Home" [*Zuhause*], said Barnabas just as quietly. "Home?"[108]

His walk with Barnabas so confuses K. that he even thinks, or hopes, that he has reached his destination, the castle. K. then reflects that despite his question of where "we" or "they" were, only Barnabas was home. The questions of where K. is and where he is going remain unanswered, perhaps unanswerable.

Related to their unreachable goals and unending investigations, K., Drogo, and Cara experience a great deal of confusion about where they are. The village's relationship to the castle, geographically and politically, confounds K. All three novels highlight problems of distance and related ones of perspective. As in *The Castle,* the beginning of Buzzati's novel emphasizes the difference between being visible and being reachable. Drogo's companion, who accompanies him for the first part of his journey, points to the fort not long after they leave the city. Despite how close the fort seems to be, Drogo rides on for hours. When he finally asks some people whether he is headed in the right direction, most of them have no idea what fort he is referring to, as though, in his approach, he were getting further away from his goal. If the story ended before Drogo

---

108 Kafka, *Castle*, 29–30. ("Wo waren sie? Gieng es nicht mehr weiter? Würde Barnabas K. verabschieden? Es würde ihm nicht gelingen. K. hielt des Barnabas Arm fest, daß es fast ihn selbst schmerzte. Oder sollte das Unglaubliche geschehen sein und sie waren schon im Schloß oder vor seinen Toren? Aber sie waren ja, soweit es K. wußte, gar nicht gestiegen. Oder hatte ihn Barnabas einen so unmerklich ansteigenden Weg geführt? 'Wo sind wir?' fragte K. leise, mehr sich als ihn. 'Zuhause,' sagte Barnabas ebenso. 'Zuhause?'"; Kafka, *Das Schloß*, 41.)

reached the fort, the work would appear even more analogous to *The Castle*. Instead, Drogo reaches the fort, but this beginning establishes that, more abstractly, he may never arrive where he wants to go. Cara, meanwhile, faces two related issues: understanding the geography of the hotel and finding an exit to leave it. While she comes to know the hotel layout better, she cannot (or chooses not to) discover a way out. In fact, her ultimate acceptance that she will not find an exit contributes to her gaining a better understanding of the hotel.

All three protagonists occupy spaces, portions of which they are not allowed to enter or even, it seems, approach, but about which they will often wonder. K., Drogo, and Cara inhabit spaces with three types of constriction. Cara's entrapment is the clearest: stuck inside a hotel, she cannot, and then chooses not to, leave. Drogo also initially would like to leave the fort, but he finds its environs, its mysteries, and its potential meaning intriguing. Although physically capable of leaving the fort, he stays. K., meanwhile, seems to be facing a different problem: a building he would like to have access to, but does not. All three protagonists, though, are stuck in a space of anticipation. The differences in their situations reveal distinct ideas about the act of waiting and interpretation, as well as the meaning of mystery, as will be discussed in the following section.

Prisons of Analysis and the Pull of Imagination

In "The Guilty Vicarage," W.H. Auden points to the function of guilt and the fact that the protagonist must search for his crime as two factors that primarily distinguish Kafka's *The Trial* from detective stories.[109] The strangeness of being accused of something one has been investigating, of being seemingly trapped in a prison of one's own making, recalls Kafka in a number of detective works.[110] In Borges's "Death and the Compass," detective Erik Lönnrot follows a series of intricate clues to find a murderer before he claims his fourth victim, but it turns out

---

109 Auden, "The Guilty Vicarage," 412.

110 Scott Turow's *Presumed Innocent* provides a more popular example of a Kafkaesque detective novel. When the protagonist is arrested for the crime he has been investigating, he references Kafka in a conversation with his defence lawyer (Turow, *Presumed Innocent*, 154). Tracing a series of acts of corruption at all levels of law enforcement, from police officers to judges, *Presumed Innocent* explores the relationship between power and the function of the law as well as who can potentially escape the law. A reader of *Presumed Innocent* could spend a portion of the detective novel wondering whether the accused, Rusty, deserves his accusation because he may have murdered his former lover.

that the clues were created to trap Lönnrot himself.[111] Having the proclivity to interpret and entering the labyrinth of analysis is what leads
Lönnrot to his death.[112] Borges "felt" and "hoped" that the story was
like Kafka.[113]

Josef K., K., Giovanni Drogo, and Cara can be seen as the investigators, victims, and perpetrators of their stories. They perhaps make
their own prisons, and the distinctions among prison, prisoner, investigator, and victim blur. *The Trial, The Castle, The Tartar Steppe,* and *The
Dual Realm* raise the question of the investigation itself as a form of
self-punishment. The novels also threaten to trap their readers in a torture chamber of interpretation. Not only is the relationship between the
investigator and the investigation problematic in Kafka, Buzzati, and
Capriolo, but the questions asked by the protagonists also raise unsolvable issues for the reader.[114]

Frank Kermode analyses how detective fiction forces an examination of hermeneutics: "Ideally, however, we are always sorting out the
hermeneutically relevant from all the other information, and doing so
much more persistently than we have to in other kinds of novel. For
although all have hermeneutic content, only the detective story makes
it preeminent."[115] The novels of Kafka, Buzzati, and Capriolo contain numerous questions that seem to make the hermeneutic context
pre-eminent. A first-time reader may ask these questions along with the
protagonists, but, unlike in most detective fiction, they will not lead to

---

111 See Bell-Villada's discussion of "Death and the Compass" in *Borges and His Fiction*,
    195–200. "He had virtually solved the problem; the mere circumstances, the reality
    (names, arrests, faces, the paperwork of trial and imprisonment), held very little
    interest for him now.... He reflected that the explanation for the crimes lay in an
    anonymous triangle and a dusty Greek word" (Borges, *Collected Fictions*, 153).
112 Borges repeatedly provides Kafka as a point of comparison in discussions of Ches-
    terton's compelling literary qualities (Borges, *Other Inquisitions*, 84). He contributed
    as both editor and author to promoting "the idea that a detective story could also ᵕ
    be literary" (Borges, *Conversations*, 24).
113 "I wrote a detective story, in a sense out of Kafka; it was called 'Death and the
    Compass.' When it was finished, I felt it was like Kafka, I hope so" (Borges, 218).
114 The role of questions in *Presumed Innocent*, as a representation of more typical,
    albeit Kafkaesque, detective fiction, contrasts with their role in Kafka, Buzzati, and
    Capriolo. Re-examining a photo, Rusty realizes how odd it is that his dead lover
    would have thirteen glasses, instead of a traditional set of twelve: "So the missing
    glass would make thirteen?" (Turow, *Presumed Innocent*, 254). Along with the law-
    yer, the accused asks where this extra glass could have come from, a question that
    leads Rusty, and perhaps also the reader, to solve the mystery. The reader can de-
    termine the significance of the thirteenth glass only if she or he can distinguish this
    information from the less important details in the narration.
115 Kermode, "Novel and Narrative," 181.

solutions. Many of the questions asked in *The Dual Realm* and *The Tartar Steppe*, as in *The Castle*, remain unanswered and unanswerable. The significance of these questions contributes to the mystery about what the mystery is, in contrast to those in works with a solvable or identifiable mystery. Robert Alter highlights this role of interpretation and uninterpretability in Kafka's novel: "His characters, especially in *The Castle* repeatedly argue or trade hypotheses about what things, or actual texts, mean. This is a world of elaborately argued conjecture constantly shadowed by the suspicion that his conjectures are wrong."[116] The novels of Kafka, Buzzati, and Capriolo demand reconsideration.

The novels make use of a technique from detective fiction, the asking of questions, to draw the reader's attention to an issue (or clue), to raise awareness of the investigator's method and thought process, and to point to issues that a traditional detective novel would generally resolve: "The special quality of the detective story, one that distinguishes it from all other fiction, is the fact that the blanks in the story are *programmed* by the genre; that is, the blanks themselves suggest methods of discovery."[117] The numerous questions in Kafka, Capriolo, and Buzzati, however, lead just to more questions, rather than conclusive answers. Many of the quotations discussed in the remainder of the chapter will contain questions and provide key moments of reflection in which the reader can ask about the village, castle, fort, or hotel, the identities of the protagonists, and the relationships between the protagonists and others dwelling in their places of exploration. The protagonists do not trust their new institutions and have questions about everyone in any way connected to the castle, fort, and hotel. At the same time, although initially unsure of their own roles in their new dwelling places, they eventually seem to become part of the societies they distrust. If literary detective novels often ask the reader to question the government or one part of society, the works of Kafka, Buzzati, and Capriolo ask the reader to question all elements of society.

The Castle contains numerous questions that reveal how K. does not trust others and does not feel trusted. Critics have asserted that we know that K. lies, although we know very little else about him.[118] Equally notable, K. constantly worries that others are lying to him or misrepresenting themselves: "To begin with he had moved close to his guest, but now he seemed to want to run away. Was he afraid of being

---

116 Alter, *Necessary Angels*, 78.
117 Dove, *The Reader and the Detective Story*, 22.
118 See Dowden, *Kafka's Castle and the Critical Imagination*, 36; and Sokel, "K. as Imposter."

interrogated about the count? Did he fear that, although he was now calling his guest 'sir,' K. was not to be relied on?"[119] Like detective work, Kafka's, Buzzati's, and Capriolo's novels evoke mistrust, but, unlike in detective fiction, the resolution of whom one can trust and why does not happen. Adorno states, "Universal suspicion, a trait etched deeply into the physiognomy of the present age, [Kafka] learned from the detective novel."[120] With their suspicions come the protagonists' imagined answers to their questions, which ultimately help ground them in their new locations.

Soon after arriving at the hotel, Cara asks, "Where is the way out [*uscita*]?"[121] The waiter's lack of knowledge causes Cara to mistrust him as well as the hotel, which no one seems to leave. Drogo similarly wonders whether he is being trapped into staying at the fort: "Supposing all Matti's hair-splitting was an act he put on? Suppose in actual fact they didn't let him go at the end of four months? Suppose they kept him from seeing the city again with excuses and quibbles about regulations? Suppose he had to stay up there for years and years, in this room, in this solitary bed, suppose he had to waste all his youth? What absurd things to think, said Drogo to himself."[122] His absurd hypothesis proves partly true: he will remain at the fort for years. What Matti's role is, exactly, remains unanswered, but Drogo and his questions, such as these, partially create the path his life took. In other words, he imagines he will stay forever, and therefore he does.[123]

The novels suggest a psychological connection between the protagonists and their potential prisons – the court, castle-village, fort, and hotel. In part because the idea of home has been destroyed, the spaces that K., Drogo, and Cara inhabit are compared to prisons, although they may be constructed by the protagonists themselves. Both protagonists of Kafka's later two novels have been accused of causing their

---

119 Kafka, *Castle*, 9. ("Zuerst hatte er sich an K. herangedrängt und nun schien es, als wolle er am libesten weglaufen. Fürchtete er über den Grafen ausgefragt zu werden? Fürchtete er die Unzuverlässigkeit des 'Herrn' für den er K. hielt?"; Kafka, *Das Schloß*, 14.)

120 Adorno, *Prisms*, 265.

121 Capriolo, *Dual*, 14. ("Dove è l'uscita?"; Capriolo, *Il doppio*, 27.)

122 Buzzati, *The Tartar*, 27. ("E se le sottilizzazioni del Matti fossero tutte una commedia? Se in realtà, anche dopo i quattro mesi, non lo avessero più lasciato partire? Se con sofistici pretesti regolamentari gli avessero impedito di rivedere la città? Se avesse dovuto rimanere lassù per anni e anni, e in quella stanza, su quel solitario letto, si fosse dovuta consumare la giovinezza. Che ipotesi assurde, si diceva Drogo"; Buzzati, *Il deserto*, 29.)

123 As Crotti has discussed, suspense structures Drogo's life (Crotti, *Tre voci sospette*, 48).

own entrapment: "Utopia means the impossibility of K. His repressed, self-absorbed, abusive nature *is* the castle that prevents him from achieving his own aim."[124] The issue of why Drogo has been assigned to Fort Bastiani, a constant but perhaps irrelevant question, raises the idea that he did something to deserve his posting, a sort of punishment: "Once it was an honour, Fort Bastiani, now it almost seems to be a punishment."[125] Since Drogo mentions the fort's physical similarities to a prison, but wants to get to know it better, he repeatedly accedes to this potential punishment.[126]

Physical spaces and mental ones mix and are confused in Kafka, Buzzati, and Capriolo. One of the strangers is concerned that Cara does not recognize that the hotel has become her prison: "Were you aware, my dear [*cara*], that convicts often become attached to their prisons?"[127] Cara herself worries that she is being punished, without knowing why: "The most terrible hell I can imagine is a place where the damned soul has forgotten the sin for which it is being punished. It would therefore not even have a sense of expiation to relieve its suffering, or the knowledge that this was ordained by some sort of justice, human or divine, something which could be understood."[128] It is not clear whether Cara is guilty and, if she is, of what. In Capriolo, the narrator makes an observation that critics have so often made about Kafka's novels: "Maybe the hotel is nothing more than the cage I've constructed for myself, the spatial translation of some unrecognized obsession."[129]

From newspaper articles to popular culture, unjust imprisonment is repeatedly associated with Kafka. In a discussion of his "Il conte di Montecristo" ("The Count of Montecristo"), Calvino agrees with his interlocutor, Luigi Baldacci, that the story is Kafka-like, especially in the parts that discuss the relationship between an innocent prisoner

---

124 Dowden, *Kafka's Castle*, 138. See also Brantlinger, "Missing Corpses," 33; and
     Grossvogel, *Limits of the Novel*, 174.
125 Buzzati, *The Tartar*, 12. ("Una volta era un onore la Fortezza Bastiani, adesso par
     quasi una punizione"; Buzzati, *Il deserto*, 14.)
126 "He thought of a prison, he thought of an abandoned palace" (Buzzati, *The Tartar*, 14).
     ("Pensò a una prigione, pensò a una reggia abbandonata"; Buzzati, *Il deserto*, 15.)
127 Capriolo, *Dual*, 77. ("Sapeva, cara, che spesso i reclusi si affezionano alla loro
     prigione"; Capriolo, *Il doppio*, 125.)
128 Capriolo, *Dual*, 28. ("L'inferno più atroce che posso immaginare è quello in cui al
     dannato sia sottratta la memoria del pecato per il quale è punito: a lenire le soffer-
     enze non avrebbe neppure il sentimento dell'espiazione, la consapevolezza che
     esse gli sono imposte da una giustizia umana o divina, ma comunque comprensi-
     bile"; Capriolo, *Il doppio*, 49.)
129 Capriolo, *Dual*, 95. ("Forse l'albergo stesso è soltanto la gabbia che mi sono fabbri-
     cata, il farsi spazio di un'ignota ossessione"; Capriolo, *Il doppio*, 153.)

and his prison: "As for the Kafkaism in 'The Count of Montecristo,' when I wrote: 'Everything that is unclear in the relationship between an innocent prisoner and his prison continues to cast shadows etc.' I was intentionally referring to Kafka, suggesting a total depersonalization as the only way out."[130] This depersonalization emphasizes the idea of analysis in the works. Calvino later writes, "You are probably right when you say that my attitude attenuates the 'dramatic nature of language,' it 'depersonalizes' it. Yes, my Montecristo wants to escape from the existential drama of the prisoner (Kafka's K.), to depersonalize his tension, as a necessary condition for escaping from the prison. And if one looks closely, K. too – or rather Kafka's style of abstract precision – was a decisive step in his direction; Kafka can be read in these two ways: as the 'story of a soul' and/or as the description of a network of objective relationships, and I think the latter approach is more important."[131]

Calvino's characterization of Kafka sheds a slightly different light on the idea of K.'s loss of identity. K., Drogo, and Cara are also the investigators, the analysers, and the interpreters of their situations. They all, in other words, try to read their situations: "If Calvino's characters, like Kafka's, tend to confront the arbitrariness of encompassing systems, successful reading invariably comprises the only escape from the prison."[132] Their situations, especially in the castle, fort, and hotel, are akin to literature that they attempt to analyse. As they are also embedded in these situations, they must necessarily depersonalize and interpret themselves.

The Castle's K. claims to be a land surveyor. Drogo is a soldier, but since he never participates in a battle, he spends a majority of his work surveying the land where an enemy might appear and the fort he resides in. These watchers not only comment on the significance of what they see, interpreting events, but their analysis also invites the reader to interpret: "The necessity to interpret engages the reader of Kafka at a particularly intimate level because it is exactly the failure of the Kafka protagonist to interpret his situation successfully that leads to his destruction within the text.... The Castle within the novel plays the same role for K. as does the text of the novel for the meaning-hungry

---

130 Calvino, *Italo Calvino*, 342. ("Quanto al kafkismo del *Montecristo* quando ho scritto 'Tutto quel che c'è di non chiaro nel rapporto tra un prigionero innocente e la sua prigione continua a gettare ombra ecc.' [p. 158] mi ricollegavo intenzionalmente a Kafka proponendo una assoluta spersonalizzazzione come unica via d'uscita"; Calvino, *Lettere*, 982.)

131 Calvino to Boselli, 23 October 1969, *Italo Calvino*, 379.

132 Sussman, *High Resolution*, 206. The relationship between the prisoner and his walls becomes a matter of interpretation and reflection in Calvino's story (Sussman, 200).

interpreter."[133] Both the unreachable castle for K. and the unreachable lands beyond the fort can be seen as representing the interpretation of literature.*The Castle* also provides the reader with an incomplete picture of K., the castle, and the village: "Because K. gains no visual high ground throughout the novel, he can never sufficiently organize the village as a view, can never frame or map it. He thus remains *inside of* what he is trying to measure and describe. He is not a distinct subject (the hero of a narrative of self-discovery detachedly observing objects) but a subject who is also an object among objects. Part of the field he attempts to survey, K. is beginning to grasp however dimly, that he is both subject and object at once."[134] Trying to escape or move forwards, K. and Cara realize how embedded they are.

The only option for potential escape appears to be analysis, which provokes the issue of self-imprisonment discussed above. Cara is more aware of and open about her dilemma than K. Cara interprets herself, her past, and the hotel in the same mode: "It's as if I were looking at my inner life in a mirror that dismantles it and rearranges it according to its own laws, altering its nature, distorting every single detail; and I myself am both the distorted and the real image, I am both eye that watches and the mirror."[135] As Cara analyses herself and the hotel, these two acts increasingly intermingle and become one. Because of Cara's inside-outside perspective, her view, like the reader's, will always be partial. Gillian Ania clarifies, "And yet Cara has no memory, no name, no identity; she is both subject and object of her account, and she constantly questions and distrusts what she writes."[136] Cara presents the impossible struggle to escape from language, which Capriolo interprets as the prison Kafka portrays: "The fundamental mechanism for Kafka becomes precisely language, which is the machine within which everyone is imprisoned."[137]

The Tartar Steppe becomes increasingly introspective towards the end, forcing the reader to be ever more aware of his or her interpretive role. While earlier chapters began with descriptions of events, later ones start more abstractly: "Another page turns, the months and the years

---

133 Bernheimer, "Symbolic Bond and Textual Play," 367–8.
134 Zilcosky, *Kafka's Travels*, 138.
135 Capriolo, *Dual*, 101. ("È come se osservassi la mia vita interiore in uno specchio che la scompone e la ricompone secondo leggi proprie alterandone l'insieme, distorcendone ogni singolo particolare, e io stessa sono l'immagine illusoria e quella vera, e sono l'occhio che guarda, e sono lo specchio"; Capriolo, *Il doppio*, 162.)
136 Ania, "Cara's 'Creative' Writing," 160.
137 "Il meccanismo fondamentale per Kafka diventa così proprio il linguaggio, che è esso stesso la macchina dentro la quale tutti sono imprigionati" (Mazza, "Intervista su Gregor Samsa").

go by."[138] Although many other books reference their own materiality, how they differ from the comments in *The Tartar Steppe* illustrates
Buzzati's modernism. Jane Austen used the material fact of pages to
mark that her novel was nearing its end: "The anxiety, which in this
state of their attachment must be the portion of Henry and Catherine,
and of all who loved either, as to its final event, can hardly extend, I fear,
to the bosom of my readers, who will see in the tell-tale compression
of the pages before them, that we are all hastening together to perfect
felicity."[139] This moment of meta-reflection in *Northanger Abbey* gives
the reader reassurance that the plot's arc will soon come to a desirable
end. Buzzati's novel provides no similar reassurances, but uses the
turning of the pages as another opportunity for imagination.

While readers of Austen know that they are reaching the end of the
story, readers of Buzzati are invited to imagine how much time has
passed between the chapter and the previous one, using the materiality
of the pages to mark an unknown period of time. The pages indicate
the passage of time for someone whose life does not follow a typical
narrative progression: "So a page is slowly turned, falls over to join the
others, the ones already finished. It is still only a thin layer. Those still to
be read are inexhaustible in comparison. But it is always another page
finished, a portion of your life."[140] The pages represent portions of a life
that could seem meaningless.

Although Drogo never engages in battle and nothing in the work has
really "happened," shortly before his death he looks out the window
into the sky and smiles: "Giovanni makes an effort and straightens his
shoulder a little; he puts right the collar of his uniform with one hand
and takes one more look out of the window, the briefest of glances,
his last share of the stars. Then in the dark he smiles, although there is
no one to see him."[141] Drogo seems to have arrived at the peace of not

---

138 Buzzati, *The Tartar*, 176. ("Si volta pagina, passano mesi ed anni"; Buzzati, *Il deserto*, 180.)
139 Austen, *Northanger Abbey*, 211.
140 Buzzati, *The Tartar*, 122–3. ("Così una pagina lentamente si volta, si distende dalla
     parte opposta, aggiugendosi alle altre già finite, per ora è solamente uno strato
     sottile, quelle che rimangono da leggere sono in confronto un mucchio inesauribile.
     Ma è pur sempre un'altra pagina consumata, signor tenente, una porzione di vita";
     Buzzati, *Il deserto*, 127.)
141 Buzzati, *The Tartar*, 198. ("Facendosi forza, Giovanni raddrizza un po' il busto, si
     assesta con una mano il colletto dell'uniforme, dà ancora uno sguardo fuori della
     finestra, una brevissima occhiata, per l'ultima sua porzione di stelle. Poi nel buio,
     benché nessuno lo veda, sorride"; Buzzati, *Il deserto*, 202.) For discussions of this
     smile, see Germani, "Il segreto e la morte," 25–32, especially as a Heideggerian an-
     ticipation of death; and Bellaspiga, *Il deserto*, 104–6.

knowing, the joy of having imagined. The description of him adjusting his uniform emphasizes his participation in fort life. He rejected taking part in what for most is seen as the normal world, but the fort represents life, as Bárberi Squarotti has argued: "The fort, the infinite and mysterious space of the desert, are the wonderfully clear and depicted allegories of the human condition."[142] Although his life could be described as a wasted one, a total dedication to an enemy he never faced, Drogo does not view his life as hopeless. He gives his own life meaning, or at least one moment of looking up and imagining meaning. Even though nothing really happens to Drogo, he dies with a smile because of what he was able to imagine could have happened. Drogo's end reveals how even the most banal moments can appear mysterious.

While there are numerous responses to the question of why Drogo does not leave the fort until he is forced to, an important one is anticipation. Nothing is as important in the fort as what he imagines could be in, or around, it. About to sign papers that would allow him to leave, he looks out the window:

> Never before had Drogo noticed that the Fort was so complicated and immense. At an almost incredible height he saw a window (or a loophole?) open on to the valley. Up there there must be men whom he did not know – perhaps even an officer like himself with whom he could be friends. In the abyss between bastion and bastion he saw geometrical shadows, frail bridges suspended among the rooftops, strange postern gates barred and flush with the walls, ancient machicolations now blocked up, long roof-trees curved with the years.[143]

The text casts doubt even on what Drogo is looking through (a window? a loophole?), or thinks he is looking through, as well as what he observes. The estranging and intriguing geography of the fort engages his imagination, keeping him there year after year. For him, more powerful than friendship is the idea of friendship. The later chapters

---

142 "La fortezza, lo spazio infinito e misterioso del deserto ... sono le allegorie mirabilmente definite e descritte della condizione umana" (Bárberi Squarotti, "Note sulle principali opera," 56).

143 Buzzati, *The Tartar*, 54. ("Mai Drogo si era accorto che la Fortezza fosse così complicata ed immensa. Vide una finestra [o una feritoia?] aperta sulla vale, a quasi incredibile altezza. Lassù dovevano esserci uomini che egli non conosceva, forse anche qualche ufficiale come lui, del quale avrebbe potuto essere amico. Vide ombre geometriche di abissi fra bastione e bastione, vide esili ponti sospesi fra i tetti, strani portoni sprangati a filo delle muraglie, antichi spiombatoi bloccati, lunghi spigoli incurvati dagli anni"; Buzzati, *Il deserto*, 57; trans. modified.)

distance the reader from passively accepting Drogo's point of view and seem to instead align the narrator with the reader. In the second half of the work, the narrator addresses Drogo with comments like, "Don't think about it any more, Giovanni Drogo."[144] The narrator also asks the reader questions at the end of the novel: "Will Drogo manage to see it or will he have to go before then?"[145] The reader must be content with what he or she has imagined could have happened to Drogo. The work represents the pull of imagination and analysis, and it increasingly invites the reader to imagine and analyse.

Buzzati and Capriolo frame differently the idea that life, like literature, is an unsolvable, unanswerable mystery. In a comment on *The Castle*, Capriolo mentions that Kafka's protagonist never realized that "who searches, does not find, who does not look is then found."[146] Cara, meanwhile, finds a certain peace in her lack of comprehension since her acceptance of the mystery becomes her understanding. At the end of *The Dual Realm*, the protagonist sits in a garden and considers her decision to remain at the hotel.[147] Not only does she accept her new role there, but the hotel itself offers opportunities for reflection on what is missing: "The garden is there to show what the hotel is *not*, and because our existence is tranquil, it makes contemplating the opposite every now and then so pleasant, as we walk among these plants which display a kind of motionless yet violent struggle."[148] While Cara will never leave the hotel and K. never reach the castle, with her acceptance Cara comes to an understanding of her position and can contemplate what she will never achieve from within the hotel. Although in many ways more trapped than K., she is also at peace with her inability to know or escape since she decides to live out her existence in one location (the hotel) as opposed to trying to reach one (the castle). She embraces the endless freedom of imagination and analysis.

Unlike *The Castle*, which leaves K. forever searching for entry to the castle and no sign that he will ever arrive, Buzzati and Capriolo provide conclusions to their works, albeit ones that rule out the reader finding most answers. Capriolo's protagonist develops a relationship

---

144 Buzzati, *The Tartar*, 122. ("Non pensarci più, Giovanni Drogo"; Buzzati, *Il deserto*, 126.)
145 Buzzati, *The Tartar*, 198. ("Farà in tempo, Drogo, a vederla o dovrà andarsene prima?"; Buzzati, *Il deserto*, 202.)
146 "Chi cerca non trova, chi non cerca viene trovato" (Capriolo, "Il simbolo opaco," 27).
147 See Ania, introduction to *The Dual Realm*, xxix.
148 Capriolo, *Dual*, 46. ("Il giardino è lì per mostrare ciò che l'albero *non* è, e proprio la tranquillità della nostra esistenza rende così piacevole contemplarne di tanto in tanto l'opposto, passeggiare fra quelle piante che offrono l'immobile rappresentazione di una lotta furibonda"; Capriolo, *Il doppio*, 76.)

with people from outside the hotel who will be leaving it. She had the chance to go with Laura, Bruno, and Guido, but does not. The reader does not discover what has happened outside the hotel or the function of the hotel itself. Drogo, ill, leaves the fort just as the long-awaited battle perhaps begins. When he abandons the fort, so does the narrative, and the reader is prevented from knowing more about what happens there. Drogo dies away from the fort, in a hotel room. In *The Tartar Steppe*, unlike in *The Dual Realm* or *The Castle*, everything appears to happen: the long-awaited battle, Drogo leaving the fort, and Drogo's death. However, these occurrences do not resolve the questions that arose during the novel. The battle may take place, but Drogo does not take part in it. The role of the much-discussed enemy remains mysterious. Drogo experiences a death that appears to have nothing to do with the fort or the life he led. His death increases rather than diminishes the mystery. In *The Tartar Steppe*, Drogo, in fact, created most of the mysteries. The novel makes clear that the questions it raises do not have easy answers and that plot twists, unlike in most detective fiction, will bring neither reassurance nor resolution.

The novels are, in part, meditations on significance, and, because of this, for some readers they are, in the end, meaningless. More than one reader has mentioned finding *The Castle* boring. In a review entitled "Kafka o il castello della noia" (Kafka or the castle of boredom), Giovanni Papini offers one of the more lively descriptions of the boredom a reader may experience in the course of completing Kafka's third novel: "I finished reading Kafka's *The Castle*. I do not want to be envied or sympathized with: I am only saying that I was able to read all the way to the end the 467 pages of Franz Kafka's *The Castle*. In my life, I have read books that are longer, deeper, and more developed than *The Castle* of Franz Kafka, but rarely have I happened to read a book more boring, more tiresome, more tedious, more fastidious, and drizzly than this one."[149]

In *The Castle*, K. encounters new people and sees new places, but never gets where he is trying to go. The protagonists of Kafka, Buzzati, and Capriolo have entered a space of stasis, and some readers think they have as well. Situations in the novels almost repeat themselves over and over again. In each chapter of *The Tartar Steppe* Drogo, and often the

---

149 "Ho finito di leggere il *Castello* di Franz Kafka. Non voglio essere invidiato né compianto: dico soltanto che son riuscito a leggere fino in fondo le 467 pagine del *Castello* di Franz Kafka. Ho letto, nella mia vita, libri più lunghi, più profondi, più nutrivi del *Castello* del *Castello* di Franz Kafka, ma rarissime volte m'è capitato un libro più noioso, più uggioso, più tedioso, più fastidioso e piovigginoso di questo" (Papini, *La loggia dei busti*, 249).

reader, think that something may happen. There is repeated anticipation and then eventual let-down as Drogo grows old and dies. For large portions of the novel time seems to have stopped: "But it seemed as if Drogo's existence had come to a halt."[150] Cara enters a world where, for the first half of the novel, the greatest changes have to do with her becoming increasingly enmeshed in the routines of the hotel: "Here, the days follow on from one another with nothing to distinguish them, so that you almost lose any sense of the passing of time."[151] Her sense that the hotel is a space out of time extends to her claiming that, in the hotel, death cannot exist.

While boredom has been associated with *The Castle*, *The Tartar Steppe*, and *The Dual Realm*, on the part of the readers' and protagonists' experiences, readers do not associate boredom with detective stories. Gadda expects the reader to enjoy detective fiction: "The public has the right to be entertained."[152] Scholars have pointed out that finding Kafka boring indicates a misreading.[153] Readers who find *The Castle* boring could be accused of trying to read the work like a mystery novel:

> The classical detective story disposes of an interestingly paradoxical economy, at once prodigal and parsimonious. On one hand, the form is based on the hypothesis that everything might count: every character might be the culprit, and every action or speech might be belying its apparent banality or literalism by making surreptitious reference to an incriminating Truth. From the layout of the country house (frequently given in all the exactitude of a diagram) to the cigar ash found on the floor at the scene of the crime, no detail can be dismissed a priori. Yet on the other hand, even though the criterion of total relevance is continually invoked by the text, it turns out to have a highly restricted applicability in the end.[154]

In *The Castle*, *The Tartar Steppe*, and *The Deal Realm*, it is the opposite: everything counts because nothing necessarily applies. The novels' suspense shifts from what will happen to consideration of what the protagonists' searches will mean when nothing happens.

---

150 Buzzati, *The Tartar*, 64. ("L'esistenza di Drogo invece si era come fermata"; Buzzati, *Il deserto*, 67.)
151 Capriolo, *Dual*, 29. ("Qui i giorni si susseguono in modo così uniforme che quasi si perde il senso di fluire delle ore"; Capriolo, *Il doppio*, 50.)
152 "Il pubblico ha diritto di essere divertito" (Gadda, "Uno scrittore e il giallo," 125).
153 "Sometimes, when one misreads Kafka's novels, one finds them systematically long and interminable, indeed boring, because one judges things summarily" (Carrouges, "The Struggle," 29).
154 Miller, *The Novel and the Police*, 33.

Albert Camus comments, "The whole art of Kafka consists in forcing the reader to reread."[155] Other authors, like Auden, have noted that a distinction between Kafka's works and detective novels is that Kafka's works require rereading, whereas detective novels are works that are read just once. A part of this contrast relates to the issue of reading "for plot," as often occurs with detective fiction as opposed to reading for other, literary, theoretical, or philosophical reasons.[156] Gramsci considers the reasons why detective fiction, as opposed to literary works, are not reread: "The question, 'Why is detective literature widely read?' is only one aspect of a more general problem: why is non-artistic literature widely read? ... In reality one reads a book because of practical impulses (and one should find out why certain impulses are more general than others) and one re-reads for artistic reasons."[157]

Not only do *The Tartar Steppe* and *The Dual Realm* prompt rereading, but they also offer reflections on reading for "artistic reasons." The castle and the fort have been read as representing literature that the protagonists attempt to fully understand or reach, but never will, whereas the hotel has been interpreted as a space that exists in literature and reality simultaneously. Capriolo's novel asks about the relationship between literature and reality most insistently, especially since Cara herself poses many of the questions that critics have of *The Castle* and *The Tartar Steppe*. Cara's ultimate acceptance of not knowing relates to how closely her experience reflects literature.

Not only can the fort and the hotel be compared to literature and Drogo and Cara to frustrated readers, but the novels also contain numerous considerations of other art forms. In both novels, there is an emphasis on the artistic expression inherent in the austerity, repetition, and mystery. Capriolo's novel meditates on the beauty of formalism in several ways. Cara enters a library full of books written in an unknown script: "In all the books the sequence of letters on each page seems to follow laws of symmetry, contrast or rhythmic alternation, rather than any need to communicate, almost as if when the printer set them out, his sole aim was to embellish the page."[158] She

---

155 Camus, *The Myth of Sisyphus*, 147.

156 For a comment on how Kafka's *The Castle* and Buzzati's *The Tartar Steppe* share this quality of being of interest more symbolically than because of plot, see Mignone, *Anormalità e angoscia*, 103.

157 Gramsci, *Antonio Gramsci*, 372.

158 Capriolo, *Dual*, 36. ("In tutti i libri la successione dei caratteri su ciascuna pagina sembra obbedire non a esigenze di comunicazione, ma a leggi ora di simmetria, ora di contrasto, ora di ritmica alternanza, quasi che il tipografo, nel disporli, avesse avuto come unico scopo la decorazione del foglio"; Capriolo, *Il doppio*, 61.)

comes to find beauty in these works and can even point to qualitative differences between them despite never deciphering their linguistic code (if they have one).

In the novels, various art forms reflect the symmetry and beauty of the repeated experiences at the fort and in the hotel. They reveal the stark power that can be found in repetition and mystery. In *The Tartar Steppe*, more important than conciliatory beauty is order and mystery: "It was not imposing, Fort Bastiani, with its low walls, nor was it in any sense beautiful, nor picturesque with towers and bastions – there was not one single thing to make up for its bareness, to bring to mind the sweets of life. Yet as on the previous evening at the foot of the defile Drogo looked at it as if hypnotized and an inexplicable feeling of excitement entered his heart."[159] The rules and regulations contribute to what makes the fort a site of fascination, even a "masterpiece": "Scores and sores of men – thought Drogo – but for whom and why? It seemed as if in the Fort the rigid formalism of the military had created an insane masterpiece [*capolavoro*]."[160] The potential pointlessness of the fort increases its power, just as the lack of clear meaning of the books in the hotel adds to their particular fascination.

The novels reflect upon the different experiences an individual can have with diverse art forms. Portrayed as the great art of community, music is the art form that Drogo and Cara feel closest to as their ties to the fort and hotel strengthen. The trumpets of the Fortezza Bastiani, which play the communal music of heroic dreams, represent one of the reasons that Drogo stays there:

> They were the famous silver trumpets of Fort Bastiani, with cords of red and gold silk hung with a great coat of arms. Their pure note filled the sky and the motionless hedge of bayonets resounded with it, like the low resonance of a bell. The soldiers themselves were motionless as statues; their faces military and expressionless. It could not be that they were preparing

---

159 Buzzati, *The Tartar,* 14. ("Non era imponente, la Fortezza Bastiani, con le sue basse mura, né in alcun modo bella, né pittoresca di torri e bastioni, assolutamente nulla c'era che consolasse quella nudità, che ricordasse le dolci cose della vita. Eppure, come la sera prima dal fondo della gola, Drogo la guardava ipnotizzato e un inesplicabile orgasmo gli entrava nel cuore"; Buzzati, *Il deserto,* 16.)

160 Buzzati, *The Tartar,* 27. ("Decine e decine – pensava Drogo – ma per chi, per che cosa? Il formalismo militare, in quella fortezza, sembrava aver creato un insano capolavoro"; Buzzati, *Il deserto,* 29; trans. modified.) For more on the fort and form, see Bárberi Squarotti, "La fortezza e la forma."

for monotonous spells of guard duty; with such heroic mien they must surely be going to face the enemy.[161]

While listening to the trumpets, all the soldiers seem to feel that they are destined for greatness, that they are invested in a communal, worthwhile project. When Drogo returns to the city, not hearing the trumpets adds to his feelings of discomfort and desire to return to the fort: "His ear waited in vain for the sound of a trumpet."[162]

Music is a source of mystery and wonderment in the hotel as well. Cara concentrates on the flute music played and feels closer to understanding it when she is closer to the hotel. In the last section of the first part, before the arrival of the new guests, she achieves a new kind of understanding of the music:

> Last night, when I heard the flute, I went to the bar, and at the door I hid myself behind one of the pillars. For some time now, the short musical phrase which is repeated no longer sounds to me like a variation on a theme, but rather a progressive deepening of it. Now, I no longer hear the multiplicity of variations; I only make out, or rather, I intuit, the unchanging unity reflected in it.[163]

In the music she discovers unity, where she used to hear just repetition. Her experience of listening to the music transforms her sense of community: "For the first time, looking at the waiters around me, captivated like me by the music, I truly thought the word 'we.'"[164] She becomes the music, in a moment of extreme community: "Instead I was them, I was us, I was the flute and the music springing from it, and each

---

161 Buzzati, *The Tartar*, 29. ("Erano le famose trombe d'argento della Fortezza Bastiani, con cordoni di seta rossa e oro, con appeso un grande stemma. La loro voce pura si allargò per il cielo e ne vibrava l'immobile cancellata delle baionette, con vaga sonorità di campana. I soldati erano fermi come statue, i loro volti militarmente chiusi. No, certo essi non si preparavano ai monotoni turni di guardia; con quegli sguardi da eroi, certo – pareva – andavano ad aspettare il nemico"; Buzzati, *Il deserto*, 32.)

162 Buzzati, *The Tartar*, 126. ("Il suo orecchio aspettò inutilmente un suono di tromba"; Buzzati, *Il deserto*, 130.)

163 Capriolo, *Dual*, 47. ("Ieri notte, udendo il flauto suonare, raggiunsi il bar e mi nascosi dietro uno stipite della porta. Da tempo il reiterarsi di quella breve frase musicale non mi appare più la ripetizione di un tema attraverso le sue variazioni, ma un progressivo approfondimento di esso. Ormai non percepisco la molteplicità di tali variazioni, percepisco soltanto, o meglio, intuisco, l'unità inalterabile che vi si riflette"; Capriolo, *Il doppio*, 77.)

164 Capriolo, *Dual*, 47. ("Per la prima volta, guardando i camerieri intorno a me, insieme con me catturati dalla musica, pensai davvero la parola 'noi'"; Capriolo, *Il doppio*, 78.)

mind totally absorbed in listening to the same sounds."[165] Cara initially refused to play the flute, but at the end, after deciding to remain at the hotel forever, she accepts her part: "I put the flute to my lips and began to play. My fingers ran over the holes, composing melody which was quite different from that of the past."[166] With the acceptance of her life at the hotel, Cara is able to add her own music to it.

While music offers a space for potential unity for Drogo and Cara, Capriolo's and Buzzati's novels present literature and writing as more problematic.[167] Both Cara and Drogo become distanced from their past writing since it appears too tied to their previous identities. When Drogo returns home, he finds that his old diary and letters do not reflect any of his current feelings: "He was amazed that he had written them – he had no recollection of them, everything referred to strange forgotten incidents."[168] He feels distanced from his past self. Cara observes that her handwriting shifts, and she worries that she soon may not understand her own penmanship: "My handwriting is changing. It's regressing to a childish form with its larger letters. If I can still recognize it, I'll probably think I tried to narrate the improbable events of a novel with a fictitious character called 'I' as protagonist, and then I'll no longer open the notebook, not even to read it. I feel a sense of anguish when I realize that I now see this possibility as a release [*una liberazione*]."[169] This personal relationship to the protagonists' writing adds another element to how the texts reflect on the connections among them, the fort and the hotel, and literature. The act of writing relates to their old identities, which erode over the course of the novels and distance them from their own writing. Writing and literature connect

---

165 Capriolo, *Dual*, 48. ("Invece ero loro, ero noi, ero il flauto e la musica che ne scaturiva, e ciascuna delle menti sprofondate in un identico ascolto"; Capriolo, *Il doppio*, 79.)

166 Capriolo, *Dual*, 104. ("Ho accostato il flauto alle labbra, e ho incominciato a suonare. Le mie dita si spostavano veloci sui fori componendo una melodia che non era quella di un tempo"; Capriolo, *Il doppio*, 166.)

167 Danielle Hipkins contrasts the universality of music in *The Dual Realm* with the more personal nature of writing; see Hipkins, Lost in the Art(ifice) of Male Language," 99.

168 Buzzati, *The Tartar*, 125. ("Stupì di aver scritto lui quelle cose, non se ne ricordava proprio, tutto si riferiva a strani fatti dimenticati"; Buzzati, *Il deserto*, 129.)

169 Capriolo, *Dual*, 25. ("La mia grafia va modificandosi, va regredendo a una forma infantile, e i caratteri si sono fatti più grandi. Se ciononostante sarò in grado di riconoscerla, riterrò probabilmente di aver tentato di narrare una vicenda romanzesca, poco verisimile, la cui protagonista è un personaggio fittizio di nome 'Io'; allora non aprirò più il quaderno, neppure per leggere. Provo un senso d'angoscia nel rendermi conto che ormai penso a questa possibilità come a una liberazione"; Capriolo, *Il doppio*, 43.)

to the personal, to identity. Writing becomes mysterious, like the novels themselves, when the characters give up their identities, other than the ones that tie them to the fort and hotel.

All three novels represent not knowing as being part of the beauty of life. The unknown creates a space for art, as Barthes has examined: "This is also Kafka's answer to all our inquiries into the novel today: that it is finally the precision of his writing (a structural not a rhetorical precision, of course: it is not a matter of 'fine writing') which commits the writer to the world: not in one of his options, but in his very defection: it is because the world is not finished that literature is possible."[170] These novels represent this unfinished quality of life and question this relationship between reality and art, as Blanchot has discussed: "What is strange about books like *The Trial* and *The Castle* is that they send us back endlessly to a truth outside of literature, while we begin to betray that truth as soon as it draws us away from literature, with which, however, it cannot be confused."[171]

At the same time that they can seem abstract and to reflect upon the various powerful elements of art, such as formalism, imagination, and distance, the novels have also been persuasively read in relation to the biographical and historical characteristics of their authors. I will briefly offer three examples of convincing interpretations of *The Castle*, *The Tartar Steppe*, and *The Dual Realm* that are, in large part, based on the authors' historical and biographical contexts and then return to a broader, but related, analysis of the works. Describing the context for understanding land surveyors in the Austro-Hungarian Empire, John Zilcosky reads the attempt to survey and the problems of vision in *The Castle* as being related to colonialism and Prague: "We could thus view K.'s struggle with the Castle as precisely a surveyor's desire to gain visual mastery: K. wants to measure, organize, and map the Castle territories according to his subjective blueprints."[172]

Ellen V. Nerenberg reads the presentation of the fort and Drogo's masculinity in light of the novel's fascist context: "The prison imagery used to characterize Fort Bastiani implicates the flow of power in the nation, whose outer reaches the garrison ostensibly protects and defends. With the fort's soldiers, Buzzati represents the instability of *amor patriae*, national character, and masculinity under Fascism."[173] Danielle Hipkins provides an interpretation of Capriolo as an author

---

170 Barthes, "Kafka's Answer," 143.
171 Blanchot, *The Work of Fire*, 1–2.
172 Zilcosky, *Kafka's Travels*, 136.
173 Nerenberg, *Prison Terms*, 194. Nerenberg also discusses Panafieu's persuasive reading: "The frontier and border emblematize the psychological struggle against bureaucracy and modernist fragmentation so characteristic of the author's fiction" (Nerenberg, 34).

and female translator of male works (such as Kafka's) in light of her own work and Cara's new self-presentation: "Thus reading the autobiographical aspect of Capriolo's text becomes a reading of her own relationship with her cultural autobiography, which emerges as conflictual and fragmented, full of unconscious resistance."[174]

While I have concentrated primarily on elements of these novels that do not require historical or biographical context, the interpretations of Zilcosky, Nerenberg, and Hipkins reveal how these novels' forms raise questions about the authors' contemporary world, just as how non-traditional detective fiction interrogates society. While literary detective novels offer critiques that are often aimed at one part of society, such as the structure of the government, the novels of Kafka, Buzzati, and Capriolo go beyond this. Functioning on multiple levels, all three novels can be examined as representing reflections on more general questions in addition to real situations.

The novels' power comes, in part, from how familiar they can seem. Who has not felt strange in a new place, like a hotel? Who has not felt uncomfortable trying to determine social expectations in a new situation? Who has not adapted to new routines and experienced one's identity shift? These novels can feel pressingly relevant. They have been read as representing a search for God or a higher power, literature, and more specific elements of society, as in the analyses above. Whereas detective novels make clear what the search is for, the three novels leave open what problems they pose, as framed by Frank Kermode: "It is possible to tell a story in such a way that the principal object of the reader is to discover, by an interpretation of clues, the answer to a problem posed at the outset. All other considerations may be subordinated to this interpretative, or, as I shall call it, hermeneutic activity."[175] These novels offer no restoration and force the reader to re-evaluate whatever he or she considered the "problem posed at the outset." All three novels bring readers to a foreign but familiar world – a world in which all the rules are new, but in which we recognize our own searches as well as those of the authors. The novels make the quotidian strange and ask us to interrogate how we find meaning and where. They also suggest the potential significance of literature and art in our attempts to find community and revisit society.

---

174 Hipkins, "Lost in the Art(ifice) of Male Language," 105. "Criticisms of it fall into two groups: the idea that it is simply 'un testo sui testi' (a text about texts), symptomatic of a general trend towards 'la serializzazione della letteratura, anche di quella colta' [the serialization of literature, including quality literature] and, in a couple of rare gender-oriented considerations of the work, a text which represses the female body" (Hipkins, *Contemporary Italian Women Writers*, 69).

175 Kermode, "Novel and Narrative," 179.

Kafka's *The Castle*, Buzzati's *The Tartar Steppe*, and Capriolo's *The Dual Realm* exemplify three ways that modern texts reflect upon the idea of interpretation, with varying kinds and levels of reflection. Comparing *The Tartar Steppe* with *The Castle*, instead of criticizing it as a Kafka copy, highlights the originality and particular modernity of Buzzati's novel. The narrator enters the text in provocative ways: the text's allusions to itself, which build as the novel reaches a close, are not fictional games but part of a structure of mystery, which remains enigmatic for the protagonist and the reader. Buzzati's novel shows that Drogo's mysteries are not answered by events that would seem to answer them.

Capriolo's novel, meanwhile, expresses the power of accepting an unreachable goal and succumbing to a loss of identity. Capriolo sees Kafka as having created the modern myth: "Today we live almost always in the midst of extreme degradations of myths, and it is because of this that perhaps it is important to find again their authentic sense, their authentic stature. For instance I think that among authors no one understood the twentieth century with the depth with which Kafka understood it, because Kafka is the only twentieth-century author who knows how to see, conceive, and express in mythic form his century."[176] Capriolo mentions *The Castle* and "Before the Law" as new, modern archetypes that are the myths of our time. Her view of Kafka as a recognizably modern mythmaker provides another perspective on the idea of Kafka's work as an "open work," as discussed by Eco, since journalists, authors, and critics use Kafka's myths to explain our modern experiences.[177] Buzzati's and Capriolo's novels build on this myth and provide new questions about modern experiences and how to find or construct meaning.

---

176 "Oggi viviamo quasi sempre in mezzo a estreme degradazioni dei miti, ed è per questo che forse è importante ritrovarne il senso autentico, l'autentica statura. Per esempio io credo che fra gli scrittori nessuno abbia capito il Novecento con la profondità con cui l'ha capito Kafka, perché Kafka è l'unico scrittore del Novecento che ha saputo vedere, concepire ed esprimere in forma mitica il proprio secolo" (Capriolo, quoted in Ania, "Gilgamesh, i miti e 'l'eterno ritorno,'" 163–4).

177 In her interviews, Capriolo is unequivocal about the importance of Kafka and has spent a considerable amount of time translating his works. Einaudi published her translation of *Das Schloss* in 2002, Il notes magico her translation of *Die Verwandlung* in 2011, and SE her translation of *Der Process* in 2015. Although Capriolo rejects the idea of direct "influence," she consistently mentions Kafka as one of the most inspiring authors; see, e.g., the interview by Gillian Ania, 160. For one of the most extensive discussions of Capriolo and Kafka (including *The Castle*, *The Trial*, *In the Penal Colony*, and *The Metamorphosis*), see Ania, *Paola Capriolo* (34, 63, 68–9, 73, 91, 104).

Kafka's Parental Bonds: The Family as Institution in Italian Literature

Ich habe die Eltern immer als Verfolger gefühlt.
I have always looked upon my parents as persecutors.
Ho considerato i genitori sempre come persecutori.

– Franz Kafka to Felice Bauer,
12 November 1912

Mothers are an important object of focus in recent Italian literary criticism. Studies have primarily analysed female writers who write about mothers and daughters, often from a psychological or biological perspective, with subheadings, articles, and chapter titles such as "The Daughter's Furious Attachment to the Maternal Body" (Adalgisa Giorgio), "Too Close, Too Far: Motherhood as a Dialogue with the Self" (Laura Benedetti), "The Renegotiation of the Mother's Body" (Patrizia Sambuco), "To Be or Not to Be a Mother: Choice, Refusal, Reluctance and Conflict; Motherhood and Female Identity in Italian Literature and Culture" (Laura Lazzari). These works reposition the earlier attention paid to intense maternal love for sons in Italian fiction and correct the problematic negation of female voices. Many of these works also exclude male authors portraying mothers, female authors portraying sons, and the portrayal of fathers altogether.[1]

This exclusion points to a problem that several of these authors themselves protested: for instance, neither Natalia Ginzburg nor Elsa

---

1 Selection criteria when dealing with the family can seem somewhat arbitrary since so many works represent familial relations. Motherhood and the family often become a primary way to examine women writers more generally: "For its poetical suggestiveness and socio-cultural significance, motherhood has been a central interpretative image for twentieth-century women writers, designed to express female existence in its personal and social dimensions" (Pickering-Iazzi, "Designing Mothers," 325).

Morante wanted to be called the best Italian female author or to be included in anthologies of women writers since they resisted a division based on their sex.[2] "Kafka's Parental Bonds" adds to the complex and rich picture of the Italian family in literature by concentrating not on gender, but on representations of the family as institution. Examining the family as an institution not only offers a new perspective on works that have been included in studies on mothers, such as those of Elena Ferrante, Natalia Ginzburg, and Oriana Fallaci, but also incorporates texts, like those of Italo Svevo, Massimo Bontempelli, and Italo Calvino, that are less often considered in examinations of the family.

Kafka's representations of the family appear throughout his oeuvre and have helped to shape our understanding of the family today. The first part of the chapter outlines his numerous portrayals of the family, with reference to how they are productive for understanding Italy's particular cultural and literary landscape. The second section provides close readings of Svevo and Ferrante, revealing how Kafka sheds new light on these authors; this analysis puts them in a new genealogy and suggests similarities between their contexts, despite their diverse backgrounds and periods. Since the family in literature includes too much material to adequately cover, critics often focus on one relationship, such as mother-daughter, or only female authors, to productively analyse significant elements of the family. Following Kafka and the themes in his work, especially his representation of the difficulty of escaping the family, offers another approach, which complements the other ones mentioned. The final part of the chapter will compare two novels, Massimo Bontempelli's *Il figlio di due madri* (*The Son of Two Mothers*, published in English as *The Boy with Two Mothers*) and Elsa Morante's *L'isola di Arturo* (*Arturo's Island*), which invite the reader to try to imagine the process of escaping from the familial unit.

The Familial Institution in Kafka and Modern Italian Literature

In the *Art of the Novel*, Milan Kundera explains, "The famous letter Kafka wrote and never sent to his father demonstrates that it was from the family, from the relationship between the child and the deified power of the parents, that Kafka drew his knowledge of the *technique*

2　Scholars have called attention to this critical tendency: "On the other hand, claims such as Garboli's inevitably isolate women writers: exceptional as they are, these women are separated from the clusters of recognized authors and schools, and doomed, at best, to follow a bright yet lonely trajectory" (Della Coletta, "The Morphology of Desire," 129).

of culpabilization, which became a major theme of his fiction."[3] While much of Kafka's literature, including *The Trial* as analysed by Kundera, can be interpreted as revealing this concept of the family as one's first, unbearable institution, "Das Urteil ("The Judgment") provides some of the clearest explorations of family oppression in Kafka's oeuvre. Georg believes he is establishing his own identity, as a businessman, as a husband-to-be, and as a friend, when he has a conversation with his father that causes him to doubt his independence in any of area of life. At the end of the story, the father orders Georg to death by drowning, and Georg obeys. His last words underline the power of parental love to drive a child over a bridge. Emphasizing his love for his demanding father and dead mother, Georg calls out to both parents as he leaps to his death: "Dear parents, I have always loved you."[4] ("Liebe Eltern, ich habe euch doch immer geliebt."[5]) Love brackets Georg's last sentence (*Liebe, geliebt*), and the parents (*Eltern, euch*) surround the child's "*ich*," leaving little space for Georg's identity in his last words. Parents love, direct, and obliterate him. Kafka's powerful depictions often highlight the link between love and domination in the family. Reading the family as an institution provides a framework for understanding the individual's predicament and guilt in Kafka's works.[6]

Kafka wished to publish "The Judgment," "The Metamorphosis," and "The Stoker" in a collection called *The Sons*. Realizing this plan, these stories, along with "Letter to His Father," have now been issued together. In the introduction to this collection in English, Mark M. Anderson observes, "Kafka's title *The Sons* defines his protagonists in terms of their families, as children still largely controlled by familial and social relations. In fact, one might say that the true subject of these stories is not the individual subject at all but the family – that social and even 'animal' organism, as Kafka once called it, through which the child first learns to define its own identity."[7] While Karl in "The Stoker," Georg in "The Judgment," and Gregor in "The Metamorphosis" are in different positions in relation to their families, all three of their stories explore the difficulty of separating from one's family and how far the bonds of familial control stretch. Kafka's "Letter to His Father" adds to

---

3 Kundera, *The Art of the Novel*, 109.
4 Kafka, "The Judgment," 16.
5 Kafka, *Erzählungen*, 60.
6 Robertson states, "The family, for Kafka, is the place where power, guilt, law and punishment originate" (Robertson, "Kafka, Goffman, and the Total Institution," 142).
7 Anderson, introduction to *The Sons*, xi.

this concern by offering an extended criticism of family dynamics and of the pressures the family puts on an individual.[8]

Kafka often addresses the family as an institution in which the parents are united. Ritchie Robertson examines "The Judgment" as a representation of a typical familial struggle and how the father "also represents the doubly unchallengeable authority of the deceased mother."[9] While the father is the most frequent point of discussion in Kafka's "Letter to His Father," the work is also a master articulation of the oppression of the entire family unit. In his letter, Kafka demonstrates how the father dominates the vision of the world he has formed: "Sometimes I imagine the map of the world spread out and you stretched diagonally across it. And I feel as if I could consider living in only those regions that either are not covered by you or are not within your reach."[10] The entire world is divided between paternal spaces and those the son is willing to occupy. Kafka's mother, considered by some the actual addressee of Kafka's letter and the only parent to read the letter, contributes to this power dynamic that Kafka finds unbearable: "If I was to escape from you, I had to escape from the family as well, even from Mother."[11] According to Kafka, his mother does not allow for an alternative space outside the father, although he claims that his mother's character contributes to his differences, which are at the root of his struggles with his father.

The strength of Kafka's father figure, as described in the "Letter to His Father," has been the reason that scholars have mentioned the letter in discussions of Ginzburg's *Lessico famigliare* (*Family Lexicon*) and Calvino's *La strada di San Giovanni* (*The Road to San Giovanni*).[12] Analysing their works in terms of the family as institution instead of father-mother

---

8 "In many ways the 'Letter to His Father' formulates explicitly the same critique of the bourgeois family that Kafka had put into literary terms seven years earlier in *The Sons*" (Anderson, xvii).

9 Robertson, *The "Jewish Question,"* 257–8. Furthermore, "An alliance between paternal and maternal forms of domination is subtly depicted in *Das Urteil*" (Robertson, 257).

10 Kafka, "Letter," 163. ("Manchmal stelle ich mir die Erdkarte ausgespannt und Dich quer über sie hin ausgestreckt vor. Und es ist mir dann, als kämen für mein Leben nur die Gegenden in Betracht, die Du entweder nicht bedeckst oder die nicht in Deiner Reichweite liegen"; Kafka, *Letter to the Father*, 110.) Robert Crumb has illustrated this memorable image with a drawing of Kafka's father stretched out over a representation of the world (Crumb, *Kafka*).

11 Kafka, "Letter," 138. ("Wollte ich vor Dir fliehn, mußte ich auch vor der Familie fliehn, selbst vor der Mutter"; Kafka, *Letter to the Father*, 54.)

12 Ginzburg's description of her father has, at times, been characterized as an act of revenge or rebellion and connected to Kafka's "Letter to His Father;" see Clementelli, *Invito alla lettura di Natalia Ginzburg*, 112–13. For Calvino, see Scarpa, "'From the Vantage Point of Hindsight,'" 162.

or father-child dynamics reveals another similarity to Kafka's: while they describe the fathers as determining their children's worlds, they frame the mothers as crucial to the family's dynamic. In Ginzburg's *Family Lexicon*, the mother and father, although they may be quite different individually and fulfil different roles within the family, act together to educate, and often dominate, the child. Ginzburg depicts the parameters of her world as determined and defined by her father's beliefs and experiences. Ginzburg's father decided that his daughter needed to be homeschooled, with her mother as the instructor. Through these lessons, the mother constructs Ginzburg's sense of the world, but based on the father's travels: "While teaching me geography, my mother told me all about the countries my father had been to when he was young. He'd been to India, where he'd fallen ill with cholera and, I believe, yellow fever. He'd been to Germany and Holland. He was also in Spitzberg."[13] Ginzburg's anecdote reveals how her father's life influences her concept of the world's layout, through her mother's descriptions. Because of the mother's choices, the places the father has been determine Ginzburg's sense of geography and the world. *Family Lexicon* combines descriptions of the controlling force of the family with nostalgia for its potential unity.

In "The Road to San Giovanni," Calvino divides the geographical area around his house into where his father believed "the world began" and where he himself saw "the world, the map of the planet" beginning.[14] Their spaces contrast, and Calvino's world occupies a different space than his father's. Calvino is forced to experience the father's world during walks to San Giovanni, and the text reflects on the differences between father and son. The mother, with her "silent authority,"[15] wakes him up for his walks and determines whether he and his brother must go with their father. The mother influences how the child and father spend time together and the parameters of the tense father-child relationship. While Calvino, Ginzburg, and Kafka frame the father as powerful *pater familias*, their mothers are also instrumental for how the family functions and the oppression the children feel, demonstrating one difference between looking at family as an institution versus concentrating on motherhood.

---

13 Ginzburg, *Family Lexicon*, 43. ("Insegnandomi la geografia, mia madre mi raccontava di tutti i paesi dov'era stato mio padre da giovane. Era stato in India, dove s'era preso il colera, e, credo, la febbre gialla; ed era stato in Germania e in Olanda. Era stato poi anche nello Spitzberg"; Ginzburg, *Lessico famigliare*, 45.)

14 Calvino, *The Road to San Giovanni*, 4 (Calvino, *La strada di San Giovanni*, 5).

15 Calvino, *The Road to San Giovanni*, 15. ("Un suo dominio silenzioso"; Calvino, *La strada di San Giovanni*, 12.)

The role of family has been discussed as an especially significant societal formation in Italy.[16] Italian society has been characterized both as an example of a strong patriarchy, in which the father rules, and as a society that venerates the mother's role as caregiver. Italian literature often depicts mothers and fathers as representing love and authority, respectively. Part of the reason for the current attention to the representations of mothers is the earlier focus on them as being subservient to their male children, including examinations of male venerations of the mother figure that ignored the mother's viewpoint.[17] Critics who focus on female authors writing about motherhood often emphasize the role of women within families and explore the tension between the male authorial role and the female nurturing role, particularly the strain this puts on women.

Considering the mother not as subservient to the son and husband, but as part of an oppressive system, this chapter discusses representations of the pressure of the family unit on the individual, especially the child, to call attention to social interactions other than gender. Considering mothers and fathers as one parental unit highlights the tensions that the bonds of family put on all family members. Critics have used Oriana Fallaci's *Lettera a un bambino mai nato* (*Letter to a Child Never Born*) in their discussions of motherhood, particularly to explore the oppression of the mother, but the narrator also emphasizes the family itself as tyrannical.[18] She writes, "Some call it the bondage of the family. I don't believe in the family. The family is a lie constructed the better to control people, the better to exploit their obedience to rules and legends, by whoever organized this world. We rebel more easily when we're alone; we resign ourselves more easily when living with others. The family is nothing but a mouthpiece for a system that cannot let you

---

16 For instance, in *The Moral Basis of a Backward Society*, Banfield famously asserted that the southern Italian society he observed was based on "amoral familism," a kind of total dedication to the family.

17 See the collection *Le madri* and Carlo Bo's preface: "Se volessimo servirci di un paradosso, dovremmo dire che soltanto grazie all'idea della madre ci sottraiamo al nostro destino" (Bo, prefazione in *Le madri*, 9). The collection contains only male authors.

18 Fallaci is a central figure in Laura Benedetti's chapter "Questioning Motherhood," which characterizes the work in this way: "Perhaps no other Italian writer has investigated in such detail pregnancy as an event that challenges a woman's notion of self-hood, while giving her a privileged perspective on the most crucial issues in human life" (Benedetti, *The Tigress in the Snow*, 90–1). Adalgisa Giorgio includes Fallaci in a list of female authors from the 1970s who focused on "women's roles and on motherhood from the mother's viewpoint" (Giorgio, "The Passion for the Mother," 121). Stefania Lucamante comments that *Letter to a Child Never Born* "reveals all of the woman's weaknesses, fears, and ambitions" (Lucamante, *A Multitude of Women*, 188).

disobey and its sanctity is nonexistent."[19] The narrator describes the family as a societal construction that aims to control, not as a natural or spiritual necessity. The family here is part of a system and a problem for all people, regardless of sex. Examining the family as an institution draws attention to the individual's struggle within society, as determined primarily by the family.

Kafka illuminates the point that Fallaci's narrator makes.[20] Family is where many of the various elements of life are first connected and questioned. Much of Kafka's work interrogates the interstitial relationship between public and private in the family. Homi Bhabha locates the interstitial in these in-between spaces, like the home: "Private and public, past and present, the psyche and the social develop an interstitial intimacy. It is an intimacy that questions binary divisions through which such spheres of social experience are often spatially opposed. These spheres of life are linked through an 'in-between' temporality that takes the measure of dwelling at home, while producing an image of the world of history."[21] Kafka's work often critiques these spheres of life, asking the reader to interrogate the foundations of society.

This interstitial relationship has been framed differently by a variety of thinkers. Deleuze and Guattari, for instance, focus on Kafka's "triangles": "In this way the family triangle connects to other triangles – commercial, economic, bureaucratic, juridical, – that determine its values. When Kafka indicates that one of the goals of a minor literature is the 'purification of the conflict that opposes father and son and the possibility of discussing that conflict,' it isn't a question of Oedipal phantasm but of a political program."[22] Discussions of the family as

19 Fallaci, *Letter to a Child Never Born*, 42. ("Alcuni la chiamano schiavitù della famiglia. Io non credo alla famiglia. La famiglia è una menzogna costruita da chi organizzò questo mondo per controllare meglio la gente, sfruttarne meglio l'obbedienza alle regole. Ci si ribella più facilmente quando si è soli, ci si rassegna più facilmente quando si vive con gli altri. La famiglia non è che portavoce di un sistema che non può lasciarti disubbidire, e la sua santità non esiste"; Fallaci, *Lettera a un bambino mai nato*, 36.)

20 "The template for Kafka's understanding of institutions was his family" (Robertson, "Kafka, Goffman, and the Total Institution," 140).

21 Bhabha, *The Location of Culture*, 19. "The family is the first institution that anyone encounters, and, for Kafka, the family is the place where oppression starts" (Robertson, 140).

22 Deleuze and Guattari, *Kafka*, 17. Scott Spector differentiated three levels of father-son conflict in Kafka: the Oedipal; the historical-political (where he positions Deleuze and Guattari's analysis); and the historiographical, or methodological. While the three categories are interconnected, studies that focus on the father-son or mother-daughter relationship often emphasize the first level, the Oedipal, or psychological (Spector, *Prague Territories*, 104).

an institution often lead to its connection with other organizing bodies, like the government, instead of Freud.[23] While Kafka alluded to Freud in writing "The Judgment," his work brings into focus a different series of the splintering elements of society that the family unit tries to control.[24] The pressure of the father's world view and of society is so overpowering in several of Kafka's stories, such as "The Judgment" and "The Metamorphosis," that the son, not the father, ends up dying, pointing to one of the great differences between how Freudian plots and Kafka's usually play out.[25]

Kafka's "Letter to His Father" reflects upon the struggle to be an individual, to be a writer, and how a family pursues its members at home, at work, and in their minds. The text, in part, examines writing as a complicated, often illusory road to freedom. Kafka describes his hope that writing will offer a way to free himself: "I was not, or, to put it most optimistically, was not yet, free. My writing was all about you; all I did there, after all, was to bemoan what I could not bemoan upon your breast."[26] While Kafka holds onto a faint hope that his writing will some day be independent from his family, he also claims that all his writing is about his father. In addition, his letter provides the author-child with a mode of shaping and presenting the parent. He includes an imagined response from his father in his letter and lessens his father's power by placing him in the familial system determined by society: "This terrible trial that is pending between us and you, to examine it in all its details, from all sides, on all occasions, from far and near – a trial in which you keep on claiming to be the judge, whereas, at least in the main (here I leave a margin for all the mistakes I may naturally make) you are a party too, just as weak and deluded as we are."[27]

---

23 Legal scholar Carol Weisbrod points to the numerous ways in which Kafka's letter illuminates the connections between family and the law: "The letter suggests the existence of a number of interacting legal regimes within the family (state law, religious-social law, father law, individual conscience)" (Weisbrod, *Butterfly, the Bride*, 73).

24 Spector distinguishes Kafka's struggle with his parents from that between son and father in Freud: concentrating especially on the "Letter to His Father," Spector notes how the struggles between father and son are based on differences relating to distinct world views, due partially to generational distinctions (Spector, *Prague Territories*, 104).

25 "Unlike Freud's narratives of *Vatermord*, these stories are about the banishment and death of children" (Anderson, introduction to *The Sons*, ix).

26 Kafka, "Letter," 150. ("Natürlich war es eine Täuschung, ich war nicht oder allergünstigsten Falles noch nicht frei. Mein Schreiben handelte von Dir, ich klagte dort ja nur, was ich an Deiner Brust nicht klagen konnte"; Kafka, *Letter to the Father*, 82.)

27 Kafka, "Letter," 142.

The works I have examined express how the narrators felt that their worlds and their parents' were distinct, and yet their works put these worlds into conversation with each other. Relatedly, in *Family Lexicon*, Ginzburg memorializes her father's many sayings, despite her father's resistance to modern writers. The father is the beginning and end of her work, but she chooses his representation. In writing about the family, there may not be freedom, but there is power.

Critics have often discussed whether to consider Kafka's letter literature or documentation. Discussing the text as simply representing Kafka's thoughts is problematic since the work sits between autobiography and fiction. Kafka may or may not have intended his father to read the letter.[28] He also may or may not have meant it to be read by the public. For instance, he sent the letter to his friend and translator, Milena Jesenká, but with the odd instruction that others should not read it, *if possible*: "Tomorrow I'll send the father-letter to your apartment, please take good care of it, I still might want to give it to my father someday. If possible [*womöglich*] don't let anyone else read it. And as you read it, understand all the lawyer's tricks: it is a lawyer's letter."[29] Regardless of the author's intentions, this autobiographical work is used as a point of reference for Kafka's life. Ginzburg's *Family Lexicon* similarly straddles multiple genres. Her introduction to her book asks that it be read as a *romanzo* (novel), not a work of non-fiction, although its contents are true since she recounts only memories that she can easily recall. Both Ginzburg's preface and Kafka's comment to Jesenká point to issues of authorial control, but the debated genre of these striking examples of familial pressure fits with the fact that discussions of family and literature are often reduced to the personal and autobiographical.

Once an author writes about the family, it becomes seemingly impossible not to discuss his or her actual family. Adrienne Rich, the author of *Of Woman Born*, did not want her identities of poet and mother to be collapsed: "Poetry was where I lived as no-one's mother, where I existed as myself."'[30] A discussion of literary families puts into focus the relationship between an author's personal and literary inspirations,

---

28 "In Kafka's case, of course, we do not really even know whether the letter is a public or private document" (Weisbrod, *Butterfly, the Bride*, 76).

29 Kafka, *Letters to Milena*, 63. ("Morgen schicke ich Dir den Vater-Brief in die Wohnung, heb ihn bitte gut auf, ich könnte ihn vielleicht doch einmal dem Vater geben wollen. Laß ihn womöglich niemand lesen. Und verstehe beim Lesen alle advokatorischen Kniffe, es ist ein Advokatenbrief. Und vergiß dabei niemals Dein großes Trotzdem"; Kafka, *Briefe 1918–1920*, 202.)

30 Randall, "Adrienne Rich's 'Clearing in the Imagination,'" 195.

and it draws attention to the relationship between the personal and the literary. As will be discussed in the last section of this chapter, this mixing is a point of focus in Arturo's development in Morante's novel *Arturo's Island*. Morante's and Bontempelli's works portray two kinds of family in the same imaginary world; this allows for a comparison that does not invite a discussion of the authors' biographical details, but rather reveals how the novels ask the reader to question the family unit. The next section examines Kafka's, Svevo's, and Ferrante's works to establish the framework of analysis for the last section. While more Italian authors could be included, this discussion suggests one way to reorient the Italian literary landscape.

Svevo's *A Life* and Ferrante's *Troubling Love*: Societal Stress and the Bonds of Family

This section examines Svevo's *Una vita* (*A Life*, 1892) and Ferrante's *L'amore molesto* (*Troubling Love*, 1992) to discuss the contextual factors that contribute to the similarities between these Italian authors' and Kafka's portrayals of the family. Discussing Kafka, Svevo, and Ferrante together reframes the view of the female author in terms that are not based on her gender and gives her a different literary genealogy. While Ferrante has become famous, one of the few modern Italian authors whose works are important enough to be considered world literature, critics often place her in a purely female lineage. Even before the debates arose about her identity as a woman known for her translations of Kafka, she herself suggested the similarities between them. Putting Kafka and Ferrante into conversation takes seriously the mentions she made in interviews about the significance of Kafka to her.

Comparing Kafka's and Ferrante's representations of the family as an institution embedded in society reveals several striking similarities. In *L'amica geniale* (*My Brilliant Friend*), the protagonist, Elena, associates her mother's feelings about her with her mother's anger at cockroaches: "Sometimes I heard her angrily crushing with her heel the cockroaches that came through the front door, and I imagined her with furious eyes, as when she got mad at me."[31] Kafka's *Ungeziefer*, at times understood and translated as "cockroach," has been connected to the language Kafka's father used to talk about his son and his son's friends.

---

31 Ferrante, *My Brilliant Friend*, 45. ("A volte la sentivo schiacciare con colpi rabbiosi di taco gli scarafaggi che arrivavano dalla porta d'ingresso, e me la immaginavo con occhi furiosi come quando se la prendeva con me"; Ferrante, *L'amica geniale*, 1:40–1.)

Ferrante and Kafka represent the intense fear that a child can feel around the parent and use the human-insect dynamic to portray the depths of this feeling. Parental anger can push the child to feel closer to the non-human creature than the parent. One reading of "The Metamorphosis" proposes that the family's oppression of Gregor led first to him physically incarnating his role as an undesired, verminous insect in the family and then, ultimately, to his death.[32] Both Elena's reactions to her mother and Gregor's transformation ask whether this boundary blurring is caused by how one is treated or based on something more internal. Is Gregor a creature because he is perceived as one or because he accepts himself as one? Does Elena connect to her mother's anger because of how she feels, or does she perceive an association that her mother would also make? She feels a moment of kinship with a cockroach because of her mother's anger, the anger that pushes her towards a blurring of boundaries, including those between humans and insects.

Ferrante mentions Kafka in a discussion of her debated term, "smarginatura," which expresses the dissolving of boundaries and which Ferrante emphatically does not associate with transcendence: "I'm drawn, rather, to images of crisis, to seals that are broken. When shapes lose their contours, we see what most terrifies us, as in Ovid's 'Metamorphoses,' Kafka's 'Metamorphosis,' and Clarice Lispector's extraordinary 'Passion According to G.H.' You don't go beyond that; you have to take a step back and, to survive, reënter some good fiction."[33] In Kafka's "The Metamorphosis," Gregor eventually dies, and the family seems to thrive without him, raising the issue of whether a family can function after the seals are broken. The familial institution cannot accommodate Gregor in his new form since the family must appear solid, and it must function economically so that it can be part of the society described in the story. Both Ferrante and Kafka explore how familial pressures contribute to the crisis Ferrante describes.

While putting Ferrante into conversation with Kafka offers another perspective on her more studied mother-daughter relationships, Svevo adds a figure not often included in discussions of the family in Italian

---

32 For an example of this in Italian criticism, see Mittner, La letteratura tedesca del Novecento, 252.

33 Lagioia, "'Writing Is an Act of Pride.'" ("Sono attratta invece dalle immagini di crisi, dai sigilli che si spezzano, e forse le smarginature vengono di lì. Lo smarginarsi delle forme è un affacciarsi sul tremendo, come nelle 'Metamorfosi di Ovidio', come in quella di Kafka e come nello straordinario 'Passione di GH' di Lispector. Oltre non si va, bisogna fare un passo indietro e, per sopravvivere, rientrare in una qualche buona finzione"; Lagioia, "'Elena Ferrante sono io.'")

literature. Although the significance of the father-son relationship in Svevo's *La coscienza di Zeno* (*Zeno's Conscience*) and his reading of Freud are frequently examined in Svevo studies, the Triestine author himself is rarely considered in analyses of the family in Italian literature. Akin to the complex relationship among family pressure, work, and sex in "The Judgment," the ties among work, artistic creation, and erotic frustration are connected to the family in Svevo's novels. The works of Kafka, Svevo, and Ferrante contain certain similarities not only because of their sensitivity to family dynamics but also because of the multiple societal pressures at play.[34] How the commonalities among these authors' portrayals of family raise questions about the similarities between their social situations and contexts is are discussed at the end of this section.

Svevo's *A Life* examines the life of a bourgeois office worker in what has, at times, been considered painstaking detail. Although it is the author's first and least-esteemed novel, it shares notable qualities with the work of Kafka, Svevo's last literary love.[35] Several critics have commented on the similarities, drawing particular attention to the fact that most of the novel takes place in an office, with workers doing seemingly useless tasks. Kafka was not even a teenager when *A Life* was published; however, not only has this novel been called Kafkaesque, but the protagonist Alfonso has also been characterized as "almost a malicious caricature of Kafka."[36] Kafka biographer Reiner Stach draws attention to the connections between Kafka and Alfonso in terms of their romantic relationships ("fails to find erotic gratification") and how work interferes with their artistic aspirations. ("His resolve is stymied by the dreary routine of endless hours at the office. He clings to the illusion of future intellectual productivity but never manages to generate anything aside from a few paltry fragments."[37]) In *A Life*, these various elements, including the ability to love and work, are portrayed as being intricately linked to the family and Alfonso's sense of being a son.

The portrayal of the power of family in *A Life* highlights how the institution works in conjunction with society to mould and oppress a child's individual identity, especially in times of transition. The novel begins and ends with letters, the first from Alfonso to his mother and

---

34 Bondanella, one of the first scholars to write in detail about Svevo and Kafka, surmises that Svevo must have read "The Judgment" before writing his most famous novel, *Zeno's Conscience* (1923), because of the striking similarities between Zeno's father's death and the bedroom scene in "The Judgment" (Bondanella, "Franz Kafka and Italo Svevo").

35 For more on Svevo's reading of Kafka, see Bondanella; and Ziolkowski, "Svevo's Dogs."

36 Stach, *Kafka*, 2.

37 Stach, 2.

the last from the company Maller & Co. about Alfonso's suicide. These letters that bracket the novel represent two of the pressures, family and work, exerted on Alfonso, which are ultimately inseparable. The last letter, signed by a firm rather than an individual, treats Alfonso's suicide as a business matter. Both letters raise questions about privacy and the barriers among the individual, the family, and work or society at large. In the first letter, Alfonso repeatedly asks his mother whether he can return home: "Wouldn't I do better at home? I could help you, work in the fields myself even, and get a chance to read poetry [*i miei poeti*] in peace under an oak tree, breathing that good undefiled air of ours."[38] In part because Alfonso is uncomfortable in his attempt to change his social status and to make a place for himself in the city, he would like to return to his mother to live out a pastoral, artistic life. The novel does not include a response from his mother, but her returns home only much later, and his suggestion remains a fantasy.

The contents of the letter, which constitutes the first chapter, are meant to be private, between mother and son, but they are made public in the first few pages of the next chapter, when Alfonso's boss reveals that he knows what Alfonso wrote his mother since she reported it to her friend, who happens to be his lover:

"Why d'you make your mother desperate by writing to her that you're not content with me or with you? Don't look so surprised! I've seen a letter from your mother to our housekeeper [*la signorina*]. The good lady complains a lot about me, but about you too. Read it and see!"

He proffered a piece of paper which Alfonso recognized as coming from Creglingi's shop. A glance told that it really was in his mother's handwriting. He blushed, ashamed of the ugly writing and bad style. In some vague way he felt offended that the letter was being made public.

"I've changed my mind now," he stuttered. "I'm quite content! You know how it is ... distance ... homesickness [*nostalgia*]."

"I understand, I understand! But we're men, you know! [*Ma via, siamo uomini!*]" He repeated the phrase a number of times.[39]

---

38 Svevo, *A Life*, 10. ("Non farei meglio di ritornare a casa? Ti aiuterei nei tuoi lavori, lavorerei magari anche il campo, ma poi leggerei tranquillo i miei poeti, all'ombra delle quercie, respirando quella nostra buona aria incorrotta"; Svevo, *Una vita*, 38.)

39 Svevo, *A Life*, 19. ("'Perché fa disperare sua madre scrivendole che è malcontento di me e io di lei? Non si sorprenda! Lo so da una lettera scritta da sua madre alla signorina. La buona signora si lagna di me, ma di lei anche e non poco. Legga per accertarsene!' Gli porse una carta che Alfonso riconobbe derivante dalla bottega del Creglingi. Vi gettò un'occhiata ed erano proprio i cari caratteri della madre. Arrossì: si vergognava di quella brutta scrittura e di quel brutto stile. C'era in lui qualche

Because his boss is having an affair with the "signorina," he has access to Alfonso's private thoughts, shared by his mother. He emphatically encourages Alfonso to act like a "man" even in a situation (writing to his mother) that could be considered private. Public persona and the performance of gender identity remain issues, even within the family unit. Alfonso feels embarrassed and irritated, not only at the signs of his mother's class, which he is supposed to rise above at his job in the city, but also that private matters have intruded upon his workplace. The almost surreal connections between family and work come together to oppress him. The imagined freedom that he explored in his letter to his mother, a life in which he will live at home, work the land, read poetry, and breathe free air is destroyed completely – not by a letter of response from his loving mother, but by how her relationship to society does not allow him to be what he wants to be, even hypothetically.

Kafka faced a similar intrusion into his life through letters that caused an unwanted break between private and public. After surreptitiously reading a letter to him from Felice Bauer, his mother secretly wrote to Bauer, asking her to keep a close eye on her son: "Question him about the way he lives, what he eats, how many meals he has, and about his daily routine in general. He must not suspect that I have written to you, nor must he learn that I am aware of his correspondence with you. Should it be within your power to change his mode of life, I would be greatly in your debt and you would be making me very happy."[40] Julie Kafka hopes to penetrate into every part of Kafka's life, even into his almost purely epistolary relationship with Bauer. She attempts to use her role as mother to persuade Bauer to help her. She understands that she is breaking a code of privacy by writing ("Jedoch darf er keine Ahnung haben, daß ich Ihnen geschrieben habe"),[41] but believes that her maternal role and insight into her son's happiness override his right to privacy.

Bauer wrote Kafka that she was upset because she felt that her privacy had been similarly invaded since her mother had apparently read Kafka's letters to her without permission. Kafka responded, "Well, there may be mothers who don't read their children's correspondence even if

---

cosa di offeso per quella lettera resa pubblica. 'Ora ho mutato di opinione,' balbettò, 'sono contento! Sa ... la lontanza ... la nostalgia.' 'Capisco, capisco! Ma via, siamo uomini!' E ripeté più volte questa frase"; Svevo, *Una vita*, 47; ellipses in original.)

40 Kafka, *Letters to Felice*, 46. ("Darum bitte ich Sie sehr, ihn auf eine Art darauf aufmerksam zu machen und ihn [zu] befragen wie er lebt, was er ißt, wieviel Mahlzeiten er nimmt, überhaupt seine Tageseintheilung. Jedoch darf er keine Ahnung haben, daß ich Ihnen geschrieben habe, überhaupt nichts davon erfahren, dass ich um seine Correspondenz mit Ihnen weiß"; Kafka, *Briefe 1900–1912*, 1:554.)

41 Kafka, *Briefe 1900–1912*, 1:554.

they have the opportunity, but I am afraid neither your mother nor mine is one of them."[42] He proceeds to analyse who, in fact, may have read his letters to Felice Bauer (her sister and her mother?) and what their reaction would have been. His humorous phrasing about hypothetical, non-intrusive mothers reveals the doubt that there exists a mother who could resist invading her child's life by reading private correspondence. For Kafka, the interventions derive not necessarily from the particular nature of their mothers, but from the nature of all families.

Kafka's mother and Bauer's mother attempt to enter into their children's romantic relationships, seemingly out of concern for their children. While Kafka's letters and Svevo's *A Life* suggest the connections between a failure to "find erotic gratification" and the family, Ferrante's *Troubling Love* and Kafka's "The Judgment" reveal more explicitly the connections between familial oppression and one's sexuality. Following his father's command, Georg drowns himself: "At that moment an almost endless line of traffic [*Verkehr*] streamed over the bridge."[43] Anderson has analysed how the German *Verkehr* connotes multiple societal exchanges, including sex, as well as how the father and the traffic are closely linked: "But one should note that, like almost all of his works, the text is structured by the opposition between paternal *Verkehr* and filial isolation."[44]

Earlier in the story, the father inhabited the role of Georg's fiancée in a terrifying moment when he imitated her lifting her skirts, superimposing the image of the desired woman on himself. His actions contribute to Georg's perception that his life, including his sex life, are not his own and lead to his ultimate decision to die instead of marry. The father lifts his shirt so high that Georg sees his war wound and is forced to consider his father's body. The father then suggests that by desiring his fiancée, Gregor has "disgraced our mother's memory." The father's use of "our" to describe the mother furthers the confusion between father and fiancée as well as mother and fiancée. The father's and son's sexualities are intertwined, with death appearing to be the only way to resolve the confusion.

---

42 Kafka, *Letters to Felice*, 105–6. ("Nun, es gibt vielleicht Mütter, welche die Briefschaften ihrer Kinder nicht lesen, wenn sie so leichte Möglichkeit dazu haben, aber ich fürchte, weder Deine Mutter noch die meine gehört zu diesen Müttern"; Kafka, *Briefe 1900–1912*, 1:334.)
43 Kafka, "The Judgment," 16. ("In diesem Augenblick ging über die Brücke ein geradezu unendlicher Verkehr"; *Erzählungen*, 60.) The pressure the son feels to follow his father's orders erases him, and his death is subsumed by society.
44 Anderson, *Kafka's Clothes*, 88. "The notion of *Verkehr* already subsumes a variety of meanings that include not only traffic, but commerce, exchange, circulation, social and sexual intercourse" (Anderson, 99).

In *Troubling Love,* Delia drastically confuses her and her mother's sexual histories and sexuality. The mother lifts her dress to show Delia how she could not possibly be sexually desirable, but Delia persists in seeing her mother as an object of desire. Delia, meanwhile, feels detached from her body. She realizes only at the end of the novel that she confused her harassment by her friend's grandfather with her mother having an affair, providing one explanation for both her relationship to her own body and her view of her mother's sexuality.[45] Many of the tensions of Ferrante's *Troubling Love* are based on the inner dialogue of the daughter attempting to understand and inhabit the mother, imagining herself as the mother. In the end, the graphic artist claims, "Io ero Amalia" ("I was Amalia") and colours the photo on her identification papers to look like her mother. The end has been interpreted both positively and negatively, in part depending on how this complete identification with the mother is read, as a sign of progress or regression.[46] Either way, it is a moment in which Delia takes control and picks up her pen to determine her relationship with her mother.

Ferrante's novels, which are partly responsible for the growth in interest in mothers and daughters in Italian criticism, often explore the parental oppression that continues into adulthood. Paying attention to the family as an institution brings to light some of the issues that have been discussed with regard to female Italian writers and characters, but several male authors and characters have also faced them. In examinations of the focus on mothers and daughters, the roles of the son and daughter are often differentiated, one representing relative freedom and the other representing sacrifice and control, but many of the same problems are reflected in Kafka's descriptions and Svevo's work, both of which reveal the pressures between various constellations of child and parent. In a letter to Bauer, Kafka comments, "All parents want to do is drag one down to them, back to the old days from which one longs to free oneself and escape; they do it out of love, of course, and that's what makes it so horrible."[47] His fictional sons, such as the ones

---

45 The drowning of her mother prompts Delia's desire to explore and then understand her past confusion. While the deaths in "The Judgment" and *Troubling Love* allow some clarity about the children's roles, they do not end the complications in the family.

46 For a reading of this final moment as positive, see, e.g., Sambuco, *Corporeal Bonds,* 129–51. For its potential dangers, see Benedetti, *The Tigress in the Snow,* 107.

47 Kafka, *Letters to Felice,* 55. ("Nichts wollen die Eltern als einen zu sich hinunterziehn, in die alten Zeiten, aus denen man aufatmend aufsteigen möchte, aus Liebe wollen sie es natürlich, aber das ist ja das Entsetzliche"; Kafka, *Briefe 1900–1912,* 1:253.)

described in "The Judgment" and "The Metamorphosis," do not experience freedom, and Alfonso is tied to his mother, even while appearing free and separate. The deaths of Georg, Gregor, and Alfonso can be attributed to, among other factors, familial pressure.

Ferrante's *Troubling Love* describes the powerful connection between parents and society that heighten the child's oppression. The narrator addresses how attempts to distance oneself from a parent can entail rejecting numerous social roles, including parenthood:

> Throughout the years, because of hatred and fear, I had wished to lose even my deepest connections with her: her expressions, the inflections of her voice, the way she held a glass or drank from a cup, her method of putting on a skirt, as if it were a dress, the arrangement of the objects in her kitchen, in her drawers, how she did her most intimate washing, her taste in food, her dislikes, her enthusiasms, and the language, the city, the rhythms of her breath. I did everything in order to become myself and detach myself from her. On the other hand, I had not wanted or managed to root anybody in me. Soon I would lose even the possibility of having children. No human being would ever detach from me with the anxiety with which I had moved away from Amalia.[48]

The adult narrator, Delia, details her efforts to distance herself from her mother, rejecting motherhood, in part, because her mother, Amalia, was a mother. This passage reveals an obsessive, detailed attention to *not* becoming the parent, an oppression as great as the parent's original oppression.[49] While Benedetti and Sambuco concentrate on Ferrante's passage in a context that emphasizes a female need to separate from

---

48 Ferrante, *Troubling Love*, 64–5. ("Accadeva dopo che negli anni, per odio, per paura, avevo desiderato di perdere ogni radice in lei, fino alle più profonde: i suoi gesti, le sue inflessioni di voce, il modo di prendere un bicchiere o bere da una tazza, come ci si infila una gonna, come un vestito, l'ordine degli oggetti in cucina, nei cassetti, le modalità dei lavaggi più intimi, i gusti alimentari, le repulsioni, gli entusiasmi, e poi la lingua, la città, i ritmi del respiro. Tutto rifatto, per diventare io e staccarmi da lei. D'altro canto non avevo voluto o non ero riuscito a radicare in me nessuno. Tra qualche tempo avrei perso anche la possibilità di avere figli. Nessun essere umano si sarebbe staccato mai da me con l'angoscia con cui io mi ero staccata da mia madre soltanto perché non ero riuscita mai ad attaccarmi a lei definitivamente"; Ferrante, *L'amore molesto*, 78.)

49 "In a moment of lucid introspection, she realizes that her decision not to become a mother herself is linked to her incapacity to deal with her relationship with Amalia, to find a middle ground between identification and rejection" (Benedetti, *The Tigress in the Snow*, 106).

one's mother, the passage reflects many similar tensions expressed by Kafka.[50] Kafka's "Letter to His Father" targets this impulse to separate from one's parent, and his literary works often concentrate on the same struggle.

Kafka outlines the difficulty with which he attempted to forge his own identity, to free himself from his parents' influence. As with Delia, the attention he pays to being not his father dominates his life and determines many of his choices: "I have made some attempts at independence, attempts at escape, with the very smallest of success; they will scarcely lead any farther; much confirms this for me. Nevertheless it is my duty or, rather, the essence of my life, to watch over them, to let no danger that I can avert, indeed no possibility of such a danger, approach them. Marriage bears the possibility of such a danger."[51] Kafka characterizes himself as avoiding not only certain jobs and words but also marriage and children because they are part of his father's world: "I fled everything that even remotely reminded me of you ... marrying is barred to me because it is your very own domain."[52]

Kafka describes his resistance to having children as stemming, in part, from not wanting to deal with a child who would react to him in the way he does to his parents: "There is a view according to which fear of marriage sometimes has its source in a fear that one's children would someday pay one back for the sins one has committed against one's

---

50 As well as other male authors, Calvino, in "Di padre in figlio" ("Father to Son," in *Adam*), reflects upon the fear of having children. The story also deals with the fear of entering an institution that fosters terror, hatred, and oppression. The narrator is apprehensive about becoming a parent, partly because he worries that the hatred he feels for his father will be replicated (Calvino, *Romanzi e racconti*, 1:183). In Calvino's story, as in Kafka's letter, the shame of the child is partially located in the awareness of the parent's position in society and the child's position vis-à-vis the parent. Calvino, although not usually framed in this way, also offered a number of important reflections on family, from "Father to Son" to "The Road to San Giovanni" and beyond.

51 Kafka, "Letter," 164. ("Ich habe schon angedeutet, daß ich im Schreiben und in dem, was damit zusammenhängt, kleine Selbständigkeitsversuche, Fluchtversuche mit allerkleinstem Erfolg gemacht, sie werden kaum weiterführen, vieles bestätigt mir das. Trotzdem ist es meine Pflicht oder vielmehr es besteht mein Leben darin, über ihnen zu wachen, keine Gefahr, die ich abwehren kann, ja keine Möglichkeit einer solcher Gefahr an sie herankommen zu lassen. Die Ehe ist die Möglichkeit einer solchen Gefahr"; Kafka, *Letter to the Father*, 112.)

52 Kafka, "Letter," 163. ("So wie wir aber sind, ist mir das Heiraten dadurch verschlossen, daß es gerade Dein eigenstes Gebiet ist"; Kafka, *Letter to the Father*, 110.)

own parents."[53] Many of Kafka's protagonists resist marriage and children, in part to avoid becoming a parent and, therefore, like the parent. Kafka's and Ferrante's works emphasize not just psychological issues but also the tensions between the self and society that originate within the family – in other words, the oppression that links the parents to the rest of society. Because of the relationship between family and society, attempting to escape the family can require rejecting entire social roles (like becoming a parent) in addition to parts of oneself.

While all families present a space in which the public and private are negotiated, the potential for pressure is highlighted by complex cultural and historical circumstances. The more options that exist – linguistic, cultural, and those relating to class, religion, and education – the more a child may feel pressured by the parents to fulfil certain roles. The parent shapes the child's values, even with regard to linguistic choice. When the child has access to more linguistic choices, he or she may feel cut off from, or choose to reject, the parent's language. Ferrante's Delia has the option to develop a language that is clearly separate from her mother's and break her ties to all that is Neapolitan. To distance herself, she changes the way she speaks and where she lives, losing not only her habits and enthusiasms but also her "language, the city." In other words, she wants to erase even the linguistic traces of her mother from her own way of speaking and is able to attempt this because of the language options that exist in Italy. She is able to escape both physical and linguistic proximity to her family.

The linguistic diversity of Kafka's Prague and of Italy contribute to the possibility that a child will feel frustrated by the parents' language, in addition to their social position, background, views, and appearance. Kafka writes about how even the word *mother* (*Mutter*) estranges him from his mother: "Yesterday it occurred to me that I did not always love my mother as she deserved and as I could, only because the German language prevented it. The Jewish mother is no 'Mutter', to call her 'Mutter' makes her a little comic."[54] Kafka describes feeling distanced from his mother because the term he uses to identify her does not seem to suit her: "'Mutter' is peculiarly German for the Jew, it unconsciously

---

53 Kafka, "Letter," 163. ("Es gibt eine Meinung, nach der die Angst vor der Ehe manchmal davon herrührt, daß man fürchtet, die Kinder würden einem später das heimzahlen, was man selbst an den eigenen Eltern gesündigt hat"; Kafka, *Letter to the Father*, 110, 112.) This comment is then undercut but also given importance in the following sentences, as Kafka analyses the particular form of guilt he feels towards his father and how it has kept him from marrying.

54 Kafka, *Diaries*, 24 October 1911, 88.

contains, together with the Christian splendor Christian coldness also."[55] This sense of separation arises partly out of Kafka's awareness of other terms, from other languages, that he could use for her. He feels trapped within the German word, but at the same time does not choose to use another one. Rejecting the word *Mutter* would, in fact, require also dismissing certain linguistic and life choices that his parents have made. As Kafka often remarked, the choices his parents made in the past set up a situation in which he felt distanced from them.[56]

Kafka saw himself as part of a group of Jewish authors writing in German who struggled with the linguistic, stylistic, and other choices that they made, but had no choice to write: "Most young Jews who began to write German wanted to leave Jewishness behind them, and their fathers approved of this, but vaguely (this vagueness was what was outrageous to them). But with their posterior legs they were still glued to their father's Jewishness and with their waving anterior legs they found no new ground. The ensuing despair became their inspiration."[57] This despair helps prompt writing. Critics, notably Spector, have described the conflicting pressures at play in Prague as a primary reason for the many authors who come from that city.[58] Similarly, the multiple pressures in Trieste, particularly for authors of Jewish origin, contribute to why Svevo's work expresses familial tensions analogous to Kafka's and why so many authors come from there. Just as Svevo's Alfonso saw literature (reading both poetry and his own writing) as a potential escape from the pressures of society, Kafka hoped to escape the parental sphere through literature. He regarded writing as a possible way to flee his family and establish his own identity, to form a different society or access a different part of it.

Kafka's representations of the institution of the family have been traced to his perception of contemporary society, which reflects both an understanding of broader societal changes and his particular cultural and social context. In an examination of nineteenth-century texts that dramatize "a family structure in which the patriarchy is breaking down and the resultant conflict,"[59] Shideler proposes that the idea of the Oedipal complex represents one of the last attempts to hold onto the traditional

---

55 Kafka, 88. See Suchoff's analysis of this passage, 85–6.

56 "This rejection of multiple origins has an estranging effect on the 'Jewish mother': refracted through the self-narrowing prism of the High German 'Mutter,' she loses the ability to take pleasure in the linguistic difference she represents" (Suchoff, 86).

57 Kafka, *Letters to Friends, Family, and Editors*, 289.

58 Spector, *Prague Territories*.

59 Shideler, *Questioning the Father*, 4.

patriarchy.[60] Calvino aligns Kafka and Freud as members of the paternal Austro-Hungarian Empire who embody the revolution against the
father: "It is not that I don't believe in interior, existential revolutions,
but the great event of the century, in this sense – and perhaps a necessary condition of the new industrial phase – was the revolution against
the father accomplished in the territories of the paternal empire of Franz
Joseph, by a medical alienist and a young visionary, Freud and Kafka."[61]

   Indicating the relationship between cultural, social, historical contexts
on the one hand and Kafka's representations of the family on the other,
Calvino not only calls attention to Kafka's and Freud's shared background but also suggests that their work may be a "necessary condition
of the new industrial phase." Kafka's and Freud's views on the family
are clearly not monolithic, but both offer powerful portrayals that have
become part of our current views of the family. Kafka's multilingual,
fin-de-siècle world contributed to how he experienced the pressures of
the family and, therefore, created works about the family that readers
still find compelling today.[62] Svevo's work can be similarly read as re-
sponding to and representing a generational shift. In Ferrante's works,
the reflections on generational shifts and language use have intensified.

Parental Bonds in Bontempelli's *The Boy with Two Mothers* and Morante's *Arturo's Island*

Both Milan Kundera and Ritchie Robertson analyse how the idea of
Kafka as a prophet of totalitarian regimes or the Holocaust relates to
his sensitive understanding of families in his own time. Examining
the ties among Kafka's work, the family, and totalitarianism, Kundera

---

60 "The Oedipus complex, one might dare to suggest, could be the last vestige of
    patriarchal dominance, an attempt at the psychological level to retain the illusion
    of the male's biological superiority" (Shideler, 12).

61 "Non che io non creda alle rivoluzioni interiori, esistenziali: ma il grande avven-
    imento del secolo, in questo senso – e forse condizione necessaria della nuova
    fase industriale –, è stata la rivoluzione contro il padre, compiuta nei territori del
    paterno impero di Francesco Giuseppe, da un medico alienista e da un giovane
    visionario, Freud e Kafka" (Calvino, *Saggi*, 113–14). See Re's discussion of this
    passage in *Calvino and the Age of Neorealism*, 391.

62 Scott Spector, in his analysis of fin-de-siècle Prague, reveals how Kafka's revolt is
    part of a larger social and historical change: "The generational conflict so clearly
    articulated in the cases of Kornfeld and Kafka must be seen within the frame not
    only of the expressionist 'revolt of the son,' but also of the more general 'postliberal
    revolt of the time.' Mary Gluck succinctly characterizes the struggle as one pitting
    Victorian moralism, utilitarian ambition, and rationality against spontaneity,
    instinct, and spirituality" (Spector, *Prague Territories*, 102).

states: "The starting point of totalitarianism resembles the beginning of *The Trial*: you'll be taken unawares in your bed. They'll come just as your father and mother used to."[63] He calls attention to the power of both parents and officials of totalitarian governments to encroach upon one's private space and disrupt the vulnerable state of sleep. While the family and the nation are generally tied together metaphorically and institutionally, certain periods stress these ties more emphatically. For instance, although obviously very different in terms of their historical roles, both Emperor Franz Joseph and Benito Mussolini were emphasized as father figures. Bontempelli's *The Boy with Two Mothers* and Morante's *Arturo's Island* ask whether the family unit is escapable and, if so, what an escape would look like. Their novels bookend the period when the family unit was glorified by the fascist state, when this question may have seemed particularly urgent.

In *How Fascism Ruled Women*, Victoria De Grazia discusses the importance of family and religion as controlling forces in fascist Italy: "The Duce's regime fell back on the traditional authority of family and religion to enforce biologically determined roles as mother and caretakers."[64] These gender roles included stricter observance of expected familial ones as well.[65] The fascist emphasis on the family put pressure on the mother and the father: "Virility was codified and normalized by Fascism, and its principal emblem was progeny: manhood meant children."[66] Relatedly, as Barbara Spackman has analysed, there was a heightened attention to gender roles under fascism: "Any redistribution of proprieties, any mixing and matching of terms – a feminine man, a masculine woman – is discounted as an unnatural monstrosity, perversion, or aberration. Fascism as discursive regime is, in this sense, merely a particularly feverish example of a more general formation."[67] Although the family as an institution was particularly important to

---

63 Kundera, *The Art of the Novel*, 111.

64 De Grazia, *How Fascism Ruled Women*, xi.

65 Important to fascist ideology was the statement, "Italians are for the family." ("L'Italiano è per la famiglia. Nessun popolo ha mai sentito in maniera più profonda la poesia del focolare.") Ellen V. Nerenberg describes how "Sarfatti's concern for the 'cell' of the family hardly disappears following the ouster of the Regime. However, rather than Fascists espousing such pro-family rhetoric, it is the Communists who deploy such language" (Nerenberg, *Prison Terms*, 220).

66 Nerenberg, 38.

67 Spackman, *Fascist Virilities*, 34. "The fascist regime subjected the family to specific interventions relating to both of its main pivots: relations between the sexes, and thus the gender structure, and relations between the generations" (Saraceno, "Redefining Maternity and Paternity," 196).

fascist politics, fascist policies certainly did not create the family unit or, in accordance with Spackman's arguments, gender roles, but rather emphasized them and their connections to the nation.[68]

While historians often favourably contrast Mussolini's dictatorship with Hitler's, part of what was insidious about Mussolini's system is how integrated the familial and religious authorities were, and are, in Italian society.[69] After the Second World War, there was a need to save the family from fascist rhetoric for the new Italian nation. For instance, the film *Roma, città aperta* (*Rome Open City*) painted anti-fascist Italians as being for the family, religious, and communist, in contrast to the homosexual and immoral Nazis.[70] Instead of attempting to claim (or reclaim) the family unit as a positive value for the Italian people, Bontempelli's *The Boy with Two Mothers* and Morante's *Arturo's Island* undertake a more complicated interrogation of the familial institution. Bontempelli's and Morante's novels present non-traditional parents whose positions help criticize the relationship between the state and the family. Their novels reveal how literature can raise powerful questions about the family, especially in political contexts that make such questioning difficult.

This chapter notes the potentially subversive elements of Bontempelli's novel, even though it was written while he was head of the National Fascist Writers' Union.[71] Both his and Morante's novels explore different family structures and the tensions between them, providing an opportunity to investigate representations of the family with two models of the institution in the same imaginary world. In addition, both novels have been left out of numerous studies on the family in Italian literature because they do not fit into many of the categories used to determine whether the stories fit the paradigm of works about motherhood. Like Kafka's stories in *The Sons*, these novels ask whether the family is escapable and explore what this escape could look like. The rest of this section concentrates on these two magnificent Italian novels, returning to Kafka at the end. The themes and ideas explored in the previous sections provide the background for my readings.

---

68 "With regard to this cultural *topos*, fascism constituted not so much a radical innovation as a pointed expression of a trend, laying down legislative, social and symbolic foundations for the pattern of the family and of the welfare state that were to last far longer than fascism itself" (Saraceno, 198).

69 "In the gruesome light of Nazi Germany, Benito Mussolini's dictatorship over Italy looks benign" (De Grazia, *How Fascism Ruled Women*, xi). How embedded fascist practices were in Italian society is still a point of discussion today.

70 See Landy, "Diverting Clichés," 98–9.

71 Wissia Fiorucci argues that the novel reveals Bontempelli's anti-fascist sentiment (Fiorucci, "Self-Censorship in Massimo Bontempelli's Magical Realism").

Morante's *Arturo's Island* describes the childhood of Arturo, whose mother died in childbirth and who grows up on the island of Procida with his often-absent father, Wilhelm Gerace. When Arturo is fourteen, his father marries a sixteen-year-old woman, who has another child. While his father is often absent, leaving Arturo to himself, his young stepmother, Nunziata, is a traditional mother confined almost completely to the home. Her love for her new son, Carmine Arturo, shows Arturo the intensity of a mother's love. Arturo, after falling in love with Nunziata and arguing with the man – whom, it turns out, his father loves – decides to leave the island with his former nanny, Silvestro, who reappears at the end of the book.

Despite the father's frequent, mysterious trips that cause him to leave the island throughout Arturo's life, his views determine Arturo's understanding of reality. As a child, Arturo developed a Code of Absolute Truth, with a list of rules: "These, and the basic certainties my father had already inspired in me, formed in my consciousness, or in my imagination, a kind of Code of Absolute Truth, whose most important laws might be listed like this: ... For a long time these childish certainties of mine were not just something I honored and loved – they made up my only possible idea of reality. It would then have seemed to me, not just dishonorable, but simply impossible, to live without my great certainties."[72] Arturo credits his father with inspiring his guidelines and, not surprisingly, many of the rules have to do with family.

In Morante's novel, the family unit functions as the establishing paradigm for how society works to control the child and determine his idea of propriety. Not only do the rules emphasize the family, but its rules also extend to others, who become part of Arturo's world, as revealed in rule 3, "The greatest baseness is betrayal, and to betray your own father, your own chief, or a friend, etc., is the very lowest depth of infamy."[73] For Arturo, his father, a chief, and a friend are all related figures to whom one owes loyalty. The relationship with the father determines the grounds for future relationships and, although his father keeps his distance from most of his community, for Arturo,

---

72 Morante, *Arturo's*, 24. ("Con essi, e in più con le prime certezze che m'aveva già ispirato la persona di mio padre, si formò dunque nella mia coscienza, o fantasia, una specie di Codice della Verità Assoluta, le cui leggi più importanti si potrebbero elencare così.... Queste mie certezze di ragazzino sono state per lungo tempo non soltanto il mio onore e il mio amore, ma la sostanza della sola realtà possibile, per me!"; Morante, *Opere*, 1:979–80.)

73 Morante, *Arturo's*, 24. ("La peggior bassezza è il tradimento. Se poi si tradisce il proprio padre o il proprio capo, o un amico ecc., si arriva all'infimo della viltà!"; Morante, *Opere*, 1:979.)

he still establishes the modes of being part of society. These "absolute" rules (*CERTEZZE*), which draw on the family and construct a restrictive idea of how society works, suggest a fascistic view.

Arturo's first rule, "Father's authority is sacred,"[74] originates primarily from his own interpretation of his life, as does, for instance, rule 4, "No one living on the island of Procida is worthy of Wilhelm Gerace. For a Gerace to become friendly with a Procidan would be degrading."[75] The next rule, "No love [*affetto*] in life equals a mother's,"[76] does not come from Arturo's experience since his mother died giving birth, but from his books: "My readings offered me many lessons and I chose to then learn what attracted me the most, what best answered my own feelings about life."[77] Arturo reveals how familial understanding and oppression come not just from his own experience but also from his reading, which influences his view of family and helps to reshape his reality. He prefers books that align with his view of life: "Needless to say, my favorite books were those that gave either real or imaginary examples of my ideal of human greatness, of which my father seemed to me the living incarnation."[78] Arturo's youthful view of his father and the importance he gives to literature for his understanding of life mean that he later has to reconsider his world view.[79]

As a child, Arturo re-conceives of both reality and literature to suit his personal understanding of the world. Initially, when stories diverge from his views, he re-imagines the literary texts. Using his reading to support his ideas of the world, he matches stories with the perception

---

74 Morante, *Arturo's*, 24. ("L'autorità del padre è sacra!"; Morante, *Opere*, 1:979.) Critics have productively examined this text in terms of Arturo's psychology, and several other passages I will mention could be too, but I want to look at these relationships in terms of the idea of an institution, as outlined by Kundera's and Robertson's discussions of Kafka.

75 Morante, *Arturo's*, 24. ("Nessun concittadino vivente dell'isola di Procida è degno di Wilhelm Gerace e di suo figlio Arturo. Per un Gerace dar confidenza a un concittadino significherebbe degradarsi"; Morante, *Opere*, 1:979.)

76 Morante, *Arturo's*, 24. ("Nessun affetto nella vita uguaglia quello della madre"; Morante, *Opere*, 1:979.)

77 Morante, *Arturo's*, 24. ("Fra i molti insegnamenti, poi, che ricevevo dalle mie letture, spontaneamente io sceglievo meglio al mio sentimento naturale della vita"; Morante, *Opere*, 1:979; trans. modified.)

78 Morante, *Arturo's*, 27. ("I libri che mi piacevano di più, è inutile dirlo, erano quelli che celebravano, con esempi reali o fantastici, il mio ideale di grandezza umana, di cui riconoscevo in mio padre l'incarnazione vivente"; Morante, *Opere*, 1:984.)

79 "The reality of perception conditioned by reading is in the eye of the beholder. In one dramatic instance in the novel Arturo learns that once fiction becomes reality, it reveals its deceptive nature" (Ruthenberg, "Romancing the Novel," 337).

he has of his father: "Just as girls imagine fairies, saints, and queens all blond, I used to imagine that great captains and warriors were all of them fair, and looked exactly like my father. If the hero of a book was described as dark and of middle size, I preferred to think the author [*storico*] had made a mistake."[80] Arturo's use of *storico* to refer to authors of all kinds of books indicates the significant role that his understanding of literature plays in his life as a template for reality. Arturo both takes his father as a model for his reading and uses his reading to create an image of his father.

Arturo's experience indicates the importance of including different models in discussions of the family. The examinations of mothers in literature has increased, in part, because of growing attention to the particular tensions of women's experiences in society and shifts in the views of motherhood itself. At the same time, critics working on topics related to motherhood have called attention to problems, not only in terms of critical lacunae in literary studies but also more broadly, in terms of societal structures. That is to say, discussions of family – one of the most crucial elements of how our society functions – frequently reveal the important interplay between literature and reality, including the power both have to influence each other. While studies of families often concentrate on how reality affects literature, the description of Arturo's world view reveals the significance of considering families from the other direction as well.

The Boy with Two Mothers is overlooked in many relevant discussions on the family, perhaps because it fits the model that many studies on mothers and daughters seek to counterbalance: it is a novel written by a man that focuses on the intense love of not just one, but two women, Arianna and Luciana, for their shared son. However, it offers an interesting view of the complex, interstitial relationship between the family unit and society. Seven-year-old Mario's apparent transformation into Ramiro (a boy who looked exactly like him and died seven years earlier on the day of Mario's birth) initially raises problems for their respective families. Quite quickly, though, everyone is involved, from those in Ramiro's community to distant letter writers. Outside interventions culminate in a court case to determine the child's future. The two (very different) mothers and child suffer due to the societal emphasis on a

---

80 Morante, *Arturo's*, 28. ("Come le ragazzine si figurano le fate bionde, le sante bionde e le regine bionde, io mi figuravo i grandi capitani e i guerrieri tutti biondi, e somiglianti, come fratelli, a mio padre. Se in un libro un eroe che mi piaceva risultava, dalle descrizioni, un tipo moro, di statura mezzana, io preferivo credere a uno sbaglio dello storico"; Morante, *Opere*, 1:984.)

traditional family unit. When the novel is put into conversation with other works that explore the oppression of the family, *The Boy with Two Mothers* reveals not only the power of the family as institution but also the vital questions it raises about the relationship between state institutions and the institution of the family.

The Boy with Two Mothers and *Arturo's Island* describe figures who do not fit the traditional role of parent (Luciana in Bontempelli's novel and Wilhelm Gerace in Morante's) as well as those that exemplify their roles (Arianna and Mariano in Bontempelli's novel and Nunziata in Morante's).[81] Being a non-traditional parent seems to indicate creativity and freedom, while the traditional parents are described as unimaginative. Arturo sees his father as heroic, in part because of his father's frequent absences. When he is gone, Arturo mistakenly believes that his father is travelling to far-off countries, like the protagonists of his books. In other words, Arturo links Wilhelm with literary heroes due to his lack of paternal attention. While Wilhelm's frequent, extended absences do not mean that Arturo is free from his control, Arturo imagines that it means his father is free. Relatedly, Wilhelm's often abandoned son and wife both associate Wilhelm with imagination. Nunziata explains to her disapproving mother why he does not fit the expected role of husband: "'He travels because he's imaginative!' she concluded proudly."[82] At the end of the novel, the father is revealed to be under the control of a young, male prisoner and has in fact never travelled very far. Wilhelm's surprising restrictions add to the question of whether Arturo's finally leaving the island represents an act of freedom and whether a child can ever be free from the family.

While Wilhelm does not fulfil a stereotypically paternal or spousal role, his wife exemplifies the doting, dominated wife and dedicated mother. Nunziata's belief in family is associated with her religious beliefs. She informs Arturo of the importance of Wilhelm's conversion, which Wilhelm does not appear to take seriously: "But ... do you know that for a real Christian to have the real ceremony of Christian marriage both the husband and wife have got to be Christians of the true Church, for the true family whose head is Our Lord."[83] For Nunziata,

---

81 For an expanded argument on how the mothers in *The Boy with Two Mothers* represent "separate aspects of a split whole," see Fiorucci, "Self-Censorship in Massimo Bontempelli's Magical Realism," 12.

82 Morante, *Arturo's*, 188. ("Viaggia perché è fantastico!"; Morante, *Opere*, 1:1180.)

83 Morante, *Arturo's*, 197. ("Voi però ... lo sapete? Che per fare la vera cerimonia delle nozze cristiane bisogna che gli sposi siano cristiani della vera Chiesa, propria della vera famiglia che per capo tiene la Santità di Nostro Signore"; Morante, *Opere*, 1:1190.)

whose name implies the Annunciation, her Christian marriage associates her directly with the holy family, suggesting its significance in Italian Catholic culture and of Maria in Italy.

In part because of her dedication to her husband and new child (Carmine Arturo), there appears to be less space for Arturo. When Nunziata's son is born, her maternal love causes her to seem almost divine: "Now that she had Carmine, she was so happy that she was singing and laughing from morning to night; when her mouth wasn't laughing, her eyes were."[84] This enthusiasm for the family, which brings Nunziata closer to God, appears to exclude her from creativity. For instance, when Arturo notices Nunziata dreaming, he imagines she is dreaming mundanely of her family and sleep: "And what about her? What dream could she possibly be having to make her laugh with joy? Maybe she thought she was home in Naples with her whole family in the one bed, and her godmother as well."[85] He believes that she is dedicated to the idea of family even in her fantasies.

While Arturo, who is narrating, only hypothesizes the content of Nunziata's dreams, the third-person narrator of *The Boy with Two Mothers* describes how the dreams of Arianna, the traditional mother, lack imagination: "Because she has no imagination [*fantasia*], her husband is still there. He looks at her with his air of superiority."[86] In both novels, the traditional mothers' dedication to motherhood and wifehood reveals their lack of creativity. Arianna, who is so limited in her thinking that even her dreams lack *fantasia*, cannot open her mind to accept a situation without a traditional family unit. Her resistance to comprehending Mario's change relates to having to understand him as developing a different relationship to society, herself, and Rome than the one he was raised to have.[87] Embracing her new reality with Ramiro/Mario would require Arianna to re-imagine the structure of her family and

---

84 Morante, *Arturo's*, 211. ("Adesso che aveva Carmine, dal mattino alla sera era ella stave sempre a cantare e a ridere, tanto era beata quando la sua bocca non rideva, ridevano i suoi occhi"; Morante, *Opere*, 1:1206.)

85 Morante, *Arturo's*, 141. ("E costei? Chi sa qual era il sogno che la faceva ridere di gioia! Forse, le pareva di ritrovarsi nella sua casa di Napoli, con tutta la sua famiglia nello stesso leto, e la comare anche?"; Morante, *Opere*, 1:1122.)

86 Bontempelli, *Separations*, 30. ("C'era ancora suo marito, perché Arianna non ha fantasia: suo marito che la guarda con occhi pieni di superiorità"; Bontempelli, *Il figlio*, 26; trans. modified.)

87 "Da sette anni non ho mai lasciato Mario un giorno solo. E da un anno solamente siamo venuti a Roma. E io non sapevo che esistesse piazza d'Italia; sono certa anche lui non è mai stato da queste parti: piazza d'Italia c'è, ed è in Trastevere. Come lo sapeva? Divento pazza" (Bontempelli, *Il figlio*, 30).

her role in it. Her inability to envision a different kind of family and happily exist in society contributes to her early death: "Arianna died for lack of imagination [*immaginazione*] when only imagination could have saved her [*ora che solo d'immaginazione avrebbe potuto vivere*]."[88] The novel depicts society as lacking imagination too, since it cannot accept Mario/Ramiro, but instead attempts to define, through arguments, letters, and a court case, a situation that is beyond societal norms.

Mariano, Mario's father, is even less receptive to Mario's transformation than his wife. Whereas Arianna struggles without success to understand the change, Mariano denies its existence. Before Mario's switch, the narrator established Arianna and Mariano's family as unquestionably traditional. Their chairs, in their picture-perfect living room, are described like those of the three little bears, with familial and gender roles embedded in the descriptions of their seats: "In this luminous space stood Mariano Parigi's deep armchair, Arianna's small soft one and, on the thickly carpeted floor, Mario's and the cat's cushions."[89] As less powerful members of the family, Arianna's and Mario's chairs take up less physical space in the house. Arianna hovers lovingly over Mario at the table, while Mariano criticizes his table manners.[90] The father, labelled the "pater familias," dominates the family, and his wife, son, and servants look to him as the ultimate authority.[91]

Both *The Boy with Two Mothers* and *Arturo's Island* contrast parents who exemplify their traditional roles with those who do not. In Bontempelli's novel, the familial situation, imagination, and behaviour of the other mother, Luciana, are diametrically opposed to those of the traditional Arianna and even more so to the family unit that includes both Arianna and Mariano. While Arianna's past is not described because her character needs no explanation besides the expectations of society, Luciana's life history occupies a significant portion of narrative space. Ramiro's mother, originally named Lucia Stirner, grew up with "little attention" and was left mostly to herself. Her mother was Neapolitan and her father, who raised her in Vienna, Austrian. She had a musical upbringing and, even when pregnant, dreamed about her musical career: "Her unborn child didn't play much of a role in

88 Bontempelli, *Separations*, 164. ("Arianna è morta, per mancanza d'immaginazione, ora che solo d'immaginazione avrebbe potuto vivere"; Bontempelli, *Il figlio*, 179.)
89 Bontempelli, *Separations*, 21. ("In quel vano luminosissimo erano la poltrona profonda di Mariano Parigi, la poltroncina morbida di donna Arianna, e per terra sopra un denso tappeti i cuscini di Mario e del gatto"; Bontempelli, *Il figlio,* 15.)
90 "Non ne faremo mai niente, di questo ragazzo" (Bontempelli, *Il figlio*, 15).
91 "Mariano Parigi, quarantenne, è il *pater familias*" (Bontempelli, 14).

her fantasies [*fantasticherie*]."[92] While Arianna appears completely dedicated to family and her familial roles, Luciana's imagination separates her from her family ties, including from her name: "The first thing she did was to choose a stage name, Luciana Veracina, to honor Francesco Maria Veracini, the composer whose heavenly sonatas she had studied with Hellmesberger. And immediately upon taking the name she was certain she had erased her past life."[93] Luciana invents a new identity for herself, and later for her son. In part because of her imagination and flexibility, she is unsurprised to see Ramiro return from the dead.

Luciana's approach to parenting Ramiro, the child of her lover, who committed suicide before she knew she was pregnant, draws on her creativity and reading. For instance, her violin playing played a crucial role in Ramiro's early days: "Sometimes when he would begin to cry she would take her violin, stand in front of him and play.... Then the baby would scream and she would compete with his screams by prying higher and higher sounds out of the violin. Ramiro would get louder. She'd get shriller, until their sounds penetrated the very walls of the apartment. She was certain they were playing a game that was enormously entertaining to the child."[94] For her the screams are not a signal of distress, but a noise and a part of her perception of the world as it relates to music and sound. Her reaction to Ramiro contrasts with the nervous, mundane, and motherly attentions of Arianna with Mario. At a key point, Luciana changes her style of parenting: "Over the years she also acquired a number of useless books on the subject of raising children. The boy was six when, perhaps as a consequence of reading one of them, she decided that it would be harmful for him to remain isolated from other children of his age."[95] Whereas Arianna mothers

---

92 Bontempelli, *Separations*, 51. ("Il figlio nascituro non aveva gran parte nelle fantas-
    ticherie"; Bontempelli, *Il figlio*, 54.)
93 Bontempelli, *Separations*, 51. ("Si scelse subito un nome d'arte, che fu Luciana
    Veracina, in onore del Veracini di cui aveva studiato con Hellmesberger le celesti
    sonate: adottò addirittura quel nome, convincendosi di cancellare così la vita pas-
    sata"; Bontempelli, *Il figlio*, 53.)
94 Bontempelli, *Separations*, 52. ("Qualche volta, quando lui cominciava a piangere,
    ella prendeva il violin, si metteva a suonare in faccia a Ramiro.... Allora il bambino
    a strillare; e lei a cercar di gareggiare con quegli strilli cavando dallo strumento
    suoni più acuti, e lui più forte, e lei acutissimi, che bucavano l'aria della stanza da
    tutte le parti: era convinta che stavano giocando e che quel gioco divertiva enorme-
    mente il bambino"; Bontempelli, *Il figlio*, 55.)
95 Bontempelli, *Separations*, 53–4. ("S'era procurata una quantità di libri inutili intorno
    all'educazione dei bambini. Il bambino aveva sei anni, quando Luciana, forse in
    seguito a una di queste letture, si convinse che gli sarebbe riuscito dannoso contin-
    uare a star così segregato dagli altri della sua età"; Bontempelli, *Il figlio*, 56.)

based on instinct and societal expectations, Luciana's behaviour is determined by her creativity and books. While the two very different mothers love their son deeply, the narrator criticizes them: Arianna for her lack of fantasy and Luciana for her nonsensicality.

Although there are many ways in which the alternative childhoods of Ramiro and Arturo can seem appealing, the absence of traditional rules does not mean that they are not subject to the demands of another. Arturo's childhood appears to be a space outside history or accountability. At the same time, however, his island, this nostalgic space, is also frequently associated with prison. He can be seen as being imprisoned on the island, which is itself the location of a prison.[96] His view of his father prevents him from interacting with others on the island or from leaving it: "But there was another reason, actually, another even more powerful reason to make me turn the prow back toward Procida when I got out into the open sea: the idea that my father might return while I was away. I felt it unbearable not to be on the island when he was there, and for this reason, although I was free and loved adventure, I never left the Procidan sea for other countries."[97]

Although Wilhelm may not purposely limit Arturo's choices, his character and his role as his father (his only family) necessarily restrict his son. Adding to Arturo's intense isolation, Wilhelm rarely allows him a glimpse of his life off the island.[98] Arturo is trapped, albeit partially by choice.[99] While Arturo is left to himself, Luciana keeps Ramiro close to her and focuses her creative energy on him. Although her obsessive attention can be attributed to intense love, his isolation borders on imprisonment: "Ramiro spent his first years in coddled solitude. Until he was six he knew only his mother."[100] While Wilhelm and Luciana offer contrasts to traditional models of parents, their power is still oppressive.

---

96 "Per molta gente, che vive lontano, il nome della mia isola significa il nome d'un carcere" (Morante, *Opere*, 1: 957).

97 Morante, *Arturo's*, 42. ("Ma in verità c'era poi un'altra ragione, ancora più forte, che, quando uscivo al largo, mi faceva presto rivoltare la prua verso Procida: il sospetto che, nella mia assenza, potesse ritornare mio padre. Mi sembrava insopportabile di non essere anch'io sull'isola quando lui c'era; e per questo, sebbene fossi libero e amassi tanto le grandi imprese, io non uscivo mai dal mare di Procida, verso altre terre"; Morante, *Opere*, 1:1001.)

98 "Lui non faceva mai parola sulla sua vita fuori dell'isola" (Morante, *Arturo's*, 38).

99 For more on the idea of entrapment in *Arturo's Island*, see Riviello, "The Motif of Entrapment."

100 Bontempelli, *Separations*, 53. ("Fino all'età di sei anni non conobbe che la madre"; Bontempelli, *Il figlio*, 56.)

Critics often describe Arturo's childhood as a nostalgic, free space, rather than one of neglect (or even abuse).[101] He idolizes his father, but his admiration does not necessarily result in filial comfort. Wilhelm's physical presence can, for instance, be overwhelming: "But if he looked up at me, his silent splendor would make me feel my littleness, and I felt like a shrimp in the presence of a great dolphin."[102] Contrasting these comments with Kafka's, whose relationship with his father is generally viewed as negative, reveal the more negative side of Arturo's upbringing. Like him, Kafka remarks upon the sense of physical domination that comes from his father's corporality. As with Arturo, it involves swimming:

> At that time, and at that time in every way, I would have needed encouragement. I was, after all, weighed down by your mere physical presence. I remember, for instance, how we often undressed in the same bathing hut. There was I, skinny, weakly, slight; you strong, tall, broad. Even inside the hut I felt a miserable specimen, and what's more, not only in your eyes but in the eyes of the whole world, for you were for me the measure of all things.... I was grateful to you for not seeming to notice my anguish, and besides, I was proud of my father's body.[103]

Kafka's long description of his father's body reflects many of the emotions Arturo expresses about his own father: most prominently, pride in his father's strength and embarrassment at his own physique – especially in contrast to the father's. This physical discomfort described by Arturo and Kafka relates not only to their fathers being physically larger but also to how the fathers fill their sons' worlds.

Wilhelm, in contrast, hardly pays attention to his son. While Arturo seemingly has a great deal of freedom, he feels the absence of his

---

101   See, e.g., Kalay's examination of *Arturo's Island*, which highlights the positive elements of Arturo's childhood: "Morante is offering the world of childhood as a counter-world in the hope that it can provide a vision of what could be and, therefore, serve to change an unacceptable status quo" (Kalay, *The Theme of Childhood in Elsa Morante*, 62).

102   Morante, *Arturo's*, 20. ("Ma se lui levava gli occhi a guardarmi, il suo splendore silenzioso mi richiamava alla coscienza della mia piccolezza. E mi pareva di essere un'alíce, alla presenza d'un grande delfino"; Morante, *Opere*, 1:974.)

103   Kafka, "Letter," 120-1. ("Damals und damals überall hätte ich die Aufmunterung gebraucht. Ich war ja schon niedergedrückt durch Deine bloße Körperlichkeit. Ich erinnere mich zum Beispiel daran, wie wir uns öfters zusammen in einer Kabine auszogen. Ich mager, schwach, schmal, Du stark, groß, breit. Schon in der Kabine kam ich mir jämmerlich vor, und zwar nicht nur vor Dir, sondern vor der ganzen Welt, denn Du warst für mich das Maß aller Dinge.... Dankbar war ich Dir dafür, daß Du meine Not nicht zu bemerken schienest, auch war ich stolz auf den Körper meines Vaters"; Kafka, *Letter to the Father*, 14, 16.)

mother, who died, and his father, who is frequently away. His laments on both counts present another side to his apparent freedom: "I longed for him to kiss me and caress me, as other fathers kiss and caress their children."[104] His father's leaving him for adventures, or so Arturo imagines, at times causes him to resent his boyhood and solitude: "I had a moment of revolt against the intransigence of life, which condemned me to a dead Siberian waste of days and nights before it removed the bitterness of being a boy."[105] Arturo here associates his life with a space connected to punishment and imprisonment: Siberia.

Arturo also suffers from not having his birth mother. In his eyes, his mother would have offered a desired point of security that he lacks: "A mother was someone who'd have waited for me to come home, who'd have thought of me day and night, someone who'd have approved of all I said, praised all I did."[106] While an imagined, non-existent mother can be idealized, when presented with Nunziata's attempts at maternal love, Arturo feels constricted. Katrin Wehling-Giorgi has examined how critics have often overlooked the more negative side of Morante's "maternal" mothers, instead emphasizing their caretaking and giving character:

> Much critical attention has thus far focused on the quintessential "nurturing" or "instinctual" function of the Morantian parent, the "real" mother for which the author herself proclaims a clear personal preference in one of her last interviews.... With the main focus on the idealised, self-sacrificing aspects of maternity, critics often ignore a central feature of Morante's portrayal of motherhood: the profound ambiguity which accompanies the maternal figure throughout her writings, depicting her as intensely loving and caring on the one hand, and as suffocating or even repulsive on the other.[107]

In contrast to Arturo, who romanticizes mothers, Wilhelm's description of experiencing a mother's love is consistent with the version of motherhood in Morante that Wehling-Giorgio discusses. Associating childhood with prison, Wilhelm claims, "No natural or historical event

---

104 Morante, *Arturo's*, 132. ("Mi venne una nostalgia ch'egli m baciasse e mi accarez-zasse, come fanno altri padri coi figli"; Morante, *Opere*, 1:1111.)
105 Morante, *Arturo's*, 33. ("Ebbi un pensiero di rivolta contro l'assolutezza della vita, che mi condannava a percorrere una Siberia sterminata di giorni e di notti prima di togliermi a questa amarezza: d'essere un ragazzino"; Morante, *Opere*, 1:992.)
106 Morante, *Arturo's*, 40. ("La madre era una che avrebbe atteso a casa i miei ritorni, giorno e notte pensando a me. Essa avrebbe provato tutte le mie parole, lodato tutte le mi imprese"; Morante, *Opere*, 1:999.)
107 Wehling-Giorgi, "Il mondo delle madri," 190–1.

means anything to her except in relation to you. And so, the whole of creation threatens to turn into a cage. That's what she wants, that's all that *love* of hers dreams of. What she'd really like would be to keep you always prisoner, the way you were when she was pregnant."[108] Nunziata contains both Wilhelm's and Arturo's understandings of mothers: her motherly love is both constricting and divine.[109]

Arturo objects to Wilhelm's negative characterization of mothers, partly based on the fact that Wilhelm experienced a German rather than Italian mother: "He was arguing from his own experience, which meant his big fat German mother. But mine was a dear little Italian."[110] In *Arturo's Island* and *The Boy with Two Mothers*, the non-traditional parent is associated with foreign, German-speaking lands. Like Luciana, Morante's Wilhelm was the product of unwed, Italian- and German-speaking parents: he grew up as the illegitimate child of a German woman until his father, Antonio Gerace, sent for him at the age of seventeen. The non-Italian identities of these parents and their unusual lifestyles are related since Wilhelm's and Luciana's non-traditional decisions are partly due to their mixed backgrounds. When Wilhelm's friend leaves him his house, the Casa dei Guaglioni, he remarks upon the fact that Wilhelm will never be able to stay in it for long: "People like you, who have mixed blood in their veins, never find rest or contentment; when they're in one place they want to be somewhere else, and as soon as they get somewhere else, they want to run away from there too."[111] His friend associates Wilhelm's multinational identity with an inability to stay in one place and, there-fore, to be a traditional husband or father. A different model of family comes from beyond the bonds of the nation.

Both Wilhelm and Luciana, although extremely different parents, shun the national institutions, like schools, that are generally consid-ered part of a regular childhood and that help integrate children into

---

108 Morante, *Arturo's*, 128. ("Qualsiasi fenomeno del cosmo, o evento della storia, a lei non si manifesta se non in relazione a te. A questo modo, il creato rischia di diventarti una gabbia. Lei ne sarebbe contenta, perché il suo *amore* non sogna altro. In realtà, essa vorrebbe sempre tenerti prigioniero, come al tempo ch'era incinta di te"; Morante, *Opere*, 1:1106.)

109 Stefania Lucamante has argued that male and female characters in Morante are exposed as having a series of faults (Lucamante, *A Multitude of Women*, 40).

110 Morante, *Arturo's*, 128. ("Lui ragionava secono la sua particolare esperienza; e cioè, secondo la madre sua, ch'era una tedesca, alta, grossa; ma la mia era un'italianuc-cia piccola"; Morante, *Opere*, 1:1107.)

111 Morante, *Arturo's*, 54. ("Quelli come te, che hanno sue sangui diversi nelle vene, non trovano mai riposo né contentezza; e mentre sono là vorrebbero trovarsi qua, e appena tornati qua, subito hanno voglia di scappar via"; Morante, *Opere*, 1:1016.)

society. Like Luciana, Wilhelm does not need to work to support himself, which allows him to remain distanced from society and to choose the ways in which he engages it. Arturo comments, "My father never bothered to send me to school; I was always on holiday, and my vagabond days, especially when he was away, had no rules or fixed hours at all."[112] These parents who push the boundaries of their expected social roles are particularly remarkable in their cultural contexts: Bontempelli's novel was written during fascist rule, and Morante's novel is set in fascist Italy. Wilhelm flouts fascist expectations of behaviour in multiple ways, including by appearing fairly uninterested in his children, prioritizing instead the male prisoner with whom he has fallen in love.

In these works, without a traditional family unit, some restrictions open up, including the boundaries of nations and expected roles. Wilhelm and Luciana are also described as not fitting into the standard view of male and female behaviour in their society. Luciana is a "dominating" woman, whom the patriarchal and traditional Mariano finds unsettling. Her imagination, intelligence, and independence contribute to this. She was never married and claims that Ramiro is more hers than Arianna's because she raised him alone and saw him die. She is the opposite of Mariano's unimaginative and dependent wife. Viewed by Arturo as an almost godly man, Wilhelm is described as powerful, handsome, and strong. Even before the end of the novel, which reveals that Arturo's idea of his father and his father's behaviour do not always align, there are signs that Wilhelm is not the stereotypically heroic male that Arturo has decided he is. As Guj has argued, "In spite of Wilhelm's proud and hero-like looks which he displays in playing with his son, when stung by a jelly-fish, he swoons like a young lady in distress."[113]

Arturo frames Wilhelm as godly, but his behaviour reveals him to be self-absorbed and perhaps weak. It becomes apparent that he can also be dominated, although never by a woman. While the taunts of a male prisoner, who calls him a parody and mocks his devotion, cast him in a new light, his relationship with his friend and benefactor, Romeo the Amalfitano, has already suggested that Arturo's father may be drawn more to men than women. Wilhelm's attraction to men is framed as related to his being German and Italian and, therefore, not held back

---

112 Morante, *Arturo's*, 12. ("Mio padre non si curò mai di farmi frequenter le scuole: io vivevo sempre in vacanza, e le mie giornate di vagabond, soprattutto durante le lunghe assenze di mio padre, ignoravano qualsiasi norma e orario"; Morante, *Opere*, 1:964.)

113 Guj, "Illusion and Literature in Morante's *L'isola di Arturo*," 151. For a discussion of Wilhelm as a "parody of the romance hero," see Guj, 151.

by traditional expectations. Related to how Arturo believes that his father's view of the family is wrong because he experienced only a German mother, Arturo initially cannot understand his father in view of societal expectations.

While the novels set up the characters with German backgrounds as being less traditional or religious than the solely Italian ones, they also associate them with a potentially more positive type of childhood, one that emphasizes imagination. All the models of family described, however, are shown to constrict the child. Like Bontempelli's novel, Morante's invites the reader to imagine the process of escaping from the familial unit, while at the same time revealing how difficult it is to accomplish, no matter how the family is configured. Extolling the family under fascism puts pressure on this unit as an organizing force for society, a line of enquiry that *The Boy with Two Mothers* and *Arturo's Island* investigate rather than attempt to eradicate.

Both novels offer ambiguous ways to escape the constricting bonds of the family. Luciana hopes to run away with her son, with the help of a "gypsy," named Solwanah, whose background is not incidental. Solwanah and his people are so removed from Italy and the idea of nations that he rarely travels to Italy and does not remember the name of the countries where he has been: "'Where did you come from? Where are you going?' 'We never know the names of places [*paesi*].'"[114] Solwanah lives beyond national boundaries. Luciana, hoping to escape the fights over family and the institutions of the Italian nation, asks Solwanah to take Ramiro. While she as the non-traditional mother pleads with the Roma Solwanah to help her and her son escape from a country that has a fixed idea of nation and family, the traditional mother, Nunziata, uses gypsies as the representation of loneliness, people she describes as anyone without a family: "And as he was born without a family, poor soul, the way he was, he'd have been alone like a gypsy his whole life through, like someone in the Foreign Legion."[115]

Solwanah does as asked, but he dies before Luciana discovers Ramiro's exact location. She is, therefore, unable to join her son. The end of Ramiro's story is also kept from the reader: Ramiro ends up, it seems, at sea, leaving no trace of how any of his family, or the institutions interested in him, can reach him. Arturo leaves his family

114 Bontempelli, *Separations*, 142. ("'Da dove siete venuti ora? dove andate?' 'Non sappiamo quasi mai i nomi dei paesi'"; Bontempelli, *Il figlio*, 154.)

115 Morante, *Arturo's*, 329–30. ("E lui, com'è nato senza una famiglia, così, poverello, sarebbe restato solo e zingaro per tutta la vita sua, uguale a un militare della Legione"; Morante, *Opere*, 1:1343.)

by the same sea. In fact, the boats in *The Boy with Two Mothers* and the boat that Arturo uses to leave are in the same waters since Procida is visible from both. As with Ramiro/Mario, Arturo's end could seem like the moment he finally escapes all models of family, from his dominating, distant father to his traditional stepmother, but neither end is purely positive.

Related to the ambiguous conclusions of the novels is the ambiguity of the sea. The watery ends of *The Boy with Two Mothers* and *Arturo's Island* can be productively compared with the watery one of "The Judgment." As Anderson argues, Georg's leap off the bridge can be seen as an attempt to achieve artistic freedom and escape into the literary: "The traffic that streams across the bridge is not just an image of urban life, but the liberated energy of the writer, the *Verkehr* of literary creation. Georg Bendemann plunges to his death, but the gymnast-writer comes to life."[116] If Georg's act is one of freedom, it is a freedom followed immediately by death. There is perhaps a moment of escape, but it ends in an unnatural death. His act separates him from his parents and, therefore, can be seen as a moment of potential freedom, but it also completely connects him to the family since he is, in fact, following his father's orders to drown himself, and his last words are about his parents.

The associations of the sea in Bontempelli's and Morante's novels are similarly multivalent, symbolizing both family and the escape from family. The sea is a place of nostalgia for Arturo, where he and his father would swim together. It also brings in visitors, like Silvestro, with news of the outside world.[117] Arturo narrates how he believed the sea's role in his life will change as he gets older: "Soon, at last, I'd reach the time I had longed for so much, when I should no longer be a boy but a man, and the sea, like a friend who had played with me and grown up beside me, would take me along to meet the oceans, and all the other countries, and the whole of the rest of life."[118] The sea opens out to different countries and paths, while always also connecting to his childhood. The sea is also related to death, as Arturo makes clear in his description of the Straits of Gibraltar.

---

116   Anderson, *Kafka's Clothes*, 89.

117   For Arturo, history comes to the island via the ocean; see Popoff, "Elsa Morante's *L'isola*," 20.

118   Morante, *Arturo's*, 162. ("Presto, ormai, per me, incomincerebbe finalmente l'età desiderata in cui non sarei più un ragazzino, ma un uomo; e lui, il mare, simile a un compagno che finora aveva sempre giocato assieme a me s'era fatto grande assieme a me, mi porterebbe via con lui a conoscere gli oceani, e tutte le altre terre, e tutta la vita!"; Morante, *Opere*, 1:1147.)

At the end of *The Boy with Two Mothers*, the sea separates Luciana from Ramiro, the same sea that she had wanted to share with him. She writes to her son: "When I can come and get you again, I'll take you back here with me and you'll see how beautiful the sea is and I'll tell you many things."[119] However, she never communicates with Ramiro again. Solwanah makes it clear that Ramiro is beyond Italy, in the sea: "'Out there.' Solwanah made a vague gesture toward the now dark, still sea. 'We've been forbidden to come back to Italy. But I can get you out there.'"[120] Later, after Solwanah's death, Luciana imagines reuniting with her son: "Solwanah said, 'Out there.' Out there is so, so big. But afterward we'll be together forever, for all our lives and then in that other life too."[121] In her imagining, she will reunite with her son in a space beyond the nation and beyond time. After Ramiro's disappearance, Luciana, who has not appeared religious earlier, talks about being united with Ramiro in the afterlife.

In *Civilization and Its Discontents*, Freud analysed the symbolic role of the ocean in terms of religion and child development, with religion offering a replacement for an infant's attachment to its parents: "It is a feeling which he would like to call a sensation of 'eternity,' a feeling as of something limitless, unbounded – as if it were 'oceanic.'"[122] Freud comments that this feeling of eternity is tied to a lack of development: "Thus we are perfectly willing to acknowledge that the 'oceanic' feeling exists in many people, and we are inclined to trace it back to an early phase of ego-feeling."[123] The last sentence of *The Boy with Two Mothers* connects the sea with early childhood since the sea is "white as milk," and it invokes a religious feeling: "At dawn the sea was a flat, gleaming expanse, white as milk, all the way to the furthest curve which encloses and seals it to the heavens."[124]

Having lost her son, again, Luciana seems to turn to religious thoughts to unite with him, whereas Arturo turns to patriotism to help

---

119 Bontempelli, *Separations*, 137. ("Quando potrò venire a prenderti ti condurrò qui e vedrai com'è bello questo mare, allora ti racconterò tante cose"; Bontempelli, *Il figlio*, 149.)

120 Bontempelli, *Separations*, 166. ("'In là...' Solwanah fece un cenno vago verso il mare, ch'era immobile e nero. 'Le hanno proibito di tornare in Italia. Ma io so andarci'"; Bontempelli, *Il figlio*, 181.)

121 Bontempelli, *Separations*, 167. ("Solwanah ha detto 'in là,' ma in là è tanto grande. Poi saremo insieme sempre, per tutta la vita, e anche dopo in quell'altra"; Bontempelli, *Il figlio*, 183.)

122 Freud, *Civilization and Its Discontents*, 11.

123 Freud, 20.

124 Bontempelli, *Separations*, 170. ("Sotto l'alba il mare tornò immobile, liscio, bianco come una distesa di latte fino all'ultimo cerchio dove si chiude e suggella col cielo"; Bontempelli, *Il figlio*, 185.)

motivate his leaving the island. After learning about the Second World War from Silvestro, Arturo decides to join him in battle. He is headed to a war, in part because of his certainties, those that emphasize family: "The people will acclaim us, and the Procidans, with our example, will become the heroes of all nations, like the Macedonians; even lots of haughty, grand people, will behave as if they were my father's brothers and be our retinue and follow us into action."[125] The only way Arturo sees himself escaping the bonds of family is through war, an experience that, like the family unit, he romanticized in his youth but finds quite different in reality. These feelings are made clear in his comments as a narrator, which Popoff has analysed.[126]

As his boat moves through the sea, Arturo turns his back on his island and his home. The book ends: "Around our ship the water was as uniform and boundless as the ocean. The island could no longer be seen."[127] The sea could appear to be a space of freedom and opportunity, of escape and change. However, although Arturo turns his back on his family, he dedicates an entire book to them. He may not be able to see the physical shape of the island, but whether he has freed himself from it mentally remains a question. In an earlier version of the novel, he is described as writing from an African prison camp, about the imprisoning experience of family that took place on an island associated with prison.[128]

Just before leaving Procida, he has a dream that connects the family he is leaving behind (Wilhelm, Nunziata, and their child) with war: "In contrast to the wonderful evening I had just spent, I had the most disturbing dreams, in which N., Carminiello, and my father all appeared muddled up. Then armored cars, black flags with skulls on them, and black-uniformed fighters all mixed up with dark kings and Indian philosophers and pale, blood-splashed women came rumbling past together, a great crowd that roared over the walled trench in which I was crouching."[129] It is ultimately unclear whether Arturo, going off to

---

125 Morante, *Arturo's*, 101. ("Tutta la gente ci acclama, e i Procidani, col nostro esem-pio, si fanno i più bravi eroi di tutte le nazioni, come i Macedoni; e anche molto alteri, e signorili, come fossero fratelli a mio padre"; Morante, *Opere*, 1:1075.)

126 Popoff, "Elsa Morante's *L'isola*."

127 Morante, *Arturo's*, 351. ("Intorno alla nostra nave, la marina era tutta uniforme, sconfinata come un oceano. L'isola non si vedeva più"; Morante, *Opere*, 1:1369.)

128 See Zagra, "Il racconto di due prigionieri."

129 Morante, *Arturo's*, 345. ("In contrasto con la serata, così bella, che avevo trascorsa, ebbi dei sogni affannosi. Accorrevano confusamente N., Carminiello, mio padre. E poi un disordine e un fracasso di carri armati, di bandiere nere stemmate di teschi, di combattenti in divisa nera, mescolate con re mori e filosofi indiani e femmine smorte e sanguinanti. Tutta questa folla passava con un rombo enorme su una trincea murata nella quale io giacevo disteso"; Morante, *Opere*, 1:1363.)

fight, has really left the bonds of family behind and, moreover, whether the violence required for his distance is in any way positive.[130] Violence also allows Ramiro to leave the family behind, and Luciana regrets having requested it, for it is ultimately what separates her from her son. Solwanah is killed in an act undertaken for Luciana: "His head is blown to pieces, but you can tell he's not from around here."[131]

As in "The Judgment" and "The Metamorphosis," death appears to be the primary mode of escape. While there may be no solution to the problems of family other than death, literature like Kafka's, Morante's, and Bontempelli's reminds readers that it is a societal structure not to be extolled unconditionally but rather interrogated.[132] In writing about the family there may not be freedom, but there is the potential to explore the ambiguities that society often clarifies, although with restrictions. As Vivian Liska has powerfully argued in terms of Kafka's uncommon German-Jewish communities, Kafka "moves into a realm where ambiguity does not need to be avoided."[133] The seemingly unavoidable dichotomies of rebellion versus submission and a child's identity vis-à-vis a parent can be left open in these texts in a way that takes a critical view of the concept of family, but does not claim to destroy it.

Family is so embedded in one's sense of reality that questioning its structure can be a difficult literary act: Kafka's, Bontempelli's, and Morante's works have been associated with literary movements that break away from reality.[134] All three authors discussed have been linked

---

130 "However, like Procida itself, home to a penitentiary, this nostalgia is a prison, a troubling retreat from adult historical consciousness" (Popoff, "Elsa Morante's *L'isola*," 20).

131 Bontempelli, *Separations*, 169. ("La testa è sfracellata, ma certo non era uno di qui"; Bontempelli, *Il figlio*, 185.)

132 For an insightful and thorough discussion of Morante as politically engaged, and of *Arturo's Island*, see Leavitt, "Una seconda fase del realismo."

133 Liska, *When Kafka Says We*, 25. As I have argued (Ziolkowski, "The Ends of an Empire," 356), her arguments about community can be productively used to discuss not only German-Jewish communities but also other groups in which the issues of community are complex and ambiguous, and they have been represented as such by a series of authors.

134 Bontempelli's questioning of the family reinforces Wissia Fiorucci's argument that his works from the 1920s can be seen as resisting many fascist ideals, although he was officially fascist at the time. She examines how his works were perhaps also not viewed as anti-fascist because of his magical realism. See also this quote from Bonsaver: "Bontempelli's surreal settings kept his narrative work away from controversy" (Bonsaver, *Censorship and Literature*, 151). Bontempelli's magical realism has been debated as being both a part of and a questioning of fascist ideology; see Jewell, "Magic Realism and Real Politics." Kafka's work has been important to many Latin American authors of magical realism because of how it combines solid

together, not because of their portrayals of the family, but because of their narrative styles: "But the immediate sources of Morante's writing are to be found in the period between the ways, in Kafka and surrealism, and, more locally in the 'magic realism' (*realismo magico*) which Massimo Bontempelli put forward in 1927–1928 as the epitome of the avant-garde under Fascism."[135] Kafka, Bontempelli, and Morante are able to include a new perspective, in part because of their narrative moments, which seem to be out of our world, perhaps surreal or magical. In doing so, they cause the reader to reflect on some of the most elemental parts of our society, such as the family. The next chapter also explores how Kafka and certain Italian authors' comparable contexts leads to literature that takes a critical look at the most elemental parts of human experience. In chapter 5, the literary representations prompt readers to question their humanity.

---

reflections on society with a way of viewing society from a completely different point of view. Morante's work also sheds light on certain societal truths because of its combination of realism and other elements. While several scholars discuss *Arturo's Island* as being fable-like, Leavitt argues persuasively that Morante did not "believe realism necessarily to be opposed to myth or fantasy" (Leavitt, "Una seconda fase del realismo," 33).

135 Caesar, "Elsa Morante," 212.

Chapter Five

The Human-Animal Boundary, Italian Style: Kafka's Red Peter in Conversation with Svevo's Argo, Morante's Bella, and Landolfi's Tombo

He would come here, sometimes, to see the animals in their cages. He said he could hear them cry at night. He lived in that house there in front, on Veneto street. He said he heard them at night and recognized them by their cries. He looked at animals as if he understood their language. When he arrived here in the afternoon, he would immediately go to the bear's cage and stay there for up to twenty minutes. After the bear, he would visit an old lioness, then he would go to find the exotic birds. Maybe I'm mistaken, but it seems to me that in front of certain animals, Buzzati took off his hat.

– A watchman at the Milan Zoo[1]

Italian Literature, Kafka, and Animal Studies

The study of animals in literature was once considered a rather frivolous topic, belonging to the realm of children and free time, but over the last few decades, it has become a notable site of interdisciplinary study. Organized under the rubric of animal studies, it has become central in debates about what being "human" means, as well as how humans should treat other animals.[2] In other interdisciplinary studies, literature

---

1 "Veniva qui, qualche volta, a vedere gli animali in gabbia. Diceva che li sentiva piangere la notte. Lui abitava in quella casa lì di fronte, in via Veneto. Diceva che li sentiva di note e li riconosceva dai loro lamenti. Guardava gli animali come se capisse il loro linguaggio. Quando arrivava qui nel pomeriggio, andava subito alla gabbia dell'orso e restava lì anche venti minuti. Dopo l'orso, visitava una vecchia leonessa, poi andava a trovare gli uccelli esotici. Forse mi sbaglio, ma mi è parso che Dino Buzzati davanti a certi animali si togliesse il cappello" (Battaglia, *Il mistero in Dino Buzzati*, 15).

2 See, e.g., a recent *New York Times* article on the rise of animal studies classes (Gorman, "Animal Studies Cross Campus to Lecture Hall"); and Kari Weil's book on the reasons for the growth in attention, *Thinking Animals*.

frequently gets pushed to the margins or occupies a position second-ary to the social sciences or sciences, but in animal studies it consist-ently plays a central role, partly because its imaginative explorations of human-animal interactions often relate to, predate, and go beyond cur-rent topics of debate in science, law, animal rights, and consumerism.[3] Certain texts, like Kafka's "Ein Bericht für eine Akademie" ("A Report to an Academy"), fulfil an especially prominent function in interdisci-plinary discussions of human and non-human animals.[4] Several critics have noted his exceptionalism within animal studies; for instance, Jean Christophe Bailly has referred to him as "the only writer, it seems to me, who has given animals speech ... and succeeded in doing so in a register that was no longer that of the fable."[5] While at times ignored by animal studies, Italian authors also wrote many narrations that give

---

3 About literature's marginal role in many interdisciplinary studies, see Marjorie
   Perloff, "It Must Change" ("Presidential Address 2006"). "But scholars of animals
   and animality today are mapping more permeable species boundaries, and, for
   reasons that are less clear, locating narrative as a zone of integration, one that
   does not end in literary studies, so much as it begins to explain how story forms
   operate centrally within shifting perceptions of species life. Through their very
   indeterminacy, narrative processes thus appear to concern the very conditions of
   possibility for human (always along with other) ways of being" (McHugh, *Animal
   Stories*, 2). To offer one more example of literature's remarkable role in animal
   studies, de Waal begins a discussion of anthromorphism with Xenophanes and
   Homer in his important article that explains his term "anthropodenial" (de Waal,
   "Anthropomorphism and Anthropodenial").
4 "A Report to an Academy" is a foundational text for Jennifer Ham and Matthew
   Senior, eds., *Animal Acts*; Nigel Rothfels, ed., *Representing Animals*; Nigel Rothfels,
   Savages and Beasts; Paul Shepard, *Thinking Animals*; and J.M. Coetzee, *The Lives of
   Animals*. Coetzee's 1997 Tanner lectures, featuring Kafka's short story "A Report
   to an Academy," prompted a fictionalized dialogue from the moral philosopher
   Peter Singer, published in *The Lives of Animals*, and were transformed into a novel,
   Elizabeth Costello. Derrida's foundational address to the 1997 Cerisy conference,
   "The Autobiographical Animal," is full of literary references, including to Kafka,
   and he claims that the difference between philosophical knowledge and poetic
   thinking is considerations of the animal; see Derrida, *The Animal That Therefore
   I Am*, which is based on the talks. Kafka also plays a notable role in Frans de
   Waal's *Are We Smart Enough to Know How Smart Animals Are?*, in which this prima-
   tologist and ethnologist sees his own animal research as linked to Kafka's writing.
   "Following in the footsteps of Kafka and Uexküll, we are trying to get under
   the skin of other species, trying to understand them on their terms" (de Waal,
   13). Kafka, particularly his "A Report to an Academy," is a special point of focus
   in Deleuze and Guattari's discussions of "becoming animal" (*Kafka*). The text is
   a central one for Weil's analysis of the animal turn: "Long before the existence of
   the Great Ape Project, the problematic was exposed in Franz Kafka's 1919 story
   'A Report to an Academy'" (Weil, "A Report on the Animal Turn," 3).
5 Bailly, *The Animal Side*, 39.

animals speech in a realistic voice. Especially since literature has been instrumental in the current rethinking of human and non-human animal relations, the wealth of Italian literary animals that tend to be overlooked by animal studies offers different perspectives on relationships between animals and humans.

The often-praised particularity of "A Report to an Academy" is best understood in the context of talking-animal stories, which I organize into three types (transformation, fable, and realistic) and outline here, with particular reference to the modern Italian literary tradition and Kafka, who wrote all three types of work. The transformation type consists of stories in which the communication between humans and animals is fantastical since the animals can speak as a result of some act of magic, bizarre science or unexplained occurrences; examples include Apuleius's *The Golden Ass*, Cervantes's "The Colloquy of the Dogs," Hoffmann's "Report of an Educated Young Man," and Kafka's "The Metamorphosis." An animal may suddenly be blessed with the ability to speak or a human may transform into an animal in these stories, but neither scenario is realistic. Even when, as in "The Metamorphosis" or Landolfi's "Il babbo di Kafka" ("Kafka's Dad"), the reaction to the transformed creature can be characterized as realistic, the transformation itself cannot be similarly described.[6] As critics have discussed about Kafka's most famous tale, the transformation in many of these stories often reveals a human's unhappiness with his or her role in society.[7] This misery with one's lot in life can be so extreme that the person ceases to be human, and it often has more to do with his or her place in society than any relationship between humans and animals.[8]

The fable type of talking-animal story, which includes many older works – *Pinocchio*, fables, children's tales, and Kafka's "Investigations of a Dog" – animals speak without describing how they found the ability to communicate or how we understand them. In several of these stories, significant attention is paid to how the species of the narrator shapes his or her narration. As one can tell even from the title, Moravia's "Gli odori e l'osso" ("Smells and Bone") focuses on what is important to the dog narrator. He begins with: "The world, this is definite, is

---

6 "Kafka's Dad" tells of Kafka's reaction to finding a spider with the head of his father in his home. The 1942 story offers a reflection on Kafka's relationship with his father as well as Kafka's influence on Landolfi. See Capek-Habekovic, *Tommaso Landolfi's Grotesque Images*, 18; and Romagnoli, "Landolfi e il fantastico," 23–4.

7 Many Marxist interpretations, e.g., concentrate on the relationship between Gregor Samsa's miserable life and his transformation; see the pieces by Fast, 12–13; Hajek, 115–116; and Suchov, 146–9; in Hughes, *Franz Kafka*.

8 Ortese's *Iguana* has been interpreted this way.

made of bones and odors."[9] Landolfi's "Favola" ("Fable") also involves a dog's concept of the world, which emphasizes smells and the significance of urinating. Landolfi's "Fable" and Moravia's "Smells and Bone" can be incorporated into a conversation about how dogs conceive of the world since these animals often reveal having a distinctly doggy vision and use vocabulary somewhat differently than a human narrator would. The works, however, do not focus on how dogs and humans communicate with each other. While often more complex than the "purely allegorical animals in Aesop's and La Fontaine's fables,"[10] these animals tend to call out for allegorical readings, and one could situate them in the long history of philosophical dogs.[11] Finally, how these animals are capable of narration is not a question.

In contrast to the transformation and fable types of stories, "A Report to an Academy" portrays an animal, an ape named Red Peter, learning to communicate in a verisimilar way due to circumstances that are potentially repeatable. Elements that contribute to his linguistic development include capture, isolation from one's own species, and desire for escape, rather than magic or inexplicable circumstances. The captured ape learns to act human in order to find a way out of his imprisonment. Red Peter reflects on his inability to communicate as ape: his story makes clear that human-animal communication is always problematic. Because of the process that leads Red Peter to develop human speech, Kafka has been read as marking a transitional point in our understanding of ourselves as human and in our relationship to other animals. Marian Scholtmeijer notes, "In a post-Darwinian world, *all* stories are stories about apes told by other apes – or at least primates. Implicitly, all stories are about the struggle of a particular species of ape to invent and preserve a nonanimal identity for itself. Only a few writers consciously incorporate that struggle into the bodies of their texts."[12] Scholtmeijer, like many other critics, views Kafka as one of these rare authors, and the typology explained above makes clear why. Kafka's story of Red Peter belongs in the rare category of realistic talking-animal story.

What distinguishes Kafka's "Report to an Academy" from the transformation and fable types of animal stories – the ape's realistic learning and the description of the process of human-animal communication – also characterizes several Italian stories. In fact, although generally uncommon among animal stories, many Italian stories describe animals that

---

9 "Il mondo, questo è sicuro è fatto di ossa e di odori" (Moravia, *Una cosa è una cosa*, 335).
10 Castaldi, "The Word Made Animal Flesh," 76.
11 On philosophical dogs, see Ziolkowski, "Talking Dogs." See Castaldi on Landolfi.
12 Scholtmeijer, "What Is 'Human'?," 139.

learn to speak in a credible manner: the point of the stories is not only what the animals say but the fact that they can talk at all and how they achieve this ability to communicate. This chapter puts Italian talking animals into conversation with Kafka's famous Red Peter from "A Report to an Academy" to examine the significance of these amazing Italian literary creatures. By highlighting these shared qualities as well as some important differences, this chapter places several Italian works into the discourse in animal studies in which Kafka's story occupies a major place.

The lack of attention that some of these stories have received indicates a persistent issue in animal studies, which has drawn primarily from French, American, English, and German literature for examples.[13] Several questions asked by studies on world literature help shed light on the sometimes limited literary selections in animal studies: considering the questions of whose world and which texts are examined alters the shape of the field.[14] The broader the range of literature included in animal studies, the more diverse the critical view of animals and animal-human animal connections will be, especially since literary traditions also affect the portrayals of animals. For instance, in Italian literature, a she-wolf (*lupa*) will recall both the *lupa* of Dante's *Divine Comedy* and the one depicted all over Rome with Romulus and Remus. In other words, both literary formation – for example, the significance of bestiaries in Italy – and cultural formation – for example, how the Catholic church's views on animals affect perspectives in Italy – contribute to the representations of animals.[15]

With Giorgio Agamben and other thinkers, Italian philosophy has been identified as being particularly receptive to the constructed nature of the human-animal boundary, but the reasons for the prominence of Italian

---

13 Since I first made this argument in 2009 and 2010, the landscape has changed somewhat. Then I was able to say that animal studies had essentially ignored Italian literature. Now there is, e.g., Past and Amberson's *Thinking Italian Animals*, which takes a range of approaches to Italian literature and animal studies, as well as a growing number of scholars working on this topic. After being on a panel together (MLA 2012), in which I presented a version of this chapter, Damiano Benvegnù published a chapter in *Creatural Fictions*, making some similar arguments to those I present here.

14 Weil, in a discussion of the rise of animal studies, states, "French, German, British, Russian, and American, these texts spring from even as they write against our Western literary and cultural heritage regarding human-animal relations" (Weil, *Thinking Animals*, xix).

15 While *bestiary* is generally defined as a "medieval" collection (e.g., in the *Oxford English Dictionary*), it has been used to label numerous modern Italian works, such as the works mentioned above and *Bestiari del Novecento*, a collection on the animals of twentieth-century authors (Biagini and Nozzoli). The emphasis on bestiaries relates, in part, to the large role that medieval literature plays in the modern Italian literary tradition.

thinkers in discussions of the human-animal boundary have just begun to be discussed.[16] While Agamben has a remarkable English *fortuna*, critics rarely note his significant Italian context. His *The End of the Poem* (in English and French), which contains a short piece on Morante and animals (a topic that will be discussed later in this chapter), was originally called *Categorie italiane* (*Italian Categories*). With the removal of the word *Italian* from the title, the Italian-ness of Agamben's book has been suppressed to render the work more appealing to an international audience.[17]

Elena Past and Deborah Amberson's *Thinking Italian Animals: Human and Posthuman in Modern Italian Literature and Film* marks an important turn towards including Italian literature and film in animal studies. My chapter adds to the work of reconsidering Italian literature in light of debates about the human-animal boundary by concentrating on communication across species. I will discuss how the way in which animals express themselves in modern Italian literature is significant for animal studies and how perspectives from this field of study shed new light on Italian literature. Stories by Italo Svevo, Tommaso Landolfi, Elsa Morante, and Dino Buzzati will be considered in terms of how animals communicate with humans and how humans try to understand them. My chapter both examines the realistically communicating animals of Italian literature and discusses why there are such notable numbers of these creatures.

While this chapter focuses on the various modes of communication that animals use in twentieth-century Italian literature, particularly as the stories relate to Kafka's "A Report to an Academy," an interpretation of the many conversing creatures of Italy could be arranged in other ways. They could be organized by author, looking at what individual authors contribute to conversations about animals and animal-human relationships.[18] This approach would allow a sustained analysis of

---

16 "Italian thought stands as a tradition that, unlike much of Western philosophy from Descartes to Heidegger, does not seek to suppresss the biological or 'animal' part of man in its construction of human identity" (Past and Amberson, "Introduction," 4).

17 The Italian circulation of Elsa Morante's materials led to Agamben's comments on Morante and animals: his piece on Morante in *The End of the Poem* begins, "I own the copy of Spinoza's *Ethics* that belonged to Elsa Morante; it was given to me by Carlo Cecchi in remembrance of Elsa" (Agamben, *The End of the Poem*, 102).

18 Several works follow this revealing path, including Trama's monograph on Landolfi and Posenato's on Buzzati. Paola Trama examines the range and power of Landolfi's animals (Trama, *Animali e fantasmi della scrittura*), as does Simone Castaldi's "The Word Made Animal Flesh." Posenato's *Il "bestiario" di Dino Buzzati* is dedicated to discussing Buzzati's animals, and the edited volume (Buzzati, *Il "Bestiario"*) brings together Buzzati's fictional and non-fictional writings on animals. A smaller volume (Svevo, *Favole*) has done the same for Svevo's animal works.

how one author's animal representations develop and give focus to the multiple, potential points of inspiration that contributed to these authors' remarkable portrayals, but it would not necessarily highlight the overarching significance of modern Italian talking animals in the broader literary landscape.

Italian animal stories could also be presented based on the types of animal: the birds of Pasolini and Palazzeschi as opposed to the dogs of Landolfi, Moravia, Svevo, and Buzzati and so on. Despite Derrida and the many debates on anthropocentrism, animal species are often lumped together in the term *animal*, as if humans have a similar relationship to birds and dogs, fleas and dolphins, and as if these creatures could reflect similar things about us. Tracing the trails of individual animals in Italian literature, as has been done, for instance, more generally for dogs, could reveal specific aspects of not only their unique representational opportunities but also our ideas of their relationship to us, as an individual species. This relationship is worth considering in this context since the species of an animal affects whether he or she can be seen to be speaking realistically.[19] For instance, a dog or cat that makes sounds that a child understands, as in Morante, differs greatly from a spider or lizard that is described doing the same. A number of animals produce sounds that we associate with speech or song, like birds. "Hearing" them differs from "hearing" an ant.

Dogs and non-human primates play a particularly significant role in this chapter, but given their different modes of being close to humans, they are also quite distinct in how they can be seen as communicating with or like us. Because of the physical similarities between apes and humans, Kafka's ape, who perhaps transformed into a man, would not be as powerful had he been a different creature. The story has elicited discussions about how much ape or human the speaker is. Theatrical representations exemplify this debate since he appears more or less apish or mannish (or even womanish), depending on the production.

Buzzati's "L'arrivista" ("The Social Climber," or "Arriviste"), meanwhile, describes a dog who has worked to become a man. This story reveals numerous parallels to "A Report to an Academy." The dog has even become a worker for an insurance company, like Kafka.[20] Like Red Peter, he states that he had wanted to become a man: "Where did I want to arrive? Here, exactly where I arrived, at man!"[21] At the same time, he

---

19 On dogs, see Giardina, "Il viaggio interrotto."

20 "Uomo! Così mi conoscete. Giovane impiegato di una grande Compagnia di assicurazioni, con discrete prospettive di carriera" (Buzzati, *Il "Bestiario,"* 140).

21 "Dove volevo arrivare? Qui, esattamente, dove arrivato sono. All'uomo!" (Buzzati, 140).

declares that the idea of progress, as defined by humans, is not necessarily appealing because dogs feel a kind of peace that humans do not.[22] Similarly, Red Peter thinks that becoming human was not a great feat, but a necessary one. His report makes clear that he lost a great deal in the process of becoming human.

While "L'arrivista" contains several similarities to "A Report to an Academy," there is a lack of focus on the dog's actual process and ability to speak (and write). To suppose that people will believe a dog in human clothing to be human requires a much greater stretch of the imagination than for an ape. The story describes the dog becoming human, rather than communicating with humans. The idea of a canine communicating with us, as will be discussed, is potentially realistic, whereas the idea of a hound being confused for a human is not. A vast, unnatural physical transformation must have occurred, although it is not clear how, unlike most stories of the transformation type.

In the Italian stories that follow, no physical transformation occurs, but a human often learns to understand another animal. In many of these works, questions remain about the exact meaning of the animal's communication, which is a significant part of what makes Kafka's ape story so powerful. The following section analyses Kafka's "A Report to an Academy" and Svevo's "Argo and His Master" to discuss their realistic communication as well as to establish points of reference for further examinations of the human-animal boundary in Svevo, Landolfi, Morante, and Buzzati.

Communication across Species: The Monologues of Kafka's Red Peter and Svevo's Argo

Primarily recognized for his novels, Italo Svevo also wrote short stories, including a remarkable animal tale that presents a crisis of what being human means and demonstrates numerous connections to Kafka's much more famous animal story.[23] In "Argo e il suo padrone" ("Argo and His Master"), a man attempts to teach Italian to his dog, Argo, after reading about an impressively expressive German dog, who, like Red

---

22 "Il progresso, come lo intendono gli uomini, li lascia indifferenti. Perché evadere, perché rinunciare a se stessi, perché rinnegare la beata ignoranza che dà la pace dell'anima" (Buzzati, 140).

23 For other considerations of "Argo e il suo padrone," see, e.g., Bondanella, "Franz Kafka and Italo Svevo"; Ziolkowski, "Svevo's Dogs" (an earlier version has been available online since 2011); Ziolkowski, "Kafka and Italy"; and Benvegnù, "The Tortured Animals of Modernity."

Peter, can "talk like a human being: in fact, rather more intelligently, as they were asking its advice. The dog pronounced difficult German words which even I would hardly be able to say."[24] The ability of the German dog to learn a human language prompts the man to reflect on his own linguistic skills, and, in the end, it is he who learns a new language: "As was to be expected, from the lessons we gave each other, the more highly evolved of the two learned more."[25]

In the first section of "Argo and His Master," the man relates the difficult process of learning to understand Argo, and the remaining sections consist of Argo's monologues, translated by the man. The man compares his experience of understanding Argo to Darwin's discoveries: "When I speak of it I am as proud of it as my predecessors – Volta, Darwin or Columbus – could ever have been in discovering other aspects of nature."[26] According to the man, understanding another species follows Darwin's analysis of the connections between the species. Darwin's discoveries prompted a continual investigation of how close we are to our animal "pasts." "A Report to an Academy" explores this closeness, in part, by describing a race to humanity, but then problematizing whether it actually represents progress.

The isolation of Svevo's narrator and Red Peter plays an important part in what enables Argo's owner and the ape to master another's language. While Red Peter is taken from his home and caged, Argo's master is banished to a mountain and scorned by the small community of people that live there. Separated from their own kind, Red Peter and the dog's owner are more likely to learn to communicate with another species. While the transformation may succeed, in part, thanks to the particular character of those involved, it is not difficult to imagine another bored master learning to understand his dog or another trapped ape imitating and "becoming" human. This repeatable, or ordinary, element of the species' changes distinguishes both stories from most tales of talking animals.

The stories are constructed so as to appear as plausible as possible. Indeed, "Argo and His Master" describes a situation that has been the focus of numerous studies in the past few years: scientists attempting to

---

24 "Argo and His Master," in Svevo, *Short Sentimental Journey and Other Stories*, 165; hereafter cited as *AM* (Svevo, *Racconti e scritti*, 2:97). The Italian original will be cited as *AP*.

25 *AM*, 167. ("Come prevedibile, dalle lezioni che ci davamo a vicenda, apprese di più l'essere più evoluto"; *AP*, 99.)

26 *AM*, 167. ("Parlandone, ne sono superbo come potevano esserlo coloro che prima di me scopersero altri lembi di natura: Volta, Darwin o Colombo"; *AP*, 99.)

understand dog language.[27] Most talking-animal stories do not portray this process of communication. As Alice Kuzniar has explained in *Melancholia's Dog*, "Given all the talking-dog stories, comic strips, and movies, it is surprisingly rare to find those that take seriously the attempt to find an adequate voice for that which remains inaccessible. For how can one possibly capture the subjective character of an animal's experience in a language foreign to it?"[28] Svevo portrays the strangeness of Argo's perspective not only through the animal's unique vocabulary but also because of the way the work is framed. Since the master translates the dog's monologues, it is difficult for the reader to know exactly what Argo himself may have meant.

"A Report to an Academy" often highlights the instability of language by drawing attention to the language being used and to problems of expression.[29] Although Red Peter may mock the discourse common in academic talks, his phrasing also emphasizes that meaning is fluid, that words construct a particular reality, and that the reader or listener may not always understand what the speaker intended to say. Red Peter consistently underscores the fact that language merely approximates what he tries to express. This philosophical problem is aggravated by his condition of being an ape: "Naturally, today I can use human words only to sketch my apish feelings of the time, and so I misstate them."[30] The ape cannot discuss his animal experience because human language lacks the proper vocabulary: "Language is at the core of Kafka's critique of assimilation as a process that gives voice only by destroying the

---

27 Barbara Smuts says, "In the language I am developing here [with her dog], relating to other beings as persons has nothing to do with whether or not we attribute human characteristics to them. It has to do, instead, with recognizing that they are social subjects, like us, whose idiosyncratic, subjective experience of us plays the same role in their relations with us that our subjective experience of them plays in our relations with them" (Smuts, "Reflections," 118). Guagnini's introduction to a Portuguese translation of Svevo's shorter works contrasts Argo's speech with modern canine language experiments (Guagnanini, "Svevo: A arte do conto").

28 Kuzniar, *Melancholia's Dog*, 54.

29 Red Peter frequently refers to the words he chooses by commenting on his own use of metaphors, idioms, and images – e.g., "to continue the metaphor" (KSS, 77) ("um in Bilde zu bleiben"; Kafka, *Erzählungen*, 322) – and "There is an excellent German saying" (KSS, 83) ("Es gibt eine ausgezeichnete deutsche Redensart"; Kafka, *Erzählungen*, 332). Red Peter also uses the word *Sinn* repeatedly to express the exact significance of his words.

30 KSS, 79. ("Ich kann natürlich das damals affenmäßig Gefühlte heute nur mit Menschenworten nachzeichnen und verzeichnen und verzeichne es infolgedessen"; Kafka, 325.)

self that would speak. What is the self, Kafka's story asks, that has no memory of its past and no means of representing it? Must that (animal) self be a blank page for others to write upon?"[31]

As opposed to representing the ape's thoughts in human language, Kafka's story leaves openly unknowable what humans cannot know: animal life. Martin Puchner observes,

> Kafka thus does not attempt, through sympathy, to represent the ape as ape, supposedly freed from all anthropological machines. As a human writing for other humans about apes, that would be impossible or naive. Instead, his story reveals the animal as a kind of gap, a gap between the ape's mode of appearance, which is necessarily anthropomorphic – using human language, modes of address, and forms of communication – and the ape's life, the unrepresentable life which Red Peter is trying to save by all means.[32]

Svevo constructs a similar "gap" in his story. Although it does represent an animal's point of view, these impressions are problematized because they are translated by a man, whose grasp of their meaning is imperfect. All the common problems of translation – lexical, syntactical, and hermeneutic – are compounded by the differences in species. Further complicating the transmission of Argo's thoughts is the fact that the dog's oral communication is transcribed into a form of writing that is completely different from the original canine form: "It is not my intention to teach it to the reader; and anyway, I haven't an adequate system of notation."[33]

Given that Argo dies before the work is finished, the master is also translating from a lost language, so there is no way to verify his translations. The language is as foreign as a language could possibly be. Although the master claims that the "general sense" was not affected by his misunderstandings, several moments of the narrative reveal the difference that a word can make. Although it is unlikely, the reader will never know, for instance, since Argo cannot be asked, whether the master was perhaps "sniffing" a woman he had encountered: "My master had stopped to chat with a woman. (Argo asserts at this point that I 'sniffed' the lady, but this is untrue and I do not hesitate to amend

---

31 Weil, "A Report on the Animal Turn," 3.
32 Puchner, "Performing the Open," 28.
33 AM, 167. ("Non è mia intenzione d'insegnarla [la lingua] ai lettori e mi mancano anche i segni grafici per notarla"; AP, 99.)

his statement. Moreover, the lady was getting on in years.)"[34] The master appears to resist the idea that Argo thought he was flirting with the woman. His parenthetical remarks remind the reader that he is not an unbiased translator of Argo's words. The narrator's comments on changing Argo's wording highlights how differently Argo perceives the world, how language reflects these differences, and how little readers can trust a translation of his language.

Svevo's tale contains impenetrable sentences, and the reader cannot be sure whether the opacity indicates that Argo's thinking is difficult for a human to understand, whether his master has misunderstood, or whether his master has purposefully mistranslated his words. Because of the gap that renders the monologues unstable, another interpretation of "Argo and His Master" is that the master does not, in fact, understand Argo at all, but has gone insane and believes that he understands his dog's barking. Since his translations cannot be verified and he never learned to reproduce Argo's speech, the text can be assessed in a number of ways, including one that questions its veracity on all levels.

Both "Argo and His Master" and "A Report to an Academy" preclude readers from feeling that they have truly understood an animal's world view. Neither work presents a dialogue. Argo speaks, and the reader is left to determine how stable his communication is, how much the translation can be trusted. The same is true for Red Peter's one-sided report. The work suggests tensions between Red Peter and his human audience more than once. The reader is in the uncomfortable position of the audience, with whom Red Peter may not feel comfortable. His report is another performance required of him to prove his humanity. The meaning of Red Peter's entire report is questionable. Does he mean what he says, or is he merely imitating academic discourse? Is his audience sincerely listening to his talk, as they would a human's, or do the audience members consider his words as they would any ape's performance? For whom, if anyone, Red Peter's words have meaning and for whom they are still merely a performance are unanswerable questions.

Readers of both stories are placed in a tenuous interpretive position, not knowing when the words expressed accurately represent what has occurred or what are even the true feelings of the dog or ape speaker. The stories portray something that "defeats our ordinary capacity to get our minds around reality, that is, our capacity to capture reality in language. That dislodges us from comfortably inhabiting our nature as

---

34 AM, 175. ("Argo dice qui ch'io annusavo quella signora ma non è vero e correggo senz'esitazione. Trattavasi anche di una signora molto vecchia"; AP, 105–6.)

speaking animals, animals who can make sense of things in the way the capacity to speak enables us."[35] Both works raise questions about what lies beyond human comprehension. Although in Kafka's story an animal learns human language and in Svevo's a human learns to understand his pet, both concentrate on the difficulties of communication between species and what this means about knowledge, about the essence of being human.

Even before the narration of the translated monologues of Argo, issues of understanding and intention complicate the dog's simple actions and reveal how much inter-species communication depends on perspective. Once his master decides to teach him to speak, his first gesture is to give him his paw, to "shake hands": "The stupid animal, finding himself assailed by gestures and sounds, mustered his entire wit and gave me his paw!"[36] Argo does what he has been trained to do, but the gesture now, instead of being a sign of comprehension, represents his failure to understand his master's efforts: "That evening I had my hands full simply ridding him of his bad habit. If he were to become human, he would have to forget the gestures of the domesticated dog, at which he had stopped as though at the farthest limits of his education."[37] Argo's and his master's means of communicating are based on training, but once the master stops assuming that this is the only way they can interact, their relationship begins to change.

Red Peter also reflects on the significance of a handshake: "The first thing that I learned was to shake hands; the handshake signifies openness. Now, today, at the high point of my career, let frank speech be coupled with that first handshake."[38] Although he claims that his words exemplify the same openness as his handshake, the reader soon learns that, in the beginning, he did not understand the meaning of any of his actions (drinking, smoking); he simply knew that they might provide an escape. This lack of comprehension raises questions about the meaning of the first clasping of hands – whether it was merely imitative, or

---

35 McDowell, "Comment on Stanley Cavell's "Companionable Thinking," 134.

36 AM, 166. ("Lo stupido animale vedendosi aggredire da gesti e suoni, raccolse tutto il suo sapere e mi porse la zampa!"; AP, 98.)

37 AM, 166. ("Per quella prima sera ebbi da fare abbastanza per levargli quel vizio. Doveva, per diventare umano, dimenticare il gesto del cane addomesticato al quale s'era arrestato come all'estremo limite della sua educazione"; AP, 98.)

38 KSS, 77. ("Das erste, was ich lernte, war: den Handschlag geben; Handschlag bezeugt Offenheit; mag nun heute, wo ich auf dem Höhepunkt meiner Laufbahn stehe, zu jenem ersten Handschlag auch das offene Wort hinzukommen"; Kafka, Erzählungen, 323.)

had meaning for the humans but not for Red Peter, or had a different meaning for both him and the humans. In addition, it can be asked whether the handshake later had meaning for him but was still viewed by the humans as imitative.

The importance of physical gestures in the two works, and their shifting meanings reveal how even non-verbal communication can be interrogated by the inclusion of an animal's perspective. Both works demonstrate that the human concept of other animals' understanding is primarily due to human perspective. Traditional modes of interaction hinder inter-species communication. Red Peter is human only if humans believe he is.[39] Similarly, Argo's master, and not Argo, has to change to understand Argo's communication. The master learns to establish a new relationship with Argo as a unique social subject, rather than as a dog to be dominated. He refers to his dog as a person and gets down on all fours, like a dog, to better relate to him.

The human view of an animal's social roles partly determines the ability to understand the dog and ape. Their hand/paw-shakes can be viewed as performative or a sign of understanding. Judith Butler's expansion of the Althusserian ideas of interpellation and the hail helps explain this issue of human and non-human greetings: "This 'I,' which is produced through the accumulation and convergence of such 'calls,' cannot extract itself from the historicity of that chain or raise itself up and confront that chain as if it were an object opposed to me, which is not me, but only what others have made of me; for that estrangement or division produced by the mesh of interpellating calls and the 'I' who is its site is not only violating, but enabling as well."[40] The animals also cannot escape the historicity of their chain, since they have no control over their constructed roles.[41]

The human handshake, both an expression of politeness and a greeting, is exposed in "Argo" as a basic, physical gesture that other species employ, like dogs smelling one other: "Men are much simpler animals than dogs, because they smell more than dogs and do so more readily. When one man meets another, they touch hands and don't seem to worry about what lies behind the other man's hand. Argo, on the other hand, when he meets another dog, cautiously advances the toothed end of his

---

39 As Philip Armstrong argues, "The immediate source of [Red Peter's] confinement is not physical but epistemological; he is held captive by how humans perceive him" (Armstrong, *What Animals Mean in the Fiction of Modernity*, 203).

40 Butler, *Bodies That Matter*, 122.

41 "The call is formative, if not *per*formative, precisely because it initiates the individual into the subjected status of the subject" (Butler, 121).

own body towards the untoothed end of the other's body and sniffs."[42] Argo contrasts a human's seemingly detached shaking of hands with the series of ways in which dog greetings could unfold, including leading to a fight, depending on the smell of the dog's "untoothed" parts. The outsider perspective of an animal opens up all the rituals of social interactions to investigation. Not only does an animal's perspective make human experiences strange, but it also draws attention to the similarities between human animals' and other animals' actions.

The communication between Argo and his master is based not on anthropomorphizing – in fact, it resists anthropomorphism – but on relating to the animal. Argo even "caninizes" human behaviour. Assuming that his master perceives the world in the same way he does, he believes that his master's most important sense is smell and, because he smells less attentively than Argo, that he has an even more acute sense of smell. Argo describes his view of the differences between himself and his master: "But my master walks in the middle of the road without taking a single step aside to enjoy the smells. His senses are more powerful than Argo's and he doesn't need to go near to enjoy them."[43] Argo believes that all creatures, from humans to birds, perceive as he does. While his views may be a cause for amusement, this cyno-centrism also asks the reader to consider anthropocentrism and the distortions of anthropomorphism. Frans de Waal's *Are We Smart Enough to Know How Smart Animals Are?* discusses how we use our senses as the measure for other animals' understanding, which is a mistake. Similarly, Argo attributes a greater sense of smell, his dominant sense, to us.

Red Peter and Argo accept inter-species communication without pleasure. In both stories, the animal participants do not especially esteem this accomplishment, which is the subject of public attention and much human interest. In Svevo's story, the master, as he is referred to throughout the work, does not set out to understand Argo, but to teach him to speak. His resulting comprehension is the only possible solution he can find for his situation: "The point was to make ourselves understood, and there were two possibilities: Argo had to learn my

---

42 AM, 182. ("L'uomo è un animale molto più semplice del cane perché sente di più e più facilmente. Quando incontra un altro uomo gli tocca la mano e sembrerebbe quasi di non curarsi di quanto sta dietro di questa mano. Invece Argo quando incontra un altro cane avvicina prudentemente la parte dentate del proprio corpo a quella sdentata dell'altro e annusa"; AP, 112.)

43 AM, 178. ("Ma il mio padrone cammina nel mezzo della via senza deviare di un passo per spiare gli olezzi. Egli ha i sensi più potenti di quelli di Argo e non ha bisogno di accostarli per goderne"; AP, 109.)

language or I had to learn his."[44] Argo himself is unenthusiastic: "Argo made his communications to me meekly and with resignation."[45] Red Peter's new ability to speak causes him no joy. The ape narrator of "A Report" learns the language of another species because he sees this new kind of communication as the only possible solution to his predicament, his only *Ausweg* (way out). Red Peter carefully qualifies that this decision, his way out, was not taken out of any desire to be like humans or interact with them; speaking was merely preferable to death.

"A Report to an Academy" and "Argo and His Master" represent the process of learning to communicate with humans as brutal. In these works, animals do not regard humans as highly as humans regard themselves. Much of what Red Peter and Argo reveal about human behaviour is hard to interpret in a positive light. Red Peter, who struggles to imitate humans only so that he can leave the cage that cuts into his flesh, is burned during his attempts to learn. Argo is repeatedly hurt without reason, and the master attempts to motivate him using violence. The works interrogate the divide that humans often assume exists between bestial animals and humane humans. "Argo and His Master" expresses more clearly than "A Report to an Academy" the similarities between humans and other animals, partly because the voice of a dog, Argo, is the focus of a large portion of the work, whereas only Red Peter the person, not Red Peter the ape, communicates with his human audience, although this communication is compromised and questioned in both works.

The dog in "Argo and His Master" and Red Peter in "A Report to an Academy" are certainly not the first communicating dog and ape of literature, but these stories of "realistically" communicating animals set them apart from animals in most other animal tales. Dogs and apes are perhaps given the fictional power of speech especially often in literature because they are close to human beings, in two senses of the word *close* (man's best friend and man's relation). This closeness further erodes the barriers between the species. As Giorgio Agamben has discussed in *The Open: Man and Animal*, this erosion creates uncertainty: "When the difference vanishes and the two terms (man and animal) collapse upon each other – as seems to be happening today – the difference between being and nothing, licit and illicit, divine and demonic also fades away, and in its place something appears for which we seem to lack even a name."[46]

---

44 AM, 167. ("Si trattava d'intendersi e perciò non c'erano che due possibili vie: Argo doveva apprendere la lingua mia oppure io la sua!"; AP, 99.)
45 AM, 167. ("Argo mi fece le sue comunicazioni mansueto e rassegnato"; AP, 99.)
46 Agamben, *The Open*, 22.

As with many of the current debates on animal perception, Kafka's
and Svevo's realistic talking animals create communicative confusion and raise the question what it means to be human. These early
twentieth-century works exemplify a modernist crisis that has gained
more attention in the late twentieth and early twenty-first centuries:
"The foundations of the reader's existence are shaken by Kafka's stories. Indeed, this is a fair description of what is occurring to human
identity in modern Western culture as animals gain power."[47] While
Red Peter's steps towards human assimilation have been read as symbolizing several groups who have experienced some sort of cultural
shift, even when not read allegorically, "A Report to an Academy"
presents a crisis of human identity.[48]

Communication across Species: Landolfi's Châli and Tombo, Morante's Bella and Immacolatella

Svevo's Argo and Kafka's Red Peter suggest how communicating
non-human animals prompt humans to reconsider not only animals'
closeness to us but also our closeness to them. Argo can be associated
with a long line of women whom Svevo's narrators attempt to educate,
but from whom they instead end up learning. How characters react to
animals can call attention to how they treat human groups that they
consider Other or insignificant.[49] These Others are often women. In
Svevo's *Senilità* (*As a Man Grows Older*, or *Emilio's Carnival*), the protagonist, Emilio, finds his friend Balli to talk to him about the stress he
is putting on Emilio's sister.[50] Balli is lost in thought behind a *canicida*
(dog killer) when Emilio approaches him: "His fondness for animals
heightened his artistic sensibility. He paid little attention to what Emilio

---

47 Scholtmeijer, "What Is 'Human'?," 130.
48 Owing partly to Kafka's background, Red Peter, with all his contradictions, has
    been viewed by some critics as an allegory for an assimilated Jew. See, e.g., Rubin-
    stein, "'A Report to an Academy.'" In Walter Sokel's *The Myth of Power and the Self*,
    the chapter "Identity and the Individual" concentrates on "Ein Bericht" as an illus-
    tration of the problems of adapting to Western society.
49 A discussion of who is Other and therefore included in this category of power-
    lessness depends somewhat on one's political and religious perspectives. Camosy,
    e.g., includes fetuses: "Human beings used other animals for their own purposes
    because they had the power to do so – just as human groups with power have
    subjugated African Americans, women, and prenatal human beings" (Camosy, *For
    Love of Animals*, 20).
50 Critics have called attention to two moments in this work that are special because
    they focus on Balli's point of view and have him standing "outside the story" (e.g.,
    Furbank, *Italo Svevo*, 168). In addition to including Balli, both scenes feature dogs.

was saying, his ears deafened by the howling of dogs."[51] Uncaringly heedless with regard to Amalia, Balli considers his passionate response to the dogs' laments, which he hopes to draw on in his art. Blinded by his compassion for the dogs, Balli's empathy does not extend to poor Amalia, whom he is helping push towards death. While Balli basically ignores Emilio's speech, Emilio reflects on the similarities between the dogs and his sister: "Emilio bitterly remembered that Amalia's lamentations also conveyed surprise and immense powerless indignation."[52]

Balli's moment of consideration for non-human animals highlights his lack of consideration for Amalia and other women. The relationship between woman and animals is a rich terrain not only in Svevo's work but in that of many other authors as well, with dogs frequently acting as a stand-in or as a foil for women. While some narrators frequently use animal imagery to describe women, others directly connect their domination of animals to that of women.[53] Landolfi's "Maria Giuseppa" provides a clear instance of this: "I got up early, practically at dawn, and fooled around with the dog or tormented him, if you will, until Maria Giuseppa came back; then I began to torment her too."[54]

Women have at times been contrasted with animals in order to degrade them: "Until fairly recently, the status of animals in scholarly work was comparable to that of women before feminism: regarded by the dominant group as inherently subordinate and defined by the dominant group in generic and reductive terms."[55] The idea that these categories must be re-examined in order for progress to occur is

---

51 Svevo, *Emilio's Carnival (Senilità)*, 129. ("Ricercava quella commozione per sentirsi, diceva lui, più artista nell'affetto agli animali. Alle parole di Emilio diede poco ascolto, avendo le orecchie intronate dai guaiti dei cani"; Svevo, *Romanzi e "continuazioni,"* 522.)

52 Svevo, *Emilio's Carnival (Senilità)*, 129. ("Il Brentani ricordò con amarezza che anche nel lamento di Amalia si era sentita una sorpresa ed un'enorme, impotente indignazione"; Svevo, *Romanzi e "continuazioni,"* 522.)

53 Elizabeth Leake describes how Cesare Pavese connects the female body with all of nature: "The female body is oftentimes more than merely a body for Pavese; it is a stand-in for the natural world – zoological, botanical, and geological – whose instincts, ripening, heat, and colors are available for manipulation and exploitation by men" (Leake, "Cesare Pavese, Posthumanism, and the Maternal Symbolic," 39).

54 Landolfi, *Words in Commotion and Other Stories*, 75. ("M'alzavo presto, quasi all'alba, e scherzavo tanto col cane, lo tormentavo anche, se vogliamo, finché non arrivava Maria Giuseppa, e allora cominciavo a tormentare lei"; Landolfi, *Dialogo dei massimi sistemi*, 14–15.)

55 Malamud, *Poetic Animals and Animal Souls*. In Adams and Donovan's *Animals and Women*, the title of the first chapter, "Species/Speciesism: Interlocking Oppressions," reveals that this connection between women and animals' roles and characteristics is not unique to Kafka's and Svevo's works or their times.

another reason that literature has remained such a vital part of conversations about the human-animal divide.[56] Literary depictions of human and non-human communication frequently ask readers to reconsider their assumptions about the differences not only between humans and non-human animals but also between various groups of humans. Martha Nussbaum interprets the impulse to animalize marginal groups, and misogyny in particular, as a particular case of *anthropodenial*, the human denial and hatred of being an animal.[57] To remove their sense of being an animal, some anthropodenialists consider a subgroup (women, Jews, Africans) truly animal-like and therefore odious, while believing that they transcend their own animal nature.

The questions of marginalization, of humans and non-humans, have increased along with the crisis of who we are as humans. Kari Weil characterizes Red Peter as a member of a minority group: apes.[58] Marianne DeKoven, meanwhile, analyses how class boundaries seem more significant than some of those between species in "A Report to an Academy": "Red Peter, through his eloquent account of his suffering, seems more 'human' than the crew. But, as I have already mentioned, this linkage of the working class with animality is a classic instance of the widespread use of animality to mark denigrated, subordinated categories of humans."[59] In Buzzati's "Il cane che ha visto Dio" ("The Dog Who Saw God"), which will be discussed in more detail at the end of the chapter, the dog has a special relationship with the poor, literally partaking of their bread and seeming to be closer to their community than the poor are to the rich.[60] Several of the stories examined

---

56 Cognitive scientist Irene Pepperberg shifts the analogy to discuss how underestimated birds have been: "People used to think birds weren't intelligent. Well, they used to think women weren't intelligent, either. They talked about the smaller circumference of our skulls as though it made us inferior to men! You know what? They were wrong on both counts" (Talbot, "Birdbrain," 64). This is also discussed by Weil (*Thinking Animals*, 9).

57 For a discussion of anthropodenial, misogyny, and racism, see Nussbaum, *Political Emotions*, 182–5.

58 "Red Peter, the story's narrator and protagonist, is presented as a representative of a minority or subaltern group: he is an ape" (Weil, "A Report on the Animal Turn," 3).

59 DeKoven, "Kafka's Animal Stories," 25. In a discussion of "A Report to an Academy" entitled "The Performing Ape: *A Report for an Academy*," Boa links racial distinctions with those of women and animals (Boa, *Kafka*, 157–8). With respect to Rotpeter in particular, Boa prefaces her first mention of "A Report" with quotations that clearly link dogs, apes, and women (Boa, 40).

60 "Mixing in perhaps with the destitute mob, who enjoyed the joke and therefore had no cause to betray him, the dog came and went with impunity." ("Mescolandosi forse alla calca dei poveretti, che godono della beffa e non hanno perciò motivo di tradirlo, il cane entra ed esce impunemente"; Buzzati, *Il "Bestiario,"* 56.)

in this chapter describe the distinctions between species as being less divisive than those between economic and social classes, or between the sexes, or in other ways that humans have devised to differentiate themselves from other members of their species.

Morante's *La Storia* (*History*) attempts to "humanize" everyone, or rather not to dehumanize anyone, from a child to the poor, from an isolated woman to dogs to a rapist. Animals in the novel, especially dogs, are treated as characters, given their own history, and shown interacting with others, even when they are not with their human companions. In other words, they are presented as subjects and protagonists, as Concetta D'Angeli has argued.[61] Not only are they a focus of attention, but they are also able to communicate with one of the human protagonists of the work, Giuseppe. His ability to communicate is described as partially arising from the amount of concentrated time he spent alone with the dog, Blitz: "These were unforgettable strokes of luck for Giuseppe; and perhaps it was in those primitive duets with Blitz that he learned the language of dogs. A knowledge that, with his understanding of other animals' languages, was to remain a valid attainment of his for as long as he lived."[62]

Although some have interpreted this aspect of Morante's work as an odd moment of magical realism in an otherwise realistic work of historical fiction, the development of Giuseppe's ability is discussed; it arises in part from isolation, as do those of Red Peter and the master. Often what is credible in stories of animal-human communication has as much to do with preconceived notions on the part of the human reader than on the animals' abilities. Defining what is realistic is complex when it comes to talking animals, and it depends partly on our cultural and personal understanding. What is realistic changes with our beliefs, and it also determines what I categorize as a potentially realistically talking animal. For instance, including as realistic stories about reincarnation would reveal a belief in reincarnation as potentially realistic. Many of these talking-animal stories, like Morante's, ask the reader to re-evaluate the understandings we may have of society, communication, and the possible.

Morante's *History* presents a world view that includes animals, in a portrayal that attempts to partially balance more official histories, which concentrate on the powerful. The narrator blurs the distinction

---

61 D'Angeli, *Leggere Elsa Morante*, 104.
62 Morante, *History*, 95. ("Quelle erano fortune indimenticabili, per Giuseppe: e forse fu in quei suoi duetti primitivi con Blitz, che imparò il linguaggio dei cani. Il quale, insieme con altri idiomi di animali, doveva restargli un acquisto valido finché fu vivo"; Morante, *La Storia*, 110.)

between human and animal characters in several ways. Davide, for instance, confuses himself not only with the human boy, Giuseppe, but also with the dog, Bella: "And Davide, meanwhile, pursued his own meditations aloud, as if he were disputing in a dream with some great Doctor, no longer realizing he was speaking to *two poor illiterates*. As if, indeed, he no longer remembered who, among the three there in the room, was the cultivated student, and who the kid and who the dog."[63] This moment can be interpreted as one in which the narrative takes seriously the presence of animals, showing how the narrator complicates the categories of human and non-human animals, and also reveals that *History* itself can be seen as addressing animals. Bella is described as illiterate, and Morante dedicates her work to the "illiterate": "Por el analfabeto a quien escribo" (For the illiterate to whom I write).[64]

Including a dog and therefore other non-human animals in this category widens the scope of those whom Morante wanted to reach and portray, beyond even the "history of humanity," as Cesare Garboli characterized it.[65] Twenty-first-century critics have discussed how official histories have neglected to include animals and could, in fact, be rewritten to focus on them. John Simons writes, "In this book I am proposing that there is yet another way of rewriting Marx: 'The history of all hitherto existing society is the history of the struggle between humans and non-humans.'"[66] While obviously an extreme way to represent history, for some the inclusion of animals naturally follows other rewritings of history, those with a greater focus on women, children, the poor, and other often marginalized members of society.

Issues of sanity surround many stories of realistically talking animals, as already discussed with regard to "Argo and His Master." One interpretation of this potential insanity points to an issue that has been of recent critical interest: humans may not really want to understand animals; we may not want them to communicate – not only because of what they might say about us but also because of what the act says about us. This resistance relates to de Waal's examinations of anthropodenial, in which humans refuse to consider animals capable of certain

63 Morante, *History*, 589. ("E Davide, frattanto, rincorreva le sue proprie meditazioni a voce alta, quasi ragionasse in sogno con qualche gran Dottore, senza piú accorgersi di parlare a *due poveri analfabeti*. Quasi non rammentava piú, anzi, chi fra i tre, là dentro, fosse lo studente colto, e chi il pischelletto e chi il cane"; Morante, *La Storia*, 524; emphasis added.)

64 Morante is referencing César Vallejo. See, e.g., Carey, "Elsa Morante: Envisioning History," 67.

65 Garboli, "Elsa Morante: La storia e le sue vittime."

66 Simons, *Animal Rights and the Politics of Literary Representation*, 7.

behaviours because those behaviours are too "human." Red Peter drove early trainers insane: crossing the boundary from non-human speech to human speech or from non-human to human crosses a boundary that many find terrifying. The dog-man of Buzzati's "L'arrivista" mentions pretending to be less intelligent so as not to frighten his human masters: "Up, up. I climbed the scale of understanding with such speed that I often was constrained to pretend sudden crises of stupidity so as not to frighten my masters."[67] Landolfi's story *"Tempesta"* ("Storm") consists of a dialogue between the dog and her master, with the narrator's thoughts interspersed; it ends with the narrator finally enunciating what he had been thinking throughout, that he was going to go mad listening to the dialogue: "(Enough enough, he's going to drive me crazy as well with his fluting and piercing voice, I want to leave!)."[68]

Whereas Svevo's master translates Argo's language into one that the reader can understand, Landolfi's "Storm" presents indecipherable dog-language, which is left for the reader to attempt to interpret. Like "Argo and His Master," "Storm" explores a dog's process of learning to speak and raises doubts about whether a human could ever really understand a dog. In the story, a man approaches the narrator and wants to show him how his dog, Châli, can "talk." The man elicits sounds from his dog in a pleading manner: "Châli, bella, my love, dear, dear one!"[69] Châli's responses seem to be slowly forming themselves into words from responses such as "Hu huh m hm uh cr cr ..." to, finally, *"Bata mail cievisal."* These sounds are untranslatable, in that their meaning is unknown, but at the same time, they would perhaps be represented in exactly the same way in most translations of the text.

In "Interpreting Animals," Umberto Eco has discussed how the inclusion of animal sounds leads quickly to an examination of the relationship between language and writing, or thought and sign: "Words stand in different relation with the thing they designate (or with the passions of the soul they signify or, in Stoic terms, with the proposition – *lekton* – they convey), and this relation is based on mere equivalence and biconditionality (as it appears also in the influential Aristotelian theory of definition)."[70] Representations of animal language, from Svevo's

---

67 "Su, su. Salivo la scala della conoscenza con tale rapidità che spesso ero costretto a fingere improvvise crisi di stupidità per non spaventare i miei padroni" (Buzzati, *Il "Bestiario,"* 139).

68 "(Basta basta! Egli farà impazzire anche me con quella sua voce piena di dolcezza, con quella sua voce flautata e penetrante! Voglio andarmene)" (Landolfi, *Il mar delle blatte e altre storie,* 110).

69 "Châli, bella, amor mio, cara cara!" (Landolfi, 110).

70 Eco, *The Limits of Interpretation,* 113.

master, who has no characters with which to transcribe Argo's speech, to the mysterious sounds of Châli, are an extreme case of untranslatability.

"Storm" focuses, in part, on how exactly an animal could be brought to speech and what this speech would look like in written form. Châli's master thinks that once his dog has formed sounds that sound like words, they must have meaning; the secret of Châli's point of view would be unlocked if only someone could decipher what exactly *"Bata mail cievisal"* means. The animal sounds in "Storm" offer a contrast to Morante's description of what a cat's meows indicate in *History*. While in "Storm" animal sounds build towards (perhaps) having meaning, in *History* animal sounds themselves are given meaning, but both approaches involve the transcription and analysis of animal sounds. Using normal sound blocks, *History* describes the sounds of a cat, which are certainly more familiar than those of a perhaps-talking dog (*meow* versus *bata mail*): "To ask for something, she said: myew or mayeu; to call, she said mau, to threaten mbrooooh, etc. etc."[71]

History offers three specific cat sounds and their meanings, calling attention to what can often already be understood in animal speech. The similarities between the cat sounds in Italian and English point to the onomatopoeic representation of many animal sounds. At the same time, their minor differences point to the added difficulties of representing animal speech and to our own linguistic representation and hearing. While *míu* and *mèu* are fairly close to *myew* or *mayeu*, they indicate the wider gap between some animal sounds, such as a rooster's *cock-a-doodle-doo* in English and *chichirichi* in Italian. Children and adults are often told that these sounds are onomatopoeic, without realizing the vast cultural and linguistic differences that come into play in what we hear. The human understanding of animal speech is not universal, but particular to different cultures and languages.

While the dog in "Storm," who almost forms words, and Morante's cat, who mews with meaning, are instances of animals whose expressions can be represented verbally, communication, of course, does not have to be oral. Morante's work raises another question in trying to determine what constitutes a talking animal: the issue of what communication entails. The question whether cat's mews are words is debatable, but the fact that they communicate something and can be represented with letters is not. The relationship between Arturo and his dog in Morante's earlier novel *Arturo's Island* can be seen as the precursor to Giuseppe's

---

71 Morante, *History*, 208. ("Per chiedere, diceva míu o mèu; per chiamare, mau, per minacciare, mbroooh, ecc. ecc"; Morante, *La Storia*, 189.)

with animals, and it offers an example of non-verbal communication. As in *History*, isolation leads to understanding another species, and the young protagonist and dog have a special bond: "What a lot of fuss about a dog, you'll say. But when I was a boy I'd no other friend, and you can't deny she was extraordinary. We'd invented a kind of deaf-and-dumb language between us: tail, eyes, movements, the pitch of her voice – all of them told me every thought of hers, and I understood."[72] This passage suggests that Arturo's and his dog's primarily non-verbal communication may be more meaningful than the spoken language most humans use with each other. The dog, Arturo's only friend, and Arturo find a mode of communication, but whether they are actually talking is another question. Giuseppe develops the ability to understand animal speech, whereas Arturo and his dog understand each other.

Landolfi's *Le due zittelle* (*The Two Old Maids*) also portrays an animal communicating without words or even sounds, but the situation is more vexed than in *Arturo's Island*.[73] Two devout unmarried sisters, Lilla and Nena, discover that their pet monkey, Tombo, has been sneaking out of his cage to eat the holy bread of the chapel of a nearby nunnery. Nena, secretly observing the altar in the chapel, sees Tombo not only doing this but also "saying" Mass and urinating on the altar. As the narrator says, "Reader, do not condemn me: *Tombo was saying Mass*. By now he was beastically devouring the consecrated host and drinking the sacred wine."[74] Tombo is acting as though he were saying Mass; he is not actually pronouncing the Latin phrases, but what he would be saying is clear to his human audience. As is the case with so many of these stories about talking animals, his ability to "say" Mass provokes questions about what constitutes communication, about language itself. The meaning of his imagined words becomes a source of great debate, related to the intentions and agency of non-human animals.

While "Argo and His Master" can be seen as a critique of anthropocentrism through cyno-centrism, the narrator of *The Two Old Maids* offers a

---

72 Morante, *Arturo's*, 35. ("Si dirà: parlare tanto d'una cagna! Ma io, quand'ero un ragazzino, non avevo altri compagni che lei, e non si può negare ch'era straordinaria. Per conversare con me, aveva inventato una specie di linguaggio dei muti: con la coda, con gli occhi, con le sue pose, e molte note diverse della sua voce, sapeva dirmi ogni suo pensiero; e io la capivo"; Morante, *L'isola*, 46.)

73 For an analysis of *Le due zittelle* in a broader context, see Anedda, "'Le due zittelle.'" For more on the story and animals beyond the matter of speech, see Trama, *Animali e fantasmi della scrittura*.

74 Landolfi, *Gogol's Wife*, 84. ("Lettore, non ne ho colpa: *Tombo diceva messa*. Esso ormai divorò bestialmente l'ostia consacrata e bevve il sacro vino"; Landolfi, *Le due zittelle*, 59.)

direct critique. The story begins with a comment on what humans are not capable of knowing about animals and the dangers of anthropomorphism:

> The monkey [*scimia*] was a rather small, vivacious animal, probably a Cercopithecus; but it will be best to give up from the start any attempt to describe him in detail and as a distinct entity – which, I can wager, will be greeted with great relief by the reader. For, in truth, all the qualities which an alert storyteller of the human species, expert as he may be in probing character, can notice in, or attribute to, an animal, are after all but mere supposition to which only our immoderate anthropomorphism lends verisimilitude. Just between ourselves: How can anyone penetrate the thoughts of a brute, the true meaning of his acts, even if we adopt the human conception of such terms?[75]

The narrator thematizes the difficulty, or impossibility, of representing non-human-animal thought. In a pursuit of veracity, he refuses to describe in detail the personal aspects of Tombo, the centre of the story. Landolfi's narrator thus points to the potential gap that Kafka and Svevo built into their own narrative structures. The narrator's amazing caution resonates with more recent concerns of anthropomorphism and our lack of knowledge about animal thought. The works of the Italian authors discussed so far in this chapter present different views on the problems of portraying animals, and these views reflect the ongoing debates about anthropomorphization versus anthropodenial.

Whereas *The Two Old Maids* raises the idea that all animal thought is beyond knowledge, Svevo and Buzzati discuss how a certain degree of animal thought is portrayable because we have some animal understanding. In Svevo's "Una burla riuscita" ("The Hoax"), the protagonist at first writes about less known animals, with poor results: "At first he repeated the mistake of his youth, and wrote about unfamiliar animals."[76] The aspiring writer soon turns to sparrows, a better subject because of his personal experience with them: "Another small step

---

75 Landolfi, *Gogol's Wife*, 61. ("Era la scimia un animale piuttosto piccolo e vivace, forse un cercopiteco; ma a presentala partitamente ed in sé sarà bene rinunziare fin d'ora, con sollievo scometto di chi legge. E invero tutte le qualità che accorto novellatore di razza umana, esparto quanto si voglia di caratteri, può rilevare in un animale o attribuirgli, non sono al postutto che mere supposizioni, cui solo il nostro smodato antropomorfismo presta verosimiglianza. Fra noi: in che modo penetrare d'un bruto i pensieri, il vero significato dei suoi gesti, anche ad adottare l'accezione umana di tali termini?"; Landolfi, *Le due zittelle*, 28.)

76 Svevo, "Hoax," 13. ("Dapprima, ripetendo l'errore commesso in gioventù, scrisse di animali che poco conosceva"; Svevo, *Racconti e scritti autobiografici*, 201.)

forward was his choice of more appropriate heroes for his fables. The exotic elephant, the fly with expressionless eyes – these disappeared, and their place was taken by the familiar little sparrows which he allowed himself the luxury (a great luxury in Trieste at that time) of feeding in his courtyard with crumbs of bread."[77] Here the protagonist successfully writes about birds, creatures he has come to know, as Svevo himself often wrote about dogs, animals he knew.

The narrator does not suggest giving up on the portrayal of animals, for that could lead to the end of literature: "So said the sparrow in its tiny brain. But if every animal in the world were obliged to mind its own business and refrain from endowing others with its own qualities and even its own organs, there would be no more fables."[78] Literature and questions about animal thought are intricately connected. Derrida has claimed, "For thinking concerning the animal, if there is such a thing, derives from poetry."[79] Like Svevo's narrator in "The Hoax," Buzzati does not argue against representing animals, but against representing their thoughts without careful consideration. In a 1957 issue of *Corriere d'Informazione*, he chastised a writer for taking too many liberties in his portrayal of the dog Laika, the first animal to orbit earth: "From Aesop on man has always been satisfied to attribute his own thoughts and emotions to beasts; and he has treated them in a number of fables. But there is a limit to everything. Even the psyche of a dog can be humanized in some ways. Up to a certain point, however. I do not say that we know dogs enough, but we know dogs a little. It is possible to establish certain points about his mind, that are not enough to reveal his whole character, but that cannot be ignored."[80]

---

77 Svevo, "Hoax," 14. ("Poi ci fu un altro piccolo progresso nella sua opera con la scelta di protagonisti più adatti. Non più gli elefanti, tanto lontani, né le mosche dagli occhi privi di ogni espressione, ma i cari, piccoli passeri ch'egli si prendeva il lusso [grande lusso, a Trieste, di quei giorni] di nutrire nel suo cortile con briciole di pane"; Svevo, *Racconti e scritti autobiografici*, 202–3; trans. modified.)

78 Svevo, "Hoax," 70. ("Così parlava il passero col suo cervellino. Ma se fosse fatto obbligo ad ogni animale di badare ai fatti proprii e non imporre le sue propensioni e perfino i suoi organi agli altri, non ci sarebbero più delle favole a questo mondo"; Svevo, *Racconti e scritti autobiografici*, 264.)

79 Derrida, *The Animal*, 7.

80 "Da Esopo in poi l'uomo si è sempre compiaciuto di attribuire alle bestie i pensieri e i sentimenti suoi; e ne ha tratto una quantità di favole. Ma c'è un limite a tutto. Anche la psiche di un cane può essere in qualche modo umanizzata. Fino a un certo punto, però. Il cane non dico che lo conosciamo abbastanza, ma un poco lo conosciamo. Circa il suo animo è ormai possibile stabilire dei punti fermi, che non bastano certo a rivelarne l'intera personalità, ma che non si possono ignorare" (originally published in *Corriere d'Informazione*, 16–17 November, reprinted in Buzzati, *Il "Bestiario,"* 125).

Buzzati points to the author's lack of knowledge in his description of Laika, a female dog, lifting her leg to urinate. This clear misunderstanding of dogs in their specificity is part of Buzzati's critique. In Landolfi's story, meanwhile, the narrator cautions against attempting to explain animal thought in any way, and much of the narrative debates whether we humans can ever be capable of understanding the place of animals in the world. All these authors considered how humans could and should represent animals as well as which boundaries between humans and other animals are surpassable and which are not.

The Language of Animals and Dialects

Like his title (*zittelle* as opposed to *zitelle*), Landolfi's passage on anthropomorphism reveals the strange nature of the linguistic choices in his story. The unusual spelling of *scimia* (monkey) with only one *m* can have various explanations: perhaps the monkey is special and not quite a *scimmia* with two *m*'s or the narrator is communicating partly in dialect. *The Two Old Maids* raises the issue of dialect at the beginning of the story: "Even the people's talk, a sort of elusive suburban dialect, was soft and unctuous."[81] In addition to questioning the boundaries between humans and animals, the work introduces a range of issues about word choices, from the monkey imitating Latin and the use of dialect in the sisters' community to Landolfi's own unusual linguistic selections.

Landolfi, Svevo, and Morante not only present communicating animals but have also been the focus of critical debate because of their linguistic choices and use, or putative use, of dialect. They had to consider carefully what type of Italian they were going to use to portray their characters' speech and their own narration. Their linguistic situations suggest one reason for the unusually large number of realistically talking animals of Italy. Efforts to communicate with an animal highlight the problem of communication more generally. The number of dialects spoken in the peninsula not only adds to the complications that already exist when two people attempt to communicate but also draws attention to these complexities. As Lorraine Daston has written, "The investigation of animal minds became only a more far-flung case of figuring out how other human minds worked, the difficulties of understanding one's dog differing only in degree from those of making sense

---

81 Landolfi, *Gogol's Wife*, 50. ("Anche la parlata della gente, una specie di dialetto indefinibilmente suburbano, era molle e un che untuosa"; Landolfi, *Le due zittelle*, 12.)

of a Frenchman."[82] Many of these Italian stories indicate the complexity of language use in Italy as well as communication more generally.

Calvino's description of his father's particular idiolect, which combines dialect, other languages, farming vocabulary, and bird language, supports my argument for one reason why there is such a wealth of Italian stories that concentrate on human-animal communication:

> And this whole Babel-like nomenclature was mashed up in an equally Babel-like idiomatic base, where various languages vied with each other, combining together as need or memory dictated (dialect for anything local and blunt – he had an unusually rich dialect vocabulary, full of words no one used anymore – ...), the result being a conversational style all woven together with stock refrains promptly trotted out in response to familiar situations, exorcizing the movements of the mind and forming once again a catalogue, parallel to that of his farming vocabulary – and to yet another catalogue of his made up not of words this time but of whistles, twitters, trills, tu-whits and tu-whoos, this arising from his great ability to mimic birdcalls.[83]

This catalogue describes a language with a world view that Calvino found impenetrable: his narration of his father's language follows the assertion that they were unable to communicate, although both were verbose, because of their different ways of perceiving the world. Calvino mentions that his inability to recognize birdsong or birds further distanced him from his father. Although they were human, he and his father faced a communicative barrier: their languages, including the father's use of dialect and *tu-whits*, are signs of their differences. This list reveals how another person's language, which includes animal noises, and perspective often remain impenetrable to others. The use of dialects in Italy aggravates the complexities of human communication.

---

82 Daston, "Intelligences," 49. "Language, as we see with Red Peter, irreparably splits the self between an experiential self and a speaking self who is never in the same place or time as the self that is to be represented" (Weil, *Thinking Animals*, 7).

83 Calvino, *The Road to San Giovanni*, 10–1. ("E tutta questa nomenclatura babelica s'impastava in un fondo idiomatico altrettanto babelico, cui concorrevano lingue diverse, mescolate secondo i bisogni e i ricordi, [il dialetto per le cose locali e brusche – aveva un lessico dialettale di ricchezza rara, pieno di voci cadute in disuso– ...] e ne veniva un discorso tutto tessuto d'intercalari che tornavano puntualmente in risposta a situazioni fisse, esorcizzando i moti dell'animo, un catalogo anch'esso, parallelo a quello della nomenclatura agricola, – e a quell'altro non di parole ma di zufolii, pispoli, trilli, zirli, chiù, che era dato dalla sua bravura ad imitare i versi degli uccelli"; Calvino, *La strada di San Giovanni*, 9–10.)

Dialects can be strong literary tools, and they can give stories new depth. But they can also be sources of confusion or even embarrassment. In a letter about obtaining a new dog, Buzzati makes a playful comment about the shame that the new English-speaking dog will experience among his current dogs, who speak only dialect.[84] While Buzzati clearly does not mean that his dogs speak dialect, he is intimating that they understand the language (dialect) of his home. Dialect here marks the dogs as part of the family, whereas the new dog comes from outside. Comments on an author's linguistic choices can make the person feel like an outsider, feel Other, as an Italian or coming from a particular region, in addition to being defensive about the literary qualities of the work being discussed. Pasolini's review of Morante's *History* critiqued her use of language because it imprecisely portrayed regional differences:[85] "The Roman spoken by Nino and his friends reminds me even (Morante has to forgive me, here I must be severe) of certain lifestyle pieces from *Il Messaggero*, while Davide's speech cannot be compared to anything: the boy presents himself as from Bologna, in reality he is from Mantua, but speaks a sort of Venetian dialect."[86] Pasolini then accuses Morante of not caring for her character Davide because she has him use the word *cader* instead of *cascare*, an indication that he is not from Bologna and a formulation no Italian would use.[87] Pasolini's extensive critique of Morante's use of language in *History* sparked a growing animosity between the two friends, and it led to a break that would last for the rest of Pasolini's life.

Especially because of Morante's powerful depiction of animals, Agamben objects to Pasolini's critique of Morante's apparent misuse

---

84 "Unico inconveniente sarà che nei primi giorni, trovandosi con i miei cani, l'angiolino che parla inglese si troverà imbarazzato. I miei parlano solo un dialetto strettissimo" (Buzzati, *Il "Bestiario,"* 6).

85 "Il corollario della povertà del contingente di lingua umoristica, è l'approssimazione e la goffaggine della 'mimesi' del linguaggio di quegli eroi, romani o napoletani che siano (per non parlare dell'alto-italiano Davide)" (Pasolini, *Descrizioni di descrizioni*, 357).

86 "Il romano parlato di Nino e dei suoi amici ricorda addirittura (la Morante mi perdoni, qui devo essere duro) quello di certi trafiletti di costume del 'Messaggero': mentre il parlato di Davide non ha riscontro in nulla: il ragazzo si presenta come bolognese, in realtà è mantovano, ma parla una specie di veneto" (Pasolini, 357). For a discussion of the relationship between Morante and Pasolini and more context for Pasolini's review, see Walter Siti, "Elsa Morante and Pier Paolo Pasolini."

87 "Dov'è il così grande amore della Morante per lui, se essa è poi così pigra da non fare il minimo sforzo per ascoltare come parla?" "Non c'è tuttavia angolo nell'Alta Italia in cui cadere si dica cader. Per ogni dove, là, nell'Alta Italia, è cascare che ha trionfato eliminando ogni altra forma concorrente. Che Davide dica cader è offensivo per il lettore: ma è soprattutto offensivo per lui" (Pasolini, 357).

of dialect. He wrote Morante a letter in which he praised the portrayal of animals in *History* as unparalleled: "Your book is unique and miraculous, that is also because in it a descent into the world of animals was accomplished. There is no similar example of this descent in the literature of this century (because of this every objection in terms of the reality and authenticity of your characters is idiotic)."[88] For Agamben, the power of Morante's animals places her work above minor linguistic criticism. The issues of animal and human communication, their interrelationships, and their debated nature comes to the fore in Pasolini's and Agamben's conflicting evaluations of Morante's novel. The complexities of literary animal communication again lead back to the complexity of human communication, oral and written, as well as the assumption and problems that are especially present in a varied country like Italy.

Unlike, for instance, Pasolini's works in dialect, the situation is less clear in Morante, Svevo, and Landolfi. All three authors play with language, but their works are not written in a clearly experimental mode, in contrast to Gadda or Pasolini. Their linguistic oddities highlight the problem of communicating more generally, rather than revealing how far literary language can be pushed. Their literature may not perfectly reproduce dialect, or standard Italian, but their aim is more to question the possibilities and limitations of human communication than to reproduce exactly how people speak or should speak. Part of this interrogation involves their inclusion of animal voices and how they further complicate ideas about communication.

Svevo's language has been a matter of intense debate from the moment his work drew broader attention.[89] Critics argued that his Italian was too Triestine, too German to be beautiful, and therefore could not be great Italian literature. Some of his early critics even claimed that he became popular abroad because he had finally been translated into a real literary language, in contrast to what he wrote in Italian. In "Argo and His Master," the master remarks upon how the German dog, who inspires him to try to teach his dog Italian, has a better German vocabulary than he does.[90] The inclusion of this German-speaking dog in the story is probably based on a real German dog, Rolf, famous for his communication, and is also fitting given Svevo's German education and life

---

88 "Il tuo libro è unico e miracoloso, ciò è anche perché in esso è stata compiuta una discesa nel mondo delle creature di cui non c'è esempio nella letteratura di questo secolo (per questo, ogni obiezione quanto alla realtà e all'autenticità dei tuoi personaggi è stolta e passa a fianco della questione)" (Agamben to Morante, included in Morante, *L'amata*, 516).

89 See Ghidetti, *Il caso Svevo*.

90 AM, 165; AP, 97.

in multilingual Trieste.[91] The quote about the dog's German vocabulary also points to the stress many Triestines experienced about their own linguistic abilities.

Svevo's best-known novel, *Zeno's Conscience* (*La coscienza di Zeno*, 1923) contains several comments on the frustrations of communication when more than one language is necessary. Suggesting some of the linguistic insecurities Svevo himself felt, his character Zeno laments his lack of proficiency in both standard Italian and German. Zeno famously claims that it is impossible for him to write Italian (or "Tuscan") that expresses his truth ("Con ogni nostra parola toscana noi mentiamo!"). The language of Svevo's narrators who write in the first person, not just Argo, whose words the man transforms from dog language into Italian, can be considered to be translated from their dialect into Italian. Some of the odd word choices may reflect a particular view of the world or issues related to this translation, with the divide between issues of language and perspective often impossible to demarcate clearly. Svevo blurs categories (humans and dogs), linguistically and conceptually, that people tend to keep separate. In "Argo and His Master," the master consistently calls his dog "Argo," a person, and in *Zeno's Conscience*, Zeno includes the office canine, also named Argo, in the same category as himself.

Kafka's communicating animals are so powerful partly because they reflect the linguistic insecurities of his culture: Kafka was a Jewish insurance worker, living in Austro-Hungarian Prague, who wrote in German. His cultural position is often used to decode his animal stories: for instance, his ape, Red Peter, has been read as an assimilated Jew.[92] To some extent due to their multicultural mix, the literature and philosophy of Austria-Hungary have been characterized as being particularly concerned with the crisis of identity, crisis of subjectivity, and crisis of language. Both Hugo von Hofmannsthal, the author of the Lord Chandos letter (which declared, "I have completely lost the ability to think or

---

91 Rolf is a prominent point of discussion in Bondeson, *Amazing Dogs*. He was not the only talking dog of Svevo's time. Svevo reported to his daughter that he was impressed by his encounter with Wilhelm Stekel (the psychoanalyst and student of Freud), who owned a dog that could say "mama" and "papa" (Benussi, *La forma delle forme*, 217; and Bertoni, quoted in Svevo, *Racconti e scritti autobiografici*, 870).

92 For an early interpretation of Red Peter converting to Christianity, see Rubinstein, "'A Report to an Academy.'" For an interpretation of the story about identity more generally, see Sokel, *The Myth of Power and the Self*, 268–92. For more on Kafka's identity and animals, see, e.g., Powell, "Bestial Representations of Otherness." For more on Kafka's writing and Jewishness, see, e.g., Suchoff, *Kafka's Jewish Languages*; and Robertson, *Kafka*.

speak coherently about anything at all"),[93] and Ludwig Wittgenstein, whose thoughts on lions ("If a lion could speak, we could not understand him")[94] echo the narrator's thoughts in *The Two Old Maids*, were born in Vienna. Following the thematic connections between Kafka's stories and those of Italian authors suggests a similar set of cultural problems: as multilingual, multi-ethnic Austria-Hungary and its language crisis partly explain Kafka's Red Peter, so Italy's complex linguistic situation contributes to Italian realistically talking animals.

Italy's linguistic situation also relates to areas of geopolitical marginality, which offers a potential space of openness for animal marginality. For instance, Buzzati's protest against the anthropomorphic representations of Laika reveals a different perspective on animals and politics than the dominant ones of the time. Whereas most journalists were concerned with the Cold War or what Laika meant for the space wars, Buzzati focused the debate on a different topic – the human treatment of other animals – which is now at the forefront of study. In part due to Italy's political marginality at that time, Buzzati was able to focus on what he viewed as truly interesting and problematic: the portrayal of animals.

Animal Bodies and Divine Presence in Morante, Landolfi, and Buzzati

Buzzati has presented his interests in animals as linked to the unknowable: "Often the animal is able to embody mystery, since it is already a mystery for us, since we do not know what is inside."[95] Both seen as being beyond human understanding, the divine and the animal are often connected, with angels and non-human animals considered the beings that humans are closest to, but whose thoughts we cannot hope to penetrate.[96] One of the reasons that Agamben views the animal representation in Morante's work as especially powerful is the animals' innocence in contrast to their human companions. Agamben believes especially in the holiness of Morante's non-human animals, who have not undergone

---

93 Hofmannsthal, *The Lord Chandos Letter*, 121.

94 Wittgenstein, *Philosophical Investigations*, 190.

95 "'Spesse volte l'animale si presta a incarnare il mistero, essendo già per noi il mistero, perché non sappiamo dentro cosa c'è'" (Buzzati to Panafieu, in Buzzati, *Bestiario*, 12).

96 Lorraine Daston's "Intelligences" explores the attempts of medieval authors to "escape anthropomorphism" when describing angels and those of post-Darwin, post-Freud authors depicting animals. She opens with a comparison of a passage from *Paradise Lost* and one from "A Report to an Academy" (Daston, "Intelligences," 37).

this loss of hope: "Pure animal life (which is clearly also present in the natural life of man) and human life, Edenic existence and the knowledge of good and evil, nature and language: these are the edges of the wound that the Judeo-Christian inheritance marked in Elsa's thought, and that separate her from her beloved cats far more than Spinoza was divided from his spiders and other so-called 'irrational beasts.'"[97]

This piece on Morante in Agamben's *The End of the Poem* concludes with a comparison to Kafka: "But, from the Kafkaesque perspective that [Elsa] fully shared, this beautiful certainty is also what deprives us of hope. The loss of hope (even of that retrospective hope, nostalgia for Eden) is the terrible price that the mind must pay when it reaches the incandescent point of certainty."[98] Max Brod believed that it was the distance from God that brought Kafka to write about animals: "The eternal misunderstanding between God and man induces Kafka to represent this disproportion again and again in the picture of two worlds which can never, never understand one another – hence the infinite separation between dumb animals and men is one of his chief themes in the numerous animal stories which his works contain, not by accident."[99]

While for Kafka the case of his representation of the divine in describing his animals is more debatable, Landolfi's *The Two Old Maids* and Buzzati's "The Dog Who Saw God" offer clear reflections on the connections between faith and animal life as well as the mysteries of both. In Landolfi's work, Tombo's actions provoke a reconsideration of what humans can understand about divine or creaturely intentions. Nena reads malicious human intentions into Tombo's actions and decides that he must be put to death for his sins, but, when her sister violently protests, she asks two priests for their opinions. The first priest, after a long monologue, agrees with Nena, the second with Lilla. The second priest questions man's ability to understand the divine and the Catholic idea of divine presence. According to him, it is human animals' inability to "know" the thoughts of an animal, to really communicate with an animal, that leads to Nena's desire to kill Tombo, not Tombo or God's intentions.

---

97 Agamben, *The End of the Poem*, 106. D'Angeli discusses the innocence of Morante's animals in detail; see "'Soltanto l'animale è veramente innocente'" (D'Angeli, *Leggere Elsa Morante*). Dell'Aia analyses this part of Agamben's argument (Dell'Aia, *La sfera del puer*, 88–91).

98 Agamben, 108.

99 Brod, *Franz Kafka*, 175. For a longer discussion of Brod's comments on Kafka and animals, an overview of the topic, and a helpful index, see Yarri, "Index to Kafka's Use of Creatures in His Writings."

The debate involves, in part, the intention behind Tombo's wordless Mass. Is he merely imitating, or must the imitation itself be somehow diabolical? When animals cross religious boundaries, what does this signify for the human sense of the divine? Regardless, the sisters ultimately kill Tombo, while Lilla screams, "I feel like we're killing our brother!"[100] Her outburst can be viewed as reflecting on the connection between Tombo and their dead brother, who had purchased the animal, or on the connection between Tombo, a primate, and the sisters, also primates. In either case, Nena wants to silence her sister: "Shut up, stupid!"[101] ("Zitta, stupida!")[102] Nena attempts to silence the doubts about God, humankind, and other animals that Tombo's actions have raised.

Like *The Two Old Maids*, Buzzati's "The Dog That Saw God" overtly combines the themes of religion (and the problems of knowing the divine) and animals (and the problems of knowing them). In each work, an animal brings to light issues of faith that a surrounding community would rather ignore. In Buzzati's story, a religious hermit settles outside a secular town, Tis, which is filled with selfish non-believers, including a man who is forced by a strange will to give bread to the poor. A dog regularly takes a piece of the grudgingly offered bread. One day the man, bothered by the dog's actions, follows the animal all the way to the hermit. Strange lights appear off in the distance where the hermit lives, and the townspeople comment that the hermit "sees" God, as does, therefore, the dog (hence the title of the story).

After the hermit's death, the hermit's dog, or a dog that appears to be the hermit's, comes down to the town, and the townspeople start changing their behaviour, out of fear of being judged by the religious dog. The dog's presence causes the people of Tis to start attending church, and the once unfrequented place becomes packed on Sundays. No one in Tis discusses the change in their behaviour, primarily out of fear of admitting that they believe in the powers of a divine dog. One night, ostensibly to scare robbers, the man shoots the dog, but the dog returns. The dog finally seems to be dying, and in the dark, the whole city helps him, essentially constructing a shrine around him. When at last he dies, they decide to bury him near the hermit, where they find another dog skeleton next to the hermit's grave. The story leaves unanswered the questions of which dog was the holy dog, can there be a holy dog, are all dogs holy, are no dogs holy, and were all the assumptions about

---

100 Landolfi, *Gogol's Wife*, 111. ("Mi pare di uccidere nostro fratello!"; Landolfi, *Le due zittelle*, 97; trans. modified.)
101 Landolfi, *Gogol's Wife*, 111; trans. modified.
102 Landolfi, *Le due zittelle*, 97.

the dog's holiness simply a figment of human imagination. The story shows how an animal can have more power to change human beings' ideas about their place in the world than any human has, including hermits and priests. Animals communicate with their very bodies how much we do not know.

While the number of Italian works that include realistically talking animals may at first be surprising, the fact that notable Italian works debate the relationship between the divine and the animal is not given the important role of the Catholic Church in Italian society. The topic of the Catholic tradition and animals is a vast one, one that lies beyond this chapter, but I will offer a brief, contradictory example of the place of dogs in the Church to suggest the complexity of the connections: the Italian expression *fortunato come un cane in chiesa* (lucky as a dog in church) is meant ironically because dogs are not allowed in church. San Rocco, who is generally depicted with a dog, is described as the patron saint of dogs.[103] This expression and San Rocco reflect the complicated relationships that humans, and here specifically Italians, have when it comes to including or excluding animals from their communities. These ambiguous relationships also contribute to the complex portrayals of communication across species that I have discussed. These Italian authors who portray animals are inspired by their own cultural and literary backgrounds as well as their personal experiences with animals. Morante is famous for her cats, while Buzzati and Svevo were both dedicated to their dogs.[104]

In addition to the significance of these authors' cultural, linguistic, historical, and personal characteristics for their extraordinary animal representations, they were also interested in Kafka's work. Svevo's wife called Kafka her husband's "last literary love";[105] Morante's husband called Kafka his wife's "master";[106] both Landolfi and Buzzati have been called "Italy's Kafka." Their animal depictions are influenced by their own literary and intellectual traditions, their personal experiences, their imagination, and their reading of Kafka. Similarly, while his Austro-Hungarian multilingualism contributed to Kafka's

---

103 Other saints are also known as patron saints of animals.

104 For instance, on Buzzati and dogs, see Posenato, *Il bestiario di Dino Buzzati*, 124–9. Mentioning that Svevo liked dogs and kept them as pets may seem superfluous to some, but not to everyone. Richard Ellman, e.g., draws attention to the commonalities between Leopold Bloom and Svevo, as opposed to Bloom and Joyce, by pointing out that Bloom and Svevo shared a fondness for dogs (Ellmann, *James Joyce*, 385).

105 Veneziani Svevo, *Memoir of Italo Svevo*, 116. For more on Svevo's reading of Kafka, see Ziolkowski, "Svevo's Dogs."

106 For more on Morante's reading of Kafka, see Ziolkowski, "Morante and Kafka."

attention to communication, many other elements contributed to his animal representations. Critics have discussed the multiple origins of Kafka's fascination with and portrayals of animals, including pets; his father's frequent use of animal expressions ("If you sleep with dogs, you'll wake up with fleas"); Darwin; the films he watched; the development of zoos in his lifetime; and his being a vegetarian.[107] Many of these elements have been credited with influencing Kafka's perception of animals and his works' ability to provoke ongoing discussion about the role of animals, in literature and more broadly.

Kafka has, in fact, been considered to represent a shift in human thinking about animals: "The foundations of the reader's existence are shaken by Kafka's stories. Indeed, this is a fair description of what is occurring to human identity in modern Western culture as animals gain power. Between Flaubert's time and Kafka's, culture had opened itself even wider to the influence of the animal."[108] Between Kafka's time and ours, another shift has occurred or is in the process of occurring, one revealed by the many animal-studies works that reference Kafka. In this century, an author who has been associated with Kafka, Pietro Grossi, published "La Scimmia" ("The Monkey"), which shares several features with "The Judgment," "The Metamorphosis," and "A Report to an Academy." Grossi's story reverses the process of sped-up evolution that Kafka narrated. In the tale, a man's friend has become a monkey. Although his outward appearance remains the same, he squats naked and has lost or rejected the ability to communicate with human words. He is still himself; no act of magic has changed him. Grossi represents the gap between human and animal in a work that includes only humans. The story suggests that a need for escape or an inability to handle the world of the twenty-first century may have led to the transformation. While these other stories of communicating animals reflect on ways that humans can potentially understand other species, Grossi's story represents how we are often unable to understand each other and that how we deal with our animality is part of this misunderstanding.

---

107 In addition to his portrayal of animals, Kafka's vegetarianism has made him a repeated point of reference for animal activists and scholars. The story of Kafka staring at fish is an oft-repeated tale: "One day while in Berlin, Franz Kafka went to visit the city's famous aquarium. According to his friend and biographer, Max Brod, Kafka, gazing into the illuminated tanks, addressed the fish directly. 'Now at last I can look at you in peace,' he told them. 'I don't eat you anymore.'" In her review of *Eating Animals*, by Jonathan Safran Foer, Elizabeth Kolbert notes that Kafka, who became what Brod calls a *strenger Vegetarianer* (strict vegetarian), is one of Foer's heroes (Kolbert, "Flesh of Your Flesh").

108 Scholtmeijer, "What Is 'Human'?," 130.

The story begins with the narrator, Nico, playing Subbuteo. He reflects, "You're not really a man if you can't play Subbuteo and table football, he had always thought, and it was a complex that had somehow stayed with him all his life."[109] Nico later goes to see his friend Piero, who has become or is acting like a monkey. Together they play with pistachios. The connections between games in the story raise questions about gender and being human as well as what determines these identities. Can something as superficial as a game determine whether someone is a man or manly (rather than womanly) or monkey (rather than man)?

While many of the stories previously discussed raise questions about how close other animals are to us because of their ability to communicate, Grossi's story examines the fear that many of us have after considering these issues. How close are we to our non-human-animal past? Have we even left it behind? Can modernity, misery, or escapism prompt a reversal? Kafka's work was not only a sign of its post-Darwinian time, but it has also contributed to the new phase of our animal understanding. As animal studies grapples with what this new phase means, it should consider Italian literature's powerful animal representations. Many of these works have taken up Kafka's questions and asked new ones in turn.

---

109 Grossi, *Fists*, 117. ("Aveva sempre pensato che non si è veramente uomini se non si
     sa giocare a Subbuteo e calcio Balilla, ed era un complesso che in qualche modo si
     era portato dietro per tutta la vita"; Grossi, *Pugni*, 159.)

Calvino's Kafka and Kafka's Italy

No poet, no artist of any art, has his complete meaning alone.

> – T.S. Eliot,
> "Tradition and the Individual Talent"

In "Kafka and His Precursors," Borges argues that reading Kafka can lead to a new understanding of past authors, forging new groups that previously would not have been considered. *Kafka's Italian Progeny* argues that Kafka can also provide a new image of modern Italian literature, one that brings together a diverse group of writers including Svevo, Romano, Calvino, Tabucchi, Capriolo, Buzzati, Bontempelli, Ferrante, Morante, Landolfi, and Manganelli. Some of these authors, like Buzzati, have been discussed with regard to Kafka, but not always productively, while other authors, like Tabucchi and Ferrante, are less frequently connected to his works. At the same time, analysing these authors together demonstrates how they shed light on different facets of Kafka: as a realist, as a lyrical writer, as playing with the strictures of detective fiction, as a questioner of the family as institution, and as a great narrator of animal fiction. *Kafka's Italian Progeny* reveals how comparison with a powerful author like Kafka, who is not frequently considered in discussions of Italian literature, adds to the critical view of that literature.

In "Calvino's Kafka and Kafka's Italy," I revisit Kafka's impact on Italian literature from the perspective of a single author who has appeared in many of these chapters, Italo Calvino. A cursory examination of Calvino's comments on Kafka suggests numerous, significant ways to read him. In chapter 1, I explored Calvino's comment, "I love Kafka because he is a realist"[1] to focus on class relations and

---

1 Baranelli and Ferrero, *Album Calvino*, 91.

narrative realism in Kafka's work, especially his first novel, *Amerika*. In chapter 2, I developed Calvino's observation that "from the lyrical Kafkaism of the forties we have moved to the (much more pseudo) sociological Kafkaism of the sixties"[2] to scrutinize the poetic elements of Kafka's short, short fiction. In chapter 3, I analysed Calvino's comment, "Kafka can be read in these two ways: as the 'story of a soul' and/or as the description of a network of objective relationships, and I think the latter approach is more important,"[3] to suggest how approaching Kafka in terms of depersonalization reveals a completely different mode than looking for the individual narrative in his works. In chapter 4, I reflected on Calvino's comment that "the great event of the century ... and perhaps a necessary condition of the new industrial phase – was the revolution against the father accomplished in the territories of the paternal empire of Franz Joseph, by a medical alienist and a young visionary, Freud and Kafka" to frame Kafka as one of the most important thinkers for understanding the transformations of the modern world.[4]

Between chasing the ghost of Kafka in Prague as a young man in 1947 and the introduction he promised to write for a new edition of *Amerika* shortly before his untimely death, Calvino kept returning to Kafka. Over the course of the book, I have also discussed Calvino's "Making Do" (1943–4), *The Path to the Spiders' Nests* (1947), "The Hanging of a Judge" (1948), "The Road to San Giovanni" (written in 1962, published 1990), "The Count of Monte Cristo" (1967), and *If on a Winter's Night a Traveler* (1979). While I did not set out to engage Calvino in every chapter, his work in the end became extremely relevant, in part because of his frequent engagements with Kafka and in part because of his large presence in the Italian literary landscape. Critics often characterize Calvino as representative of twentieth-century Italian literature, moving from neorealism in the 1940s to postmodernism in the 1970s and 1980s.[5] Some critics have lamented the place where Calvino's supposed trajectory ends, with postmodernist literature apparently far from his earlier communist beliefs.[6] In "Pasolini vs. Calvino, One More Time: The Debate on the Role of Intellectuals and Postmodernism in Italy

---

2 Translated from Calvino, *Lettere*, 872–3.

3 Calvino to Boselli, 23 October 1969, *Italo Calvino*, 379.

4 Calvino, *Saggi*, 113–14.

5 Eugenio Bolongaro claims that Calvino's "fictional and critical writings profoundly shaped the very notion of what constitutes valid literary narrative within the Italian cultural milieu" (Bolongaro, *Italo Calvino*, 55).

6 See Alessia Ricciardi's chapter on Calvino in *After La Dolce Vita*.

Today," Lucia Re ends with a call to assess Italian authors in their own contexts, beyond labels, since critical parameters can limit how Italian literature is understood.[7]

Calvino's central place in this book reveals not only his diverse opinions on literature but also how comparing him to Kafka can disrupt some of the labels that have been placed on him, revealing what is missed when his apparent trajectory becomes the primary way to understand him. Even though Calvino's interest in Kafka spans his entire writing career, Kafka's presence is so small in many thorough monographs on Calvino that he is either mentioned only briefly or not at all.[8] Scholars perhaps frequently ignore Calvino's debt to Kafka because of the focus in Italian studies, discussed in the introduction, on Italian authors' regional backgrounds, their national significance, and then, when put in a comparative perspectives, their connections to France and the United States. An entire monograph could be dedicated to Calvino and Kafka. In a discussion of "La formica argentina" ("The Argentine Ant," 1952), this epilogue adds to the picture of Calvino's Kafka presented in earlier chapters and also suggests other connections between the two authors.

Interpretations of Calvino's "The Argentine Ant" rival those of Kafka's works in their number and range. The story follows a husband, wife, and baby who arrive in a new land, hoping to escape their problems, and instead find ants covering everything. Their neighbours have developed a series of mechanisms to deal with the insects, but none are successful. Do the ants represent the forces beyond human reason? Do they symbolize a catalogue of attitudes about how humans face problems? Do they represent the struggle to combat capitalism? Do they reveal the irrelevance of humanity, the inescapability of death, everyone's alienation, the power of nature, the power of the government, the human conflict between fantasy and need, or the fight against injustice? Or are they just ants?

---

7 "Although each [Calvino and Pasolini] in his own way has left us with a rich heritage of texts and images and inspiration for how to read and think through the complexities of the present and to approach the future, neither can be labeled simply a 'postmodernist' or a 'realist'" (Re, "Pasolini vs. Calvino, One More Time," 117).

8 Kafka, e.g., does not make an appearance in the index of McLaughlin, *Italo Calvino*; Carter, *Italo Calvino*; Cavallaro, *The Mind of Italo Calvino*; Jeannet, *Under the Radiant Sun and the Crescent Moon*; Pilz, *Mapping Complexity*; or Modena, *Italo Calvino's Architecture of Lightness*. While anglophone authors of journal or newspaper articles are more likely to reference Kafka while trying to frame the author for an English-speaking audience that does not know Calvino, Italian monographs are more likely to mention Kafka a few times as one of Calvino's favourite authors.

Calvino resisted the way the story was contrasted with Kafka because, for him, the ants were real: "Watch out because *The Ant* is not 'abstractly symbolic,' but totally realistic: British critics talked a lot about Kafka in connection with it, probably thinking that the Argentine ant was an imaginary creature. Whoever has been in the Riviera knows that there is nothing exaggerated in my story."[9] Although the story may not be "like Kafka's" in terms of how the critics interpreted it, Calvino himself stated that in trying to create an allegory, Kafka had created the most realistic works that best expressed modern alienation.[10] Similarly, in "The Argentine Ant," Calvino may have begun with a real situation, but he ended up creating a work that was also open to a myriad of symbolic interpretations.

Gore Vidal suggests that the openness and precision of "The Argentine Ant" are part of what makes the story a masterpiece: "Or, put another way, if 'The Argentine Ant' is not a masterpiece of twentieth-century prose writing, I cannot think of anything better. Certainly it is as minatory and strange as anything by Kafka."[11] Part of the strangeness in the story comes from how the ants force a change in perspective in the characters. The ants seem perhaps even more horrible than they are because they become everyone's obsession: "But we could no longer find peace in bed, with the thought of those insects everywhere, in the food, in all our things, perhaps by now they had crawled up the legs of the chest of drawers and reached the baby."[12]

Like the soundtrack of a horror movie, the thought of the ants accompanies everything, making even the ordinary appear potentially terrifying. For critics of this story, as for critics of so many of Kafka's works, how realistic, surreal, or frightening the story appears depends, in part, on readers' expectations. Readers approach works with different soundtracks. Both because of how the neighbours approach the ants and also how a reader might approach the story, "The Argentine Ant" reflects on a multiplicity of perspectives. That, and the significance of hypothesis, discussed in chapter 2, could be used to connect numerous works by Kafka and Calvino.

The ants cause particular unpleasantness because of how they change the family's sense of home: "But the more I looked, the more

---

9　Calvino, *Italo Calvino*, 171.
10　Calvino, *Saggi*, 1381.
11　Vidal, "Calvino's Novels," 106. The article originally appeared in the *New York Review of Books*, 30 May 1974.
12　Calvino, "The Argentine Ant," 148. ("Ma a letto non ci riusciva più d'aver pace, con l'idea di quelle bestie dappertutto, nei cibi, nella roba; forse ora stavano risalendo dal pavimento per i piedi del comò fino al bambino"; Calvino, *Romanzi e racconti*, 1:453.)

new ways I discovered by which the ants came and went. Our new home, although it looked so smooth and solid on the surface, was in fact porous and honeycombed with cracks and holes."[13] The focus on vision and the narrator's discovery of the house's porousness reveal that while the home has not changed, the narrator's perspective of it has. The husband portrays his wife as limiting his imagination and ability to deal with problems, including the ants: "What prevented me from entering their state of mind, I was thinking on my way home, was my wife, who had always been opposed to any fantasy. And I thought what an influence she had on my life, and how nowadays I could never get drunk on words and ideas any more."[14]

The tensions between family and creativity suggest a reason for the isolated narrators that are found in so many of Kafka's and Calvino's works. While more subtly than the works discussed in chapter 4, Calvino's story questions how the family restricts creativity. The husband's uncle, who has remained single, lived happily in the land of the ants years ago and did not emphasize the insects as a problem. Kafka's and Calvino's works frequently suggest the dangers of human relationships. They present some of the most solitary figures in literature. Calvino discussed the difficulty of writing about sex, an act that often requires reflection on human closeness, in the twentieth century. He claimed, "Ours is the century – of Kafka, the chaste writer."[15]

In "The Argentine Ant," the humans are set in opposition to the ants. The "ant man," who may be helping the ants (to keep himself in business), resembles an ant himself and calls into question the human-versus-nature interpretation of the story. "The Argentine Ant" presents several upsets in the balance between human relationships and those between humans and nature. These shifts focus on descriptions of the home, its construction, and how to potentially protect it from the outside world. Several of Kafka's works, such as "Der Bau" ("The Burrow"), and Calvino's other works, from his early story "La

---

13 Calvino, "The Argentine Ant," 150. ("Ma più guardavo e più scoprivo nuove direzioni nelle quali le formiche andavano e venivano, e come la nostra casa, in apparenza liscia ed omogenea come un dado, fosse invece porosa e tutta solcata da fessure e crepe"; Calvino, *Romanzi e racconti*, 1:454.)

14 Calvino, "The Argentine Ant," 165–6. ("L'ostacolo per me a entrare in quella mentalità, – pensavo ritornando a casa, – era mia moglie, sempre nemica delle cosa fantastiche. E pensavo pure a quanto essa avesse inciso nella mia vita, così che ormai io non riuscivo più a ubriacarmi di parole e pensieri"; Calvino, *Romanzi e racconti*, 1:468.)

15 Calvino, from a 1961 interview on eroticism, discussed in detail and translated by Tommasina Gabriele; see Calvino, *Italo Calvino*, 44. ("Il nostro è il secolo di Kafka, scrittore casto"; Calvino, "Otto domande sull'eroticismo," 22.)

casa degli alveari" ("The House of the Beehives") to *Invisible Cities*, can be analysed in terms of the architecture of protection.

Walter Benjamin draws attention to the centrality of building in Kafka's oeuvre: "No human art appears as deeply compromised as the art of building in Kafka. None is more essential and none makes perplexity more perceptible."[16] The analysis of one's space makes evident one's mental confusion. "The Argentine Ant" emphasizes how art and focus, not a solution, may be the aim of human endeavours: "I couldn't get used to the idea of so much art and perseverance being needed to carry out such a simple operation as catching ants; but I realized that the important thing was to carry on continually and methodically."[17] The neighbours take pride in their methods of combatting the ants, even though none are successful. The constructing, not the finished construction, may be the goal. The connection between construction and thought suggests how these stories also reflect upon literature, its making and its interpretation. All of Kafka's works have been analysed as representing the process of understanding and creating literature. His similarities to Calvino reveal how the Italian author's works also reflect on literature.[18]

For Jonathan Lethem, Calvino's work was a living bridge "between Pliny the Elder, Franz Kafka, and Italian neorealist cinema."[19] For Cynthia Ozick, "Calvino occurring in any span of decades other than those vouchsafed him is inconceivable. He was meant to flourish on the heels of Kafka."[20] Making clear that he did think he wrote *after*, or "on the heels of," Kafka, Calvino explains that Kafka combines literary style with a strong point of view, an approach that both changes the common understanding of what being human is and contributes to philosophical thought more broadly. He writes,

> The names of Dostoyevsky and Kafka remind us of the two supreme examples in which the authority of the writer – that is, the power to transmit an unmistakable message by means of a special intonation of language

---

16 Benjamin, quoted in Thiel, "Architecture," 141.

17 Calvino, "The Argentine Ant," 161. ("Io non riuscivo ad abituarmi al pensiero che per compiere un'operazione così semplice come schiacciare una formica si dovesse impegnare tanta arte e costanza, ma capivo che l'importante era farlo con metodo, incessantemente"; Calvino, *Romanzi e racconti*, 1:464.)

18 While for the earlier works this may be less obvious, Calvino's later works often make more explicit that they are reflecting on literature than Kafka's work does.

19 Lethem, *The Ecstasy of Influence*, 75. Sander L. Gilman claims, "Italo Calvino (1923–1985), in his *Invisible Cities*, rethinks Kafka's fantasy world" (Gilman, *Franz Kafka*, 137).

20 Ozick, "Mouth, Ear, Nose."

and a special distortion of the human figure and of situations – coincides with the authority of the thinker on the highest level. This also means that "the Dostoyevsky man" and "the Kafka man" have altered the image of man, even for those who have no particular inclination toward the philosophy that lies more or less explicitly behind such representations.[21]

Kafka is one of Calvino's examples of a great philosophical author, an author who alters the way the reader sees the world. While Kafka's modernist experimentations helped early Calvino develop his literary style and perspective, later Calvino also used Kafka to analyse literature itself. Alluding to Kafka's "Silence of the Sirens," Calvino explains one way in which modern fiction can build on older fiction in "Levels of Reality in Fiction" (1978): "'I write that Homer tells that Ulysses discovers that the Sirens are mute.' In this case, in order to obtain a particular literary effect, I apocryphally attribute to Homer my own inversion, or distortion, or interpretation of the Homeric narrative."[22] Adding another level of complexity to his statement, Calvino then mentions that Kafka did attain this literary effect: "In fact, the idea of the silent Sirens is Kafka's, and we must realize that the 'I' who is the subject of the sentence is Kafka."[23] In this essay on reality in literature, on how literature engages literature, Calvino inhabits Kafka's narration: "I" for Calvino here is Kafka.

This brief analysis of Calvino and Kafka reveals how putting the two authors into conversation with one another could result in an entire reconsideration of Calvino's oeuvre. It also demonstrates how the topics discussed in the chapters – what the realism of Kafka potentially reveals about Italian works, the power of Italian short, short fiction, the relationship between mysteries and analysis, family as an institution, and the human-animal boundary – could be expanded upon, in regard to Calvino's work and others. While Kafka can contribute to readings of Calvino that aim to show consistencies rather than changes in his writings, it is harder (unless Calvino is taken as *the* representative Italian author) to show what this means about Italian literature more broadly.

---

21 Calvino, *The Uses of Literature*, 41–2.
22 Calvino, *The Uses of Literature*, 107. ("'Io scrivo che Omero racconta che Ulisse scopre che le Sirene sono mute.' In questo caso per ottenere un determinato effetto letterario io attribuisco apocrifamente a Omero un mio capovolgimento o deformazione o interpretazione del racconto omerico"; Calvino, "I livelli della realtà in letteratura," *Saggi*, 386.)
23 Calvino, *The Uses of Literature*, 107. ("In realtà l'idea delle Sirene silenziose è di Kafka; facciamo conto che l'*io* soggetto della frase sia Kafka"; Calvino, *Saggi*, 386.)

The chapters aimed to show the variety of Italian literature by concentrating on multiple authors. Shifting how authors are grouped leads to new views of them and therefore of the character of modern Italian literature. The chapters do not exhaust the way that Kafka and Italian authors could be grouped: Jewish themes, Trieste, fascism, and loneliness in Italian literature could all be traced with the help of Kafka.

This book takes the limited circulation of the debated category of modernism in Italy as an opportunity to rethink the contours of the modern Italian canon. In "Whom Do We Write For?," Calvino re-imagines Borges's "Kafka and His Precursors" using the image of the bookshelf: "A book is written so that it can be put beside other books and take its place on a hypothetical bookshelf. Once it is there, in some way or other it alters the shelf, expelling certain other volumes from their places or forcing them back into the second row, while demanding that certain others should be brought up to the front."[24] By analysing a few of the large number of Italian authors who produced works worthy of study, *Kafka's Italian Progeny* aims to propel more of them onto the shelves of non-Italianists, where they may receive more consideration.[25] More than perhaps any other modern author, Kafka, the "Dante of our time," shows the vitality of literature. As Calvino commented, Kafka's writing not only helps readers understand the world but also helped create it. *Kafka's Italian Progeny* does not aim to be the last word on Italian authors and Kafka, let alone Italian authors or Kafka, but it means to contribute to dialogues that reveal the great variety of modern Italian literature and how modern Italian literature can help us understand the world.

---

24 Calvino, *The Uses of Literature*, 81. ("Un libro viene scritto perché possa essere affiancato ad altri libri, perché entri in uno scaffale ipotetico e, entrandovi, in qualche modo lo modifichi, scacci dal loro posto altri volume o li facia retrocedere in seconda fila, reclami l'avanzamento in prima fila di certi altri"; Calvino, *Saggi*, 199.) Both Borges and Calvino build on ideas that T.S. Eliot proposed in "Tradition and the Individual Talent," which explored how a work of art changes the view of artworks that preceded it, in addition to building on them.

25 While Calvino could potentially support a monograph dedicated solely to his work and Kafka's, most of these Italian authors could not – not for want of material, but because they are not well enough known to be the primary subject.

Works Cited

Adams, Carol J., and Josephine Donovan, eds. *Animals and Women: Feminist Theoretical Explorations*. Durham, NC: Duke University Press, 2006.

Adamson, Walter L. *Avant-Garde Florence: From Modernism to Fascism*. Cambridge, MA: Harvard University Press, 1993.

Adorno, Theodor W. *Prisms*. Translated by Samuel and Shierry Weber. Cambridge, MA: MIT Press, 2007.

Agamben, Giorgio. *Categorie italiane: Studi di poetica e di letteratura*. Venice: Marsilio, 1996.

– *The End of the Poem: Studies in Poetics*. Translated by Daniel Heller-Roazen. Stanford, CA: Stanford University Press, 1999.

– *Nudità*. Rome: Nottetempo, 2010.

– *Nudities*. Translated by David Kishik and Stefan Pedatella. Stanford, CA: Stanford University Press, 2011.

– *The Open: Man and Animal*. Translated by Daniel Hellen-Roazen. Stanford, CA: Stanford University Press, 2012.

Aisenberg, Nadya. *A Common Spring: Crime Novel and Classic*. Bowling Green, OH: Bowling Green University Popular Press, 1980.

Ajello, Epifanio. "Photographs Illustrating and Photographs Telling: Exercises in Reading Lalla Romano and Elio Vittorini." In *Enlightening Encounters: Photography in Italian Literature*, edited by Nancy Pedri and Alù Giorgia, 191–214. Toronto: University of Toronto Press, 2015.

Alter, Robert. *Necessary Angels: Tradition and Modernity in Kafka, Benjamin and Scholem*. Cambridge, MA: Harvard University Press, 1991.

Anceschi, Luciano. *L'esercizio della lettura*. Edited by Liliana Rampello. Parma: Pratiche, 1995.

–, ed. *Lirici nuovi: Antologia*. Milan: U. Mursia, 1964.

Anderson, Mark M. Introduction to *The Sons*, by Franz Kafka, vii–xxx. New York: Schocken Books, 1989.

- "Kafka, Homosexuality and the Aesthetics of 'Male Culture.'" In *Gender and Politics in Austrian Fiction*, edited by Ritchie Robertson and Edward Timms, 79–99. Austrian Studies 7. Edinburgh: Edinburgh University Press, 1996.
- *Kafka's Clothes: Ornament and Aestheticism in the Habsburg Fin de Siècle*. Oxford: Clarendon Press, 2002.

Anedda, Antonella. "'Le due zittelle.'" In *Landolfi libro per libro*, edited by Tarcisio Tarquini, 77–80. Alatri: Hetea, 1988.

Angioletti, Giovanni Battista. "Il poeta Kafka." In *Introduzione a Kafka: Antologia di saggi critici*, edited by Ervino Pocar, 44–5. Milan: Il Saggiatore, 1974.

Ania, Gillian. "Cara's 'Creative' Writing: The Fiction of Originality in Capriolo's Il Doppio Regno." In *Essays in Italian Literature and History in Honour of Doug Thompson*, edited by George Talbot and Doug Thompson, 156–71. Dublin: Four Courts Press, 2002.
- *Fortunes of the Firefly: Sciascia's Art of Detection*. Market Harborough, UK: University Texts, 1996.
- "Gilgamesh, i miti e 'l'eterno ritorno': Intervista con Paola Capriolo, Milan, September 2003." *Italianist* 25, no. 1 (2005): 144–72. http://usir.salford.ac.uk/1255/1/s7.pdf.
- Introduction to *The Dual Realm*, by Paola Capriolo, ix–xxx. Market Harborough, UK: Troubador, 2000.
- *Paola Capriolo: Mitologia, musica, metamorfosi, 1988–1998*. Florence: F. Cesati, 2006.

Antonello, Pierpaolo, and Florian Mussgnug, eds. *Postmodern impegno: Ethics and Commitment in Contemporary Italian Culture*. Oxford: Lang, 2009.

Apter, Emily S. *Against World Literature: On the Politics of Untranslatability*. London: Verso, 2013.

Ara, Angelo, and Claudio Magris. *Trieste: Un'identità di frontiera*. Turin: Einaudi, 1983.

Arac, Jonathan. "Global and Babel: Language and Planet." In *Shades of the Planet: American Literature as World Literature*, edited by Wai Chee Dimock and Lawrence Buell, 19–38. Princeton, NJ: Princeton University Press, 2011.

Argento, Micol. *Giorgio Manganelli: Indagine per una riscrittura infinita*. Naples: Liguori, 2012.

Armstrong, Philip. *What Animals Mean in the Fiction of Modernity*. London: Routledge, 2008.

Arslan, Antonia. *Invito alla lettura di Dino Buzzati*. Milan: Mursia, 1974.

Asquer, Renata. *La grande torre: Vita e morte di Dino Buzzati*. Lecce: Manni, 2002.

Auden, W.H. "The Guilty Vicarage: Notes on the Detective Story, by an Addict." *Harper's Magazine*, May 1948, 406–12.
- *Prose*. Edited by Edward Mendelson. Vol. 2. Princeton, NJ: Princeton University Press, 2002.

Austen, Jane. *Northanger Abbey*. Modern Library paperback ed. New York: Modern Library, 2002.

Bahr, E. "Kafka and the Prague Spring." *Mosaic*. Special issue, *New Views on Franz Kafka* 3, no. 4 (Summer 1970): 15–30.

Bailly, Jean Christophe. *The Animal Side*. New York: Fordham University Press, 2011.

Baioni, Giuliano. *Kafka: Letteratura ed ebraismo*. Rome: Edizioni di storia e letteratura, 2008.

– *Kafka: Romanzo e parabola*. Milan: Feltrinelli, 1962.

Baldacci, Alessandro. "Amelia Danza Kafka." *Trasparenze* 17 (2003): 119–32.

– *Amelia Rosselli*. Rome: Laterza, 2007.

– *Fra tragico e assurdo: Benn, Beckett e Celan nella poetica di Amelia Rosselli*. Cassino: Università degli studi di Cassino, 2006.

Baldini, Anna. "Il Neorealismo: Nascita e usi di una categoria letteraria." In *Letteratura italiana e tedesca 1945–1970: Campi, polisistemi, transfer / Deutsche und italienische Literatur 1945–1970; Felder, Polysysteme, Transfer*, edited by Irene Fantappiè and Michele Sisto, 109–28. Rome: Istituto Italiano di Studi Germanici, 2013.

Banfield, Edward C., and Laura Fasano Banfield. *The Moral Basis of a Backward Society*. New York: Free Press, 1975.

Banville, John. "A Different Kafka." *New York Review of Books*, 24 October 2013. http://www.nybooks.com/articles/2013/10/24/different-kafka/.

Baranelli, Luca, and Ernesto Ferrero, eds. *Album Calvino*. Milan: A. Mondadori, 2003.

Barberio Corsetti, Giorgio. *America*. Milan: Vita e Pensiero, 1993.

Bárberi Squarotti, Giorgio. *Dal tramonto dell'ermetismo alla neoavanguardia*. Brescia: Editrice La Scuola, 1984.

– "Forme simboliche del romanzo del Novecento." In *Lezioni sul Novecento: Storia, teoria e analisi letteraria*, edited by Andrea Marino and Stefano Agosti, 111–37. Milan: Vita e Pensiero, 1990.

– "La fortezza e la forma: *Il deserto dei Tartari*." In *Dino Buzzati*, edited by Alvise Fontanella, 139–56. Florence: Olschki, 1982.

– "Note sulle principali opere di Buzzati." In *L'attesa e l'ignoto: L'opera multiforme di Dino Buzzati*, edited by Mauro Germani, 53–60. Forlì: L'arcolaio, 2012.

Barenghi, Mario. "Narrazione." In *Giorgio Manganelli*, edited by Marco Belpoliti and Andrea Cortellessa, 408–25. Milan: Marcos y Marcos, 2006.

Barilli, Renato. *Comicita di Kafka*. Milan: Bompiani, 1982.

Barthes, Roland. "Kafka's Answer." In *Franz Kafka: A Collection of Criticism*, edited by Leo Hamalian, 140–4. New York: McGraw-Hill, 1974.

Battaglia, Romano. *Il mistero in Dino Buzzati*. Milan: Rusconi, 1980.

Baumann, Barbara. *Dino Buzzati: Untersuchungen zur Thematik in seinem Erzählwerk*. Heidelberg: Carl Winter, 1980.

Bellaspiga, Lucia. *Il deserto dei Tartari, un romanzo a lieto fine: Una rilettura del capolavoro di Dino Buzzati*. Milan: Àncora, 2014.

Bell-Villada, Gene H. *Borges and His Fiction: A Guide to His Mind and Art*. Austin: University of Texas Press, 2000.

Belpoliti, Marco. "Ping Pong Calvino-Manganelli, Manganelli-Calvino." In *Le foglie messaggere: Scritti in onore di Giorgio Manganelli*, edited by Viola Papetti, 92–113. Rome: Editori riuniti, 2000.

Benco, Silvio. *Scritti di critica: Lettteraria e figurativa*. Edited by Oliviero Honore Bianchi, Bruno Maier, and Silvio Pesante. Trieste: LINT, 1977.

Benedetti, Carla. *Pasolini Contro Calvino: Per una letteratura impura*. Turin: Bollati Boringhieri, 1998.

– *Una trappola di parole: Lettura del "Pasticciaccio."* Pisa: ETS, 1988.

Benedetti, Laura. *The Tigress in the Snow: Motherhood and Literature in Twentieth-Century Italy*. Toronto: University of Toronto Press, 2009.

Ben-Ghiat, Ruth. "Fascism, Writing, and Memory: The Realist Aesthetic in Italy, 1930–1950." *Journal of Modern History* 67, no. 3 (1995): 627–65.

Benjamin, Walter. *Charles Baudelaire: A Lyric Poet in the Era of High Capitalism*. London: Verso, 1989.

– *Illuminations*. Edited by Hannah Arendt. Translated by Harry Zorn. London: Pimlico, 1999.

Benussi, Cristina. *La forma delle forme: Il teatro di Italo Svevo*. Trieste: EUT, 2007.

Benvegnù, Damiano. "The Tortured Animals of Modernity: Animal Studies and Italian Literature." In *Creatural Fictions*, 41–63. New York: Palgrave, 2016.

Bergel, Lienhard. "*Amerika*: Its Meaning." In *Franz Kafka Today*, edited by Angel Flores and Homer Swander, 117–26. Madison: University of Wisconsin Press, 1962.

Bernheimer, Charles. "Symbolic Bond and Textual Play: Structure of *The Castle*." In *The Kafka Debate: New Perspectives for Our Time*, edited by Angel Flores, 367–84. New York: Gordian Press, 1977.

Bertoni, Federico. *Realismo e letteratura: Una storia possibile*. Turin: G. Einaudi, 2007.

Bhabha, Homi K. *The Location of Culture*. London: Routledge, 2010.

Biagini, Enza, and Anna Nozzoli. *Bestiari del Novecento*. Rome: Bulzoni, 2001.

Bianco, Monica. "The Murder in Via Merulana: Presenze di Poe nel Pasticciaccio." In *Un meraviglioso ordegno: Paradigmi e modelli nel "Pasticciaccio" di Gadda*, edited by Maria Antonietta Terzoli, Cosetta Veronese, and Vincenzo Vitale, 89–111. Rome: Carocci, 2013.

Billiani, Francesca. *Modes of Censorship and Translation: National Contexts and Diverse Media*. London: Routledge, 2016.

Billiani, Francesca, Daniela la Penna, and Mila Milani, eds. "Special Issue: National Dialogues and Transnational Exchanges across Italian Periodical Culture, 1940–1960." *Modern Italy* 21 (2016): 122–225.

Blanchot, Maurice. *The Work of Fire*. Translated by Charlotte Mandell. Stanford, CA: Stanford University Press, 1995.

Bloom, Harold. *Italo Calvino*. Philadelphia: Chelsea House Publishers, 2001.

Bo, Carlo. *Della lettura*. Urbino: Quattro venti, 1987.

– "Prefazione" to *Le madri*, edited by Riccardo Bacchelli, 7–12. Milan: Bramante, 1972.

– *Riflessioni critiche*. Florence: Sansoni, 1953.

Boa, Elizabeth. *Kafka: Gender, Class, and Race in the Letters and Fictions*. Oxford: Clarendon Press / Oxford University Press, 1996.

Bock, Gisela, and Pat Thane, eds. *Maternity and Gender Policies: Women and the Rise of the European Welfare States, 1880s–1950s*. London: Routledge, 2008.

Bolongaro, Eugenio. *Italo Calvino and the Compass of Literature*. Toronto: University of Toronto Press, 2003.

Bondanella, Peter E. "Eco and the Tradition of the Detective Story." In *New Essays on Umberto Eco,* edited by Peter Bondanella, 90–112. Cambridge: Cambridge University Press, 2009.

– *The Films of Federico Fellini*. Cambridge: Cambridge University Press, 2002.

– "Franz Kafka and Italo Svevo." In *Proceedings of the Comparative Literature Symposium: "Franz Kafka: His Place in World Literature,"* edited by Wolodymyr Zyla, 17–34. Lubbock: Interdepartmental Committee on Comparative Literature, Texas Tech University, 1971.

Bondeson, Jan. *Amazing Dogs: A Cabinet of Canine Curiosities*. Ithaca, NY: Cornell University Press, 2011.

Bondy, François. *European Notebooks: New Societies and Old Politics, 1954–1985*. New Brunswick, NJ: Transaction Publications, 2005.

Bonsaver, Guido. *Censorship and Literature in Fascist Italy*. Toronto: University of Toronto Press, 2007.

Bontempelli, Massimo. *Il figlio di due madri*. Macerata: Liberilibri, 2005.

– *Separations: Two Novels of Mothers and Children*. Translated by Estelle Gilson. Kingston, NY: McPherson, 2004.

Borges, Jorge Luis. *Collected Fictions*. Translated by Andrew Hurley. New York: Penguin Books, 2009.

– *Conversations*. Edited by Richard Burgin. Jackson: University Press of Mississippi, 1998.

– Foreword to *Stories 1904–1924, by Franz Kafka*, 5–8. Translated by J.A. Underwood. London: Abacus, 2002.

– "Kafka and His Precursors." In *Labyrinths: Selected Stories and Other Writing*, edited by Donald A. Yates and James E. Irby and translated by James E. Irby, 199–201. New York: New Directions, 1964.

– *Other Inquisitions: 1937–1952*. Translated by Ruth L.C. Simms. Austin: University of Texas Press, 2000.

Borgese, Giuseppe Antonio. "In Amerika con Kafka." In *Da Dante a Thomas Mann*, 253–9. Milan: Mondadori, 1958.

Botta, Anna. "The Journey and the Quest." In *Antonio Tabucchi: A Collection of Essays*, edited by Bruno Ferraro and Nicole Prunster, 143–74. Melbourne: La Trobe University, 1997.

Brantlinger, Patrick. "Missing Corpses: The Deconstructive Mysteries of James Purdy and Franz Kafka." *NOVEL: A Forum on Fiction* 20, no. 1 (1986): 24–40.

Briziarelli, Susan. "Of Valiant Knights and Labyrinths: Leonardo Sciascia's *Il Cavaliere e la Morte*." *Italica* 68, no. 1 (1991): 1–12.

Brizio-Skov, Flavia. *Antonio Tabucchi: Navigazioni in un arcipelago narrativo*. Cosenza: Pellegrini, 2002.

Brod, Max. *Franz Kafka: A Biography*. Translated by G. Humphreys-Roberts. New York: Schocken Books, 1970.

Butler, Judith. *Bodies That Matter: On the Discursive Limits of "Sex."* New York: Routledge, 1993.

Buzzati, Dino. *I capolavori di Dino Buzzati*. Edited by Giulio Carnazzi. Milan: Oscar Mondadori, 2005.

– *Il "Bestiario" di Dino Buzzati: Cani, gatti e altri animali*. Edited by Lorenzo Viganò. Milan: Oscar Mondadori, 2015.

– *Il deserto dei Tartari*. Novara: Mondadori, 1989.

– "Il giallo in biblioteca: Non sono capace di scrivere un giallo." *Il giornale d'Italia* (21 January 1966): 30.

– "Kafka's Houses." In *The Siren: A Selection from Dino Buzzati*, translated by Lawrence Venuti, 142–7. San Francisco: North Point Press, 1984.

– *La "nera" di Dino Buzzati: Crimini e misteri*. Edited by Lorenza Viganò. Milan: Mondadori, 2002.

– "Le case di Kafka." *Corriere della Sera*, 31 March 1965. http://www.corriere.it/parole_in_viaggio/articoli/buzzati/praga.htm.

– *Lettere a Brambilla*. Edited by Luciano Simonelli. Milan: A. Mondadori, 1988.

– *Restless Night: Selected Stories of Dino Buzzati*. Manchester: Carcanet, 1987.

– *The Siren: A Selection from Dino Buzzati*. Translated by Lawrence Venuti. San Francisco: North Point Press, 1984.

– *The Tartar Steppe*. Translated by Stuart C. Hood. Jaffrey, NH: Verba Mundi, 2005.

Buzzati, Dino, and Yves Panafieu. *Dino Buzzati, un autoritratto: Dialoghi con Yves Panafieu, luglio-settembre 1971*. Milan: A. Mondadori, 1973.

Caesar, Ann Hallamore, and Michael Caesar. *Modern Italian Literature*. Cambridge: Polity, 2007.

Caesar, Michael. "Elsa Morante." In *Writers & Society in Contemporary Italy: A Collection of Essays*, edited by Michael Caesar and Peter Hainsworth, 211–34. New York: St. Martin's Press, 1984.

Caetani, Marguerite. *La rivista* Botteghe oscure *e Marguerite Caetani: La corrispondenza con gli autori italiani, 1948–1960*. Edited by Stefania Valli. Rome: Erma di Bretschneider, 1999.

Caillois, Roger. *The Mystery Novel*. Translated by Roberto Yahni and A.W. Sadler. Bronxville, NY: Laughing Buddha Press, 1984.

Calasso, Roberto. *K*. New York: Vintage, 2012.

– "Marginalia." In *The Zürau Aphorisms of Franz Kafka*, by Franz Kafka, vii–x. Translated by Geoffrey Brock and Michael Hofmann. New York: Schocken Books, 2006.

Calvino, Italo. *Adam, One Afternoon & Other Stories*. Translated by Archibald Colquhoun and Peggy Wright. London: Minerva, 1992.

– "The Argentine Ant." In *The Watcher and Other Stories*, translated by Archibald Colquhoun, 139–181. San Diego, CA: Harcourt, 1971.

– *If on a winter's night a traveler*. Translated by William Weaver. New York: Harcourt Brace, 1981.

– *Il sentiero dei nidi di ragno*. Milan: Oscar Mondadori, 1993.

– *Invisible Cities*. Translated by William Weaver. New York: Harcourt, 1978.

– "Italo Calvino, The Art of Fiction No. 130." Interview by William Weaver and Damien Pettigrew. *Paris Review* 124 (Fall 1992). https://www.theparisreview.org/interviews/2027/italo-calvino-the-art-of-fiction-no-130-italo-calvino.

– *Italo Calvino: Letters, 1941–1985*. Edited by Michael Wood. Translated by Martin McLaughlin. Princeton, NJ: Princeton University Press, 2014.

– *La strada di San Giovanni*. Edited by Cesare Garboli. Milan: Oscar Mondadori, 2011.

– *Le città invisibili*. Milano: A. Mondadori, 2006.

– *Lettere: 1940–1985*. Milan: Mondadori, 2001.

– *Lezioni americane: Sei proposte per il prossimo millennio*. Milan: Mondadori, 2002.

– *The Literature Machine: Essays*. London: Secker & Warburg, 1987.

– "Main Currents in Italian Fiction Today." *Italian Quarterly (of Los Angeles)* 4, no. 13–14 (Spring/Summer 1960): 3–14.

– *Mondo scritto e mondo non scritto*. Edited by Mario Barenghi. Milan: Oscar Mondadori, 2011.

– *Numbers in the Dark*. New York: Houghton Mifflin Harcourt, 2014.

– "Otto domande sull'eroticismo." *Nuovi argomenti* 51–2 (July–October 1961): 21–4.

– *The Path to the Spiders' Nest*. Translated by Archibald Colquhoun and Martin McLaughlin. New York: HarperCollins, 2000.

– *Perché leggere i classici*. Milan: Mondadori, 1991.

– *The Road to San Giovanni*. Translated by Tim Parks. Toronto: Vintage Canada, 1995.

— *Romanzi e racconti*. Vol. 1. Edited by Mario Barenghi and Bruno Falcetto. Milan: A. Mondadori, 2005.

— *Romanzi e racconti*. Vol. 3, *Racconti sparsi e altri scritti d'invenzione*. Edited by Mario Barenghi and Bruno Falcetto. Milan: Mondadori, 2005.

— *Saggi: 1945–1985*. Edited by M. Barenghi. Milan: Mondadori, 2015.

— *Se una notte d'inverno un viaggiatore*. Milan: Mondadori, 2002.

— *Six Memos for the Next Millennium*. Translated by Patrick Creagh. New York: Vintage Books, 1993.

— *Sono nato in America: Interviste 1951–1985*. Edited by Luca Baranelli and Mario Barenghi. Milan: Mondadori, 2012.

— *Ultimo viene il corvo*. Edited by Geno Pampaloni. Milano: Mondadori, 2012.

— *The Uses of Literature: Essays*. Translated by Patrick Creagh. San Diego: Harcourt Brace, 1986.

— *Why Read the Classics?* Translated by Martin McLaughlin. New York: Houghton Mifflin Harcourt, 2000.

— "The Written and Unwritten Word." Translated by William Weaver. *New York Review of Books* 12 (1983): 38–9.

Camilleri, Andrea. *La mossa del cavallo*. Palermo: Sellerio, 2017.

Camosy, Charles Christopher. *For Love of Animals: Christian Ethics, Consistent Action*. Cincinnati, OH: Franciscan Media, 2013.

Camus, Albert. *The Myth of Sisyphus and Other Essays*. Translated by Justin O'Brien. New York: A.A. Knopf, 1975.

Cannon, JoAnn. *The Novel as Investigation: Leonardo Sciascia, Dacia Maraini, and Antonio Tabucchi*. Toronto: University of Toronto Press, 2006.

Capek-Habekovic, Romana. *Tommaso Landolfi's Grotesque Images*. New York: Lang, 1986.

Capriolo, Paola. *The Dual Realm*. Translated by Gillian Ania and Doug Thompson. Market Harborough, UK: Troubador, 2000.

— *Il doppio regno*. Milan: Bompiani, 1991.

— "Il simbolo opaco." In *La metamorfosi*, by Franz Kafka, 9–28. Translated by Paola Capriolo. Padova: Il notes magico, 2011.

Caputo-Mayr, Maria Luise. "Introduction: Present Kafka Research; An Outlook." *Journal of Modern Literature* 6, no. 3 (1977): 331–6.

— "Kafka and Romance Languages: A Preliminary Survey." *Journal of the Kafka Society of America: New International Series* 27, no. 1–2 (2003): 4–20.

Caputo-Mayr, Maria Luise, and Julius M. Herz. *Franz Kafka: Internationale Bibliographie der Primär- und Sekundärliteratur; Eine Einführung*. Bd. 2, Tl. 2 / *Franz Kafka: International Bibliography of Primary and Secondary Literature; An Introduction*. Vol. 2, Part 2. München: Saur, 2000.

Carey, Sarah. "Elsa Morante: Envisioning History." In *Elsa Morante's Politics of Writing: Rethinking Subjectivity, History, and the Power of Art*, edited by Stefania Lucamante, 67–74. Madison, NJ: Fairleigh Dickinson University Press, 2015.

Carloni, Massimo, and Roberto Borbolini. *L'Italia in giallo geografia e storia del giallo italiano contemporaneo*. Reggio Emilia: Diabasis, 1994.

Carrouges, Michel. "The Struggle against the Father." In *Franz Kafka: A Collection of Criticism*, edited by Leo Hamalian, 27–38. New York: McGraw-Hill, 1974.

Carter, Albert Howard. *Italo Calvino: Metamorphoses of Fantasy*. Ann Arbor, MI: UMI Research Press, 1987.

Casanova, Pascale. *The World Republic of Letters*. Translated by M.B. DeBevoise. Cambridge, MA: Harvard University Press, 2007.

Cases, Cesare. "L'uomo buono." In *Il Marxismo della maturità di Lukács*, edited by Miklós Almási and Guido Oldrini, 11–22. Naples: Prismi, 1983.

Castaldi, Simone. "The Word Made Animal Flesh." In *Thinking Italian Animals: Human and Posthuman in Modern Italian Literature and Film*, edited by Deborah Amberson and Elena Past, 75–92. New York: Palgrave Macmillan, 2014.

Catalfamo, Antonio. *Cesare Pavese: La dialettica vitale delle contraddizioni*. Rome: Aracne, 2014.

– *Cesare Pavese: Mito, ragione e realtà*. Chieti: Solfanelli, 2012.

Caute, David. *Politics and the Novel during the Cold War*. New Brunswick, NJ: Transaction, 2016.

Cavallaro, Dani. *The Mind of Italo Calvino: A Critical Exploration of His Thought and Writings*. Jefferson, NC: McFarland, 2010.

Cecchi, Emilio. "Introduzione" to *Americana: Raccolta di narratori dalle origini ai nostri giorni*, edited by Elio Vittorini, ix–xxiii. Milan: Bompiani, 1943.

Ceserani, Remo. "Sulle curiosità intellettuali di Tabucchi e i suoi modelli, non solo letterari." In *Adamastor e dintorni: In ricordo di Antonio Tabucchi; Con un frammento inedito*, edited by Valeria Tocco, 57–69. Pisa: ETS, 2013.

Chandler, Charlotte. *I, Fellini*. New York: Cooper Square Press, 2001.

Citati, Pietro. "Giorgio, malinconico tapiro." In *Giorgio Manganelli*, edited by Marco Belpoliti and Andrea Cortellessa, 256–61. Milan: Marcos y Marcos, 2006.

– *Kafka*. Milan: Mondadori, 2000.

Clementelli, Elena. *Invito alla lettura di Natalia Ginzburg*. Milan: Mursia, 1974.

Coetzee, J.M. *Elizabeth Costello*. New York: Penguin, 2003.

– *The Lives of Animals*. Edited by Amy Gutmann. Princeton, NJ: Princeton University Press, 2001.

Comparini, Alberto. "Una proposta per il modernismo italiano: La mitologia esistenziale modernista." In *Rassegna europea di letteratura italiana* 41 (2013): 103–24.

Contarini, Silvia. "The 'New' Novel of the *Neoavanguardia*." In *Neoavanguardia: Italian Experimental Literature and Arts in the 1960s*, edited by Paolo Chirumbolo, Mario Moroni, and Luca Somigli, 99–122. Toronto: University of Toronto Press, 2010.

Corngold, Stanley. "Aphoristic Form in Nietzsche and Kafka." In *Kafka und die kleine Prosa der Moderne / Kafka and Short Modernist Prose*, edited by Manfred Engel and Ritchie Robertson, 133–50. Würzburg: Königshausen & Neumann, 2011.

– "Kafka's Later Stories and Aphorisms." In *The Cambridge Companion to Kafka*, edited by Julian Preece, 95–110. Cambridge: Cambridge University Press, 2006.

Corngold, Stanley, and Ruth Vera Gross, eds. *Kafka for the Twenty-First Century*. Rochester, NY: Camden House, 2011.

Corti, Maria. "Gli infiniti possibili di Manganelli." In *Giorgio Manganelli*, edited by Marco Belpoliti and Andrea Cortellessa, 241–6. Milan: Marcos y Marcos, 2006.

– *Il Viaggio Testuale*. Torino: Einaudi, 1978.

Crespi, Alberto. "Kafka ha due soli registi: Noi." *L'Unità*, 23 February 1984.

Crespi, Guido. "Kafka e l'Italia." In *Miti e Contromiti: Cent'anni di relazioni culturali italo-austriache dopo il 1861*, edited by Alida Fliri, 107–12. Fasano: Schena, 1990.

– *Kafka Umorista*. Brescia: Shakespeare, 1983.

Crotti, Ilaria. *Tre voci sospette: Buzzati, Piovene, Parise*. Milan: Mursia, 1994.

Crumb, Robert. *Kafka*. Northampton, MA: Kitchen Sink Press, 1999.

Culler, Jonathan. "Comparative Literature, at Last." In *Comparative Literature in an Age of Globalization*, edited by Haun Saussy, 237–48. Baltimore, MD: Johns Hopkins University Press, 2006.

Cusatelli, Giorgio. "Kafka e i suoi lettori italiani." In *Kafka oggi*, edited by Giuseppe Farese, 1–10. Bari: Adriatica, 1986.

Dainotto, Roberto. "World Literature and European Literature." In *The Routledge Companion to World Literature*, edited by Theo d'Haen, David Damrosch, and Djelal Kadir, 425–34. New York: Routledge, 2015.

Damrosch, David. *What Is World Literature?* Princeton, NJ: Princeton University Press, 2006.

D'Angeli, Concetta. *Leggere Elsa Morante:* Aracoeli, La storia *e* Il mondo salvato dai ragazzini. Rome: Carocci, 2003.

Daston, Lorraine. "Intelligences: Angelic, Animal, Human." In *Thinking with Animals: New Perspectives on Anthropomorphism*, edited by Lorraine Daston and Gregg Mitman, 37–58. New York: Columbia University Press, 2005.

Davis, J. Madison. "Noir, Italian Style." *World Literature Today* 85, no. 4 (7 July 2011): 9–11.

De Angelis, Luca. *Qualcosa di più intimo: Aspetti della scrittura ebraica del Novecento italiano; Da Svevo a Bassani*. Florence: Giuntina, 2006.

De Grazia, Victoria. *How Fascism Ruled Women: Italy, 1922–1945*. Berkeley: University of California Press, 1993.

Deidier, Roberto, ed. "Scrittori d'Italia." In *La penombra mentale: Interviste e conversazioni, 1965–1990*, 164–74. Rome: Editori Riuniti, 2001.

DeKoven, Marianne. "Kafka's Animal Stories: Modernist Form and Inter-species Narrative." In *Creatural Fictions: Human-Animal Relationships in Twentieth- and Twenty-First-Century Literature*, edited by David Herman, 19–40. New York: Palgrave Macmillan, 2016.

Deleuze, Gilles, and Félix Guattari. *Kafka: Toward a Minor Literature*. Translated by Dana Polan. Minneapolis: University of Minnesota Press, 1986.

Della Coletta, Cristina. "The Morphology of Desire in Elsa Morante's *L'isola Di Arturo*." In *Under Arturo's Star: The Cultural Legacies of Elsa Morante*, edited by Stefania Lucamante and Sharon Wood, 129–56. West Lafayette, IN: Purdue University Press, 2006.

Dell'Aia, Lucia. *La sfera del puer: Il tempo dei ragazzini di Elsa Morante*. Rome: Aracne, 2013.

Del Monte, Alberto. *Breve storia del romanzo poliziesco*. Bari: Editori Laterza, 1962.

Demetz, Peter. *The Air Show at Brescia, 1909*. New York: Farrar, Straus and Giroux, 2002.

Derrida, Jacques. *The Animal That Therefore I Am*. Translated by Marie-Louise Mallet. New York: Fordham University Press, 2010.

de Waal, Frans. "Anthropomorphism and Anthropodenial: Consistency in Our Thinking about Humans and Other Animals." *Philosophical Topics* 27, no. 1 (1 April 1999): 255–80.

– *Are We Smart Enough to Know How Smart Animals Are?* W.W. Norton, 2017.

Diffley, Paul. "The Figure of the Detective in the Novels of Antonio Tabucchi." In *Crime Scenes: Detective Narratives in European Culture since 1945*, edited by Anne Mullen and Emer O'Beirne, 110–2. Amsterdam: Rodopi, 2000.

Dimock, Wai Chee, and Lawrence Buell. *Shades of the Planet: American Literature as World Literature*. Princeton, NJ: Princeton University Press, 2011.

Dini, Andrea. *Il Premio nazionale "Riccione" 1947 e Italo Calvino*. Cesena: Il Ponte Vecchio, 2007.

Dolfi, Anna, ed. *I "notturni" di Antonio Tabucchi: Atti di seminario, Firenze, 12–13 maggio 2008*. Rome: Bulzoni, 2008.

Dombroski, Robert. *Creative Entanglements: Gadda and the Baroque*. Toronto: University of Toronto Press, 1999.

– "The Foundations of Italian Modernism: Pirandello, Svevo, Gadda." In *The Cambridge Companion to the Italian Novel*, edited by Peter E. Bondanella and Andrea Ciccarelli, 89–103. Cambridge: Cambridge University Press, 2003.

Douthwaite, John. "Montalbano: Type and Prototype of the Detective." In *Lingua, storia, gioco e moralità nel mondo di Andrea Camilleri: Atti del seminario, Cagliari, 9 marzo 2004*, edited by Giuseppe Marci. Cagliari: CUEC, 2004.

Dove, George N. *The Reader and the Detective Story*. Bowling Green, OH: Bowling Green State University Popular Press, 1997.

Dowden, Stephen D. *Kafka's Castle and the Critical Imagination*. Columbia, SC: Camden House, 1995.

Dunnett, Jane. "Translation and Concealment: The Lost Voice of Lucia Rodocanachi." *Journal of Romance Studies* 4, no. 2 (2004): 37–53.

Eckert, Elgin. "Murder in Sicily: Commissario Montalbano Talks about His Author's Literary Traditions." In *Differences, Deceits and Desires: Murder and Mayhem in Italian Crime Fiction*, edited by Mirna Cicioni and Nicoletta Di Ciolla, 67–82. Newark: University of Delaware Press, 2008.

Eco, Umberto. *The Limits of Interpretation*. Bloomington: Indiana University Press, 1997.

– *The Open Work*. Translated by Anna Cancogni. Cambridge, MA: Harvard University Press.

– *Opera aperta: Forma e indeterminazione nelle poetiche contemporanee*. Milan: Bompiani, 1962.

– *The Role of the Reader: Explorations in the Semiotics of Texts*. Bloomington: Indiana University, 1997.

– *Six Walks in the Fictional Woods*. Cambridge, MA: Harvard University Press, 2004.

Elbeshlawy, Ahmed. *America in Literature and Film: Modernist Perceptions, Postmodernist Representations*. Burlington, VT: Ashgate, 2011.

Ellmann, Richard. *James Joyce*. New York: Oxford University Press, 1986.

Emrich, Wilhelm. *Franz Kafka: A Critical Study of His Writings*. Translated by Sheema Zeben Buehne. New York: Frederick Ungar, 1968.

Engel, Manfred, and Dieter Lamping, eds. *Franz Kafka und die Weltliteratur*. Göttingen: Vandenhoeck & Ruprecht, 2006.

Engel, Manfred, and Ritchie Robertson. Preface to *Kafka und die kleine Prosa der Moderne (Kafka and Short Modernist Prose)*, edited by Manfred Engel and Ritchie Robertson, 7–14. Würzburg: Königshausen & Neumann, 2011.

Eysteinsson, Ástráður. *The Concept of Modernism*. Ithaca, NY: Cornell University Press, 1994.

Faeti, Antonio. "Note su Italo Calvino e la scuola." In *Italo Calvino: Atti del convegno internazionale (Firenze, Palazzo Medici-Riccardi, 26–28 febbraio 1987)*, edited by Giovanni Falaschi and Luigi Baldacci, 53–81. Milan: Garzanti, 1988.

Falaschi, Giovanni, and Luigi Baldacci, eds. *Italo Calvino: Atti del convegno internazionale (Firenze, Palazzo Medici-Riccardi, 26–28 febbraio 1987)*. Milan: Garzanti, 1988.

Falkoff, Rebecca R. "Giorgio Manganelli and the Illegible Obscene." *Italian Studies* 70, no. 1 (2015): 131–47.

Fallaci, Oriana. *Lettera a un bambino mai nato*. Milan: BUR Rizzoli, 2014.

– *Letter to a Child Never Born*. Translated by John Shepley. New York: Simon and Schuster, 1976.

Farrell, Joseph. *Leonardo Sciascia*. Edinburgh: Edinburgh University Press, 1995.

– "Literature and the Giallo: Gadda, Eco, Tabucchi, and Sciascia." In *Italian Crime Fiction*, edited by Giuliana Pieri, 48–72. Cardiff: University of Wales Press, 2012.

Fernandez, Dominique. *Il mito dell'America negli intellettuali italiani: Dal 1930 al 1950*. Translated by Alfonso Zaccaria. Caltanissetta: Salvatore Sciascia, 1969.

Ferrante, Elena. *L'amica geniale*. Vol. 1. Rome: Edizioni e/o, 2011.

– *L'amore molesto*. Rome: Edizioni e/o, 1992.

– *My Brilliant Friend*. Translated by Ann Goldstein. New York: Europa Editions, 2013.

– *Troubling Love*. Translated by Ann Goldstein. New York: Europa Editions, 2006.

Ferrari, Fabio. *Myths and Counter-Myths of America: New World Allegories in 20th Century Italian Literature and Film*. Ravenna: Longo, 2008.

Finzi, Gilberto. *Come leggere "La luna e i falò" di Cesare Pavese*. Milan: Mursia, 1999.

Fiorucci, Wissia. "Self-Censorship in Massimo Bontempelli's Magical Realism." *Between* 5, no. 9 (1 May 2015). http://ojs.unica.it/index.php/between/article/view/1398/1522.

Fischer, Ernst. "Kafka Conference." In *Franz Kafka: An Anthology of Marxist Criticism*, edited and translated by Kenneth Hughes, 76–94. Hanover, NH: University Press of New England, 1981.

– "Kafka-Konferenz." In *Franz Kafka aus Prager Sicht*, edited by Paul Reimann and Zdeněk Vančura, 157–68. Prague: Voltaire Verlag, 1966.

Forti, Marco, and Sergio Pautasso, eds. *Il Politecnico: Antologia*. Milan: Rizzoli, 1980.

Fortini, Franco. "Capoversi su Kafka." In *Il Politecnico: Antologia critica*, edited by Marco Forti and Sergio Pautasso, 682–93. Milan: Lerici, 1960.

Franchetti, Leopoldo. *Politica e mafia in Sicilia: Gli inedita del 1876*. Edited by Antonio Jannazzo. Rome: Bibliopolis, 1995.

Freud, Sigmund. *Civilization and Its Discontents*. Translated by James Strachey. New York: W.W. Norton, 1989.

Friedlander, Saul. *Franz Kafka: The Poet of Shame and Guilt*. New Haven, CT: Yale University Press, 2013.

Fuchs, Anne. "Why Smallness Matters: Smallness, Attention and Distraction in Franz Kafka's and Robert Walser's Short Prose." In *Kafka und die kleine Prosa der Moderne / Kafka and Short Modernist Prose*, edited by Manfred Engel and Ritchie Robertson, 167–80. Würzburg: Königshausen & Neumann, 2011.

Furbank, P.N. *Italo Svevo: The Man and the Writer*. London: Secker & Warburg, 1966.

Fusco, Florinda. *Amelia Rosselli*. Palermo: Palumbo, 2007.

Gabriele, Tommasina. *Italo Calvino: Eros and Language*. Rutherford, NJ: Fairleigh Dickinson University Press, 1994.

Gadda, Carlo Emilio. *A un amico fraterno: Lettere a Bonaventura Tecchi*. Edited by Marcello Carlino. Milan: Garzanti, 1984.

– *Lettere a una gentile signora*. Edited by Giuseppe Marcenaro. Milan: Adelphi, 1983.

– "Uno scrittore e il giallo." In *Il punto su: Il romanzo poliziesco*, edited by Giuseppe Petronio, 125–9. Rome: Laterza, 1985.

Galinetto, Carla. "Alberto Spaini germanista." Thesis. Lingue e letteratura straniere moderne, Università di Pavia, 1986.

– "Alberto Spaini germanista." *Metodi e ricerche* 8, no. 7 (January–June 1989): 124–43.

Garboli, Cesare. "Elsa Morante: La storia e le sue vittime." *Il Grillo*, 23 April 2002. http://www.emsf.rai.it/grillo/trasmissioni.asp?d=906.

Gentile, Emilio. *The Struggle for Modernity: Nationalism, Futurism, and Fascism*. Westport, CT: Praeger, 2003.

Germani, Mauro. *L'attesa e l'ignoto: L'opera multiforme di Dino Buzzati*. Forlì: L'arcolaio, 2012.

Ghidetti, Enrico, ed. *Il caso Svevo: Guida storica e critica*. Bari: Editori Laterza, 1984.

Giardina, Andrea. "Il viaggio interrotto: Il tema del cane fedele nella letteratura italiana del Novecento." *Paragrafo* 1 (2006): 145–66.

Gilman, Sander L. *Franz Kafka*. London: Reaktion, 2005.

Gilmour, David. *The Pursuit of Italy: A History of a Land, Its Regions and Their Peoples*. London: Allen Lane, 2011.

Ginzburg, Natalia. *Family Lexicon*. Translated by Jenny McPhee. New York: New York Review Books Classics, 2017.

– *Lessico famigliare*. Turin: Einaudi, 1999.

Gioanola, Elio. *Cesare Pavese: La realtà, l'altrove, il silenzio*. Milan: Jaca Book, 2003.

Giorgio, Adalgisa. "The Passion for the Mother: Conflicts and Idealisations in Contemporary Italian Narrative." In *Writing Mothers and Daughters: Renegotiating the Mother in Western European Narratives by Women*, edited by Adalgisa Giorgio, 119–54. New York: Berghahn Books, 2002.

Giraldi, William. "Internal Tapestries: Conversation with Louise Glück." *Poets & Writers*, October 2014, 42–9.

Golino, Carlo L. "On the Italian 'Myth' of America." *Italian Quarterly* 3, no. 9 (Spring 1959): 19–33.

Gorman, James. "Animal Studies Cross Campus to Lecture Hall." *New York Times*, 2 January 2012.

Gramsci, Antonio. *Antonio Gramsci: Selections from Cultural Writings*. Edited by David Forgacs and Geoffrey Nowell-Smith. Translated by William Q. Boelhower. London: Lawrence & Wishart, 2012.

Gray, Richard T. *Constructive Destruction: Kafka's Aphorisms; Literary Tradition and Literary Transformation*. Tübingen: M. Niemeyer, 1987.

Gray, Richard T., Ruth V. Gross, Clayton Koelb, and Rolf J. Goebel. *A Franz Kafka Encyclopedia*. Westport, CT: Greenwood Press, 2005.

Gross, Ruth V. "Fallen Bridge, Fallen Woman, Fallen Text." *Literary Review* 26 (1983): 577–87.

– "Hunting Kafka out of Season: Enigmatics in the Short Fictions." In *A Companion to the Works of Franz Kafka*, edited by James Rolleston, 247–62. Columbia, SC: Camden House, 2006.

Grossi, Pietro. *Fists*. Translated by Howard Curtis. London: Pushkin, 2010.

– *Pugni*. Palermo: Sellerio, 2009.

Grossvogel, David I. *Limits of the Novel: Evolutions of a Form from Chaucer to Robbe-Grillet*. London: Cornell University Press, 1971.

Guagnanini, Elvio. "Svevo: A arte do conto." In *Argo e seu dono*, by Italo Svevo. Translated by Liliana Laganá, 13–14. São Paulo: Berlendis & Vertecchia Editores, 2001.

Guj, Luisa. "Illusion and Literature in Morante's *L'isola Di Arturo*." *Italica* 65, no. 2 (1988): 144–53.

Gumpert, Carlos, and Antonio Tabucchi. "La letteratura come enigma ed inquietudine: Una conversazione con Antonio Tabucchi." In *Dedica a Antonio Tabucchi*, edited by Claudio Cattaruzza, 17–105. Pordenone: Associazione provinciale per la prosa, 2001.

Ham, Jennifer, and Matthew Senior, eds. *Animal Acts: Configuring the Human in Western History*. New York: Routledge, 1997.

Haring, Ekkehard W., ed. "Kafka-Atlas." https://www.kafka-atlas.org.

Harrison, Thomas. *1910: The Emancipation of Dissonance*. Berkeley: University of California Press, 1998.

Haycraft, Howard. *Murder for Pleasure: The Life and Times of the Detective Story*. New York: Carroll & Graf, 1984.

Hayes, Aden W., and Khachig Tololyan. "The Cross and the Compass: Patterns of Order in Chesterton and Borges." *Hispanic Review* 49, no. 4 (1981): 395–405. https://doi.org/10.2307/472745.

Heiney, Donald. *America in Modern Italian Literature*. New Brunswick, NJ: Rutgers University Press, 1965.

Hipkins, Danielle E. *Contemporary Italian Women Writers and Traces of the Fantastic: The Creation of Literary Space*. London: Legenda, 2007.

– "Evil Ambiguities: The Fantastic Flight from Interpretation in Dino Buzzati's Il Deserto Dei Tartari and Paola Capriolo's Early Fiction." *Spunti e ricerche* 13, no. 1 (1998): 81–98.

– "Lost in the Art(ifice) of Male Language: Finding the Female Author in Paola Capriolo's 'Il doppio regno.'" *Modern Language Review* 101, no. 1 (January 2006): 90–105.

Hofmann, Michael. Introduction to *Amerika (The Man Who Disappeared)*, by Franz Kafka. Translated by Michael Hofmann, vii–xiv. New York: New Directions, 1996.

Hofmannsthal, Hugo von. *The Lord Chandos Letter and Other Writings*. Translated by Joel Rotenberg. New York: New York Review of Books, 2005.

Holquist, Michael. "Whodunit and Other Questions: Metaphysical Detective Stories in Post-War Fiction." *New Literary History* 3, no. 1 (1971): 135–56.

Hösle, Johannes. *Cesare Pavese*. Berlin: Walter de Gruyter, 1964.

– *Die italienische Literatur der Gegenwart: Von Cesare Pavese bis Dario Fo*. Munich: Verlag C.H. Beck, 1999.

– "Italien." In *Das Werk und seine Wirkung*. Vol. 2 of *Kafka-Handbuch*, edited by Hartmut Binder, 722–32. Stuttgart: A. Kröner, 1979.

– *Italienische Literatur des 19. und 20. Jahrhunderts in Grundzügen*. Darmstadt: Wissenschaftliche Buchgesellschaft, 1990.

Hughes, H. Stuart. *Prisoners of Hope: The Silver Age of the Italian Jews, 1924–1974*. Cambridge, MA: Harvard University Press, 1996.

Hughes, Kenneth. *Franz Kafka: An Anthology of Marxist Criticism*. Hanover, NH: Published for Clark University Press by University Press of New England, 1981.

Hutcheon, Linda. *Narcissistic Narrative: The Metafictional Paradox*. Waterloo, ON: Wilfrid Laurier University Press, 2013.

Huyssen, Andreas. *Miniature Metropolis: Literature in an Age of Photography and Film*. Cambridge, MA: Harvard University Press, 2015.

Ioli, Giovanna. *Dino Buzzati*. Milan: Mursia, 1988.

Isotti Rosowsky, Giuditta. *Giorgio Manganelli: Una scrittura dell'eccesso*. Rome: Bulzoni, 2007.

Jeannet, Angela M. *Under the Radiant Sun and the Crescent Moon: Italo Calvino's Storytelling*. Toronto: University of Toronto Press, 2000.

Jewell, Keala. "Magic Realism and Real Politics: Massimo Bontempelli's Literary Compromise." *Modernism/Modernity* 15, no. 4 (15 January 2009): 725–44.

Jossa, Stefano. *L'Italia letteraria: Come poeti e scrittori hanno costruito l'identità nazionale*. Bologna: il Mulino, 2006.

Kadarkay, Arpad. *Georg Lukács: Life, Thought, and Politics*. Cambridge, MA: B. Blackwell, 1991.

Kafka, Franz. *America*. Translated by Amelia De Rosa. Milan: Dalai, 2011.

– *Amerika (The Man Who Disappeared)*. Translated by Michael Hofmann. New York: New Directions, 1996.

– *Amerika: The Missing Person; A New Translation, Based on the Restored Text*. Translated by Mark Harman. New York: Schocken Books, 2008.

– *Briefe 1900–1912*. Vol. 1. Edited by Hans-Gerd Koch. Frankfurt am Main: S. Fischer, 1999.

– *Briefe 1914–1917*. Vol. 3. Edited by Hans-Gerd Koch. Frankfurt am Main: S. Fischer, 2005.

– *Briefe 1918–1920*. Vol. 4. Edited by Hans-Gerd Koch. Frankfurt am Main: S. Fischer, 2013.

– "The Bucket Rider." In *Complete Stories*, edited by Nahum Norbert Glatzer. Translated by Willa and Edwin Muir, 412–14. New York: Schocken Books, 1983.

– *The Castle*. Translated by Anthea Bell. Oxford: Oxford University Press, 2009.
– *Contemplation*. Translated by Kevin Blahut. Prague: Twisted Spoon Press, 1997.
– *Das Schloß*. Edited by Malcolm Pasley. Frankfurt am Main: Fischer, 2008.
– *Der Proceß*. Edited by Malcolm Pasley. Frankfurt am Main: Fischer, 2010.
– *Der Verschollene*. Frankfurt am Main: Fischer, 2008.
– *Der Verschollene*. Edited by Jost Schillemeit. Vol. 1. Munich: S. Fischer, 1983.
– "Description of a Struggle." In *Complete Stories*, edited by Nahum Norbert Glatzer and translated by Tania and James Stern, 9–51. New York: Schocken Books, 1983.
– *The Diaries, 1910–1923*. Edited by Max Brod. New York: Schocken Books, 1988.
– *Erzählungen*. Frankfurt am Main: Fischer Taschenbuchverlag, 1996.
– *Il fochista*. Translated by Magda Olivetti. Genoa: Il melangolo, 1993.
– *Il fochista: Racconto*. Rome: La Repubblica, 1997.
– *Il processo*. Translated by Primo Levi. Turin: Einaudi, 1983.
– "The Judgment." In *The Sons*, translated by Willa and Edwin Muir and Arthur Wensinger, 1–16. New York: Schocken Books, 1989.
– *Kafka's Selected Stories: New Translations, Backgrounds and Contexts, Criticism*. Translated by Stanley Corngold. New York: W.W. Norton, 2007.
– *Letter to the Father / Brief an den Vater*. Translated by Eithne Wilson and Ernst Kaiser. New York: Schocken Books, 2015.
– "Letter to His Father." In *The Sons*, translated by Eithne Wilkins, Ernst Kaiser, and Arthur Wensinger, 113–67. New York: Schocken Books, 1989.
– *Letters to Felice*. Edited by Erich Heller and Jürgen Born. Translated by James Stern and Elisabeth Duckworth. New York: Schocken Books, 1988.
– *Letters to Friends, Family, and Editors*. Translated by Richard Winston and Clara Winston. New York: Schocken Books, 1990.
– *Letters to Milena*. Translated by Philip Boehm. New York: Schocken Books, 1990.
– *The Metamorphosis*. Translated by Susan Bernofsky. New York: W.W. Norton, 2014.
– *Nachgelassene Schriften und Fragmente*. Vol. 1. Frankfurt am Main: S. Fischer, 1993.
– *Tagebücher*. Edited by Hans-Gerd Koch, Michael Müller, and Malcolm Pasley. Frankfurt am Main: S. Fischer, 1990.
– *The Transformation and Other Short Stories*. Translated by Malcolm Pasley. London: Penguin Books, 1992.
– *The Trial: A New Translation, Based on the Restored Text*. Translated by Breon Mitchell. New York: Schocken Books, 1998.
– *The Zürau Aphorisms of Franz Kafka*. Translated by Geoffrey Brock and Michael Hofmann. New York: Schocken Books, 2006.
Kafka, Franz, and Giuseppe Menassé. "Franz Kafka." Translated by Giuseppe Menassé, with notes. *Il Convegno* (1928): 383–90.

Kalay, Grace Zlobnicki. *The Theme of Childhood in Elsa Morante*. University: University of Mississippi, Department of Modern Languages, 1996.

Karst, Roman. "Kafka and the Russians." In *Perspectives and Personalities: Studies in Modern German Literature; Honoring Claude Hill*, edited by Ralph Ley and Claude Hill, 181–97. Heidelberg: Winter, 1978.

Kermode, Frank. "Novel and Narrative." In *The Poetics of Murder: Detective Fiction and Literary Theory*, edited by Glenn W. Most and William W. Stowe, 175–96. San Diego, CA: Harcourt Brace Jovanovich, 1983.

Kezich, Tullio. *Fellini*. Milan: Biblioteca universale Rizzoli, 1988.

Klopp, Charles. "Antonio Tabucchi: Postmodern Catholic Writer." *World Literature Today* 71, no. 2 (Spring 1997): 331–4.

–, ed. *Bele Antiche Stòríe: Writing, Borders, and the Instability of Identity; Trieste, 1719–2007*. New York: Bordighera, 2008.

Koelb, Clayton. *Kafka's Rhetoric: The Passion of Reading*. Ithaca, NY: Cornell University Press, 1989.

– "The Turn of the Trope: Kafka's 'Die Brücke.'" *Modern Austrian Literature* 22, no. 1 (1989): 57–70.

Kolbert, Elizabeth. "Flesh of Your Flesh: Should You Eat Meat?" Review of *Eating Animals*, by Jonathan Safran Foer. *New Yorker*, 9 September 2009. Accessed 23 August 2018. https://www.newyorker.com/magazine/2009/11/09/flesh-of-your-flesh.

Kübler-Jung, Tilly. *Einblicke in Franz Kafkas "Betrachtung": Analyse und literaturgeschichtliche Einordnung*. Marburg: Tectum, 2005.

Kundera, Milan. *The Art of the Novel*. Translated by Linda Asher. New York: Harper Perennial, 2006.

Kusin, Vladimir V. *The Intellectual Origins of the Prague Spring: The Development of Reformist Ideas in Czechoslovakia 1956–1967*. Cambridge: Cambridge University Press, 2002.

Kuzniar, Alice A. *Melancholia's Dog: Reflections on Our Animal Kinship*. Chicago: University of Chicago Press, 2015.

La Ferla, Manuela. *Diritto al silenzio: Vita e scritti di Roberto Bazlen*. Palermo: Sellerio editore, 1994.

Lagioia, Nicole. "'Elena Ferrante sono io': Nicola Lagioia intervista la scrittrice misteriosa." *La repubblica*, 4 April 2016. http://www.repubblica.it/cultura/2016/04/04/news/_elena_ferrante_sono_io_nicola_lagioia_intervista_la_scrittrice_misteriosa-136855191/.

– "'Writing Is an Act of Pride': A Conversation with Elena Ferrante." *New Yorker*, 19 May 2016. http://www.newyorker.com/books/page-turner/writing-is-an-act-of-pride-a-conversation-with-elena-ferrante.

Landolfi, Tommaso. *Dialogo dei massimi sistemi*. Edited by Idolina Landolfi. Milan: Adelphi, 2007.

– *Gogol's Wife & Other Stories*. Translated by Raymond Rosenthal. Norfolk, CT: New Directions, 1963.

– *Il mar delle blatte e altre storie*. Edited by Idolina Landolfi. Milan: Adelphi, 1997.

– *Le due zittelle*. Edited by Idolina Landolfi. Milan: Adelphi, 2012.

– *Words in Commotion and Other Stories*. Translated by Kathrine Jason. Harmondsworth, UK: Penguin, 1988.

Landy, Marcia. "Diverting Clichés: Femininity, Masculinity, Melodrama, and Neorealism in *Open City*." In *Roberto Rossellini's Rome Open City*, edited by Sidney Gottlieb, 85–105. Cambridge: Cambridge University Press, 2004.

La Penna, Daniela. "Authoriality in Poetic Translation: The Case of Amelia Rosselli's Practice." *Translation Studies* 7, no. 1 (2014): 66–81.

Lauretano, Gianfranco. *La traccia di Cesare Pavese*. Milan: Biblioteca universale Rizzoli, 2008.

Lazzarin, Stefano. *Il Buzzati "secondo": Saggio sui fattori di letterarietà nell'opera buzzatiana*. Rome: Vecchiarelli, 2008.

– "Il Cantiniere Dell'Aga Khan: Ovvero, Buzzati tra Kafka e Borges." *Italianist* 25, no. 1 (2013): 55–71.

– "Note sulla contaminazione delle fonti nella narrativa breve di Buzzati." *Spunti e Ricerche* 13 (1998): 9–37.

Leake, Elizabeth. "Cesare Pavese, Posthumanism, and the Maternal Symbolic." In *Thinking Italian Animals: Human and Posthuman in Modern Italian Literature and Film*, edited by Deborah Amberson, 39–56. New York: Palgrave Macmillan, 2014.

– *Tex Willer: Un cowboy nell'Italia del dopoguerra*. Bologna: il Mulino, 2018.

Leavitt, Charles L. "Cronaca, Narrativa, and the Unstable Foundations of the Institution of Neorealism." *Italian Culture* 31, no. 1 (1 March 2013): 28–46.

– "'Una seconda fase del realismo del dopoguerra': The Innovative Realism of Elsa Morante's L'Isola di Arturo." *Italianist* 32, no. 1 (2012): 32–52.

Le Rider, Jacques. *Modernity and Crises of Identity: Culture and Society in Fin-de Siècle Vienna*. Translated by Rosemary Morris. Cambridge: Polity Press, 2007.

Lethem, Jonathan. *The Ecstasy of Influence*. London: Vintage, 2013.

Levi, Carlo. *Christ Stopped at Eboli*. Translated by Frances Frenaye. London: Penguin Books, 1982.

– *Cristo si è fermato a Eboli*. Turin: Einaudi, 1990.

– *Un volto che ci somiglia: Ritratto dell'Italia. Fotografia di János Reismann*. Turin: Einaudi, 1960.

Liska, Vivian. "Kafka's Other Job." In *The Book of Job: Aesthetics, Ethics, Hermeneutics*, edited by Leora Batnitzky and Ilana Pardes. Berlin: De Gruyter, 2015.

– *When Kafka Says We: Uncommon Communities in German-Jewish Literature*. Bloomington: Indiana University Press, 2009.

Löwy, Michael. "'Fascinating Delusive Light': Georg Lukács and Franz Kafka." In *Georg Lukács: The Fundamental Dissonance of Existence,* edited by Timothy Hall and Timothy Bewes and translated by Zachary Sng, 178–87. New York: Continuum, 2011.

Lucamante, Stefania. *Elsa Morante e l'eredità proustiana.* Fiesole: Edizione Cadmo, 1998.

–, ed. *Elsa Morante's Politics of Writing: Rethinking Subjectivity, History, and the Power of Art,* 2015.

– *A Multitude of Women: The Challenges of the Contemporary Italian Novel.* Toronto: University of Toronto Press, 2016.

Lucamante, Stefania, and Sharon Wood, eds. *Under Arturo's Star: The Cultural Legacies of Elsa Morante.* West Lafayette, IN: Purdue University Press, 2006.

Lukács, Georg. "An Entire Epoch of Inhumanity." In *Georg Lukács: The Fundamental Dissonance of Existence: Aesthetics, Politics, Literature,* edited by Timothy Bewes and Timothy Hall and translated by Zachary Sng, 221–6. New York: Continuum, 2011.

– *Il significato attuale del realismo critico.* Translated by Renato Solmi. Turin: G. Einaudi, 1957.

– *Realism in Our Time: Literature and the Class Struggle.* Translated by John and Necke Mander. New York: Harper & Row, 1971.

Luperini, Romano, and Massimiliano Tortora, eds. *Sul modernismo italiano.* Naples: Liguori, 2012.

Lupo, Giuseppe. "Calvino, Kafka e il romanzo olivettiano." In *Studi di letteratura italiana in onore di Claudio Scarpati,* edited by Eraldo Bellini, Maria Teresa Girardi, and Uberto Motta, 973–1000. Milan: Vita e Pensiero, 2010.

Luzzatto, Guido Lodovico. "Franz Kafka." *La Rassegna Mensile di Israel* 10, no. 11/12 (April 1936): 506–12.

Maek-Gérard, Eva. "La ditta di Manganelli." In *La penombra mentale: Interviste e conversazioni 1865–1990;* Interviews with Giorgio Manganelli. Edited by Roberto Deidier, 175–84. Rome: Editori Riuniti, 2001.

Maffia, Dante. *Nel mondo di Antonio Tabucchi.* Rome: Lepisma, 2011.

Magris, Claudio. *Danube.* Translated by Patrick Creagh. New York: Farrar, Straus and Giroux, 1990.

– *Danubio.* Milan: Garzanti, 2003.

– "Genesi di un 'mito': Colloquio con Claudio Magris." In *40 anni di mito absburgico: Mostra della Biblioteca Civica Vincenzo Joppi di Udine e del Musil-Institut dell'Università di Klagenfurt; 28 maggio–27 giugno 2003,* edited by Luigi Reitani, 13–23. Udine: Comune di Udine-Biblioteca civica V. Joppi, 2003.

– *Il mito absburgico nella letteratura austriaca moderna.* Turin: G. Einaudi, 1988.

– *Itaca e oltre.* Milan: Garzanti, 1982.

Malamud, Randy. *Poetic Animals and Animal Souls.* New York: Palgrave Macmillan, 2003.

Malaparte, Curzio. *Battibecco: 1953–1957*. Milan: A. Palazzi, 1967.

Mallac, Guy de. "Kafka in Russia." *Russian Review: An American Quarterly Devoted to Russia Past and Present* 31 (1972): 64–73.

Manganelli, Giorgio. "6." In *Gruppo 63 il romanzo sperimentale: Palermo 1965*, edited by Nanni Balestrini, 173–4. Milan: Feltrinelli, 1966.

– *Centuria: Cento Piccoli Romanzi Fiume*. Milan: Adelphi, 2012.

– *Centuria: One Hundred·Ouroboric Novels*. Translated by Henry Martin. Kingston, NY: McPherson, 2005.

– *Encomio del tiranno: Scritto all'unico scopo di fare dei soldi*. Milan: Adelphi, 1990.

– "Giorgio Manganelli presenta Franz Kafka." *Rai Cultura*. Includes video, 6:25. http://www.letteratura.rai.it/articoli/giorgio-manganelli-presenta-franz-kafka/1057/default.aspx.

– *Il rumore sottile della prosa*. Edited by Paola Italia. Milan: Adelphi, 1994.

– "Iperipotesi." In *Gruppo 63: La nuova letteratura; 34 scrittori, Palermo ottobre 1963*, 259–63. Milan: Feltrinelli, 1964.

– *L'impero romanzesco: Letture per un editore*. Edited by Viola Papetti. Turin: N. Aragno, 2003.

Mann, Klaus. "Introduction to *Amerika*." In *Franz Kafka: A Collection of Criticism*, edited by Leo Hamalian, 133–9. New York: McGraw-Hill, 1974.

Marcenaro, Giuseppe. *Una amica di Montale: Vita di Lucia Rodocanachi*. Milan: Camunia, 1991.

Marcus, Laura. "Detection and Literary Fiction." In *The Cambridge Companion to Crime Fiction*, edited by Martin Priestman, 245–68. Cambridge: Cambridge University Press, 2012.

Marcus, Millicent. *Italian Film in the Light of Neorealism*. Princeton, NJ: Princeton University Press, 1987.

Marino, Andrea, and Stefano Agosti. *Lezioni sul Novecento: Storia, teoria e analisi letteraria*. Milan: Vita e Pensiero, 1990.

Martini, Cristian. *La vendetta di Kafka*. Rome: Robin, 2005.

Maslow, Vera. "Lukacs' Man-Centered Aesthetics." *Philosophy and Phenomenological Research* 27, no. 4 (1967): 542–52.

Mattioni, Stelio. *Storia di Umberto Saba*. Milan: Camunia, 1989.

Mauro, Walter. *Il ponte di Glienicke: La letteratura della disfatta; Saggi su Gadda, Morante, Pasolini, Moravia, Turoldo, Calvino, Fortini, Ginzburg*. Marina di Belvedere: Grisolia, 1988.

Mazza, Giuseppe. "Paola Capriolo: Intervista su Gregor Samsa." *Doppiozero*, 1 September 2014. http://www.doppiozero.com/rubriche/1468/201409/paola-capriolo-intervista-su-gregor-samsa.

Mazza, Maria Serafina. *Not for Art's Sake: The Story of* Il Frontespizio. New York: King's Crown Press, 1948.

Mazzetti, Lorenza. *Diario londinese*. Palermo: Sellerio, 2014.

Mazzuchetti, Lavinia. "Franz Kafka e Il Novecento." *I libri del giorno* 10, no. 1 (January 1927): 10.

– *Novecento in Germania.* Milan: Mondadori, 1959.

McDowell, John. "Comment on Stanley Cavell's 'Companionable Thinking.'" In *Philosophy and Animal Life*, 127–38. New York: Columbia University Press, 2009.

McHugh, Susan. *Animal Stories: Narrating across Species Lines.* Minneapolis: University of Minnesota Press, 2011.

McLaughlin, Martin. *Italo Calvino.* Edinburgh: Edinburgh University Press, 1998.

Medin, Daniel L. *Three Sons: Franz Kafka and the Fiction of J.M. Coetzee, Philip Roth, and W.G. Sebald.* Evanston, IL: Northwestern University Press, 2010.

Meldolesi, Claudio. "Per una storia del teatro nel romanzo in Europe: Gli apici del 'Pasticciaccio' e del 'Castello.'" In *La letteratura in scena: Gadda e il teatro*, edited by Alba Andreini and Roberto Tessari, 11–60. Rome: Bulzoni, 2001.

Menechella, Grazia. "Centuria: Manganelli Aspirante Sonettiere." *MLN* 117, no. 1 (2002): 207–26.

– *Il felice vanverare: Ironia e parodia nell'opera narrativa di Giorgio Manganelli.* Ravenna: Longo, 2002.

Messina, Davide. "Qfwfq as Kafka? Possible-Worlds Interpretations." *Modern Language Review* 106, no. 4 (2011): 1001–27.

Mignone, Mario B. *Anormalità e angoscia nella narrativa di Dino Buzzati.* Ravenna: Longo, 1981.

Miles, David H. "'Pleats, Pockets, Buckles, and Buttons': Kafka's New Literalism and the Poetics of the Fragment." In *Probleme der Moderne: Studien zur deutschen Literatur von Nietzsche bis Brecht; Festschrift für Walter Sokel*, edited by Benjamin Bennett, Anton Kaes, and William J. Lillyman, 331–2. Tübingen: Niemeyer, 1983.

Miller, D.A. *The Novel and the Police.* Berkeley: University of California Press, 1988.

Mittner, Ladislao. *La letteratura tedesca del Novecento e altri saggi.* Turin: Einaudi, 1966.

Modena, Letizia. *Italo Calvino's Architecture of Lightness: The Utopian Imagination in an Age of Urban Crisis.* New York: Routledge, 2014.

Montale, Eugenio. *Lettere Italo Svevo con gli scritti di Montale su Svevo.* Bari: De Donato editore, 1966.

– *Poetic Diaries, 1971 and 1972.* Translated by William Arrowsmith. New York: W.W. Norton, 2013.

Montanelli, Indro. "Nella malattia." In *Il Mistero in Dino Buzzati*, edited by Romano Battaglia, 71–8. Milan: Rusconi, 1980.

Morante, Elsa. *Arturo's Island: A Novel.* Translated by Isabel Quigly. South Royalton, VT: Steerforth Italia, 2002.

– *Diario 1938*. Edited by Alba Andreini. Turin: G. Einaudi, 2005.
– *History: A Novel*. Translated by William Weaver. Hanover, NH: Zoland Books, 2007.
– *L'amata: Lettere di e a Elsa Morante*. Edited by Danièle Morante and Giuliana Zagra. Turin: Einaudi, 2012.
– *La Storia. Romanzo*. Turin: Einaudi, 1995.
– *Lo scialle andaluso*. Turin: Einaudi, 2011.
– *Opere*. Edited by Carlo Cecchi and Cesare Garboli. Vol. 1. Milan: Mondadori, 1988.
– *Opere*. Edited by Carlo Cecchi and Cesare Garboli. Vol. 2. Milan: Mondadori, 2003.
Moravia, Alberto. *Diario europeo: Pensieri, persone, fatti, libri, 1984–1990*. Milan: Bompiani, 2007.
– "Kafka scrittore realista." In *Introduzione a Kafka*, edited by Ervino Pocar, 227. Milan: Il Saggiatore, 1974.
– *Una cosa è una cosa*. Milan: Bompiani, 1967.
Moravia, Alberto, and Alain Elkann. *Life of Moravia*. Translated by William Weaver. Vermont, CA: Steerforth; London: Turnaround, 2001.
– *Vita di Moravia*. Milan: Bompiani, 2007.
Moretti, Franco. *Distant Reading*. London: Verso, 2015.
– *The Way of the World: The "Bildungsroman" in European Culture*. Translated by Albert Sbragia. London: Verso, 2000.
Morrison, Iano. "*Il giorno della civetta* to *Il Cavaliere e la Morte*: Continuity and Change in the Detective Fiction of Leonardo Sciascia." In *Differences, Deceits and Desires: Murder and Mayhem in Italian Crime Fiction*, edited by Mirna Cicioni and Nicoletta Di Ciolla, 99–114. Newark: University of Delaware Press, 2008.
Morson, Gary Saul. *The Long and Short of It: From Aphorism to Novel*. Stanford, CA: Stanford University Press, 2012.
Muir, Edwin. "Introductory Note." In *The Castle*, by Franz Kafka. Translated by Edwin and Willa Muir, i–vii. New York: Alfred A. Knopf, 1930.
Mullen, Anne. "Leonardo Sciascia's Detective Fiction and Metaphors of Mafia." In *Crime Scenes: Detective Narratives in European Culture since 1945*, edited by Anne Mullen and Emer O'Beirne, 88–99. Amsterdam: Rodopi, 2000.
Musolino, Walter. "The Failure of the Female Experiment: A Study of Women in Cesare Pavese's *La luna e i falò*." In *Visions and Revisions: Women in Italian Culture*, edited by Mirna Cicioni and Nicole Prunster, 71–88. Providence, RI: Berg, 1993.
Mussgnug, Florian. *The Eloquence of Ghosts: Giorgio Manganelli and the Afterlife of the Avant-Garde*. Bern: Peter Lang, 2010.
Necco, Giovanni. *Realismo e idealismo nella letteratura tedesca moderna*. Bari: Laterza, 1937.

Nekrasov, Viktor. *Both Sides of the Ocean: A Russian Writer's Travels in Italy and the United States*. Translated by Elias Kulukundis. New York: Holt, Rinehart and Winston, 1964.

Nelles, William. "Microfiction: What Makes a Very Short Story Very Short?" *Narrative* 20, no. 1 (12 January 2012): 87–104.

Nerenberg, Ellen V. *Prison Terms: Representing Confinement during and after Italian Fascism*. Toronto: University of Toronto Press, 2016.

Nussbaum, Martha Craven. *Political Emotions: Why Love Matters for Justice*. Cambridge, MA: Belknap Press, 2015.

O'Neill, Patrick. *Transforming Kafka: Translation Effects*. Toronto: University of Toronto Press, 2014.

Ozick, Cynthia. "Mouth, Ear, Nose." *New York Times*, 23 October 1988. http://www.nytimes.com/1988/10/23/books/mouth-ear-nose.html.

Pacifici, Sergio J. "Existentialism and Italian Literature." *Yale French Studies*, no. 16 (1955): 79–88.

Panebianco, Beatrice, Simona Seminara, and Mario Gineprini, eds. "Percorso Tema, Le figure sociali: Il mercante e la cultura laica." In *LetterAutori*, vol. 3. Bologna: Zanichelli, 2011.

Paoli, Rodolfo. "Spavento dell'infinito." In *Il Frontespizio: 1929–1938*, edited by Luigi Fallacara, 209–14. Rome: Luciano Landi, 1961.

Paolone, Marco. *Il cavaliere immaginale: Saggi su Giorgio Manganelli*. Rome: Carocci, 2002.

Papetti, Viola. Introduzione a *L'impero romanzesco: Letture per un editore*, edited by Viola Papetti, ix–xiii. Turin: N. Aragno, 2003.

Papini, Giovanni. *La loggia dei busti: Pensieri sopra uomini di genio, d'ingenio, di cuore*. Florence: Vallecchi, 1956.

Pappalardo La Rosa, Franco. *Cesare Pavese e il mito dell'adolescenza*. Milan: Laboratorio delle arti, 1973.

Paris, Renzo. *Ritratto dell'artista da Vecchio: Conversazioni con Alberto Moravia*. Rome: minimum fax, 2001.

Parks, Tim. "Throwing Down a Gauntlet." *Threepenny Review* (Winter 2001). https://www.threepennyreview.com/samples/parks_w01.html.

Pasolini, Pier Paolo. *Descrizioni di descrizioni*. Turin: Einaudi, 1979.

– *Poesia in forma di rosa*. Milan: Garzanti, 2015.

Past, Elena. *Methods of Murder: Beccarian Introspection and Lombrosian Vivisection in Italian Crime Fiction*. Toronto: University of Toronto Press, 2012.

Past, Elena M., and Deborah Amberson. "Introduction: Thinking Italian Animals." In *Thinking Italian Animals: Human and Posthuman in Modern Italian Literature and Film*, edited by Elena M. Past and Deborah Amberson, 1–20. Basingstoke, UK: Palgrave Macmillan, 2014.

Past, Elena M., and Deborah Amberson, eds. *Thinking Italian Animals: Human and Posthuman in Modern Italian Literature and Film*. Basingstoke, UK: Palgrave Macmillan, 2014.

Pavese, Cesare. *American Literature: Essays and Opinions*. Translated by Edwin Fussell. Berkeley: University of California Press, 1970.

– *Il mestiere di vivere: Diario 1935–1950*. Edited by Marziano Guglielminetti and Laura Nay. Turin: Einaudi, 2014.

– *La letteratura americana e altri saggi*. Turin: Einaudi, 1991.

– *La luna e i falò*. Turin: Einaudi, 1950.

– *Lettere, 1924–1944*. Edited by Lorenzo Mondo. Turin: Einaudi, 1968.

– *The Moon and the Bonfires*. Translated by R.W. Flint. New York: New York Review Books, 2003.

– *Officina Einaudi: Lettere editoriali; 1940–1950*. Edited by Silvia Savioli and Franco Contorbia. Turin: Einaudi, 2008.

– *This Business of Living: Diaries, 1935–1950*. New Brunswick, NJ: Transaction Publishers, 2009.

Pavese, Cesare, and Anthony L. Chiuminatto. *Cesare Pavese and Anthony Chiuminatto: Their Correspondence*. Edited by Mark Pietralunga. Toronto: University of Toronto Press, 2007.

Pecoraro, Aldo. *Gadda*. Rome: Laterza, 1998.

Pedri, Nancy, and Alù Giorgia. *Enlightening Encounters: Photography in Italian Literature*. Toronto: University of Toronto Press, 2015.

Perloff, Marjorie. "Presidential Address 2006: It Must Change." *PMLA* 122, no. 3 (2007): 652–62.

Petrignani, Sandra. "Benvenuto giocoliere." In *La penombra mentale: Interviste e conversazioni, 1965–1990*, edited by Roberto Deidier, 204–8. Rome: Editori Riuniti, 2001.

Petrignani, Sandra, and Lalla Romano. *Le signore della scrittura: Interviste*. Milan: Tartaruga, 1996.

Pezzin, Claudio. *Antonio Tabucchi*. Caselle di Sommacampagna: Cierre, 2001.

Pickering-Iazzi, Robin. "Designing Mothers: Images of Motherhood in Novels by Aleramo, Morante, Maraini, and Fallaci." *Annali d'Italianistica* 7 (1989): 325–40.

Pilz, Kerstin. *Mapping Complexity: Literature and Science in the Works of Italo Calvino*. Leicester: Troubador, 2005.

Pizzi, Katia. *A City in Search of an Author: The Literary Identity of Trieste*. Sheffield: Sheffield Academic Press, 2001.

Polcini, Valentina. *Dino Buzzati and Anglo-American Culture: The Re-use of Visual and Narrative Texts in His Fantastic Fiction*. Newcastle upon Tyne: Cambridge Scholars, 2014.

Politzer, Heinz. *Franz Kafka: Parable and Paradox*. Ithaca, NY: Cornell University Press, 1979.

Popoff, Gabrielle. "Elsa Morante's *L'isola di Arturo* and *Aracoeli*: Remembering and Reconciling with the Fascist Past." *Quaderni Del '900* 11 (2011): 19–26.

Porter, Dennis. *The Pursuit of Crime: Art and Ideology in Detective Fiction*. Ann Arbor, MI: Books on Demand, 1999.

Posenato, Cinzia. *Il "bestiario" di Dino Buzzati*. Bologna: Inchiostri associati, 2009.

Powell, Matthew T. "Bestial Representations of Otherness: Kafka's Animal Stories." *Journal of Modern Literature* 32, no. 1 (2008): 129–42.

Preve, Costanzo. "Lukács in Italia (Dalla commemorazione del centenario della nascita al bilancio critico della sua influenza)." *Rivista di Studi Ungheresi* 2 (1967): 78–84.

Puchner, Martin. *The Drama of Ideas: Platonic Provocations in Theater and Philosophy*. New York: Oxford University Press, 2010.

– "Goethe, Marx, Ibsen and the Creation of a World Literature." *Ibsen Studies* 13, no. 1 (2013): 1–19.

– "Performing the Open: Actors, Animals, Philosophers." *TDR: The Drama Review* 51, no. 1 (2007): 21–32.

– *Poetry of the Revolution: Marx, Manifestos, and the Avant-Gardes*. Princeton, NJ: Princeton University Press, 2006.

Pugliese, Stanislao G., and Raniero M. Speelman, eds. "Italian-Jewish Literature from World War II to the 1990s." In *The Most Ancient of Minorities: The Jews of Italy*, 177–90. Westport, CT: Greenwood Press, 2002.

Pulce, Graziella. *Giorgio Manganelli: Figure e sistema*. Florence: Le Monnier Università, 2004.

Pupo, Ivan. *Passioni della ragione e labirinti della memoria: Studi su Leonardo Sciascia*. Naples: Liguori, 2011.

Pyrhönen, Heta. *Murder from an Academic Angle*. New York: Camden House, 1994.

Rabaté, Jean-Michel. *Crimes of the Future: Theory and Its Global Reproduction*. New York: Bloomsbury, 2014.

Ragusa, Olga. *Narrative and Drama: Essays in Modern Italian Literature from Verga to Pasolini*. The Hague: Mouton, 1976.

Raddetz, Fritz J. *Georg Lukács in Selbstzeugnissen und Bilddocumenten*. Hamburg: Rowohlt, 1972.

Ram, Harsha. "Futurist Geographies: Uneven Modernities and the Struggle for Aesthetic Autonomy: Paris, Italy, Russia, 1909–1914." In *The Oxford Handbook of Global Modernisms*, edited by Mark A. Wollaeger and Matt Eatough, 313–40. New York: Oxford University Press, 2013.

Rambelli, Loris. *Storia del "giallo" italiano*. Milan: Aldo Garzanti, 1979.

Randall, D'Arcy. "Adrienne Rich's 'Clearing in the Imagination': *Of Woman Born* as Literary Criticism." In *From Motherhood to Mothering: The Legacy of Adrienne Rich's Of Woman Born*, edited by Andrea O'Reilly, 195–208. Albany: State University of New York Press, 2004.

Raquel Ribeiro, Rossella M. "Marginal, Nomadic and Stateless: Pessoa, Musil and Kafka in the Works of Maria Gabriela Llansol." In *The Poetics of the Margins: Mapping Europe from the Interstices*, edited by Rossella M. Riccobono, 157–86. Bern: Lang, 2011.

Raveggi, Alessandro. *Calvino americano: Identità e viaggio nel nuovo mondo.* Florence: Le lettere, 2012.

Re, Lucia. *Calvino and the Age of Neorealism: Fables of Estrangement.* Stanford, CA: Stanford University Press, 1991.

– "Pasolini vs. Calvino, One More Time: The Debate on the Role of Intellectuals and Postmodernism in Italy Today." *MLN* 129, no. 1 (2014): 99–117.

Regazzioni, Enrico. "E il premio Manganelli? A Petrarca." In *La penombra mentale: Interviste e conversazioni, 1965–1990*; Interviews with Giorgio Manganelli, edited by Roberto Deidier, 49–50. Rome: Editori Riuniti, 2001.

Ria, Antonio, and Lalla Romano. *Il silenzio tra noi leggero: Lalla Roma in pittura, scrittura, fotografia.* Piacenza: Galleria Ricci Oddi, 2008.

Ribatti, Domenico. *Italo Calvino e l'Einaudi.* Bari: Stilo, 2010.

Ricci, Franco. "The Quest for Sonship in *Le città invisibili* and 'La strada di San Giovanni' by Italo Calvino." *Forum Italicum* 29, no. 1 (1 March 1995): 52–75.

Ricciardi, Alessia. *After* La Dolce Vita: *A Cultural Prehistory of Berlusconi's Italy.* Stanford, CA: Stanford University Press, 2012.

Riccobono, Rossella M., ed. *The Poetics of the Margins: Mapping Europe from the Interstices.* Bern: Lang, 2011.

Riccobono, Rossella, and Doug Thompson, eds. *"Onde di questo mare": Reconsidering Pavese.* Market Harborough, UK: Troubador, 2003.

Riviello, Tonia Caterina. "The Motif of Entrapment in Elsa Morante's *L'isola di Arturo* and Dacia Maraini's *L'età del Malessere*." *Rivista di studi italiani* 8, no. 1–2 (1990): 70–87.

Robert, Marthe. *The Old and the New: From Don Quixote to Kafka.* Berkeley: University of California Press, 1977.

Robertson, Ritchie. Introduction to *The Man Who Disappeared (America)*, by Franz Kafka, xi–xxvii. Translated by Ritchie Robertson. Oxford: Oxford University Press, 2012.

– *The "Jewish Question" in German Literature 1749–1939: Emancipation and Its Discontents.* Oxford: Oxford University Press, 2004.

– "Kafka, Goffman, and the Total Institution." In *Kafka for the Twenty-First Century*, edited by Stanley Corngold and Ruth Vera Gross, 136–50. Rochester, NY: Camden House, 2011.

– *Kafka: Judaism, Politics, and Literature.* Oxford: Clarendon Press, 1987.

– "Reading the Clues: Franz Kafka, *Der Proceß*." In *The German Novel in the Twentieth Century: Beyond Realism*, edited by David R. Midgley, 59–79. Edinburgh: Edinburgh University Press; New York: St. Martin's Press, 1993.

Robey, David, and Peter Hainsworth, eds. *The Oxford Companion to Italian Literature.* Oxford: Oxford University Press, 2006.

Romagnoli, Sergio. "Landolfi e il fantastico." In *Le lunazioni del cuore: Saggi su Tommaso Landolfi*, edited by Idolina Landolfi, 15–26. Florence: La Nuova Italia, 1996.

Romano, Lalla. *Le Lune di Hvar*. Turin: Einaudo, 1991.

– *Le metamorfosi*. Edited by Antonio Ria. Turin: Einaudi, 2005.

– *Lettura di un'immagine*. Turin: Einaudi, 1975.

– *Opere*. Vol. 1. Milan: Mondadori, 2001.

– *Opere*. Vol. 2. Milan: Mondadori, 1997.

Romano, Lalla, Ernesto Ferrero, and Antonio Ria. *Vita di Lalla Romano raccontata da lei medesima*. San Cesario di Lecce: Manni, 2006.

Rosselli, Amelia. *È vostra la vita che ho perso: Conversazioni e interviste, 1964–1995*. Edited by Monica Venturini and Silvia De March. Florence: Le lettere, 2010.

– *Una scrittura plurale: Saggi e interventi critici*. Novara: Interlinea, 2004.

– *War Variations / Variazioni belliche*. Translated by Lucia Re and Paul Vangelisti. Los Angeles: Otis Books / Seismicity Editions, 2016.

Rothfels, Nigel, ed. *Representing Animals*. Bloomington, IN: Indiana University Press, 2002.

– *Savages and Beasts: The Birth of the Modern Zoo*. Baltimore, MD: Johns Hopkins University Press, 2012.

Rubinstein, William C. "Franz Kafka's 'A Report to an Academy.'" *Modern Language Quarterly* 13, no. 4 (1 December 1952): 372–6.

– "'A Report to an Academy.'" In *Franz Kafka Today*, edited by Angel Flores and Homer D. Swander, 55–60. Madison: University of Wisconsin Press, 1964.

Ruland, Richard. *America in Modern European Literature: From Image to Metaphor*. New York: New York University Press, 1976.

Ruthenberg, Myriam Swennen. "Romancing the Novel: Elsa Morante's *L'Isola Di Arturo*." *Romance Languages Annual* 9 (1997): 336–41.

Ryder, Frank. "Kafka's Language 'Poetic'?" In *Probleme der Moderne: Studien zur deutschen Literatur von Nietzsche bis Brecht; Festschrift für Walter Sokel*, edited by Benjamin Bennett, Anton Kaes, and William J. Lillyman, 319–30. Tübingen: Niemeyer, 1983.

Saba, Umberto. *Prose scelte*. Edited by Giovanni Giudici and Guido Piovene. Milan: A. Mondadori, 1976.

Sambuco, Patrizia. *Corporeal Bonds: The Daughter-Mother Relationship in Twentieth Century Italian Women's Writing*. Toronto: University of Toronto Press, 2012.

Sandbank, Shimon. *After Kafka: The Influence of Kafka's Fiction*. Athens: University of Georgia Press, 1989.

– "Parable and Theme: Kafka and American Fiction." *Complete Comparative Literature* 37, no. 3 (1985): 252–68.

Sanguineti, Edoardo, and Giuliano Galletta. *Sanguineti/Novecento: Conversazioni sulla cultura del ventesimo secolo*. Genoa: Il melangolo, 2005.

Sanguineti, Edoardo, and Fabio Gambaro. *Colloquio con Edoardo Sanguineti: Quarant'anni di cultura italiana attraverso i ricordi di un poeta intellettuale*. Milan: Anabasi, 1993.

Saraceno, Chiara. "Redefining Maternity and Paternity: Gender, Pronatalism and Social Policies in Fascist Italy." In *Maternity and Gender Policies: Women and the Rise of the European Welfare States, 1880s–1950s*, edited by Gisela Bock and Pat Thane, 196–212. London: Routledge, 2008.

Sartre, Jean Paul. "Die Abrüstung der Kultur: Rede auf dem Weltfriedenskongreß in Moskau," translated by Stephan Hermlin. *Sinn und Form* 15, no. 5 (1962): 805–15.

Saussy, Haun. "Exquisite Cadavers Stitched from Fresh Nightmares." In *Comparative Literature in an Age of Globalization*, edited by Haun Saussy, 3–42. Baltimore, MD: Johns Hopkins University Press, 2006.

Savelli, Giulio. "Una struttura del destino in Buzzati." *MLN* 108, no. 1 (1993): 125–39.

Sayers, Dorothy. "The Omnibus of Crime." In *Detective Fiction: Crime and Compromise*, edited by Dick Allen and David Chacko, 351–83. New York: Harcourt Brace Jovanovich, 1974.

Sbragia, Albert. *Carlo Emilio Gadda and the Modern Macaronic*. Gainesville: University Press of Florida, 1997.

Scarpa, Domenico. "'From the Vantage Point of Hindsight': Viewing Calvino's Landscape." In *Image, Eye and Art in Calvino: Writing Visibility*, edited by Birgitte Grundtvig, Martin McLaughlin, and Lene Waage Petersen, 152–70. London: Legenda, 2007.

Scholtmeijer, Marian. "What Is 'Human'? Metaphysics and Zoontology in Flaubert and Kafka." In *Animal Acts: Configuring the Human in Western History*, edited by Jennifer Ham and Matthew Senior, 127–44. New York: Routledge, 1997.

Schuman, Rebecca. *Kafka and Wittgenstein: The Case for an Analytic Modernism*. Evanston, IL: Northwestern University Press, 2015.

Sciascia, Leonardo. "Breve storia del romanzo poliziesco." In *Opere 1971–1983*, Vol. 2, Tome 2: 1181–96. Milan: Bompiani, 1989.

– *Il cavaliere e la morte: Sotie*. Milan: Adelphi, 2009.

– *The Knight and Death: Three Novellas*. Translated by Joseph Farrell and Marie Evans. London: Harvill, 1992.

Segre, Cesare, ed. "Nota biografica." In *Opere*, by Lalla Romano, Vol. 1, LXVI–XCIX. Milan: Mondadori, 2001.

Sereni, Vittorio. "Sogni che parlano da sé." In *Le metamorfosi*, by Lalla Romano, vii–xiv. Milan: Mondadori, 1986.

Serpell, C. Namwali. "Of Being Bridge." *Comparatist* 36 (2012): 4–23.

Settis, Salvatore. "Antonio Tabucchi contro l'eclisse dell'impegno intellettuale." In *Adamastor e dintorni: In ricordo di Antonio Tabucchi*, edited by Valeria Tocco, 25–31. Pisa: ETS, 2013.

Sgorlon, Carlo. *Kafka narratore*. Venezia: N. Pozza, 1961.

Shideler, Ross. *Questioning the Father: From Darwin to Zola, Ibsen, Strindberg and Hardy*. Stanford, CA: Stanford University Press, 2000.

Sica, Paola. "Ermetismo." In *Encyclopedia of Italian Literary Studies*, edited by
    Gaetana Marrone, 929–31. London: Routledge, 2007.
Siddique, Haroon. "How to Spot Whodunnit: Academics Crack Agatha
    Christie's Code," *Guardian* (Manchester). 2 August 1995. https://www.
    theguardian.com/books/2015/aug/02/academics-unlock-formula-agatha-
    christies-mysteries.
Simons, John. *Animal Rights and the Politics of Literary Representation.*
    Basingstoke, UK: Palgrave, 2002.
Siti, Walter. "Elsa Morante and Pier Paolo Pasolini." In *Under Arturo's Star: The
    Cultural Legacies of Elsa Morante*, edited by Stefania Lucamante and Sharon
    Wood, 268–89. West Lafayette, IN: Purdue University Press, 2006.
Smith, Agnes W. "The Castle." In *Twentieth Century Interpretations of The Castle*,
    edited by Peter F. Neumeyer, 106–7. Englewood Cliffs, NJ: Prentice-Hall, 1969.
Smith, Lawrence G. *Cesare Pavese and America: Life, Love, and Literature.*
    Amherst: University of Massachusetts Press, 2011.
Smuts, Barbara. "Reflections." In *The Lives of Animals* by J.M. Coetzee, edited
    by Amy Gutmann, 107–120. Princeton, NJ: Princeton University Press, 2001.
Snoek, Anke. *Agamben's Joyful Kafka: Finding Freedom beyond Subordination.*
    New York: Bloomsbury, 2014.
Sofri, Adriano. *Una variazione di Kafka.* Palermo: Sellerio, 2018.
Sokel, Walter. "K. as Imposter: His Quest for Meaning." In *Twentieth Century
    Interpretations of The Castle: A Collection of Critical Essays*, edited by Peter F.
    Neumeyer, 32–5. Englewood Cliffs, NJ: Prentice-Hall, 1969.
– *The Myth of Power and the Self: Essays on Franz Kafka.* Detroit, MI: Wayne
    State University Press, 2002.
Somigli, Luca. "Form and Ideology in Italian Detective Fiction." *Symposium:
    A Quarterly Journal in Modern Literatures* 59, no. 2 (2005): 67–9.
Somigli, Luca, and Mario Moroni, eds. *Italian Modernism: Italian Culture between
    Decadentism and Avant-Garde.* Toronto: University of Toronto Press, 2004.
Spackman, Barbara. *Fascist Virilities: Rhetoric, Ideology, and Social Fantasy in
    Italy.* Minneapolis: University of Minnesota Press, 1997.
Spaini, Alberto. "Prefazione" to *America*, by Franz Kafka. Translated by
    Alberto Spaini, vii–xii. Turin: Einaudi, 1945.
Spanos, William V. *Repetitions: The Postmodern Occasion in Literature and
    Culture.* Baton Rouge: Louisiana State University Press, 1987.
Spector, Scott. *Prague Territories: National Conflict and Cultural Innovation in
    Franz Kafka's Fin de Siècle.* Berkeley: University of California Press, 2002.
Stach, Reiner. "Death by Data: How Kafka's The Trial Prefigured the
    Nightmare of the Modern Surveillance State." *New Statesman*, 16 January
    2014. http://www.newstatesman.com/2014/01/death-data-how-kafkas-
    trial-prefigured-nightmare-modern-surveillance-state.

– *Is That Kafka? 99 Finds*. Translated by Kurt Beals. New York: New Directions, 2017.
– *Kafka: The Decisive Years*. Translated by Shelley Frisch. Princeton, NJ: Princeton University Press, 2013.
– *Kafka: The Early Years*. Translated by Shelley Frisch. Princeton, NJ: Princeton University Press, 2017.
Stellardi, Giuseppe, and Emanuela Tandello Cooper, eds. *Italo Svevo and His Legacy for the Third Millennium*. Vol. 1. Leicester: Troubador, 2014.
Stimilli, Davide. *Fisionomia di Kafka*. Turin: Bollati Boringhieri, 2001.
Strelka, Joseph P. "Kafkaesque Elements in Kafka's Novels and in Contemporary Narrative Prose." *Comparative Literature Studies* 21, no. 4 (1984): 434–44.
Suchoff, David Bruce. *Kafka's Jewish Languages: The Hidden Openness of Tradition*. Philadelphia: University of Pennsylvania Press, 2012.
Surdich, Luigi. "Il principio della letteratura, raccontare il sogno di un altro": Forma e sostanza dei sogni nella narrative di Tabucchi. In *I "notturni" di Antonio Tabucchi: Atti di seminario, Firenze, 12–13 maggio 2008*, edited by Anna Dolfi, 25–63. Rome: Bulzoni, 2008.
Sussman, Henry. *High Resolution: Critical Theory and the Problem of Literacy*. New York: Oxford University Press, 2011.
Svevo, Italo. *Emilio's Carnival*. Translated by Beth Archer Brombert. New Haven, CT: Yale Nota Bene, 2002.
– *Favole: Uomini e bestie*. Rome: Edizioni dell'Altana, 2003.
– "The Hoax." In *Short Sentimental Journey, and Other Stories*, translated by Beryl de Zoete, 11–72. Berkeley: University of California Press, 1967.
– *A Life*. Translated by Archibald Colquhoun. London: Pushkin Press, 2006.
– *Racconti e scritti autobiografici*. Milan: Arnoldo Mondadori, 2004.
– *Romanzi e "continuazioni."* Edited by Nunzia Palmieri and Mario Lavagetto. Milan: A. Mondadori, 2004.
– *Short Sentimental Journey and Other Stories*. Translated by Beryl de Zoete, L. Collison-Morley, and Ben Johnson. Berkeley: University of California Press, 1967.
– *Una vita*. Edited by Mario Lunetta. Rome: Newton & Compton, 2003.
Tabucchi, Antonio. *Conversazione con Antonio Tabucchi: Dove va il romanzo?* Rome: Omicron, 1997.
– *Di tutto resta un poco: Letteratura e cinema*. Edited by Anna Dolfi. Milan: Feltrinelli, 2013.
– *Dreams of Dreams: And, The Last Three Days of Fernando Pessoa*. Translated by Nancy J. Peters. San Francisco: City Lights Books, 2000.
– "Il mio tram attraverso il Novecento." In *Parole per Antonio Tabucchi: Con quattro inediti*, by Roberto Francavilla, 51–4. Rome: Artemide, 2012.

- "Incontro con Antonio Tabucchi: A Louvain-la-Neuve il 6 maggio
  1993 (modetrice: Alberte Spinette)." In *Gli spazi della diversità: Atti
  del Convegno Internazionale; Rinnovamento del codice narrativo in Italia
  dal 1945 al 1992*, vol. 2, edited by Serge Vanvolsem, Franco Musarra,
  and Bart Van Den Bossche, 651–68. Leuven: Leuven University Press,
  1995.
- *La testa perduta di Damasceno Monteiro*. Milan: Feltrinelli, 2014.
- *The Missing Head of Damasceno Monteiro*. Translated by J.C. Patrick.
  New York: New Directions, 2005.
- *Racconti con figure*. Edited by Thea Rimini. Palermo: Sellerio, 2011.
- *Requiem: A Hallucination*. Translated by Margaret Jull Costa. New York:
  New Directions, 2002.
- *Sogni di sogni*. Palermo: Sellerio, 2012.
Tabucchi, Antonio, Claudio Cattaruzza, Davide Benati, and Carlos Gumpert.
  Dedica a Antonio Tabucchi. Pordenone: Associazione provinciale per la prosa,
  2001.
Tabucchi, Antonio, Carlos Gumpert, and Javier González Rovira.
  Conversaciones con Antonio Tabucchi. Barcelona: Anagrama, 1995.
Talbot, George, and Doug Thompson. *Essays in Italian Literature and History in
  Honour of Doug Thompson*. Dublin: Four Courts Press, 2002.
Talbot, Margaret. "Birdbrain: A Woman and Her Chatty Parrots." *New Yorker*,
  12 May 2008, 64–75.
Tambling, Jeremy. *Lost in the American City: Dickens, James and Kafka*.
  New York: Palgrave, 2001.
Tani, Stefano. *The Doomed Detective: The Contribution of the Detective Novel
  to Postmodern American and Italian Fiction*. Carbondale: Southern Illinois
  University Press, 1987.
Tellini, Gino. *The Invention of Modern Italian Literature: Strategies of Creative
  Imagination*. Toronto: University of Toronto Press, 2007.
Testa, Carlo. *Masters of Two Arts: Re-creation of European Literatures in Italian
  Cinema*. Toronto: University of Toronto Press, 2002.
Thiel, Roger. "Architecture." In *Franz Kafka in Context*, edited by Carolin
  Duttlinger, 137–48. Cambridge: Cambridge University Press, 2018.
Thomas, James, Robert Shapard, and Christopher Merrill. *Flash Fiction
  International: Very Short Stories from around the World*. New York:
  W.W. Norton, 2015.
Todorov, Tzvetan. *The Poetics of Prose*. Translated by Richard Howard. Ithaca,
  NY: Cornell University Press, 1995.
Trama, Paolo. *Animali e fantasmi della scrittura: Saggi sulla zoopoetica di Tommaso
  Landolfi*. Rome: Salerno, 2006.
Trentini, Nives. *Una scrittura in partita doppia: Tabucchi fra romanzo e racconto*.
  Rome: Bulzoni, 2003.

Turow, Scott. *Presumed Innocent.* New York: Farrar, Straus, Giroux, 1987.

Tyler, Parker. "Kafka's and Chaplin's *Amerika.*" *Sewanee Review* 58, no. 2 (1950): 299–311.

Vecchi, Maria Luisa. "Giorgio Manganelli." *Belfagor; Firenze* 37 (1 January 1982): 41–54.

Veneziani Svevo, Livia. *Memoir of Italo Svevo.* Translated by Isabel Quigly. Marlboro, VT: Marlboro Press, 1990.

Vertone, Saverio, trans. *Franz Kafka da Praga 1963: Una serie di rapporti della cultura marxista sulla vita e sull'opera di Kafka.* Bari: De Donato, 1966.

Vidal, Gore. "Calvino's Novels." In *The Selected Essays of Gore Vidal*, edited by Jay Parini, 101–22. New York: Vintage Books, 2009.

Viganò, Lorenzo. *Album Buzzati.* Milan: Mondadori, 2006.

Vighi, Fabio. *Traumatic Encounters in Italian Film: Locating the Cinematic Unconscious.* Bristol: Intellect Books, 2006.

Vincenti, Fiora. *Lalla Romano.* Florence: La Nuova Italia, 1974.

Virgil. *The Aeneid.* Translated by Robert Fagles. London: Penguin, 2010.

Vittorini, Elio. *Diario in Pubblico.* Milan: Bompiani, 1957.

– "Politica e cultura: Lettera a Togliattti." In *Il Politecnico: Antologia critica*, edited by Marco Forti and Sergo Pautasso, 165–94. Milan: Lerici editori, 1960.

Vogt, Ursula. "Carlo Bo e Franz Kafka." *Studi Urbinati, B: Scienze Umane e Sociali* 82 (2012): 41–57.

Vollenweider, Alice. "Il mondo tedesco fra sogno e esperienza." In *Le foglie messaggere: Scritti in onore di Giorgio Manganelli*, edited by Viola Papetti and Marco Belpoliti, 193–8. Rome: Editori riuniti, 2000.

Wagenbach, Klaus. *La libertà dell'editore: Memorie, discorsi, stoccate.* Palermo: Sellerio, 2013.

Wehling-Giorgi, Katrin. "'Il mondo delle madri': Pre-Oedipal Desire and the Decentered Self in Elsa Morante's *La Storia* and *Aracoeli.*" In *The Fire Within: Desire in Modern and Contemporary Italian Literature*, edited by Elena Borelli, 190–209. Newcastle upon Tyne: Cambridge Scholars, 2014.

Weil, Kari. "A Report on the Animal Turn." *Differences* 21, no. 2 (2010): 1–23.

– *Thinking Animals: Why Animal Studies Now?* New York: Columbia University Press, 2012.

Weinberg, Helene Barbara. *The New Novel in America: The Kafkan Mode in Contemporary Fiction.* London: Cornell University Press, 1979.

Weinstein, Philip M. *Unknowing: The Work of Modernist Fiction.* Ithaca, NY: Cornell University Press, 2005.

Weisbrod, Carol. *Butterfly, the Bride: Essays on Law, Narrative, and the Family.* Ann Arbor: University of Michigan Press, 2004.

Wellek, Rene. *Concepts of Criticism.* Edited by Stephen G. Nichols. New Haven, CT: Yale University Press, 1963.

Whitlark, James. *Behind the Great Wall: A Post-Jungian Approach to Kafkaesque Literature*. Rutherford, NJ; London: Fairleigh Dickinson University Press, Associated University Presses, 1991.

Wilson, Rita. "On the Margins: Antonio Tabucchi's Investigative Reflections." In *Differences, Deceits and Desires: Murder and Mayhem in Italian Crime Fiction*, edited by Mirna Cicioni and Nicoletta Di Ciolla, 13–26. Newark: University of Delaware Press, 2008.

Wittgenstein, Ludwig. *Philosophical Investigations: The German Text, with a Revised English Translation*. Translated by G.E.M. Anscombe. Malden, MA: Blackwell, 2008.

Wood, Sharon. "The Bewitched Mirror: Imagination and Narration in Elsa Morante." *Modern Language Review; Cambridge* 86, no. 2 (1 April 1991): 310–21.

– *Italian Women's Writing, 1860–1994*. London: Athlone, 1995.

Woodhouse, John Robert. "The Fascist Era and Beyond." In *A Short History of Italian Literature*, by John Humphreys Whitfield, 289–325. Baltimore, MD: Penguin Books, 1980.

Woods, Michelle. *Kafka Translated: How Translators Have Shaped Our Reading of Kafka*. New York: Bloomsbury, 2014.

Yarri, Donna. "Index to Kafka's Use of Creatures in His Writings." In *Kafka's Creatures: Animals, Hybrids, and Other Fantastic Beings*, edited by Marc Lucht and Donna Yarri, 269–83. Lanham, MD: Lexington Books, 2012.

Zagra, Giuliana. "Il racconto di due prigionieri: I manoscritti di *Menzogna e sortilegio* e *L'isola di Arturo*." In *Le stanze di Elsa: Dentro la scrittura di Elsa Morante; Biblioteca nazionale centrale di Roma, 27 aprile–3 giugno 2006*, edited by Giuliana Zagra and Simonetta Buttò, 23–36. Rome: Colombo, 2006.

Zangrilli, Franco. *Dietro la maschera della scrittura: Antonio Tabucchi*. Florence: Polistampa, 2015.

– *Le muse di Buzzati: Realtà e mistero*. Pesaro: Metauro, 2012.

Ziegler, Alan, ed. *Short: An International Anthology of Five Centuries of Short-Short Stories, Prose Poems, Brief Essays, and Other Short Prose Forms*. New York: Persea Books, 2014.

Zilcosky, John. *Kafka's Travels: Exoticism, Colonialism, and the Traffic of Writing*. New York: Palgrave Macmillan, 2004.

Ziolkowski, Saskia Elizabeth. "The Ends of an Empire: Pier Antonio Quarantotti Gambini's *Il Cavallo Tripoli* and Joseph Roth's *Radetzkymarsch*." *Comparative Literature Studies* 52, no. 2 (29 July 2015): 349–78.

– "Kafka and Italy: A New Perspective on the Italian Literary Landscape." In *Kafka for the Twenty-First Century*, edited by Stanley Corngold and Ruth Vera Gross, 237–49. Rochester, NY: Camden House, 2011.

– "Morante and Kafka: The Gothic Walking Dead and Talking Animals." In *Elsa Morante's Politics of Writing: Rethinking Subjectivity, History, and the*

Power of Art, edited by Stefania Lucamante, 53–66. Madison, NJ: Fairleigh Dickinson University Press, 2014.

– "Primo Levi and Jewish Kafka in Italy." *Journal of the Kafka Society of America* 35/36 (2012): 76–89.

– "Svevo's Dogs: Kafka and the Importance of Svevo's Animals." In *Italo Svevo and His Legacy for the Third Millennium*, edited by Giuseppe Stellardi and Emanuela Tandello Cooper, 2:58–71. Leicester: Troubador, 2014.

– "Svevo's Last Love: Kafka in Trieste and the Remapping of Italian Modernism." In *Diversity, Otherness, and Pluralism in Italian Literature, Cinema, Language, and Pedagogy: Yesterday, Today, and Tomorrow*, edited by Filomena Calabrese, Lucia Ghezzi, Teresa Lobalsamo, and Wendy Schrobilgen, 87–109. Ottawa: Legas, 2009.

Ziolkowski, Theodore. *Lure of the Arcane: The Literature of Cult and Conspiracy*. Baltimore, MD: Johns Hopkins University Press, 2013.

– "Talking Dogs: The Caninization of Literature." In *Varieties of Literary Thematics*, 86–122. Princeton, NJ: Princeton University Press, 1983.

Zyla, Wolodymyr T., ed. *Franz Kafka: His Place in World Literature*. Lubbock: Interdepartmental Committee on Comparative Literature, Texas Tech University, 1971.

Index